The Leopard, the Lion, and the Cock

The Leopard, the Lion, and the Cock

Colonial Memories and Monuments in Belgium

Matthew G. Stanard

LEUVEN UNIVERSITY PRESS

© 2019 by Leuven University Press / Presses Universitaires de Louvain / Universitaire Pers Leuven. Minderbroedersstraat 4, B-3000 Leuven (Belgium).

ISBN 978 94 6270 179 3
e-ISBN 978 94 6166 280 4
D / 2019/ 1869 / 10
NUR: 688

Layout: Crius Group, Hulshout
Cover: Anton Lecock
Cover illustration: *Tireur à l'arc* by Arthur Dupagne, Etterbeek, 2018
Unless otherwise noted, all photographs are by the author

Contents

List of Illustrations

To Jean-Luc Vellut

Acknowledgements

Although this is a sole-authored book, several people and institutions helped make it possible, and I am happy to recognize them here. It was Idesbald Goddeeris who first suggested that I publish this study, and for that I am much obliged. The research that went into this book was supported by funding and sabbatical leave from Berry College, which made multiple trips to Belgium possible. During my visits to Brussels, Meredith and Adolf Spangenberg were welcoming and generous to a fault, always. A 2016 Festschrift conference in honor of John M. MacKenzie helped me think through several aspects of the historiography of Belgian colonial culture, and I am grateful to Bryan Glass, John MacKenzie, and Nigel Dalziel for that opportunity.

Several other individuals and institutions were generous with their assistance as I researched and worked on this study: Jason Lantzer, Noemí Sarrión, Daniel Cabral, Vincent De Santis, Maëline Le Lay, Mathilde Leduc-Grimaldi, Martine Boucher, Tobias Alain Gérard, David Hensley, Tom Kennedy, Pierre Dandoy, Brad Adams, Els De Palmenaer, Moïse Cohen, Lydia Burton, Hannah Brunner, Els Vande Kerckhove, Patricia Van Schuylenbergh, Zana Aziza Etambala, Maarten Couttenier, Tobias Wendl, Anne Cornet, Bambi Ceuppens, Veerle Soens, Vincent Grégoire, Pierre Lierneux, Sarah Van Beurden, Boris Wastiau, Florence Gillet, Todd Timberlake, Kayla Fuss, Anne-Sophie Gijs, Jon Atkins, Larry Marvin, Ivan and Marlon Stanard, and the staff at the hôtel de ville in Liege. I appreciate all the help I received from staff at the archives and libraries I visited while at work on this subject: the Bibliothèque royale in Brussels; the Archives Africaines at the Belgian Federal Public Service for Foreign Affairs (Brussels); the Archives historiques privées at the AfricaMuseum in Tervuren; the BOZAR archives (Brussels); the Archives de la Ville de Bruxelles; and at the Berry College Memorial Library. Thank you also to Nathalie Tousignant, who generously agreed to read an earlier version of the book, and who provided useful feedback. It has been a pleasure working with Veerle De Laet, Mirjam Truwant, Annemie Vandezande, and the layout designers at Leuven University Press, all of whom helped bring the book to fruition.

I owe an especially fond debt of gratitude to Guy Vanthemsche, who in addition to being an inspirational scholar of the first order is also invariably welcoming, helpful, and kind. What is more, Guy read the entire manuscript.

His extensive feedback and key insights—several of which are indicated in the book's references—have improved the final work substantially.

This book is dedicated to Jean-Luc Vellut. Nearly twenty years ago now, as a graduate student on my first research trip to Belgium, I reached out to Jean-Luc for guidance, and he warmly invited me into his home. He has been unfailingly generous to me over the years; much more so than I deserve. His work is of the very highest quality, as is his advice, even if I have not always followed it. Although I suspect he might take issue with some of the conclusions presented in this book, it is dedicated to him with affection, gratitude, and great admiration.

Naturally, any errors or shortcomings in the text are the responsibility of the author alone.

Acronyms and Abbreviations

AA	Archives africaines, Federal Public Service Foreign Affairs, Brussels
ACED	Association citoyenne pour un espace public décolonial
AIA	Association internationale africaine
ARSOM/KAOW	Académie royale des sciences d'outre-mer/ Koninklijke Academie voor Overzeese Wetenschappen
BCB	*Biographie Coloniale Belge/Belgische Koloniale Biografie* and *Biographie Belge d'Outre-mer/ Belgische Overzeese Biografie*
BOZAR	Palais des Beaux-Arts/Paleis voor Schone Kunsten, Brussels
BRT	Belgische Radio- en Televisieomroep (today VRT)
BRUNEAF	Brussels Non-European Art Fair
CADTM	Comité pour l'abolition des dettes illégitimes
CD&V	Christen-Democratisch en Vlaams
CEGESOMA	Centre for Historical Research and Documentation on War and Contemporary Society
CFS	Congo Free State (État indépendant du Congo)
CRAOCA	Cercle royal des anciens officiers des campagnes d'Afrique/Koninklijke Kring van de Oud Officieren en Kaders van Afrika
CVC	Corps des volontaires congolais
IBERSOM	Institut belge pour l'encouragement de la recherche scientifique outre-mer
IMNC/Z	Institut des musées nationaux du Congo/Zaïre
Inforcongo	Office de l'information et des relations publiques pour le Congo belge et le Ruanda-Urundi
KADOC	Katholiek Documentatie- en Onderzoekscentrum
KVS	Koninklijke Vlaamse Schouwburg
MAS	Museum aan de Stroom
MRAC	Musée royal de l'Afrique centrale (AfricaMuseum), Tervuren
RTBF	Radio Télévision belge francophone

STIB	Société des transports intercommunaux de Bruxelles
UFRACOL	Union royale des fraternelles coloniales
ULB	Université libre de Bruxelles
UMHK	Union minière du Haut-Katanga
UN	United Nations
UROME	Union royale belge pour les pays d'Outre-mer/ Koninklijke Belgische Unie voor de Overzeese Landen
VLD	(Open) Vlaamse Liberalen en Democraten
VRT	Vlaamse Radio- en Televisieomroeporganisatie (formerly BRT)
VUB	Vrije Universiteit Brussel

Introduction

"Of all the former colonial powers, we are probably the nation which has been happiest to shed light, with no concessions or taboos, on our past history in Africa."[1] — Belgian Foreign Minister Louis Michel, 2004

"No colonial master has more to apologise for, or has proved more reluctant to acknowledge and accept its guilt, than Belgium."[2] — British journalist Michela Wrong, 2005

Some people still like King Leopold II of Belgium. In 2015, the city of Brussels planned to celebrate the king with "un hommage sur la place du Trône, devant la statue de Léopold II" (a tribute at the place du Trône, in front of the statue of Leopold II),[3] a large equestrian monument that sits just outside the Royal Palace along the capital city's inner ring road.[4] The event was meant to observe the 150th anniversary of the king's ascent to the throne on 17 December 1865, and to honor his contributions to the cityscape of Brussels, of which there are many. The commemoration was planned despite the fact that Belgium's second king was infamous both in his home country and abroad for a colonial misrule in Africa so brutal that he had been compared to Adolf Hitler and Joseph Stalin. Planners must also have been oblivious to the "Rhodes Must Fall" campaign that began months earlier in South Africa, which initially centered on the presence of a statue to arch-imperialist Cecil Rhodes at the University of Cape Town, and which led to its removal by the university in April. Two months afterward, in June 2015, a mass shooting by a deranged white supremacist in Charleston, South Carolina, led to soul-searching in the U.S. about that country's history of white oppression of blacks. Some states began taking down Confederate monuments and other symbols of the country's history of slavery and oppression. South Carolina and Alabama removed the Confederate battle flags from their state capitols, and the University of Texas took down a statue of Confederate president Jefferson Davis, which students had voted to remove the previous March.

In Belgium's capital, however, authorities decided to honor a world-historical colonialist with a December celebration at the city's most prominent monument to him, accompanied by a conference on the subject of Leopold II's contributions to the urban space of Brussels. In the end, the conference took place, but the tribute before the statue did not. As word spread of the planned commemoration, protests emerged, and then grew to such an extent that the city cancelled it. Brussels MP Bruno De Lille (Green Party) came forward to say that such an event would have been "morally reprehensible," and would have mocked "the suffering of the genocide victims and their families."[5] What happened instead was a counter-protest at the same place du Trône, during which the equestrian statue was vandalized, including being sprayed with red paint to symbolize Leopold II's bloody colonial rule.[6]

As these events in 2015 suggest, the colonial legacy in Belgium is complex. The colonial era had numerous long-term effects on Belgian culture, some of them profound, and most of them poorly understood, if recognized at all. This book examines the long-term effects and legacies of the colonial era on Belgium and its cultures after 1960, which was the year the Congo gained its independence, even if these legacies were almost always overshadowed by other factors such as the country's north-south language divide. The three animals of this book's title refer to the Congo (the leopard, symbol of the authority of Mobutu Sese Seko, dictator in the Congo from 1965-1997), Flanders (the iconic lion of the Flemish Community), and Wallonia (the region's symbol, the *coq hardi*). Although the entire country dealt with the colonial past, there were significant differences in how its French- and Flemish-language communities grappled with memories and other aftereffects of the colonial experience. Ongoing relations with the Congo after 1960 and remembrances of the colonial era interrelated with developments within and between Belgium's two main language communities after 1960.

The significance of "colonial culture"

In the very title of their 2005 book, Benno Barnard, Tony Judt, and their co-authors rightly asked, "How Can One Not Be Interested in Belgian History?"[7] The story of Belgium, including its colonial rule in Africa, is fascinating. The country's history arguably stretches back more than two millennia to when the area we know today as the Kingdom of Belgium was conquered along with the rest of Gaul in the last century BCE by Julius Caesar, turning it into the "Gallia Belgica" region of the Roman world. The area was central to the Carolingian Empire, whose former capital, Aachen, is today located just a few kilometers from Belgium's border with Germany. Following the collapse of Charlemagne's empire the area became an economic, religious, cultural, political, and linguistic crossroads of medieval and early modern Europe. Towns like Bruges became leading centers of commerce, and the larger region was the base of the northern Renaissance. The Low Countries straddled the linguistic frontier between Germanic- and Romance language-speaking Europe. Throughout the early modern period the Continent's major powers fought over this rich crossroads as the Low Countries changed hands among Holy Roman emperors, Burgundy's powerful dukes, Iberian or French Catholic monarchs, and Habsburg Austrians. Following the Reformation, the Low Countries found themselves on the front lines of Europe's Protestant-Catholic conflict, leading to a split between a mostly Protestant north—which became the Dutch Republic—and a mostly Catholic south, which later emerged as the Kingdom of Belgium. At the time of Belgium's independence in 1830, the country led the shift to industrialism on the Continent, beginning its transformation into one of the globe's richest and most industrialized countries. In 1914, Belgium found itself at the very center of a global war, and then suffered conquest, occupation, and devastation during the Second World War, including being centrally involved in that conflict's fundamental issues: ideological competition, collaborationism, and the war on Europe's Jews. After 1945, the country's service sector took off, which was related to twentieth-century bureaucratization, including the move toward European unification. Indeed, Brussels became Europe's "capital." Another late-twentieth-century transformation resulted from waves of migration, as Belgium typified the Western European experience by seeing its population reshaped by non-European immigration. In sum, this one small country embodies many if not most of the central strands of European history: Rome and its legacies; Charlemagne's rule; the medieval revival of trade; the Renaissance; early modern wars of religion; Great Power rivalries; industrialization; two world wars; the Holocaust; the rise of the service sector; and post-war immigration.

Along the way Belgium also played a role in yet another fundamental stage in Europe's long history, namely late-nineteenth century overseas expansion, a development that left significant cultural legacies in the country. Examining the inheritances of Belgian overseas colonialism, and of the decolonization that ended it, entails delving into Belgian culture and identity—or cultures and identities—which are complex subjects. The country was an "artificial creation" when it emerged in 1830, so-called because it was a buffer state negotiated among the Great Powers rather than a nation-state that, supposedly, would have emerged more naturally or organically. It was divided between a Dutch-speaking Flanders in the north and a francophone Wallonia in the south, meaning the country lacked a single language that unified all Belgians. French was the language of politics, of the state administration, and of the country's elite, and Flemish was discriminated against. Whereas Marquis d'Azeglio said after Italian unification that, "we have made Italy, now we must make Italians," in 1912, after more than eight decades of Belgium's existence, Walloon socialist politician Jules Destrée wrote in an open letter to King Albert I, his famous *Lettre au roi*: "permit me to tell You the truth, the great and horrifying truth: there are no Belgians."[8] As the late Simon Leys (Pierre Ryckmans) put it, "at bottom, Belgianness is a diffuse awareness of a lack."[9]

With the rise of mass nationalism in the late 1800s, north-south divisions emerged to the forefront, especially Flemish resentment at the dominant francophone bourgeoisie's discrimination against Flemish culture and language; the supremacy of that class had only strengthened as industrial Wallonia's economic growth boosted its financial, social, and political power. World War I unified the country and pushed the language question into the background, but also added a new dimension with the annexation of German-speaking Malmedy and Eupen in 1920.[10] World War II toned down the language dispute again; some French speakers perceived it as a threat when it emerged renascent in the 1960s, around the same time that the country's economic center began to shift decisively northward.[11] In that same decade, former Foreign Minister Pierre Wigny (1905-1986) quoted a stand-up comedian who said, "Belgium is the only country in the world where various oppressed majorities coexist, three groups that each have a certain supremacy and that feed an inferiority complex."[12]

Identity and culture are not only determined by language, and Belgium has had multiple, historically overlapping layers that have shaped the ways in which its peoples have assigned their loyalties and how they have self-identified. Added to the three language communities are four regions: the Flemish-speaking north; the French-speaking south; the German-speaking East Cantons of Eupen and Malmedy; and the predominantly francophone but officially bilingual Brussels, which is geographically situated within Flanders. Politically and socially, three political and social pillars—socialist, liberal, and Catholic—gave shape to social and political life in the nineteenth and much of the twentieth century. Although Belgium's Catholicism contributed to its independence from the Protestant Netherlands in 1830, the late 1800s witnessed growing secularism and anti-clericalism, which was strongest among urban industrial workers, who formed a new social class often at odds not only with the bourgeoisie but also with those living and working in rural areas. As time passed, a shared history as well as a myth of oppression by foreign nations and a general disassociation from nearby neighbors came to comprise other layers of Belgian identity, including opposition to those with whom Belgians shared a language: French speakers did not generally see themselves as French, and many Flemish speakers found the Dutch language and culture foreign. These many overlapping layers made national identity in Belgium a "lasagna," as one writer put it.[13]

Up to the 1960s, the unitary state, the unifying force of the monarchy, and to a lesser extent Catholicism—sapped as it was by growing secularism—acted as the pan that held the Belgian lasagna together. A shared identity further coalesced around the experience of two foreign occupations in less than three decades, and perhaps to a degree around a shared national project in the form of a massive central African colony. After World War II, questions of collaborationism and left-right ideological conflict tore into the national fabric. Since the loss of the Congo in 1960, the breakdown of the unitary state and the creation of separate government jurisdictions have both tracked longstanding cultural and language divisions, and deepened them. In 1963, the language border between the French-speaking south and Dutch-speaking north was fixed. A first major state constitutional reform, passed in 1970, created three cultural communities (Dutch-, French-, and German-speaking) and enshrined language divisions into the kingdom's constitution. A second reform in 1980 created Flemish and Walloon regions and devolved further governance competencies to them and the communities. In 1988-1989, yet another state reform was passed, which both created a third community—the Brussels-Capital Region—and transferred responsibility for education to the communities. This was followed four year later by another major state reform, in 1993, which turned Belgium into a full-blown federal state, with directly-elected parliaments in each of the three communities. This fourth state reform also led to the division of the province of Brabant into Flemish Brabant and Walloon Brabant. Further modifications in 2001 and 2011 transferred additional competencies to the communities and regions.

The multiplication of overlapping governmental entities continued to the point of absurdity. Belgium is today a kingdom with a federal government (based in Brussels) that has three regions (the Flemish Region, the Brussels-Capital Region, and the Walloon Region, the latter including German-speaking cantons in the east), three communities (Dutch-speaking, French-speaking, and German-speaking), and four language areas (the Flemish-speaking north, bilingual Brussels, the French-speaking south, and the small German-speaking area in the east). Whereas the Flemish Community and Flemish Region opted for one unified government and parliament (based in Brussels), the French Community embraces French speakers in Brussels and Wallonia (with a capital also in Brussels), whereas the Brussels-Capital and Walloon regions have their own parliaments, the latter based in Namur, and also representing German-speaking Eupen-Malmedy. And all this is not to mention the country's ten provinces (not counting the

Brussels-Capital area), and its hundreds of communes. When June 2010 elections famously led to a protracted government crisis in 2010-2011, it was said the country broke records for going the longest without a government. In truth, the country was governed throughout, it was just that government was on the regional, community, and local level rather than the national one. The experience suggested that the Kingdom of Belgium might not survive without a federal government, but that Belgians seemed capable of doing so with little problem.

At what level and to what extent has the colonial experience fed into regional and national identity in the country? Prominent histories of Dutch- and French-speaking identity, memory, and the Walloon and Flemish movements take into account neither the effects of overseas rule nor how memories of the colonial era might have played into those identities and movements post-1960.[14] And it is true that militants of neither the earlier-developing Flemish movement nor the later, more reactionary movement for Wallonia's independence or *rattachement* to France picked up and used "colonialism" to mobilize their respective movements after 1960. Instead, as we will see, overseas colonial rule acted at the margins of identity and nationalism in Belgium in multiple ways. Up until the 1950s, when the language divide was "exported" to the colony, the Congo acted as a unifying force to underpin Belgian nationalism, albeit not a particularly powerful one. The country was then unified, in a sense, by the shared trauma of decolonization and the end of empire. By contrast, as the years unfolded following the Congo crisis, Flemish- and French-speaking Belgians increasingly diverged in their memories of the colonial experience, and some actors occasionally instrumentalized the country's colonial legacies to accentuate differences between the country's two main language communities, although in particular ways.

Historiography of European colonial culture

How the colonial experience has figured into the recent history of Belgium and Belgian culture is not a historical problem that boasts an extensive pedigree. Indeed, the long-term effects of the colonial era on Belgian culture, or cultures, has only recently become a subject of interest to historians and other scholars.[15] One reason this subject did not draw attention until recently is because people long believed that the colonial experience mainly affected non-European parts of the world. It is well known that sixteenth-century European maritime empire building and the Columbian Exchange remade the Americas, creating "neo-Europes" there, and then later in Australia and

New Zealand.[16] Subsequently, a massive new wave of expansionism beginning in the second half of the 1800s in many ways reshaped sub-Saharan Africa, south Asia, Oceania, and to a lesser extent north Africa, the Middle East, and east Asia. The degree to which more recent overseas expansion and its end in the second half of the 1900s affected Europe itself was for long underappreciated, including its effects on Belgian history and culture. Half a century removed from the era of decolonization, European countries are only now coming to terms with the fact that they have not come to terms with decolonization, and that what is noteworthy about European culture and empire is not only the presence of empire but also its notable absence in Europeans' understandings of their past history. In the Netherlands, for example, "despite having a colonial history in South East Asia that extends over 350 years, the crucial years of decolonization in the Dutch East Indies are particularly notable for their absence in the nation's cultural narrative."[17]

There are reasons for the delayed coming to terms with Europe's imperial past and its aftereffects in Europe specifically. Into the mid-twentieth century, comparatively little had been written about the more recent European overseas colonialism. Then, with the era of decolonization—from India's independence until the end of Portugal's empire in the mid-1970s—history writing about Africa and Asia tended to focus on recently independent countries, not on imperialism per se, as newly-independent peoples tended toward the writing of national histories that legitimized emergent nation-states. Partly as a result, by the early 1980s the subfield of imperial history declined dramatically. In some cases it had never really taken off. As regards the historiography of German imperialism, for instance, scholars had almost completely neglected overseas colonialism, dwelling instead on historical problems of German empire-building in Europe, especially under the Nazi Empire. In the case of Italy's overseas colonialism, Angelo del Boca was for many years almost alone in his extensive efforts to delve into that country's colonial past. Into the 1970s Portugal's "third empire" was still a going concern, and thus not much of an object for historical research. Generally speaking, research into the history of European overseas empire tended to focus on earlier subjects, such as the British East India Company, or seventeenth and eighteenth century competition among the European maritime powers for territories in the Americas, India, and southeast Asia. The focus tended to fall on strategy, diplomacy, governance, and economics, and by the early 1980s the field had become a backwater for historical research, a subfield in decline. At the time, historian David Fieldhouse compared the field to Humpty Dumpty, asking whether imperial history, fallen and broken, could ever be put back together again.[18]

The appearance of major works in the late 1970s and early 1980s initiated a revival, among the most notable being Edward Said's *Orientalism* (1978). Said's work showed how studies of the Arab and Eastern worlds by European "Orientalists" in the eighteenth and nineteenth centuries revealed more about Europe itself than the ostensible subjects at hand. Instead of Europe being one fixed entity that had projected itself outward during the era of imperialism to leave its imprint on distant lands—and learning about and mastering those places as a result—Europe had in fact itself been shaped by imperialism, in no small part by defining itself against non-European "Others." Studies followed, branching out beyond the economics, diplomacy, and administration of empire to embrace new realms, many of them concerned with questions of culture, difference, and the exercise of power. As social and Marxist history frameworks to study the past fell out of favor with some, historians turned toward anthropology, structuralism, the work of French philosopher Michel Foucault, and language for insights into the workings of power. Some moved in new directions with the advent of cultural studies, the rediscovery of Antonio Gramsci's writings, and the coming into being of Subaltern Studies.

By the 1990s, the study of the history of recent overseas imperialism was flourishing. The return of the history of imperialism as a vibrant area of study was not due to mere chance. Much of the world by the late 1970s had suffered a protracted economic downturn as the *trentes glorieuses* came to an end, and this included a drop in commodity prices that hurt much of the developing world. The hopeful expectations of the decolonization era had morphed into disappointment as neo-colonialism, slow economic growth, corruption, and military rule plagued so many parts of the former colonial world. More and more scholars turned to the past to explain the world of the late 1970s and 1980s. In addition, immigration into Europe from the Caribbean, Africa, and south Asia increased the numbers of people of non-European origin living there, which roused memories of the colonial past. With 1989 and the end of the Soviet empire in eastern Europe, some turned their attention to other forms of domination, discarding a Cold War or ideological framework for viewing the past in favor of one centered on empire building in its various guises, a shift only given further impetus by the threat of unrestrained U.S. global power after 1989. In addition, by the 1990s history writing on the Second World War had developed such that many more had come to better terms with Nazi empire building and the Holocaust (as much as that was possible), which opened up intellectual "space" to revisit overseas empire building.

In addition to Said another pioneering figure was John M. MacKenzie, who argued in *Propaganda and Empire* that British culture had been profoundly reshaped by empire by the twentieth century.[19] MacKenzie's initial work in the field became a touchstone for innumerable others that followed, many appearing in the *Studies in Imperialism* series that MacKenzie founded, and which now boasts some 150 titles.[20] The literature that has emerged is enormous; it mostly addresses single nation-states in Europe and the impact of empire, with many contributions focusing on Britain and France and their imperial experiences.[21] Pascal Blanchard, Sandrine Lemaire, Nicolas Bancel, and Dominic Thomas' *Colonial Culture in France since the Revolution*, for example, includes nearly fifty essays on France, and runs to nearly 650 pages.[22] Lora Wildenthal did pioneering work on Germany.[23] Gert Oostindie, among others, has recently tackled the long-term effects of the colonial era in the Netherlands.[24] In sum, the intersection of European culture and empire has become a now well-established and burgeoning subfield of study.

Thus the emerging historiography of Belgian "colonial culture" follows recent shifts in the study of European history more generally, namely the growing interest in Europe's "colonial cultures" deriving from overseas empires in the nineteenth and twentieth centuries. Much ink has been spilled regarding the colonial period's cultural and other legacies in Africa and Asia,[25] much less so empire's effects in Belgium. Some have considered the economics of decolonization, or how the Congo affected Belgium in terms of politics and foreign relations after 1960, but fewer have considered culture.[26] Examinations of imperialism's lingering affects on Belgian culture and memory are many but disparate. The subject of the francophone-Flemish cultural divide has been paramount in the years after 1960, but rarely does anyone incorporate an understanding of the loss of the Congo or the colonial past's enduring influence into studies of it. In general, the literature on the impact of the colonies on Europe is dominated by the former powers of France and Britain to the detriment of our understanding of legacies of empire among the "lesser" colonial powers, including Belgium.

In ways it is surprising that the cultural ramifications in Belgium of the country's overseas imperialism took so long to become a serious subject of study.[27] After all, even if other European states, most notably Britain, claimed greater and longer-lasting status as imperial states, Belgium ruled the Congo—one of the world's largest countries by area—for more than three-quarters of a century, meaning that for much of its history since independence in 1830, Belgium was a colonial power. As we will see, spillover effects of the colonial experience showed up in Belgian culture early on in the colonial era, from the intimate association of the country's monarchy with colonialism, to *bandes dessinées* like Hergé's *Tintin in the Congo* (1930-1931), to clergy preaching about Congo missions from the pulpit, to pro-colonial monuments. Right at the end of the colonial era, in 1960, a chaotic and traumatic decolonization led to an immediate influx of thousands of Belgian (now former) colonials from the Congo, who brought physical objects as well as their memories, experiences, and own physical selves back home with them.

Yet, when landmark works on European culture, overseas imperialism, and "colonial culture" appeared beginning in the 1970s and 1980s, they initially had little impact in Belgium, including milestones like Said's *Orientalism* and MacKenzie's *Propaganda and Empire*. Those scholars who pioneered work on colonial culture rarely paid much attention to "little Belgium," and when they did, it was mostly to the sensational Leopoldian era of atrocities, *mains coupées*, and "red rubber," which gained the lion's share of attention despite the fact that the Belgian state-rule era (1908-1960) lasted more than twice as long as the Leopoldian period. In short, the Belgian case remained an outlier that was rarely incorporated into the growing historiography of European colonial culture.

This began to change only recently with the appearance of works explicitly tackling questions of Belgian culture and the colonial experience. Bambi Ceuppens explored colonialism's effects both in central Africa and on Flanders in her 2003 *Congo Made in Flanders?*, for instance Frans Deckers and Flemish-language "colonial literature."[28] Ceuppens joined forces with Vincent Viaene and David Van Reybrouck to produce the 2009 collection *Congo in België*, whose several essays argued that the colony had a limited impact on culture in Belgium.[29] With *European Empires and the People* (2011), John MacKenzie married his knowledge about the British empire and culture with that of historians working on the Belgian, French, German, Italian and Dutch colonial experiences.[30] This author's own *Selling the Congo* (2011) approached the subject of colonial culture via an analysis of pro-empire propaganda in Belgium before 1960. A recent addition, *Europe after Empire*, by Elizabeth Buettner (2016), includes Belgium alongside Portugal, Britain, France, and the Netherlands, making it suggestive of the shift toward inclusion of Europe's "smaller" imperial powers as well as the burgeoning interest in the field.[31]

This said, MacKenzie's comparative collection, Viaene et al.'s *Congo in België*, and Buettner's book are only very recent additions after years of near silence on the topic, a silence that can be chalked up to several factors. One is the fact that it was only late that Belgian colonial history and African history *tout court* developed as fields of study in Belgium, which really was not until the 1960s.[32] Similar to many others in Europe, Belgians had viewed sub-Saharan Africa as a place without history. One of the most prominent scholars of Belgian involvement in Africa, the late Jean Stengers, pursued "colonial" history only as a secondary interest. Even the country's pre-eminent scholar of the history of colonialism in central Africa, Jean-Luc Vellut, is in essence an Africanist rather than a historian of empire. Nevertheless, Vellut has produced a massive and diverse body of work unveiling the workings of Belgian overseas rule. Among the many subjects of his meticulous research and prodigious output are the nature of the CFS, colonial medicine, African resistance, the inner workings of the colonial state, economics, African artwork, memories and representations of the colonial era, the image and self-image of the "white" in the colonial situation, the end of Belgian empire, religious movements, and the death penalty, in addition to major contributions in the realms of historiography and bibliography.[33] Other scholars did investigate the colonial era, many of whose publications appeared in the main journal of the Académie royale des sciences d'outre-mer/Koninklijke Academie voor Overzeese Wetenschappen (ARSOM/KAOW), initially called the Institut royal colonial belge/Koninklijk Belgisch Koloniaal Instituut. As its original name suggests, ARSOM/KAOW was a colonialist institution, and many specialists who published with it tended toward a more traditional, pro-colonial approach.[34]

In short, Belgian historians who studied the country's colonial history for long fell outside the mainstream of academic history in the country. What is more, historical analysis of the colonial situation, such as it was, tended to stick to a more "aloof" or detached scientific method, epitomized by Stengers, who maintained that it was not the historian's duty to pass judgment on the past but to explain what happened and why. Former diplomat and amateur historian Jules Marchal and anthropologist Daniel Vangroenweghe wrote significant and much more critical works in the 1980s. The 1985 centenary of the Congo Free State (CFS) led to a number of other publications about this past, some of which dealt with cultural effects on Belgium.[35] In short, no one took up as an object of study the colony's consequences for Belgian culture specifically. Many if not most people continued to believe well into the post-colonial era that cultural transfers had been essentially one-way: Europe's cultures spread outward from Belgium, France, Britain, and other countries to their respective colonies. In retrospect this makes sense, because the diffusion of European culture had been part and parcel of what was called the "civilizing mission," which was a justification for empire. This took multiple forms: education, urban planning, Protestant and Catholic Christianity, sports, technology, medicine, language, and so forth. To remake Belgian culture via colonialism in Africa was never anyone's objective. In this sense, the disregard of overseas colonialism's cultural repercussions in Belgium was a holdover from the colonial era and itself a symptom of Europeans' belief in their own cultural superiority.

If European cultural superiority was assumed as true, other forces more specific to the Belgian case were at work causing an inattention to colonial culture in the country. One was the longstanding focus on the main aspect marking Belgian cultural (and other) history, namely the country's north-south divide between Flanders and French-speaking Wallonia. In the twentieth century, two world wars only refocused attention on the "Flemish Question" after German occupying authorities pursued a *Flamenpolitik* to "conquer and divide" Belgians by tapping into Flemish nationalism to drive a wedge between the country's language groups.[36] Another factor: few people had direct experience in the colony. Many of those who worked in the Congo before 1908—merchants, missionaries, doctors, administrators, Force publique officers—were not Belgian, but rather from Scotland, England, Wales, Russia, Italy, Germany, Scandinavia, the U.S., or Switzerland.[37] Not until 1893 did Belgians comprise a majority of whites working in the CFS, and as late as 1920 barely half of all Europeans in what was then the Belgian Congo were actually nationals of the colonial power.[38] There was little circulation of people between metropole and colony—during both world wars, movement back and forth slowed to a trickle—and because comparatively few Belgians lived or worked in the Congo, there was no massive influx of former colonials at the time of decolonization; nothing approaching the million-plus *pieds noirs* who left Algeria for metropolitan France in the early 1960s, or the 500,000 *retornados* who returned to Portugal in 1974-1975 (and who increased that country's population by five percent as a result). Numerous scholars working in other national contexts had had first-hand exposure to the colonies, for instance Benjamin Stora, born in French Algeria in 1950, or John M. MacKenzie, who at around twelve years of age moved to Northern Rhodesia.[39] Almost no Belgian scholars had similar experience.

Another issue of major significance was the historically small size of the Congolese community in Belgium. The colonial state's policy of severely restricting the movements of colonial subjects kept the Congolese presence in the metropole to a minimum before 1960, and their numbers increased only slowly thereafter. There was nothing comparable in Belgium to the so-called Windrush Generation in Britain beginning in 1948 and the arrival of *Empire Windrush*, which saw Britain's population noticeably reshaped by colonial migration.[40] It has not been until very recently that Congolese in Belgium addressed the colonial past head-on, in large part because historically many Congolese, Rwandans, and Burundians only lived in Belgium temporarily, either as students or exiles, and always planned to return home. Not until the 1994 Rwandan genocide and the 1997 collapse of the Mobutu regime did the number of permanent residents of central African background in

Belgium grow significantly; even then, many of them remained much more concerned about contemporaneous problems in their home country than the distant past.[41] Moreover, they were seldom in a strong position from which they might raise impolitic questions about past oppression; many Congolese, Rwandans, and Burundians occupied marginal positions in European society. An example is Paul Rusesabagina, who saved thousands of lives at the Hôtel Mille Collines in 1994, and who is well known thanks to the film *Hotel Rwanda* (2004) and his memoir *An Ordinary Man*. But at the time Rusesabagina's story was "discovered," he was just getting by driving a taxi cab in Brussels, after having sought asylum there in 1996.[42] Compared to other former imperial powers, colonial migrants in Belgium did not propel any extensive reconsideration of the colonial past, at least not until recently.

As all of the above mentioned factors suggest, the relatively longstanding inattention to colonialism's effects on Belgium is not due to Belgians simply forgetting their colonial past because of the shame felt at its darker chapters. Numerous commentators, including Adam Hochschild and Michela Wrong, have at least insinuated that Belgians chose to forget or deliberately ignore their past overseas rule, Hochschild going so far as to call it the "Great Forgetting."[43] But as James Young has put it, "to suggest that a society 'represses' memory because it is not in its interest to remember, or because it is ashamed of this memory, is to lose sight of the many other social and political forces underpinning national memory."[44] This study shows that there were ebbs and flows in terms of remembering the colonial past in Belgium, and numerous factors at work in this change over time.

Indeed, the situation has changed just over the past two decades, which have witnessed a significant growth in interest in colonial history, including its cultural aftereffects. In ways, it was American Adam Hochschild who led the way by publishing *King Leopold's Ghost* in 1998, which was right away translated into French and Dutch.[45] This American journalist blasted Belgians for having forgotten their atrocious colonial misdeeds, and alleged a history of genocide that caused ten million deaths during Leopold's rule, placing the king alongside Hitler and Stalin on history's roster of worst rulers. Many Belgians greeted Hochschild's claims with astonishment and hostility. The American's riveting storytelling and the controversy over his book stimulated much interest, and were followed by other developments that brought the "colonial" to the forefront. Notably, sociologist Ludo de Witte's *The Assassination of Lumumba* (1999) revisited the 1961 murder of Patrice Lumumba and pinned much of the blame for it on Belgium.[46] This was followed by a 2000-2001 parliamentary inquiry that led to an admission of state complicity in Lumumba's death by then-Foreign Minister Louis Michel. Then, just as

1985 and the centenary of the declaration of the CFS had raised awareness of the colonial past, so too did the years 2008, 2009, and 2010—respectively the centenary of Belgium's takeover of the Congo, the centennial of Leopold II's death, and the fiftieth anniversary of Congo's independence. These years produced a variety of cultural events related to the Congo, as well as a flurry of scholarly activity.[47] 2010 was also the centenary of a frequent object of criticism, the Musée royal de l'Afrique centrale (MRAC), today called the AfricaMuseum.[48] Critics looked into the museum's past and took Belgium to task for harboring a dusty colonialist institution frozen in time.[49]

Important also have been the passage of time, generational change, and a certain coming to terms with Belgium's controversial World War II experience, which opened up intellectual and psychic "space" in which colonial issues might be contemplated. The fundamental questions being asked about the country's colonial history have changed as greater distance has developed between that past and those asking the questions. As we will see, for decades, few Belgians even took up the colonial past as a subject of historical inquiry; as mentioned, these included Jean Stengers, Jean-Luc Vellut, Jules Marchal, and Daniel Vangroenweghe. Another equally modest generation followed them—some of whose works are cited below—but historical studies of Belgian colonialism sensu stricto remained generally outside the mainstream of historical inquiry.[50] Important work on the colonial era's effects was carried out in scholarly fields aside from history writing. Pierre Halen and Marc Quaghebeur produced major studies of the francophone literature of Belgian imperialism.[51] Beginning in the late 1980s, Sabine Cornelis began exploring "colonial" influences on Belgian artists, and Bogumil Jewsiewicki, a prominent Polish-Canadian historian of the Congo, turned his attention to popular artwork in the Congo.[52]

It is only in recent years that a new generation of historians has emerged, delving into Belgium's colonial past with gusto. Perhaps typifying this generational change is David Van Reybrouck (b. 1971) and his blockbuster Congo: A History.[53] Van Reybrouck also edited, along with Bambi Ceuppens and Vincent Viaene, Congo in België (2009), the first full-length treatment of the cultural effects of the colonial experience on contemporary Belgian culture, broadly speaking.[54] Congo in België suggested a growing consensus that, although overseas colonialism's influence on the country's culture has not been overwhelming, it was important, and greater than anyone suspected. In any case, a younger generation of scholars not personally implicated in the colonizing of their forebears is exploring the subject with greater freedom, and with greater access to sources due to the passage of time and the lifting of restrictions on previously off-limit archival sources. Unfortunately, a serious lack of institutional support, including a dearth of teaching and/or research posts at universities focused on the history of Africa and Belgium's past there, threatens to undermine this recent outpouring of productive research.

Themes and structure of the book

In the space of several chapters the present study seeks to build on the existing historiography by showing fundamental ways in which Belgian culture was reshaped into the post-1960 era by the colonial experience. The book's structure is straightforward, divided as it is into several chronological chapters. It begins with a chapter providing an overview of the colonial "adventure" before 1960, including a sketch of the kind of colonial culture that had developed in Belgium prior to 1960. Belgium was one of Europe's "lesser" imperial powers, and the culture of the country was never as imbued with imperialist sentiment or colonialist themes as was the case in some other European colonizing states, in particular Britain, France, and Portugal. Nonetheless, decades of pro-imperial propaganda fostered among Belgians a widespread acceptance of—and an important degree of pride in—their country's colonial undertaking in central Africa. The first chapter sketches this history, which is important for understanding what followed the Congo's independence in 1960.

The book continues with a second chapter examining Belgian culture from 1960-1967, which was a time of turmoil in central Africa and a period during which Belgian memories of and feelings about the colonial era were affected by the immediacy of the glory years of the 1950s and the trauma that capped that decade when the Congo suddenly became independent. The second chapter's analysis begins, logically enough, with the caesura of 1960, and it draws to a close in 1967, for a number of reasons. It was around the mid- to late-1960s that the turmoil of the Congo crisis had largely died down. Also, by 1967, many Belgians who had moved to central Africa had returned home, and many had found their footing. Moreover, by 1967 army chief Joseph-Désiré Mobutu was firmly in charge in the Congo. That year his government asserted a new series of claims against Belgium, opening, in a sense, a new era in Belgian-Congolese relations.

The third chapter's analysis spans nearly two decades, from 1967 to 1985, a period that coheres because it was a time of quiescence. A hallmark of this time period is how Belgium in many ways "moved on" from the colonial era. Colonialist narratives continued to predominate, thanks in no small part to former colonials' work to sustain a positive history of the colonial past, and the fact that there existed only a very small Congolese immigrant community in the country that did not challenge that pro-colonialist narrative. The milestone year of 1985 opens yet another chapter. The year 1985 marked not only the centenary of the declaration of Leopold II's CFS but also a quarter century of independence for the Congo, which Mobutu had renamed Zaire in 1971. The year 1985 also marked thirty years since King Baudouin's first royal visit to the Congo, and it was occasioned by yet another visit by the sovereign, which would turn out to be his last. More significantly, 1985, being an anniversary year, led to an important unearthing of knowledge, history, and memories of the colonial past, but almost always bathed in nostalgia.

The book's fifth chapter explains how the colonial era came roaring back to the forefront in Belgium beginning in the mid-1990s because of the 1994 Rwandan genocide, the subsequent collapse of the Mobutu regime in 1997, the emergence of explosive historical studies, and the commissioning of a parliamentary inquiry. As with chapter four, the final chapter begins with a major anniversary, namely fifty years of Congolese independence, which Belgium and the former colony celebrated in 2010. Even more so than in 1985, the half-century milestone of 2010 led to an outpouring of reconsiderations of the colonial past, among them exhibitions, concerts, and abundant other cultural events. The final chapter on Belgian culture and the colonial experience that addresses the period from the 2010 anniversary to more recent times is followed by a brief epilogue that not only draws conclusions, but also discusses some very recent developments.

A key component of the analysis that follows is the foregrounding of the enduring presence of "empire" in everyday life in Belgium in the form of permanent colonial markers in bronze and stone, *lieux de mémoire* of the country's history of overseas expansion.[55] Still today dozens if not hundreds of colonial monuments and memorials dot the Belgian landscape. This book includes high-quality photographs of many of them, all framed within inset boxes, each providing a kind of "biography" of the relevant marker: a concise explanation of its origins, materials, meanings, legacies, and afterlife in the post-colonial era. The stories behind colonial monuments in Belgium have much to teach us about the country's overseas rule, decolonization, and Europe's cultures after empire. Because these monuments and their "life stories" are so central to the story told here, each inset box is placed deliberately such that the photographs and stories of individual monuments connect to the running text of the book, and vice versa. Naturally, anyone interested in a particular monument can go directly to its photograph(s) and "biography." Yet the inset boxes and the surrounding text are complementary, and are designed to be read in tandem.

As will be seen, although memorials in Belgium that bear some connection to the colonial era convey multiple meanings, they also share many qualities. Virtually all of them are rather classical in design and figural in their representations, as opposed to being abstract works bearing little resemblance to things in the real world. The earliest ones date back to 1887-1888, which is to say they were put up in the very first years following the foundation of the CFS. Unsurprisingly, few were put up during the world wars, and very few were erected after 1960. Most celebrate military men, with fewer to missionaries, administrators, or figures from the world of business. Inaugurations and commemorations fostered Belgian nationalism and celebrated the CFS and Leopold II. Mainly put up by colonial interest groups like the Ligue du souvenir congolais, as well as veterans and local government—often with subsidies from the Ministry of Colonies—they upheld empire as warranted, underpinned as it was by the fight for civilization.[56] In his classic study of Holocaust memorials, James Young showed how such markers in several countries expressed a desire to put the past to rest, pointing to "Germans' secret desire that all these monuments just hurry up and disappear."[57] Belgian pro-colonialist markers, like those put up by other colonial powers, were in contrast designed to keep the past alive.

There have been only muted calls for the removal of colonialist statues in Belgium, in contrast to what happened in the Congo after 1960, where numerous colonial-era monuments were torn down, destroyed, or severely damaged. The "Rhodes Must Fall" campaign in South Africa, mentioned earlier, has spread beyond the initial demand to take down a statue of Rhodes to calls to bring down other colonial- or apartheid-era markers as well as to "decolonize" life not just in South Africa but also in the United Kingdom, for example in university curricula. In Spain, the physical presence of sites and monuments commemorating the Franco regime continues to agitate people on either end of the political spectrum. In recent years in the U.S., the place of Confederate monuments has stirred a fierce debate, which has included protests, people being killed, and the removal of a number of Confederate statues. All this is not to mention the extensive destruction and relocation of monuments in formerly communist eastern Europe after 1989.

In Belgium, colonial monuments remain in place, with very few exceptions. *The Leopard, the Lion, and the Cock* includes numerous photographs of these memorials, with explanations, capturing the colonial era's enduring presence. Permanent public markers and memorials only generate meaning if the people who see and talk about them derive meaning from them, be it through the activation of memories or feelings, or by informing. By reproducing and explaining many major pro-colonial memorials as well as several obscure ones, the book reveals the surprising degree to which Belgium had become infused with the colonial spirit during the colonial era as pride in the colony took center stage in many towns and cities while also reaching even remote corners of the country. Some have suggested that monuments can have the paradoxical effect of allowing people to forget, by doing their memory work for them.[58] This might be more true in certain cases and much less so in others, where a memorial might remind, or teach, or serve as a gathering point more than anything else. Because not all monuments are alike, what follows both generalizes across these historical markers and examines individual ones in detail: their construction, alteration, use, representation, and reception. The analysis of each monument will also show the varied ways inhabitants of Belgium have approached the colonial past since 1960, treating memorials variously as objects of veneration, with indifference, or as symbols to be attacked or torn down.

This book is aimed primarily at the general reader while also addressing those with a more academic interest in monuments, memories, and empire. To that end, the analysis that follows avoids jargon while also building on the rich literature on post-colonial history and European culture. Although it is only recently that scholars have developed a serious interest in Belgian "colonial culture," the subject is so expansive that there already exists a large literature that at least touches on the subject. Although readers will find references to that literature in each chapter's notes, the book is not encyclopedic, and a specialist in any given field, be it *bandes dessinées* or Dutch-language television or food and postcolonialism, might put the book down somewhat dissatisfied with the treatment of any one specific subject. Likewise, even though the author himself has visited more than eighty Belgian colonial memorials, and although this book includes photos of dozens of them, many have been excluded, either because of space or to avoid a certain repetition. Rather than being encyclopedic, the book is intended as a thought-provoking reflection on culture, colonialism, and the remainders of empire in Belgium after 1960. Towards that end, the book develops several arguments.

One contention that unfolds across the following pages is that the post-1960 effects of the colonial experience, memories of the colonial past, and enduring remnants of empire in Belgium have been much more significant than previously believed. While not a dominant presence, recent studies of Britain, France, the Netherlands, and other former colonial powers have shown how the colonial past reshaped those countries' cultures in numerous ways, just one example being how their populations changed as a result of colonial and post-colonial migration. In the Belgian case, too, the colonial past was not the predominant shaper of culture post-1960, because other domestic or international issues were more significant: the Dutch-French language divide, post-World War II American cultural influences, the Cold War, immigration, and so forth. But when it comes to the effects of the colonial past, they have been much greater than heretofore believed. Particularly prominent is how Belgians upheld a positive view of their colonial history, at least until the end of the twentieth century. The ongoing presence of colonial monuments is both constitutive and suggestive of this enduring positive interpretation of the country's colonial past. This book will explain how and why this vision endured, and why opinions began to shift around the turn of the twenty first century.

As suggested by its title, a central question this book raises is how the colonial experience—and then interactions between Belgium and the Congo after 1960—affected relations between, and culture within, the country's two language communities. To a degree, overseas colonial rule had acted as a unifying factor—albeit a subtle and complex one—for much of Belgium's history: the *mission civilisatrice* in the Belgian Congo was a kind of shared "project" that both the northern, Flemish half of the country and the southern, French-speaking half shared. As Vincent Viaene has shown, the 1908 takeover of the colony helped strengthen national identity by adding an overseas, "African" component to it in the form of a shared colonial project.

> Het was een kristallisatiepunt—van België's heerschappij over Congo, maar ook van de stempel die Congo of de Congolese onderneming op de Belgische samenleving drukte. Het was nooit anders bedoeld. Van België een ander soort natie maken was immers de ultieme doelstelling van Leopold II in Congo.
> (It was a crystallization point—of Belgium's dominion over the Congo, but also of the imprint that the Congo and the Congolese undertaking made on Belgian society. It was never meant otherwise. To make Belgium another sort of nation was always the ultimate goal of Leopold II in the Congo.)[59]

After 1960, Dutch- and French-speaking Belgians shared both memories of the colonial past as well as a common colonial history. The loss of the Congo then removed this unifying force, and in the years afterward some even "deployed" the colonial past to advance current political goals, some oriented around the language issue. Certain Dutch-speaking Belgians came to frame their views of the colonial past through a contemporary pro-Flemish lens and were quicker to castigate the African administration—closely associated with the dynasty and francophone elites—while viewing Church action in central Africa more charitably. Some French speakers, by contrast, were more inclined to view the dynasty favorably and to defend the colonial past, closely connected as it was to the kingdom's ruling house. One goal in the analysis that follows will be to point out similarities and differences in how Dutch and French speakers dealt with colonial inheritances in order to raise the question as to empire's longer-term impact on memory and identity in Belgium.

The book develops other arguments, one being that the decade of the 1950s had a disproportionate impact on Belgians' post-1960 views of colonialism. Most people, if they know anything about Belgium's colonial past, are aware of the history of Leopoldian rule and the atrocities it led to in central Africa. For several reasons, however, it was the history and experience of imperialism in the decade of the 1950s that more than any other fundamentally underpinned Belgian memories and knowledge of the colonial era into the post-1960 era. Crucial to alter understandings of the colonial past has been generational change. Not only has a younger generation—by necessity uninvolved in colonialism—begun to tackle the colonial past with renewed vigor and new questions, but changing demographics have remade "the colonial" in the country.

Another proposition developed in the pages that follows is that empire affected artistic creation and the art market in Belgium. The evidence presented demonstrates how colonial, Congolese, and more generally African influences have been significant, in particular in the realm of "high culture," as Congolese artwork had a much greater impact upon upper class elites in Belgium than it affected culture more generally. The book also raises the question as to whether the decline of the Catholic Church after 1960 was accelerated by the end of empire. The colonial era had boosted the influence not only of the French-speaking bourgeoisie and the monarchy, but also of the Church. After 1960, all three declined; for example, the number of Belgian missionaries to central Africa, which had jumped dramatically after World War I, dropped significantly and steadily in the post-1960 period.

The Leopard, the Lion, and the Cock also shows how colonial-era rhetoric about Belgian altruism and the so-called civilizing mission was mainly just that: rhetoric. Education about the colony dropped off dramatically beginning in 1960, evidenced both in school textbooks and university curricula. This suggests that, despite many good intentions as well as the actions of well-meaning colonials and specialists, Belgians in general had been interested in what whites did in the colony, not in Africans themselves, and this despite their own professions to the contrary. Although Belgians had claimed they were involved in central Africa out of a kind of altruism—for the benefit of the Congolese—the drop off in education in the colony beginning in 1960 belies the reality that Belgians were in it for themselves. This shift in education does not mean that Belgians completely forgot their colonial history, including the abuses of the Leopoldian period, an allegation that has been leveled many times in the past. Rather, memories of atrocities and other aspect of the colonial past recurred or were unearthed in different forms post-1960, in particular around the moments of commemoration, like anniversaries.

Movements of people, that is, migration, played a key role in shaping Belgium's post-colonial culture, and this comprises another of the book's major themes. Unlike in Britain, France, Portugal, or the Netherlands, for most of Belgium's post-colonial existence, the number of former colonials—Belgians who had lived in the Congo and then relocated home—greatly outnumbered the small number of former subjects (and their descendants) living in Belgium. What is more, Congolese immigrants to the former metropole have always been vastly outnumbered by other non-European immigrants, in particular from the Maghreb. There were few former colonial subjects (or their descendants) to raise issues about the past and comparatively little concern regarding their numbers living in Belgium. Simultaneously there was a larger number of former colonials promoting a positive vision of the country's imperial history, which dampened any questioning of it.

Chapter 1
Belgians and the Colonial Experience before 1960

"I undertook the work of the Congo in the interest of civilization and for the good of Belgium."[1] — King Leopold II

Leopold II's Congo

The Belgian experience with overseas colonialism dates back to the country's second king, Leopold II, whose efforts to secure a colony coincided with the late-nineteenth century New Imperialism that witnessed a renewed overseas expansionism by European states.[2] Industrial might and technological advances were married with Europeans' faith in their cultural and racial superiority to drive a wave of conquests above all directed at North Africa, sub-Saharan Africa, and south and East Asia. Leopold II ascended the throne in 1865 with a full-blown desire to acquire a colony overseas. Autocratic by nature, he felt hemmed in within the confines of Belgium, which was a small, neutral constitutional monarchy. He took the Dutch colony in the East Indies as a model: a colony to make profits redounding to the benefit of the metropole. A key step was the convening of an international geographical conference in Brussels in 1876, which led to the establishment of a supposedly neutral association of exploration directed toward central Africa that the king then manipulated to achieve his own ends. Through various such schemes, by financing expeditions to central Africa, and by using wily diplomacy, Leopold managed by 1885 to gain the Great Powers' recognition of him as sovereign over a vast colony in central Africa, which was baptized the État Indépendant du Congo, or Congo Free State (CFS), a massive territory encompassing most of the Congo River basin and adjoining areas. Once its borders were fleshed out through further exploration, negotiation, and outright conquest and military occupation, Leopold's Congo comprised a territory some 80 times the size of Belgium.

Unlike other European overseas territories, the CFS was not a state possession but instead the personal colony of one person, the Belgian king. When parliament recognized Leopold II as ruler of the Congo—the constitution required parliamentary approval for the king to reign over another country, a legacy of German and other princes taking up various thrones in the

IN THE RUBBER COILS.

Scene—*The Congo "Free" State.*

"In the Rubber Coils," Linley Sambourne, Punch, 28 November 1906

nineteenth century—it specifically disassociated the Belgian state from
the king's colonial endeavor. Leopold II relied on many Belgians to run his
new, African state, but he also employed numerous foreigners. Polish boat
captain and *Heart of Darkness* author Joseph Conrad is but one prominent
example; numerous officers in the colonial army, the Force publique, were
from Switzerland or Scandinavia, and most doctors in the CFS were Italian.[3]
Leopold's European subjects remained largely indifferent to his colonial
efforts. Belgian financiers and industrialists preferred investing at home
or in other European markets. The country's Catholic missionaries, such
as they were, generally went to work places elsewhere than sub-Saharan
Africa, for instance Asia. For most Belgians, other issues took precedence
over colonialism, including the late-nineteenth "social question" regarding
the accommodation of a rapidly expanding industrial working class.

Having secured a colony, Leopold modeled his administration, in part,
on his understanding of Dutch rule in the East Indies, meaning he focused
above all on profit seeking. In short, the CFS developed into a system designed

to extract the maximum profit at minimum cost by means of armed force and the threat of physical abuse, which CFS and concessionary company employees used to coerce African labor, in particular for the harvesting first of ivory, then of wild rubber during the fin-de-siècle rubber boom. The Force publique squelched on-the-ground indigenous resistance and the king (and his agents) characterized their takeover as the "pacification" of Congo territories, not conquest. They also claimed victory over "Arab" slaving in eastern Congo, that is to say the military defeat of east African Arab-Swahili merchants, including slavers, who dominated the eastern Congo. In this way Leopold II cast his colonial rule as a humanitarian struggle of civilization against cruel, foreign, Arab Muslims who were preying on hapless Africans.

The anti-slavery narrative might have stuck had it not been eclipsed by the horrific news and images of abuses that missionaries and others disseminated of the CFS system of killing, torture, kidnapping, village burning, mutilation, and whipping that compelled Africans to work for the benefit of the colonial state. In reaction, a powerful international movement developed, spearheaded by the Congo Reform Association and its driving force, Anglo-Frenchman E. D. Morel. This sparked intense international and eventually also domestic condemnation of Leopold II that eventually forced the king's hand.[4] Various plans were mooted as to how to end Leopoldian rule in Africa, for instance dividing the CFS up among neighboring colonial powers, but it was a Belgian takeover that won the day, leading to the 1908 *reprise* whereby the Belgian state gained control over the king's massive central African colony.

Early cultural influences

The Leopoldian era was important for laying the foundation of Belgian under-standings of colonialism in the Congo, and numerous cultural productions, for instance of visual imagery, appeared. It is hard to gauge whether the overall effect was positive or negative by 1908, the year Belgium took control of the Congo. The scandal over Leopold's colonial misadministration, the monarch's haughty comportment, his financial machinations, alongside his many dubious dalliances: all combined to make him into an unloved figure. After his death in 1909, the public is said to have booed his funeral cortège as it passed through the streets of the country's capital. Leopold II is today almost universally reviled by those familiar with the history of Belgian colonialism, and atrocity images of the Congo reform campaign still predominate when it comes to views of the king and his colonial rule. Often forgotten, or simply not known, is the tremendous extent to which *positive* images of colonialism circulated during the Leopoldian era, both ones made before photographic evidence of violence emerged, and afterward, as the monarch and his collaborators created propaganda to tell a positive story about the CFS. Leopold II had always claimed he wanted to turn the Congo over to his "other" kingdom, a sentiment he expressed in an 1889 letter to prime minister Auguste Beernaert, which was later often quoted to support a positive view of the king. Critics have rightly focused on the stubborn, years-long fight the king mounted as he refused to surrender his colony, and of course the profits extracted from it. Nevertheless, the king's promotion of the Congo among his European subjects suggests he was speaking at least some truth in that 1889 letter. In any case, early efforts to promote overseas rule in Africa did somewhat familiarize the public with colonialism while also introducing a number of themes to Belgian pro-colonial discourse that would endure for decades.

Pro-colonial efforts before 1908 took several forms, one being publications promoting the nascent empire including *Le Mouvement géographique* (from 1884) and *Le Congo illustré* (from 1891); many were either subsidized or directly run by the CFS administration.[5] Many so-called pioneers went to the CFS and returned home to promote the colonial idea in published articles and public talks. In some cases, colonial devotees organized photographic exhibits, although these were few and far between. Early efforts to bring Africa back home on film reels were largely unsuccessful because of the technical difficulties involved in sending equipment and developing and transporting film. Indeed, most of the few motion pictures that were made in the CFS have been lost to the historical record. Another medium of propaganda was colonial exhibits, of which there were major ones at the 1885 and 1894 Antwerp world's fairs, and at the 1897 Tervuren colonial exposition, which took place in conjunction with the universal exposition that year in Brussels.[6] Millions of Belgians were introduced to central Africa and Congolese at these fairs, which often included not only informational and entertaining pavilions, but also live displays of Leopold II's African subjects.[7]

Another influence came in the form of Africana and African art, even if African artwork was not recognized as "art" for many years.[8] As soon as Leopold II had begun funding voyages of exploration, "massive shipments of art from the Congo" started to arrive to Antwerp, the country's main sea port, leading to the assemblage of vast collections of African artwork and objects.[9] On royal grounds around the village of Tervuren, just east of Brussels, the king and his collaborators built a large museum to the colony to act as a "window" onto Africa. Tervuren accepted so many objects that collections rapidly exceeded the available space, leading to construction of a larger museum building, opened in 1910. In Antwerp, where ships from and

Pierre Ponthier (1858-1893)
Location: Marche-en-Famenne, place roi Albert Ier
Sculptor: Alphonse de Tombay[10]
Inauguration: 1897
Funded/built by: public subscription

Ponthier was born in Ouffet, about 30 kilometers north-northeast of the town that became his adoptive home, Marche-en-Famenne. He served as a Force publique officer in the CFS and was involved in numerous military operations there, including the 1892-1894 anti-slavery war against east coast Arab-Swahili slave traders. It was in combat during that conflict that Ponthier was wounded around 18-20 October 1893, at the battle of Kasongo. He died a few days later, and was buried on site.[11]

The monument in Marche-en-Famenne, known as the "Fontaine Ponthier," is one of few colonial memorials built in Belgium during the period of Leopoldian rule in the Congo. It comprises a fountain built on one side of the town's hôtel de ville, a building that today houses a restaurant. At the fountain's center is a large bust of the mustachioed Ponthier in military uniform. It reads, in French only, "Au Commandant Pierre Ponthier, tué au combat de Kassongo le 19 Octobre 1893." (To commanding officer Pierre Ponthier, killed in the battle of Kasongo on 19 October 1893.) Above the bust are outspread wings surrounding the star of the CFS.[12] According to one account, the monument is of Egyptian inspiration, as the bust is "posé sur un socle entouré d'une porte de temple égyptisant. Un bossage irrégulier évoque une pyramide." (set on a pedestal surrounded by the doorway of an Egyptian-style temple. An uneven bossage [stone projecting from the building] evokes a pyramid.)[13]

As one local website points out, the monument commemorates multiple things, not all of them obvious to the observer. It not only celebrates a native son and military figure, it also highlights the provision of clean water to the town, a relatively new achievement at the time it was built. The fountain's waters flowed through the mouths of six lions—also evocative of Egypt, or Africa more generally—three each into two concentric basins: "c'est là que l'on voit, sur les cartes postales anciennes, les habitantes de la localité remplir leur seau ou laver le linge." (It is there that one sees on old postcards local inhabitants filling their buckets or washing laundry.)[14] Perhaps even more, the Fontaine Ponthier is a monument to the 1892-1894 anti-slavery campaigns that Belgians characterized as a fight against east coast Arab slavers, and early postcards of the monument explicitly named the anti-slavery fight.

M. Coosemans' hagiographic entry for Ponthier in the *Biographie Coloniale Belge/Belgische Koloniale Biografie* (*BCB*, later the *Biographie Belge d'Outre-*

mer/Belgische Overzeese Biografie)
praised him as energetic and audacious,
placing him among the "most illustrious
artisans of the colonial undertaking."[15] As
Guy Vanthemsche has explained, the *BCB*
(nine volumes, 1948-2015) is a reference
work on colonial figures begun during
the colonial era that was controlled and
indeed censored in order to produce a
positive impression of Belgian colonialism and its agents. This makes the *BCB*
part of the pro-colonial propaganda of
the state-rule era that relied on tropes
such as the "anti-slavery campaigns" that
underpinned the legitimacy of Belgian in-

*Memorial fountain for Pierre
Ponthier, Marche-en-Famenne, 2003*

tervention in central Africa.[16] Coosemans'
biographical note on Ponthier continues
by not only identifying the man as a "glorious conqueror," but by calling his life
"heroic" and his death "noble." Along the way, Coosemans lauds the CFS officer
further by emphasizing that, "Ponthier embodied hatred of the Arab."[17] Thus,
in addition to highlighting water delivery and the accomplishments of a native
son, the fountain and bust are also a kind of anti-Arab marker that has stood in
the town for well more than a century.

to the Congo loaded and unloaded every day, collector Henry Pareyn began
amassing items beginning in 1903, eventually putting together a collection
so large and valuable that it was worth perhaps as much as 2 million francs
when it was sold at auction in 1928 after his death.[18] One estimate places at
"between 70,000 and perhaps as many as 100,000" the number of objects
pillaged from the Congo in the years before World War I.[19]

The period before 1908 also witnessed the building of the first monuments
in Belgium to so-called colonial pioneers. The term "pioneer" was applied to
those Belgians, all of them men, who left for the Congo "as of the first hour,"
who built the CFS, and who were said to have served the civilizing mission.
Even if for many years Belgians comprised only a fraction of whites in the
Congo, colonial monuments in the metropole only celebrated Belgians, for
instance the one raised in March-en-Famenne in 1897 to Pierre Ponthier. In
all, few colonial monuments were erected in the metropole before 1908, and
it was not until the Belgian state rule period beginning that same year that
the building of such memorials took off.

The circulation of images and of information about central Africa had varied effects. Negative news about the CFS reshaped the Belgian psyche, contributing to critiques of their own king—for instance Félicien Cattier's *Étude sur la situation de l'État indépendant du Congo*[20]—but simultaneously to resentment at foreign influence in the nation's colonial affairs. After 1908, fears of foreign influence transmutated into the rehabilitation of Leopold II as "the internationally tarnished image of the colony was relentlessly restored."[21] For years, even decades, the myth survived that attacks on the CFS by the British and others were motivated by their jealousy, and that they coveted the resource-rich overseas territories of "little Belgium," which might be easily pushed around.

Positive imagery about Leopold and the Congo led to other myths or themes, one early one being the idea that the Belgian takeover of the Congo was good and justified because Belgians had fought uncivilized, non-Christian Arab slavers. This narrative represented a continuation of the abolitionism that had underpinned the end of the Atlantic slave trade, now embellished with a decidedly anti-Arab bent, which was fixed in imagery, sometimes subtly so, such as in the monument in Marche-en-Famenne to Pierre Ponthier. Nineteenth-century exploration travelogues had already underlined the viciousness of "Arab" slave raiding.[22] Many such accounts were printed years or even decades before the century's end, and many remained influential, including the images of violent Arab slavers they contained, either because of their wide circulation or because publishing houses reprinted them, or both. A generic image of Africa south of the Sahara emerged, as a place given over to danger, violence, and primitiveness, begging the question of European intervention. According to this narrative, CFS pioneers brought Catholicism and civilization, and ended the Arab slaving that plagued central and east Africa, epitomized in the lives and deaths of Henri De Bruyne and his commanding officer Joseph Lippens. Those two Belgians were murdered during the anti-slavery campaigns of 1892-1894 by men under the command of Sefu bin Hamid, son of Tippu Tip, the powerful Zanzibari leader who had established a raiding and trading state in eastern Congo, which put him in conflict with the CFS. De Bruyne and Lippens became heroes, and were memorialized for their sacrifice, as discussed in chapter 4.

The narrative of heroic sacrifice against so-called Arab cruelty created a dichotomy at the heart of CFS visual culture, that of heroism and violence. Depictions of European valor sublimated the violence of European conquest of African territories and peoples, transforming the narrative of the CFS from one of conquest into a positive history of the extension of a superior European civilization—even salvation—to backward, helpless Congolese.

This made foreign rule into something not vicious and unjust but necessary, even welcome.

In sum, the king and his collaborators tried to raise awareness and interest among the Belgian public for colonial endeavors in central Africa. By 1908, however, popular interest was only just awakening, and Belgians felt no real attachment to the colony. In fact, the colony played almost no role during the elections of 1908.[23] As noted, Leopold died in 1909, largely unloved. The king's successor, King Albert I, sustained the connection between the colony and the Belgian monarchy by taking a trip there even before ascending the throne—unlike Leopold II, who never stepped foot in the Congo. Nonetheless, interest remained restricted to a small group of ardent colonial supporters, some members of the country's elite (mainly francophone), and among some missionary orders.

The Belgian state rule era

After 1908, a limited but significant colonial culture developed in the metropole such that by 1960, many people embraced a positive vision of their colonial "mission" in Africa. Upon Leopold's 1908 turnover of the Congo, Belgians suddenly found themselves supposed masters of a massive overseas colonial possession, yet under siege because of the international condemnation that the horrific abuses of the CFS regime had elicited. The pressure remained: E. D. Morel's Congo Reform Association was not disbanded in 1908, when Leopoldian rule ended, but rather not until 1913. The government instituted reforms to transform the colonial administration and distance it from the Leopoldian past, although more transformative was World War I. Germany invaded Belgium—which fought back fiercely, perhaps derailing Germany's Schlieffen Plan—and resistance at the forts of Liege and elsewhere led to great praise from the country's Entente allies. A Force publique victory in German East Africa at Tabora handed Belgium its greatest field victory of the entire war, and suffering at the hands of German invaders helped recast the country as victim in the eyes of its western partners. The extent of the transformation is suggested by how in 1919, Belgium increased its colonial holdings by gaining the former German territories of Ruanda-Urundi as League of Nations mandates, something unthinkable before the war. The Bolshevik Revolution in Russia—a country that had been a major target of Belgian foreign investment—sent Belgian investors in search of new outlets for their investment outlays, and many steered funds toward the colony. And there were new profits to be made there. Copper, gold, and other mining enterprises grew significantly from 1914-1918 as wartime demands encouraged mining industries, which eventually eclipsed other activities to form the backbone of the colonial economy. In this sense, World War I acted as the foundation of twentieth-century Belgian overseas rule.[24]

In the immediate post-war years, interest in the colony grew. The number of missionaries going there increased dramatically, most of them hailing from Flanders. The total white population in the Congo grew significantly. As noted, colonial investing and economic activity accelerated, especially in mining, at least up until the onset of the Great Depression, which hit mining and other economic activity hard. Although imports from the colony dropped significantly, exports continued to grow.[25] There was no widespread, organized violent African resistance, and such instances of resistance as there were, were largely kept quiet through close control over information flows to and from the colony. Instead, a significant production of positive imagery propelled a shifting, much more positive view of the colony, for example in lavish photo layouts in the magazine *L'Illustration congolaise*.[26] The 1930s nevertheless witnessed a decline in the white population. Most Belgians never traveled to or lived in the Congo—there were fewer than 12,000 there in 1935—and therefore their ideas about Africa and colonial rule were formed in Europe. Because mainstream newspapers reported little on colonial affairs, people's views were shaped largely by information shared by priests and missionaries, private companies, state information offices, and imperial enthusiasts, including colonial veterans. This is not to say it was all-pervasive; far from it. Consider Stefan Hertmans' retelling of his grandfather Urbain Martien's life (1891-1981) in his recent *War & Turpentine*: the Congo is not mentioned once.[27] Nonetheless, the Congo increasingly "came home" to Belgium in more and more varied ways.

One constant was the Tervuren Museum of the Congo, which served as a "window" onto Africa, and which became a leading center of education about the colony. It developed into not only one of the most popular museums in the country but became the starting point for most people when it came to understanding the Congo. Those in favor of promoting the colonial idea, including many in the Ministry of Colonies (under which the museum fell), targeted Belgian youth in particular: the museum encouraged school visits and set up a so-called Journées d'Études Coloniales at the museum just for school teachers. Although Tervuren was not an "art" museum as such, by the 1950s Tervuren had pulled together a massive collection of Africana and African artwork—museum director Guido Gryseels noted in 2017 that the museum held a collection of 500 Pende masks alone.[28]

Several other realms came to be influenced by colonial stimuli. The colony showed up on some currency, stamps, coins, and medals, albeit rarely.[29]

Colonial themes slowly seeped into literature more generally, including juvenile literature.[30] Hergé's *Tintin in the Congo*, which appeared first in serial form before being published as a book in 1931, is well-known today, but other authors also drew on colonial themes in their writing. Bambi Ceuppens calls Frans Demers (pseudonym of Frans Deckers) the "founder" of Flemish colonial writing. Author Sylva de Jonghe expressed in his works how spreading Christianity was the greatest motivation for colonialism. These authors are largely forgotten today, de Jonghe in part because of his wartime collaboration, for which he was sentenced to prison in 1945, where he died in 1950.[31] There were no Belgian "colonial" writers who achieved the renown of British and French authors stirred by empire, like Rudyard Kipling, E. M. Forster, André Gide, or Pierre Loti. With perhaps the exception of David Van Reybrouck's 2010 *Congo: A History* (discussed below), all of the most famous bestsellers about the Congo have been written by non-Belgians: Henry Morton Stanley's *Through the Dark Continent*; Joseph Conrad's *Heart of Darkness*; V. S. Naipaul's *A Bend in the River*; Adam Hochschild's *King Leopold's Ghost*; and Barbara Kingsolver's *The Poisonwood Bible*.

When it came to expositions of empire in the metropole, Belgium held its own. France hosted the massive 1931 Colonial Exposition, and Britain the 1924-1925 Wembley colonial fair, in addition to another in Glasgow in 1938. Belgian fair organizers also "brought the empire home" to the metropole by means of large colonial pavilions at universal expositions in Brussels in 1910, Ghent in 1913, Antwerp in 1930, and Brussels in 1935. All told these fairs drew in many millions of visitors; more than four million people visited the *pavillon du Congo belge* in Antwerp in 1930 alone.[32]

Just as colonial-themed pavilions grew in prominence at world's fairs during the Belgian state rule period, so did the story of Belgian imperialism increase its presence in classroom education, in textbooks, and in Church publications. Belgium was a young country, independent only in 1830, and educators used the colony in textbooks and lessons to root national identity. Already by the end of Leopold II's reign, the colony had begun to contribute to Belgian self-representations in the country's history texts. After 1908, and especially after World War I, the CFS was transformed into the heroic period of the empire's foundation, further incorporating the colony into the country's history.[33] Catholic missionary orders edited publications to spread news about their activities abroad, and to raise money. Into the post-war era, missions were themselves affected by the colonial encounter as the Catholic Church in Belgium was forced, in a sense, to become more active rather than reflective because of the growing possibilities for action abroad, in the colony. Colonial missionizing influenced the Church by sustaining its prestige into the twentieth century, during an era in which it was beset by threats to its status, in particular following Belgium's late-nineteenth century "culture wars."[34] In a parallel way, the fact that the colonial administration and capital were long dominated by the country's French speakers meant that the colony gave the predominant influence of the country's francophone middle classes an extra lease on life.

Although mainly the province of an elite, the circulation of African artwork only increased as more and more Belgians began to collect it into the interwar era.[35] Some voyages to the Congo had as their main goal the collection of ethnographic objects. Joseph Maes, head of the Tervuren Museum's department of ethnography from 1910-1946, voyaged to the colony in 1913-1914, visiting 120 locations, and collecting 1,293 objects. Some of Henry Pareyn's collection formed the basis of what became Antwerp's ethnographic museum. The city acquired some 1,500 pieces from him in the early 1920s, and further contributions from Minister of Colonies Louis Franck led to the "Volkenkundige verzamelingen en Kongoleesche Afdeeling" (Ethnographic collections and Congolese division) at Antwerp's Vleeshuis in the 1920s. Antwerp's Etnografisch Museum was established in 1952, even if it was always more than just a colonial museum because only around 12,000 of its estimated 40,000 objects originated in Africa.[36]

It remained true that few recognized African artwork as *art*, at least until the end of the colonial era, seeing African art objects instead as creations of handicraft workers, not artists expressing abstract ideas.[37] A few believed otherwise as early as the 1920s, but they were exceptions that proved the rule, for instance Antwerp's Pareyn, George Thiry, and Gaston-Denys Périer.[38] Thiry was a Belgian colonial functionary in the Congo who encouraged indigenous artistic production, and who discovered Congolese artists who were to become major figures, including Albert Lubaki. Unlike Thiry, Périer did not travel to the Congo, but he was intimately connected to the world of colonial affairs through his position within the Ministry of Colonies in Brussels, where he eventually headed the "Bibliothèque-Documentation-Presse et Propagande" (Library-Documentation-Press and Propaganda) office. Périer became an enthusiast and tireless promoter of the culture and art of central Africa; "un grand amateur d'art nègre" (a great lover of negro art) who "felt that Congolese art needed to come out of the ghetto of primitivism in which it had been confined for too long."[39]

It was army officers, missionaries, and colonial administrators who brought the majority of Africana to Belgium before 1960. Some was exhibited at world's fairs, much was put on display in expected places such as the well-known Tervuren Congo museum, but much other work was displayed in private homes, other museums, businesses, galleries, art dealerships, and religious institutions. Statues, masks, ceramics, and weapons—being substantial material culture—reshaped three dimensional space in those places where they were shown. Some missionaries became admirers of African culture, and some became collectors. Scheutist Leo Bittremieux, who lived among the Mayombe (Lower Congo) from 1907 until his death in 1946, sent items to the Catholic University of Leuven, to his family, and to his congregation's "Musée de Fétiches" in Kangu.[40] Some items Bittremieux collected ended up in the Tervuren Congo museum as well.[41] In her memoir *Back to the Congo*, Lieve Joris recalls her uncle, a missionary, who sent objects home, some of which ended up on being put on display in the house, others going into storage in the attic.[42]

The country's large collections of Congolese art and Africana were intimately connected to colonial rule. Much Congolese Africana in Belgium, especially weaponry, was seized after victory in battle, and subsequently endured the trip back to Belgium and years-long storage or display precisely because of its durability. Nearly all early oil and other paintings by Congolese, such as there were, were made of vegetable and other materials, and have been lost.[43] Collecting, categorizing, and preserving artwork—and later the promotion of indigenous artistic production—intrinsically asserted European expertise over African culture as collectors set themselves up as experts, assuming a position from which they judged which art was "authentic." After years of colonial rule in the Congo, some Europeans came to the conclusion that Congolese culture, including authentic artistic creation, was disappearing because of the onslaught of modernity. "Il était d'ailleurs urgent de récolter ou de sauvegarder ces témoignages, car, pensait-on, il s'agissait d'un monde menacé par la décadence et la ruine." (It was moreover urgent to collect or to safeguard these expressions because, so it was thought, this was a world threatened by decadence and ruin.)[44] This argument to preserve Congolese cultures paralleled similar assertions elsewhere in the colonial world including in British India and French Indochina.[45]

In African art displays, school textbooks, the Tervuren Museum, literature, and from the pulpit: the Congo loomed larger, and became nationalized. This was only reinforced by a wave of monument building beginning around 1930, part of a surge of Belgian nationalism following World War I. The erection of memorials across the country to the nation's colonial pioneers—in Anderlecht, Bonlez, Borgerhout, Gedinne, Lens, Leuven, Lodelinsart, Mons, Ostend, Verviers, and many dozens if not hundreds of other towns and villages—asserted the country's claim over the Congo while demonstrating and reinforcing post-war nationalism. In this way, colonial themes became woven into the fabric of everyday life, in particular in urban areas.

Colonial pioneers
Location: Anderlecht, inside the city hall
Inauguration: 5 October 1930[46]
Funded/built by: commune of Anderlecht

Plaque to colonial pioneers, Anderlecht, 2018

This plaque to native sons of Anderlecht who died "voor de beschaving" (for civilization) in the Congo during the Leopoldian era is located in the foyer of Anderlecht's city hall. It was inaugurated in 1930, part of a wave of memorial building spearheaded by Belgian pro-colonial groups, in particular the Ligue du souvenir congolais and the Vétérans coloniaux.[47]

Many pro-colonials in Belgium characterized such men as "pioneers" and "heroes," although what little is known about the eleven commemorated on the Anderlecht plaque suggests that the deaths of many of them, if terrible, were hardly heroic. Take Arthur-François Declerck, who is listed third on the memorial, and who served in the CFS administration beginning in 1892. As Declerck's period of service in the Congo neared its end, he died, in February 1895. The cause of death is recorded as *fièvre hématurique*, or fever and hematuria (blood in the urine), which likely meant malaria, and probably blackwater fever.[48] Seventh on the plaque is Charles-Louis-Jules Fichefet, who joined the Force publique as an officer in 1899 at the age of twenty-four. He served one year in the Congo, from March 1899 to March 1900, at which point he had to depart for Belgium because of illness. Fichefet returned to central Africa in September of the same year, but died of fever before the year was out.[49] Also listed on the plaque is Jean-Charles Croes, a sergeant in the Force publique who spent nine months in the Congo before killing himself at Befidji in early 1895.[50] Jean-Quirin Verlooy, also in the Force publique, served at various posts before dying suddenly of dysentery in December 1899, one month shy of his twenty-fourth birthday.[51]

Whatever one's view of the so-called civilizing mission, the Anderlecht memorial reveals the risks Europeans took when leaving for the Congo. Suicide, which ended the life of Croes, was not uncommon, as suggested by Joseph Conrad's short story, "An Outpost of Progress," based in part on the author's time in the Congo. Conrad's tale tells of two European men posted to a remote location in the colony who eventually get into a dispute that leads one of the two to kill the other before taking his own life, by hanging.[52] A conservative estimate of the suicide rate for Europeans in the CFS would be 464 per 100,000, compared to about 12 per 100,000 in Europe today.[53] Much more dangerous was disease, especially malaria and dysentery. Viral and bacterial infections killed Europeans at such a rate in nineteenth-century tropical sub-Saharan Africa that some called West Africa "the White Man's Grave." As one scholar put it, "during the whole of the nineteenth century, the most important problem for Europeans in West Africa was simply that of keeping alive."[54] As the experiences of the young men from Anderlecht memorialized in the commune's hôtel de ville suggest, the same could just as easily have been said of Europeans venturing to the Congo.

Joseph-Émile Villers (1866-1898) and Charles-Eugène Edouard Chevalier de Meulenaer (1873-1920)
Location: Bonlez, église Sainte-Catherine, rue de Bonlez
Inauguration: 8 August 1930[55]

This plaque in the village of Bonlez remembers two native sons "morts au Congo pour la civilisation" (who died in the Congo for civilization). Villers was a tramway steam engine operator before he left for the Congo in 1894, becoming a deputy stationmaster on the first rail line that was being built between Matadi and Kinshasa. He returned home in the spring of 1896, only to depart for the Congo again in February 1897, where he died of unspecified causes a year later.[56] Villers was one of hundreds who lost their lives during the construction of the Matadi-Kinshasa railway, most of whom were Africans. De Meulenaer, six years Villers' junior, joined the military at the age of eighteen and left for the Congo in 1898 as a Force publique officer, where he worked for the CFS administration. He enjoyed an illustrious military career, moving back and forth between the metropole and the Congo. He was in central Africa at the outbreak of World War I, and supported wartime efforts there behind the lines. His term of colonial service ended while the war raged on, and when he returned to Europe, he went to the Western Front, suffering grievous injuries in June 1918. Having recovered, he returned to the colony before suddenly dying of unspecified causes at Leopoldville in September 1920. He was 47 years old.[57]

Plaque to native sons who died in the Congo, Bonlez, 2018

The memorial plaque in Bonlez formed part of the wave of nationalistic and pro-colonial memorialization of Congo "pioneers" during the interwar years. Different than most, the plaque commemorates someone, namely de Meulenaer, who died *after* 1908. Like many others, the plaque clearly ties the two men to the CFS by means of a star engraved on it, a large star being a key CFS symbol that adorned the colonial state's flag. The plaque is also somewhat unusual in that it was placed on a church. These memorial plaques were less often placed on or near churches, although it did happen not only in Bonlez but also Bovigny, Elsaute, and Thisnes, among other sites—churches were normally centrally located, after all. This plaque also shows how commemoration of colonial heroes, as they were called, reached into even small and rather remote villages, like Bonlez.

Colonial pioneers
Location: Borgerhout (Antwerp), Moorkensplein
Inauguration: unknown
Funded/built by: commune of Borgerhout

This plaque honoring eight locals from Borgerhout who died in the Congo reads, "Aan de Borgerhoutse Kolonialen gestorven in Congo vóór 18 October 1908." (To the Borgerhout colonials who died in the Congo before 18 October 1908.)[58] The plaque is unusual in that among the dead it honors is a woman, a rarity for such memorials. This was Joanna (or Jeanne) Crauwels, known as Sister Vincentia, who was of the congregation the Sœurs du Sacré Cœur de Marie. She left for the Congo in autumn 1899, becoming one of the very first white women to reach the Uele River. She died in January 1904.[59] The memorial is typical in that it explicitly connects local pioneers with Leopold II's colonial rule by including the

Borgerhout plaque to colonial pioneers, 2018

CFS symbol, a star, along with the date of 18 October 1908; this the day the parliament passed the *Charte coloniale*, which annexed the Congo as a colonial territory.

Many colonial plaques and monuments spell out exact dates in order to specifically associate those being honored with the Leopoldian period of rule in the Congo: usually either 1876-1908 or 1885-1908. The year 1876 witnessed the Brussels Geographical Conference, which many took to signal the very beginning of the Leopoldian colonial endeavor, whereas the year 1885 was the year the CFS was declared. 1908, as noted, was the year Leopold II surrendered or "gifted" his colony to Belgium. Because there were Belgians who died in the Congo after 1908, highlighting that year specifically glorified Belgians who died serving Leopold II, creating a kind of colonial tradition for a country that did not have one. Unlike the Portuguese, Spanish, French, British, and the Dutch, Belgians had no longstanding history of overseas expansionism or colonial rule. Singling out the pre-1908 period and honoring Leopold II was an attempt to legitimize the country's young colonial rule that had been born in controversy. Hearkening back to the Leopoldian "heroic" era rooted the contemporaneous Belgian colony in some kind of longer and thus legitimate colonial history.

This rooting of Belgium's interwar colonialism in a supposedly historical and therefore valid tradition of national overseas expansion in memorials such as the one in Borgerhout was profoundly and doubly ironic. First, before 1908, not only were Belgians largely indifferent to Leopold's African rule, in practice the CFS was as much an international enterprise as it was a homegrown one. In fact in 1908, when Belgium took over the colony, a mere 58 percent of whites in the colony were Belgian. These interwar memorials—which exclusively honor Belgians who died in the colony before 1908, not any foreigners—implicitly recast an international colonial endeavor as one that was strictly Belgian. A second irony is that these monuments heap praise on the glorious "civilizing mission" of Leopold II and his agents, when in reality it was because the king's administration was so terrible that an international campaign emerged in the first place, which brought it to an end. It was Leopold II's colonial misrule that caused the king to be forced to turn the colony over to Belgium in the first place, and yet interwar memorials turned around and heaped praise on him and his colonial rule.

Local colonial "pioneers"[60]
Location: Verviers, rue du Théâtre
Inauguration: 5 July 1931[61]
Funded/built by: Amicale des anciens coloniaux

This memorial plaque to local sons who died in the Congo bears several names, and reads as follows:

LA VILLE DE VERVIERS A SES ENFANTS
(The City of Verviers to its children)

F. BODSON	F. PATERNOSTER
J. COLLARD	F. PIRON
J. DELHEY	A. PROTIN
J. GENICOT	N. YUNCKER
J. GEORGE	CAMPAGNE 1914-1918
R. GUEQUIER	A. DOMKEN
P. LECROMPE	E. TODT
G. DORTU	F. LEFEBVRE

MORTS AU CONGO AU SERVICE DE LA CIVILISATION
(Died in the Congo in the service of civilization)

An inset image with the caption "Pro Patria Belgica" shows a woman laying a wreath on a dead man. Like the memorial to Anderlecht's colonial dead, this one in Verviers shows how going to the Congo was an inherently risky undertaking. J. Collard arrived to the Congo on 26 February 1891, and was dead, in Matadi, by 7 April 1891, little more than a month later.[62] Reneldes Guéquier, whose death by hematuria assured that "sa place est, dans le martyrologe de l'E.I.C., parmi les courageux pionniers de l'âge héroïque," (in the martyrology of the CFS, he is to be found among the courageous pioneers of the heroic age,) first arrived to the Congo on 10 January 1895; he was dead by August 1897.[63] Guillaume Dortu arrived to the colony on 5 May 1893 and was dead before the year was out.[64] Félix Piron manned a battery at the Shinkakasa fort. When they

Verviers plaque to native sons who died in the Congo, 2018

tested a new cannon in 1892, the gun burst into pieces, killing Piron.[65] Somewhat unusual is that three of the men listed, A. Domken, F. Lefebvre, and E. Todt,
died not during the so-called heroic period, but rather during World War I.

The funds to raise the plaque were put together by a local association of former colonials in the Congo. This Verviers group, created in 1921, originally had
the name "Groupement des anciens coloniaux," which became in 1925, "Amicale
des anciens coloniaux," and then after independence the Royale Amicale des
Anciens d'Afrique de Verviers et environs (RAAAV). Their plaque is located on
a wall along stairs called the "Chic-Chac," not far from the city's train station.
Small, rather obscure, and in 2018 on a much-deteriorated stairway, one would
not suspect that the plaque was once a center of attention. But in fact, photos
from the 1930s show hundreds gathered at the site to celebrate the men listed
on the memorial on the occasion of the country's summertime "colonial days."[66]

Beginning in 1940, Belgium again suffered German invasion, leading to
defeat, occupation, collaboration, resistance, and waiting. Even if the country
was cut off from its central African possessions, and even if colonial issues
retreated from the national consciousness as navigating everyday life took
precedence, the Congo was of critical importance during the war. Colonial
revenue sustained the government in exile in London, thereby preserving the
country's sovereignty, and uranium for the U.S. atomic bombs dropped on
Japan came from Katanga's mines.[67] But this was known to few at the time,
and if anything the conflict represented a caesura in Belgian connections with
the colony as exchanges were suspended, the terms of colonial administrators
were extended, and most Belgians remained preoccupied with mere survival.

The 1950s: The apogee of empire

With liberation in 1944, reconstruction, and post-war economic growth, the Belgian Congo emerged as more influential and important than ever. Still, other issues loomed larger. Although this was an era of economic growth, the 1950s were also a decade of transition, tensions, and strife. The country had to rebuild not only physically but also psychically after the trauma of war, and the reestablishment of the pre-war governmental system was problematic and contentious.[68] The *Question royale* loomed large: this was the question as to Leopold III's suspected collaborationist leanings during the war, and whether they would prevent him from returning to the country to once again reign after the war's end. The crisis of the *Question royale* was only partially resolved after a five-year regency and Leopold III's 1950 abdication in favor of his son, Baudouin, who took the oath in August 1950 and ascended the throne the following year. Leopold III and his second, morganatic wife Princess Lilian continued to live at the Château de Laeken until 1960, casting a shadow over the young Baudouin's reign, and the whole episode called into question the prestige, influence, and significance of the monarchy. Another burning issue was *la question scolaire* and state support for *écoles libres*, that is, non-state (usually Catholic) schools. This was a debate that was not resolved until elections, strife, and negotiations resulted in the November 1958 *pacte scolaire*. This agreement formally confirmed the existence of state and "free" schools, guaranteed parental choice in schooling, and assured tuition-free schooling (for required, compulsory education), which meant both continued government underwriting of official schools as well as subsidies for religious schools.[69] Another development was a catastrophic mining accident at Marcinelle on 8 August 1956 that killed hundreds and shocked the public. Internationally, there were moves toward greater European cooperation, in no small part to deal with "the German problem." Those included the *plan Schuman* of 1950 and the signing of the Treaty of Rome of 1957. In 1958, Brussels opened further to Europe and the world, hosting the first universal exposition since New York's 1939-1940 World's Fair, and becoming the provisional seat of the European institutions that were to become the Communauté européenne, and, eventually, the European Union.

Throughout the 1950s, the country's African territories gained in importance not only economically and diplomatically but also psychologically and culturally as the colony assumed a greater place in everyday life and as Belgians became more aware of themselves as colonial rulers. This was paralleled by a heightened colonial state penetration of the Congo, even if the Belgian administration never completely mastered its vast African territories. World War II and then the Korean War underlined the importance of raw commodities and boosted faith in the colony's mining sector, which produced copper, uranium, gold, tin, cobalt, and diamonds. A signal of confidence in a colonial future was that Belgium, like Europe's other colonial powers, launched an ambitious development plan, the *plan décennal*, to direct colonial investments. There was a spike in emigration to central Africa: the number of Belgians residing there grew from 23,643 in 1945 to 39,006 in 1950 and 88,913 in 1959.[70] This is not to say the floodgates opened for anyone to relocate. Most whites living there, as in the pre-war years, were comparatively well off because both official policy and unofficial practice hindered and sometimes even prohibited "undercapitalized" individuals from traveling to or staying in the colony. In fact, the colonial administration booted at least 1,450 whites out of the Congo during the colonial period, probably in most cases because they did not have enough capital.[71] Political elites expressed satisfaction with their achievements in Africa and studiously rejected any interference in the country's colonial affairs, for instance by the U.N. or the U.S.[72] A 1956 poll revealed everyday people felt pride in their colony and believed in the legitimacy of their country's control over the Congo.[73]

It is hard if not impossible to distill all the factors contributing to Belgian views by the post-World War II era, but surely they resulted in part from decades of pro-colonial propaganda, which only ramped up during the 1950s. By that decade such propaganda had achieved a complete rehabilitation of the previously maligned Leopold II, and had gone further by successfully associating the Leopoldian era with Belgian state rule. Those parts of 1950s-era history textbooks that dealt with colonialism focused on Leopold II and the explorers and adventurers who had worked for him, and almost completely passed over the period after 1908. Textbooks depicted Leopoldian rule as a Belgian affair, even though the CFS administration, the Force publique officer corps, missionary posts, and colonial companies all had been staffed by many foreigners.[74] Leopold's rehabilitation extended beyond the classroom to film, exhibits, museums, and annual summer celebrations during the country's "journées colonials" or "koloniale dagen" (colonial days). Popularization efforts included ramped-up pro-colonial photography and filmmaking, much of it coordinated by the Ministry of Colonies' Office de l'Information et des Relations publiques pour le Congo Belge et le Ruanda-Urundi, or Infor-congo.[75] The country's second king was remembered in major new monuments in Mons, Hasselt, Halle, and Ghent, in addition to the re-inauguration of yet another one in Namur. Other pro-colonial monuments were also unveiled, such as one to Baron Tombeur de Tabor in St. Gilles. One statue to Leopold unveiled in the 1950s in Arlon bore the words that form this chapter's epigraph, placing the king in a favorable light. This quote from Leopold also adorned a temporary bust of him displayed at a pavilion entrance at the 1958 Brussels World's Fair.[76] An unpopular monarch at the time of his death in 1909, Belgians were full of praise for Leopold a half century later.

Two major events in the 1950s reveal the degree to which people had embraced the colonial project. The first was a 1955 royal tour of the Congo

---

Leopold II (1835-1909)

Location: Arlon

Sculptors: Victor Demanet and Arthur Dupagne

Architect: J. Ghobert[77]

Inauguration: 17 June 1951

Funded/built by: public subscription and the Cercle colonial arlonais[78]

Located outside Arlon at the carrefour de la Spetz, this monument is the work of Victor Demanet, the same sculptor behind Namur's statue of Leopold II. It is one of three colonial memorials in Arlon, the others being a 1931 plaque to colonial pioneers near Arlon's city hall and a 1937 plaque to Pierre Van Damme, who was killed in German East Africa in 1917.

"Before" plaque, Arlon monument to Leopold II, 2003

"After" plaque, Arlon monument to Leopold II, 2003

Arlon monument to Leopold II and colonialism, 2003

Above a towering Leopold II at the center of the memorial's scene is the quotation attributed to him, in French only, which also shows up on other monuments: "I undertook the work of the Congo in the interest of civilization and for the good of Belgium." Panels to the king's left and right tell a didactic "before and after" story of colonizing success. The "before" scene to the left shows several Africans in miserable shape, driven by Arab slavers. All are nude or semi-naked; some are bound; one cowers; and a woman, kneeling on the earth, holds her child tightly, in fear. The "after" scene to the right portrays the glorious results of the civilizing mission. Gone are the Arab slavers. Now, essentially all the African figures are clothed. One seated Congolese man peers through a microscope; others work materials with tools; yet another wears a European suit and carries a book. One woman, standing, holds her child in her arms, while another female figure wearing a cross around her neck guides a child standing at her feet.

Similar to monuments to Leopold II inaugurated in the 1950s in Halle, Hasselt, and elsewhere, this one in Arlon can be considered not only a colonial site, but one that promoted the Saxe-Coburg dynasty. Belgium's monarchy emerged from World War II damaged, and was undermined by the *Question royale*. Celebrating Belgium's second king in bronze and stone in the 1950s was one way to bolster the country's ruling house at a difficult moment. The dynastic connection was made explicit at the monument's inauguration, which was attended by Princess Joséphine-Charlotte, the daughter of King Leopold III.[79]

Charles Tombeur (1867-1947)
Location: St. Gilles (Sint-Gillis), avenue du Parc
Sculptors: Jacques Marin (bust, 1922), and André Willequet
Architect: Georges Dewez[80]
Inauguration: 24 June 1951

Tombeur's claim to fame was his role conquering Tabora in German East Africa during World War I. He was born in Liege in 1867, and died in Brussels eighty years later, where he was buried, in St. Gilles cemetery. Tombeur began his service in the Congo under Leopold II with a first term of duty in the CFS from 1902 to 1905, returning there again in 1907. During World War I, he became a lieutenant-general, and was placed in charge of Belgian African troops. He launched the successful spring 1916 offensive against German colonial forces in German East Africa, which led to victory and the taking of the German East Africa capital, Tabora, by September of that same year. Albert I granted Tombeur his title of nobility in 1926, and Tombeur was given the honor of being able to

St. Gilles monument to Baron Tombeur de Tabora, 2018

add "of Tabora" to his name following a 1936 royal decree. After retirement, he headed the Union colonial belge then the Cercle royal africain in Brussels. There was a state funeral upon his death.[81]

This major colonial figure was memorialized a number of times in his home country: a street in Etterbeek bears his name, and busts of him were displayed in the Tervuren Congo Museum's *salle de mémorial*, in the Musée Africain de Namur, and in the Liege city hall's *salle des pas perdus*. The St. Gilles monument is by far the largest of these memorials to him. Photographs from its 1951 inauguration show an honor guard and crowds lining the avenue du Parc for the event.[82]

The St. Gilles monument itself consists of a bust of Tombeur in bronze framed by a large backdrop of bluestone, with the inscription: AU LIEUTENANT GENERAL BARON TOMBEUR DE TABORA 1867-1947. On the reverse are the words TOMBEUR DE TABORA above a downward-pointing sword surrounded by a wreath. The monument has remained essentially unchanged over the years, aside from upkeep, such as the reguilding of its inscriptions. Recently, the commune of St. Gilles added an explanatory plaque, in French, Dutch, German, and English, calling attention to Tombeur's leadership role in east Africa during World War I, which led to Belgium's takeover of Ruanda-Urundi. It is surprising that in what is a diverse commune where many people of African descent live, the plaque leaves unquestioned the "how" and "why" of Belgium's presence in Africa.

Belgium's victory in east Africa represented its greatest battlefield success of World War I, aside from its fierce defense at the outset of the conflict that hindered German forces, perhaps derailing the Schlieffen Plan. The successful east Africa campaign under Tombeur's leadership contributed to Belgium's takeover of the former German territories of Ruanda-Urundi as League of Nations Mandates after the war. Because Tombeur made his name above all else through his role as a commander in World War I, the monument is as much a commemoration of the country's role in that conflict as it is a celebration of empire.

The timing of Tombeur's death and the inauguration of the monument might also have lent them significance, coming as they did on the heels of the creation of the U.N. in the fall of 1945, which transformed Ruanda-Urundi into UN Trust Territories. Belgium had to report on those territories before a special U.N. committee, and Belgium, along with the other colonial powers, came under intense criticism in that forum. The large monument to Tombeur, in the country's capital region, and celebrated with great fanfare, could have acted as a subtle assertion of Belgian authority over the territories of Ruanda-Urundi.

In any case, the Saint-Gilles monument became a site of commemoration for pro-colonials. The "salut aux drapeaux des campagnes d'Afrique" (salute to the flags of the African campaigns) became a mainstay of annual national "colonial day" celebrations each summer. After the inauguration of Tombeur's monument in 1951, laying wreaths at the monument became a key moment of annual colonial day celebrations, even into the post-1960 period.[83]

by their young king, Baudouin, which was a huge success.[84] The monarchy was trying to recover from the *Question royale*, and Baudouin emerged as a popular figure as photographs and news reel showed him beaming as he received his Congolese subjects. It was said that the king, who often appeared taciturn, "found his smile" in Africa. The visit resulted in a major propaganda film by André Cauvin, *Bwana Kitoko*. The title was a European creation combining Lingala and Swahili. During the visit, in Lingala-speaking areas of the Congo, some called the young king *mwana kitoko*, meaning "handsome young man." Many Congolese, having heard the king was coming, expected an older man, and were surprised at the monarch's youth. (He was 25 at the time.) But "handsome young man" would not do for Belgians, because it was not respectful enough. So they combined the Lingala expression with the Swahili word for master, "bwana," to come up with *bwana kitoko*.[85] As this focus on the young king might suggest, the home audience's attention in 1955 was on their white, European king, not so much on Congolese or the Congo itself. Aside from colonial newspapers and the relatively small European population in the Congo, press reports on the 1955 visit were read and interpreted within the framework of metropolitan concerns much more than being understood from a "colonialist" let alone African perspective.[86]

The 1955 royal tour showed again how Belgian views of the monarchy—and the dynasty's influence on Belgian politics and society—were linked to the colony, as they had been going back to Leopold II. All monarchs after Leopold II toured the Congo, meaning the 1955 trip was only the latest and greatest of various trips to the colony that strengthened the monarchy's ties to it. Innumerable critics have blasted Leopold II for never having set foot in the Congo, even though he ruled that area, and with devastating consequences, for nearly a quarter century. Yet this was not entirely unusual. Other European heads of state or of government rarely visited their colonies; a single reigning monarch visited India during the British Raj, George V in 1911.[87] And all of Leopold's successors went to the Congo either before, during, or after their reign, including Regent Charles.[88] These many royal tours of the Congo—including, as we will see, into the post-1960 era—were followed with interest in both the French- and Flemish-language press.[89] Just as the colony extended the power of the Church and the country's French-speaking middle classes, so did it offer an opportunity to enhance the monarchy's influence in Belgium.

The second major event indicative of the degree to which Belgians had embraced the civilizing mission was the 1958 Brussels World's Fair, which included a large Congo section.[90] This first universal exposition since 1939-1940 showcased modern technology, with a large gleaming "Atomium" acting as its centerpiece. With the recent launch of Sputnik and continuing tensions in Berlin and elsewhere, the Cold War loomed large. The fair attracted some 40 million visitors, many of whom experienced a major display of colonial paternalism and self-assuredness in the large Congo section, which was designed and created almost exclusively by Europeans, and which included seven pavilions to showcase achievements in the realms of missionary activity, mining, health care, agriculture, and other aspects of the civilizing mission. Outside the pavilions, a tropical garden evoked central Africa, and a "native village" held artisans working before the eyes of a curious public; one more and perhaps the last such show in a long line of "human zoos" in Europe and the U.S. Those artisans were among the hundreds of Congolese authorities brought to or allowed to travel to Europe for the fair, most housed under strict conditions in segregated quarters next to the Tervuren Museum. In sum, the fair reinforced colonial stereotypes, highlighted Belgian achievements, and denied African history.

By the 1950s, the colony was something on which virtually all Belgians agreed, regardless of gender, social class, language spoken, or even political leanings; even socialists had long ago abdicated their opposition to colonialism.[91] Belgians coalesced around ideas of European, white supremacy over backward Africans. Being rulers of what they believed was an envied colonial regime stoked anxieties: that Belgium might be pushed around by bigger powers, a perennial fear reinforced by invasion in 1914 and 1940, and the outsized power of the U.S. after 1945. Belgians of all political stripes and regional attachments felt confident their country was doing an exceptional job in Africa, something reinforced by and reflected in pro-colonial propaganda displays such as the 1958 Congo pavilions. In a turbulent world in which neighboring colonial powers suffered setbacks like India's 1947 partition, Ghana's independence in 1957, the Mau Mau uprising in Kenya, or France's war in Algeria, the Belgian Congo was by contrast an "oasis of stability" in the colonial world.

Conclusion

Belgian views of the colony and of their history there, and the way in which these fed into the country's culture, underwent major transformations across the state rule period after 1908. Indifference—even opposition—shifted to widespread pride in the colony, if not profound attachment to it. Visual imagery, for instance in explorer travelogues, were reprinted and circulated to construct a generic image of an Africa that was dangerous, violent, and primeval. This was reinforced in stone and bronze in monuments that emphasized European civilization and Christianity, Arab predation, and African primitiveness, all of which justified colonization and a European presence in central Africa that rationally exploited its untapped resources. Leopold went from worst to first: once a maligned villain, he had become transformed into a prescient genius who had gifted a great empire to his country, making it the envy of a jealous world. The colonial past had been nationalized. Belgians ignored both their own predecessors' indifference to colonial affairs, and the fact that Leopold II had relied heavily on foreigners to run the CFS. Leopold's CFS agents had been converted from an international band of violent conquerors into Belgian pioneers of civilization who had ended the brutal domination of foreign, Muslim Arab slavers. Most striking of all, the colonial system of the CFS, which had been so horrific its ruler had been forced to surrender it to Belgium, became foundational to contemporaneous colonial rule.

The rosy picture Belgians enjoyed in the 1950s was not to last, however. On June 30, 1960, the Congo became independent. It turned out that Belgian rule was not immune to the vast changes sweeping the colonial world. The radicalism of African nationalism—embodied in the Congo's first prime minister, Patrice Lumumba—and the Congo crisis that followed the colony's independence, would for many Belgians ruin nearly everything for which they and their forebears had sacrificed so much, in the process reshaping Belgium's culture in significant ways.

Chapter 2
Reminders and Remainders of Empire, 1960-1967

"The independence of the Congo is the crowning of the work conceived by the genius of King Leopold II undertaken by him with firm courage, and continued by Belgium with perseverance."[1] — King Baudouin, 30 June 1960

"Nous ne sommes plus vos macaques!" (We are no longer your monkeys!)[2] — Attributed to Patrice Lumumba, 30 June 1960

The Congo's independence and the crisis that followed garnered much attention in Belgium through the mid-1960s and influenced people's views of their country's colonial history. As historian Guy Vanthemsche puts it, "the crisis in the Congo reverberated throughout Belgian society and shocked public opinion."[3] This is not to say that "colonial" issues predominated over all others. After all, for all the trauma of the end of empire, the total population of Belgians living in the Congo before 1960 never exceeded 90,000 in any given year, meaning that most of the country's population was impacted by decolonization at a remove. Moreover, developments closer to home remained of paramount importance. The country continued to develop as a bi-lingual state at the center of West European post-war recovery efforts, with a multi-layered, centuries-old culture framing people's everyday lives, be it the neatly-tended countryside, a deep heritage of both classical and cutting-edge painting and literature, Catholicism, the country's culinary inheritance, or its declining but still crucial industrial backbone. One specific, dramatic event grabbed everyone's attention beginning in December 1960, namely a massive industrial strike that essentially shut down Wallonia. It turned out to be one of the largest strikes, if not the largest, in the nation's twentieth-century history. This harbinger of change to come—namely a decline in and then halt to coal production in the Borinage—created shockwaves. This connected to related shifts in the country's economy as its center shifted northward to Flanders, and as the workforce transformed from one divided among farmers, industrial workers, service sector employees, and civil servants, to one where service sector employees predominated. As World War II collaboration receded in time, the language issue re-emerged, most dramatically in two Flemish "marches on Brussels" in 1961 and 1963. In politics, this was an era in which Flemish-language parties were ascendant: from 1954 to 1973, all first ministers were to be Flemish-speaking except Pierre Harmel (1965-1966) and Vanden Boeynants (1966-1968).[4]

Decolonization and the Congo Crisis

The Congo's independence in 1960 came suddenly and revealed that despite much rhetoric to the contrary, Belgians had done little to prepare their colony (or themselves) for self-rule. As we have seen, paternalistic colonial displays like the one at the 1958 World's Fair and its human zoo reflected confidence in the endurance of the *mission civilisatrice*, as did the continued unveiling of colonialist memorials throughout the 1950s, for example a new statue to Leopold II erected in Mons in 1958. To all appearances, it seemed independence must be decades away. In 1957, "that is a little more than three years before the independence of the Congo," one study says, "at that moment, no one in Belgium believed it to be so close."[5]

Thus, it is in retrospect no surprise that when riots broke out in January 1959 in the colony's capital, Leopoldville, the colonial establishment was shocked, as it was again when shortly afterward Baudouin took to the radio airwaves to address the situation and actually pronounced the word "independence." Few appreciated how quickly Congolese nationalism had developed in the previous years, and nationalist leaders now pushed for negotiations. At a roundtable conference in January-February 1960, Congolese delegates wrested independence from their Belgian counterparts, who acquiesced to a rapid timetable in hopes it would leave the Congo unprepared, and in need of indefinite Belgian tutelage. Elections took place, and an independence ceremony was held on 30 June. As the contrasting quotes in this chapter's epigraph reveal, Belgian and Congolese leaders took decidedly different views on the past: Baudouin saw the colonial epoch as a glorious page in his kingdom's history, while newly-elected prime minister Lumumba saw it as an era of humiliation and oppression.

Independence was almost immediately followed by what came to be called the Congo crisis: an army mutiny; the secession of the rich provinces of Katanga and Kasai; violence; and foreign interventions, including by the former colonial power. The president, Joseph Kasavubu, and the prime minister, Patrice Lumumba, each dismissed the other, and the Armée nationale congolaise seized power under its chief, Joseph-Désiré Mobutu. In January 1961, Lumumba was assassinated by Katanga's leaders, with encouragement from

Leopold II (1835-1909)

Location: Mons (Bergen), behind église Sainte-Elisabeth

Sculptor: Raoul Godfroid

Inauguration: ca. 14 September 1958

Funded/built by: Cercle royal congolais de Mons et de la région and the Ministry of Colonies[6]

The bronze statue of Leopold II in Mons reveals both how the monarch had been fully rehabilitated by the 1950s, and how colonial monuments mobilized the public during and after the colonial era. The building of a large statue to the founder of the Belgian overseas empire entailed the creation of a board to do so; a committee membership list includes more than 150 names, showing how such efforts involved large numbers of people. What is more, much of the funding for the monument was raised through public subscription, another way in which such efforts mobilized a broader public, and not merely pro-colonial enthusiasts.

The statue itself, by sculptor Raoul Godfroid, was inaugurated in 1958 in the presence of a large crowd composed of people from "patriotic groups," schools, the army, and the gendarmerie, as well as a representative of the king. According to one report, the statue rose seven meters above ground-level and dominated the entrance to Mons via the chaussée de Bruxelles at the city's northern end. It was one Mr. Marquette, the president of the Vétérans coloniaux as well as president of the monument organizing committee, who presented the statue to the city.[7] Godfroid's towering creation perhaps more than any other statue to Leopold II captures the monarch's great height. Leopold's breast bears typical medals; a sword hangs in a scabbard by his side; one hand grips his gloves; and his other hand, hanging at his side, holds his hat. Over his shoulders he wears a large greatcoat, completing a regal picture.

Statue of Leopold II in Mons, 2018

Statue of Leopold II in
Mons in 2002 and 2018

The Mons memorial to Leopold II reveals the surprising degree to which Belgians remained confident in their colonial control in the Congo, right down to its sudden and largely unanticipated end. Within just four months of the statue's inauguration, riots had broken out in the Congo's capital, Leopoldville, a key moment that propelled events toward the colony's independence a mere 18 months later.

The large bronze Leopold II in Mons is also suggestive of how colonial monuments retained their importance over time. Even though the statue suffered numerous contextual and literal displacements, it was never taken down. First, the colony came to an end within months of the statue's inauguration. Second, road work forced the city to relocate the monument. It was moved from its original location at la place Régnier au Long Col, where it had been for several years; up until 1966, at least.[8] The reason for the move seems to have been road construction, including the removal of the *rond-point* of place Régnier au Long Col in 1968-1969.[9] The statue was then moved to its present location behind the église Sainte-Elisabeth at the juncture of rue des Fossés and rue Boulangé de La Hainière. The monument's inscription also changed. When this author first visited the monument in 2002, the inscription on its base read, in French, "A sa Majesté Léopold II et aux Pionniers Coloniaux Hennuyers." (To His Majesty Leopold II and to the colonial pioneers of Hainaut.)[10] At some point that plaque was removed, leaving the monument with none. By 2018, the plaque had been replaced with another that read, more simply, "Léopold II. Roi des Belges," making no reference to the colonial past.[11]

Despite the removal of a reference to colonialism, the Mons statue of Leopold II has retained its colonialist association for many. As with other such markers honoring the king, the one in Mons has turned into a site for protest against the colonial past, in 2017, for instance, by the group Mémoire coloniale.[12]

Belgian and U.S. authorities. Rebellions broke out elsewhere as the central government struggled to control the country. To outside observers, it seemed that a cascade of violent and disorderly events followed one after the other until army leader Mobutu seized power in a coup in 1965, with backing from the U.S. and Belgium.[13] The Congo crisis and Mobutu's power grab not only allowed Belgium to exercise some continuing influence in the Congo, it kept the newly-independent country in the headlines and on people's minds.

Even if there were hints before 1960 that change was coming, attitudes had developed such that most Belgians were mentally incapable of envisioning independence, which meant it came as a shock. Such signs of impending change included tensions within the Congo itself, between Belgium and the Congo, and on the international scene. For example, the *question scolaire* of the 1950s and the language issue were increasingly "exported" to the colony, contributing to greater inter-linguistic and inter-cultural tensions.[14] While the *question scolaire* was settled by 1958, the damage had been done, and there was a growing knowledge among colonizers and the colonized that Belgians did not represent one united group. There were tensions between whites and blacks, despite the aura of confidence Belgians maintained within the colony and the rosy picture they projected at home and abroad.[15] In any case, pro-empire propaganda and long-held paternalistic views meant, "'Mental decolonization' was practically non-existent among many Belgians involved in the colonial enterprise, not least King Baudouin."[16]

The mental limits within which Belgians operated included a generally racist outlook that denigrated black Africans and considered them incapable of ruling their own independent state absent Belgian overlordship. The colonial situation did not create racialist thinking in Belgium, but it provided an object for the expression and reinforcement of it. What is more, the colonial experience strengthened Belgian identity as being "white" as Europeans set themselves off and apart from the blacks of the Congo in innumerable ways, both on the ground in the colony and in the colonial imaginary in the metropole. This helped create what one scholar calls a "national identity framed in terms of white supremacy," which joined the country's two main language communities insofar as it made "whiteness (...) a trope for (real) Belgian citizenship."[17]

Racist attitudes and episodes abounded, perhaps most famously in *Tintin in the Congo*, a creation of the colonial era that has remained in print, albeit in different forms, down to today.[18] The creation of cartoon artist Hergé, *Tintin in the Congo* first appeared in serialized form over several months in 1930 in *Le Petit Vingtième* before being published together in book form in 1931. In Hergé's story, Africans are in awe of the young Tintin, hailing him, and even his dog Milou (Snowy) as a hero. In one scene, when Tintin decides to set up camp, he sends his "boy" off to put up the tent while he leaves to hunt for their dinner. This repeated the oft-depicted scenario of the in-command European leading the hunt with an African as a mere helper, even though we know that Europeans depended on African hunters for their success, and that it was colonial restrictions, for example on firearms possession, that curbed African hunting.[19] In Hergé's creation, Tintin's true antagonist is another white man, leaving locals to fill the role of bit players, suggesting that central Africa was a place for whites to take action, and for Africans to act as background. Hergé, although not a particularly devout Catholic, depicts the missionary in *Tintin in the Congo* favorably, while Africans, in contrast, are portrayed not only as superstitious, but as not even being able to speak properly. And in one well-known Eurocentric scene, when Tintin steps in to substitute for the missionary at his school, he opens his lesson to a classroom full of black African children by saying, "My dear friends, today I'm going to talk to you about your country: Belgium!"[20] Hergé later recognized and lamented the Eurocentric and colonialist spirit in which he had created the original *Tintin in the Congo*, and he toned down the racism and Eurocentrism in revised editions that appeared after World War II, but only slightly. These racist, Eurocentric depictions were consumed by readers young and old, for years.[21]

The racist portrayal of Africans in *Tintin in the Congo* is but one example among many. Numerous depictions of Congolese in colonialist memorial sculpture depicted them as semi- or completely naked, signaling backwardness, often casting them as needy supplicants at the mercy of powerful white European figures. At least as late as the interwar years, school textbooks described Congolese as cannibals.[22] African artisans on display in the *village indigène* at the 1958 Brussels World's Fair returned to the Congo early because of the abuse they had received, including members of the public throwing bananas and chocolates at them and asking if they could examine their teeth.[23] Some Belgians openly portrayed Africans as lazy, or as monkey-like, or simply as monkeys. One political cartoon in *De Standaard* at the time of the 1960 *table rond* conference, for instance, depicted Africans as monkeys in suits.[24] Many Belgians sustained the view that central Africa was utterly backward, that Africans lived in trees before the arrival of European colonists, or were still "jumping up in the trees."[25] Patrice Lumumba reported that a white woman had called him a *sale macaque* after he accidentally bumped into her on a Leopoldville street in the 1950s, surely not an isolated incident.[26] As seen in this chapter's epigraph, Lumumba turned the tables in his independence day speech, underscoring to the audience, which included King

Baudouin, "We are no longer your monkeys!"[27] Racist views of Africans were not exclusive to Belgians, of course. After a 1959 trip to Africa that included a stop in Leopoldville, U.S. official Maurice Stans reported privately that many Africans "still belonged in the trees."[28] Naturally, such attitudes did not simply fade away upon the Congo's political independence. A Belgian former colonial official told this author in 2001 that before the Belgians arrived, the Congolese "were like monkeys living in the trees."[29] Several years ago in Brussels, this author heard a white man insult a black man, in public, by shouting at him, "macaque!"[30] Among other things, such mental views on race meant that many if not most Belgians before 1960, including many who knew the colonial situation best, presumed it would take decades for the Congolese to be ready for self-rule.

The former colony's descent into chaos beginning in 1960 contrasted only too sharply with the stability and prosperity that seemed to have reigned there during the 1950s, producing Belgian resentment and disappointment. Although Belgium did not fight a war of decolonization, the advent of self-rule entailed violence nonetheless, especially after the new national army (the former Force Publique) mutinied just days after independence. Whereas Belgians expected to continue on as close advisors and experts to guide the newly self-governing state, Lumumba's cutting of ties with Belgium and the drawing of the crisis into the Cold War conflict made clear this was not going to happen. The disappointment that resulted was tinged with melancholy resentment. Belgium had long guarded control over its massive colony: from foreign attacks against Leopoldian rule; from the post-World War I threat of German irredentism and Nazi expansionism; to supposed post-World War II U.S. designs on the Congo's riches; to growing international criticism at the U.N. After navigating such hazards for decades, Belgium saw its domination in central Africa evaporate in a matter of days as decolonization morphed from a Belgian-Congolese affair to an international crisis between independence on June 30 and U.N. resolution 143 on July 14 authorizing U.N. intervention.[31]

Belgian press reporting intensified as events spun out of control. Newspapers reported on whites who were killed, including French-speaking Belgian missionary Nicolas Hardy, and closely followed those who fled and returned home. That the public in the former metropole was above all focused on the fate of whites—either "refugees" returning home or those who remained behind after independence—was not unusual, as the same occurred elsewhere, for example in the British press when covering the end of empire in Kenya.[32] Photojournalists and their editors filled front pages of newspapers with photographs of pathetic, white refugees, which contrasted sharply with the many official images that had been taken and disseminated by the colonial

Nicolas Hardy (1919-1964)
Location: Elsaute, Saint-Roch church
Funded/built by: parish of Elsaute

A plaque on the village church of Elsaute dedicated to Nicolas Hardy remembers
him as a missionary and a martyr.[33] Its simple inscription reads "Missionnaire
au Congo, Martyr à Kilembe." (Missionary in the Congo, Martyr at Kilembe.)[34]
The town also renamed a nearby street after this local son who was a member
of the Oblats de Marie order, the first members of which arrived to the Congo
beginning only in 1931, although Hardy himself arrived many years later. Hardy
was murdered at the outset of the Kwilu rebellion that began in January 1964,
along with fellow missionaries Pierre Laebens (1920-1964) and Gérard Defever
(1920-1964), after a crowd attacked their missionary post at Kilembe. When
Hardy's body was found, it was in pieces, suggesting he had been hacked to
death.[35] Perhaps Jef Geeraerts was making reference to the attack at the end
of *Het Verhaal van Matsombo* (1966), in a post-1960 scene in which all Belgian
priests and sisters at a mission post are attacked and murdered.[36] The plaque
in Elsaute is a rarity in Belgium: a memorial to the "civilizing mission" that was
put up after 1960.

Memorial plaque to Nicolas
Hardy, Elsaute, 2018

Saint-Roch d'Elsaute, 2018

administration in the 1950s, which had created a picture of peace and prosperity. Now, in the nation's newspapers one saw photographs of violence, refugees, fear, and corpses. Some action took place in the streets of Brussels as former colonials, some organized by associations like the Comité action et défense des Belges d'Afrique, took to the streets to protest the descent into violence in the former colony.[37] Accounts of white Belgian soldiers who returned home in summer 1960, parading through the streets and welcomed as heroes, contrasted sharply with the anarchy that seemed to reign in Africa. Press accounts seeking to explain the former colony's descent into chaos resorted to clichés of a Stone Age and uncivilized Africa, or of irrational Africans, for example when discussing prime minister Lumumba.[38] The effect was greater than the cause, because, "While some Belgians clearly did suffer terribly at the hands of Congolese soldiers, and many were killed, scholars have suggested that actual instances of physical brutality were nowhere near as widespread as the media or official investigations implied."[39]

A pivotal break

The independence of the Congo was more of a decisive cultural break for Belgium than those of other colonies for other European powers because the country's overseas imperialism was essentially directed toward only one overseas territory.[40] Britain claimed a vast empire, and for Britons, twentieth-century decolonization stretched over decades, from India's 1947 independence to multiple independences around 1960, to Rhodesia's 1965 Unilateral Declaration of Independence, to the turnover of Hong Kong to China in 1997. France also possessed many colonies, and fought multiple wars to hang onto them, making decolonization develop, in a sense, in stages. Portugal also dealt with protracted anti-colonial wars, and the end of empire for the Netherlands stretched from a four-year war capped by the 1949 surrender of the Dutch East Indies (Indonesia), to the negotiated handover of New Guinea in 1962, to Suriname's independence in 1975. With the sudden loss of the Congo in 1960 and its quick absorption into the international Cold War conflict, Belgium experienced a perhaps uniquely sudden termination of its role as colonial master.[41] This was certainly true politically, as Belgians, who believed they would be able to mold the new state, found themselves largely sidelined by Cold War competition as the crisis in the Congo became internationalized.[42] Economically, Belgian authorities quickly passed laws on the eve of independence that allowed for the repatriation of much colonial capital. Although these might have been aimed at safeguarding economic activity in the Congo, they put somewhat more distance between Belgium and the now-former colony. This was followed by the Congo government's contentious nationalizations of major remaining investments in the 1960s. Another caesura was demographic as most Belgians living in the colony simply left in the weeks and months after June 1960, with few returning to replace them. Education about the colony for all intents and purposes ground to a halt, a break made all the more dramatic because of how it had actually intensified in the 1950s. "The more the moment of decolonization approached, the more did the provision [*l'offre*] of teaching and research grow richer and more diverse."[43] Also coming to an abrupt halt was production of pro-colonial material such as pro-empire exhibitions or colonial films. Colonial tourism, which had been on the rise, stopped.[44]

Aside from the psychological shock of Congo's independence there was the challenge of reincorporating former colonial functionaries, company employees, and their families back into Belgian society, something for which neither repatriates nor the country had prepared. Although leaving the (former) colony was traumatic, many had relocated to Africa only temporarily in the first place because the Congo was not a colony of settlement, unlike, say, Algeria, Australia, Kenya after World War I, or Angola from the 1950s. Still, whites both in Europe and in the colony expected that those living in the Congo before 30 June 1960 would remain on afterward to assist the newly-born nation.[45] The number of Belgians who left the Congo beginning around June 1960, either for other colonies or to repatriate, was not massive in absolute terms—some 38,000 in the initial post-independence period—but it was significant for a country (Belgium) with a population of barely more than nine million at the time. Historian Guy Vanthemsche characterized the flight "a mass exodus."[46] Returnees nonetheless represented a much smaller proportion of the country's population than the influx of *pieds noirs* into France in the early 1960s or the hundreds of thousands of *retornados* who left Africa for Portugal in the 1970s.

Similar to former colonists who returned to the U.K., France, and other countries during the decolonization era, Belgian returnees from the Congo believed themselves to be disadvantaged. In the months and years to follow, many were to be motivated by two things: upholding the "correct" version of colonial history and defending themselves and their interests in a difficult new situation. Many felt unwelcome upon their return, some even as victims. Former colonials organized, protested, and wrote letters to obtain compensation for their displacement, as none seemed to be forthcoming. That said, legislation was passed to ease the reincorporation of some former colonials. In March 1960, the Belgian parliament already had passed a law with an eye toward the eventual integration of former colonial functionaries into the metropolitan administration. When the stream of returnees turned into a flood beginning in June 1960, however, parliament passed a law (27 July 1961) of broader scope but more modest accommodation, which was later modified by a 3 April 1964 law, all of which advanced "the integration of former colonial officials into the Belgian public service," at least.[47] Even so, for many the transition back home left a bitter taste in their mouths. They felt the sting of having achieved so much—in their own eyes, at least—only to suffer a traumatic ejection. There followed a lingering suspicion that their fellow citizens back home believed it was the former colonials' failures that had somehow unleashed the chaos of 1960.[48]

Other than the legislation of 1960, 1961, and 1964, the number of specific, organized efforts in Belgium to reintegrate returning colonials was vanishingly small. There was the "home des vétérans coloniaux" or "Gui Home" near Genval Lake, which the group les Vétérans coloniaux had opened on 28 May 1949.[49] By 1961 it housed some thirty colonial veterans, more than half having served in the Congo before 1908.[50] There was some housing built near the Tervuren Museum in a neighborhood where street names like Katangabinnenhof echoed a colonial connection.[51] The case of returnees to Tervuren's Congo museum illustrates the ad hoc process. The institution was surprised in 1960 by the "sudden return of a large number of scientific researchers from the Congo."[52] It could not have come at a worse time since the institution's very existence was at risk. Its director, Lucien Cahen, created the Institut Belge pour l'Encouragement de la Recherche Scientifique Outre-Mer (IBERSOM) in order to place researchers from the Congo, returning in a flood back home, into workable positions in Belgium, including at the MRAC.[53] In sum, coordinated efforts to reintegrate former colonial settlers were few, leaving many of them disoriented and some resentful, even if most landed on their feet before long.

It is important to pause for a moment to consider how former colonials acted through their own interest groups after the Congo's independence, and thereby formed a kind of "pro-colonial lobby." This meant oddly enough that these groups were advocating for "colonial" interests in a post-colony era. Former colonials became "imperialists without an empire" who crafted and sustained a positive narrative and image of Belgian overseas rule, which of course reflected positively on themselves.[54] National and local pro-colonial groupings were nothing new post-1960; the first ones had formed as early as the late 1800s during the early years of the Leopoldian colonial endeavor.[55] During the post-1908 Belgian state rule period, a whole slew of these groups sprang up, often called *cercles coloniaux* or *koloniale verenigingen* (colonial clubs or associations): the Koloniale en maritieme kring van Brugge; Cercle africain borain; Cercle colonial arlonais; Cercle colonial de Hal; Koloniale kring van Leuven; and the umbrella Royale Union coloniale belge, among many others. Membership tended to be drawn from those who had worked in the colony and then returned home, and people who wanted to promote colonialism, or network with fellow former colonials, or both. Promotion of colonialism included publishing periodicals with a focus on colonization in the Congo; the holding of *concours colonials* (colonial competitions) for schoolchildren, which tended to be imbued with colonialist ideas; arranging empire- or Congo-themed exhibits; and coordinating outings to the colonial sections of Belgium's several World's Fairs or to Tervuren's museum of the Congo. A number of these groups received subsidies from the Ministry of Colonies or city or regional governments.[56]

Although the number of former colonials perforce declined over time after 1960, the number of associations of former colonials paradoxically grew. In 1912, the Royale Union coloniale belge brought together 11 associations, whereas its post-colonial successor the Union royale belge pour les pays d'outre-mer (UROME) grouped together 27 such associations in 2008, encompassing some 10,000 former colonials.[57] They engaged in numerous actions and public relations endeavors that altogether conveyed a highly positive history of Belgian action in central Africa, including the colonial rule of Leopold II. Former colonials and even UROME itself published apologias of Leopoldian and Belgian rule in central Africa both on its website and in hard copy.[58] By the 1980s, they were collectively producing some two dozens pro-colonial publications, even if such publications were largely geared toward former colonials and their families and therefore did not circulate in large numbers. Some former colonials did reach a broader public by publication of their letters to the editor in mainstream newspapers on occasions when issues of the colonial past or contemporary disputes with Congo's Mobutu entered the news. Local colonials in Namur kept up the Musée Africain de Namur (discussed below), and many from colonialist associations across the country commemorated Leopold II and the Belgian empire each year at memorials in bronze and stone. Such associations also kept close tabs on the goings-on at the MRAC in Tervuren and exerted pressure behind the scenes to ensure it hewed to a pro-colonial line. Some have argued that the effects that former colonials had on public debates about the colonial past were negligible.[59] But by means of their steady, stalwart, and oftentimes unseen defense of colonialism, they held the line to sustain a positive view of the colonial past, including that of the CFS era.

As the preceding discussion of returnees suggests, what one saw about the colony in Belgium immediately after 1960 was overwhelmingly focused on the trauma of decolonization rather than events further back in the past. Instead of celebrating their former charges' newfound independence, Belgians were much more concerned with "whites": their own and their fellow citizens' shock; the plight of refugees; and the fate of those who had remained in the former colony. Such focus was suggestive of how the "civilizing mission" had always been less about its purported target, namely Africans; it was more a motto justifying colonialism and a slogan to explain foreign, European domination in Africa. This could be seen elsewhere, such as the great interest in King Baudouin's trip to the Congo in 1955, which revealed less about Belgians' interest in Africa and Africans and more about their interest in their king.[60] Similarly, earlier royal voyages to the Congo, such as that of Albert I and Queen Elisabeth in 1928, garnered press attention because of the monarchs themselves, less so because of anything they did in the colony, or because of the colonized themselves.[61] During the 1950s, newspapers had regularly carried "interest" pieces on the Congo written by Europeans, such as the socialist Le Peuple's "Chronique Coloniale." Some of these were articles on pressing current affairs, for example a 1953 piece investigating the political future of the colony, which asked whether blacks or whites would be in power in the Congo in the future.[62] But many other "colonial chronical" pieces in Le Peuple were mere informational pieces to inform Belgians about their Congo.[63] When school history texts discussed the colony they carried illustrations of visits by the royals, which, of course, was a highly uncommon rather than everyday occurrence in the Congo.[64]

Congolese in Belgium

Although it was not unusual for the press in different European countries to focus on the fate of whites during the decolonization era, this was perhaps even more the case in this instance because there were so few Congolese living in the now-former metropole who might otherwise have driven greater coverage of Africans and their concerns. The contrast with Britain and France was especially striking; in the latter there was already by the interwar years a significant presence of subjects from across the colonial world, especially in Paris.[65] The small community of colonial migrants in Belgium had been the case from the earliest days of the CFS, when authorities severely restricted Congolese immigration. Very early attempts at education of Africans in Belgium, for instance, were limited before being halted completely.[66] It became illegal for colonials to bring Africans home, for example as servants. Unlike France, Britain, and to a lesser degree Italy, Belgium refused to mobilize its

Louis-Napoleon Chaltin (1857-1933) and
the Corps des Volontaires Congolais
Location: Erpent (Namur)
Sculptor: Harry Elström (sometimes Elstrøm)
Inauguration: ca. 1937

Although white, European officers of the Force publique are commemorated
dozens if not hundreds of times in Belgium, African soldiers of the Force publique are only remembered in the country on one public monument, that being
the Force publique memorial in Schaerbeek, inaugurated after the colonial
period, in 1970. But Schaerbeek is not the only monument in Belgium to Africans who fought for the country, for there is another: the monument to Colonel
Chaltin and the Corps des Volontaires Congolais (CVC), today located in Erpent,
an area of Namur.[67] The monument reads, in French, Dutch, English, and
German, "To the Belgian Colonial Volunteers who, under Colonel Chaltin, took
part in the defence of Namur, August 1914." The bas-relief shows six soldiers,
apparently heading into battle, led by two bare-headed white soldiers, probably
officers. Among the four other men being led, at least one face is recognizable
as African. It seems likely that the four figures behind the two leading white
men—all of whom are wearing military hats with a star on the front, evoking
the colony—represent the four Congolese soldiers who joined Chaltin's nearly
all-white CVC, which was comprised of former colonials living in Belgium at the
time of war's outbreak in August 1914.[68] Formed by royal decree in August 1914,

Detail of monument to Chaltin and the CVC, 2018

Monument to Colonel Chaltin and the CVC, Erpent, 2018

the CVC was led by Colonel Louis Chaltin, at the time 57 years old. They saw very brief fighting in August in the defense of Namur, and many were captured and interned by Germany in POW camps for the remainder of the war. Among those Africans who volunteered for the CVC and who ended up in Germany was Paul Panda Farnana, who went on to become the first Congolese "nationalist."[69]

As many as twenty eight other Congolese fought on the Western Front. A number of them died, some returned to the Congo, while others remained in Belgium where they generally eked out marginal existences. Some had to count on charity assignments from the Ministry of Colonies, including Antoine Manglugi, Honoré Fataki, Jules Mokweke, and Léon De Cassa, who were hired by the ministry to do some work. That Ministry's Office Colonial hired Africans to be present at least one of the *quinzaines coloniales*—a two week-long colonial exhibit—to form an honor guard, and Jean Balamba found work at the Tervuren Museum.[70]

African subjects to serve in Europe during World War I, and those few who did fight on the Western Front were only those couple dozen or so Congolese who just happened to be living in the metropole in August 1914. The largest group of Congolese who traveled to and from Belgium were mariners, usually sailing from the port of Matadi to Antwerp and back. In Antwerp, they were required to remain on board ship, or were housed in Ndako Ya Biso—"Ons Huis" (Our House)—living quarters set up by the Compagnie Maritime Belge.[71] Because some of the sailors started taking their salaries into town to buy goods to bring home with them, the missionary overseeing the home, Father Nuyens, decided to set up a store *inside* Ndako Ya Biso so that sailors would not have an excuse to go into the city, further isolating them.[72] Authorities could not completely quarantine the home country from its colonial subjects, but they tried, and before 1960 there were probably never more than perhaps a couple hundred Congolese living in Belgium at any one time.

Beginning in 1960 this changed, albeit gradually, as some Congolese relocated to Belgium, leading to a slowly growing African presence. In absolute terms, the number of Congolese immigrants remained small: from 2,585 by 1961 to 5,244 by 1970, not including 534 Rwandans and 339 Burundians.[73] About a thousand of those Congolese who came to Belgium in the 1960s were students provided scholarships through an aid scheme, and who, presumably, returned to Africa once their course of studies was complete.[74] Even if such small numbers created a situation atypical both of migrants to Belgium more generally and of African immigrants to other western European countries, Congolese immigration did increase. As a result, Monique Vanderstraeten-Wayez, whose brother was a missionary to Africa, established "La Maison africaine," or *Maisaf*, in 1960 in Ixelles as a center for Congolese who were residing in or traveling through Brussels.[75] Other *Maisons africaines* followed in Liege, Anvers, Charleroi, although the latter closed in the 1970s. Most Congolese who lived or settled in Belgium chose to do so in Brussels, and the Congolese area of Ixelles, located off the Porte de Namur, became known as Matonge (sometimes Matongé) after a Kinshasa neighborhood of the same name known for its nightlife. The number of African students in the country grew, even if their presence remained limited. Writer Lieve Joris wrote of her university days at Leuven that, "Black students were part of the landscape in this city, yet they remained strangers, we knew so little about them."[76] As students, they were in Belgium perforce for short-term stays, which made them like most other Congolese, since most were temporary workers interested in returning home, even if many did not manage to do so because of the turbulence of the 1960s. The provisionality of their presence was reflected in their absence from Belgian domestic politics, in contrast to the situations in France, Britain, and the Netherlands. Even if some were politically active, their attention was focused almost exclusively on their country of origin, especially under the Mobutu regime.[77]

The Congo crisis continues

Attention to whites was sustained in press coverage as the situation in the Congo deteriorated. Any stability in the early 1960s was short-lived, and by 1964 further rebellion threatened the Kinshasa government and led to attacks on whites (among other problems), which exacerbated trauma for many Belgian families.[78] The Simba rebellion in the Congo's eastern provinces included the taking of hostages in Paulis (Isiro) and Stanleyville, or "Stan" (Kisangani), leading to the rescue operations *Dragon Rouge* and *Dragon Noir*.[79] Belgium, with U.S. assistance, sent paratroopers into Paulis and Stan in November to evacuate Europeans and Americans there, as well as some Congolese. The return of refugees in the days that followed filled front pages of newspapers as the country's main French- and Flemish-language news outlets reported on the operations and their aftermath, or, as *Het Laatste Nieuws* put it, "Het Drama van Stan." Photographs of refugees being met at the airport by royals once again tied the Congo to the Saxe-Coburg dynasty, as members of the royal family including Baudouin, Fabiola, and the Prince and Princess of Liège appeared on front pages across the country.[80] Whereas colonial rule had long been associated with manliness, the obverse—the disintegration of European rule—was gendered, too, and photographers and editors focused heavily on the fate of women and children, casting them as the preeminent victims of the chaos in the Congo.[81]

Although the rebels killed hostages—the press reported they executed hundreds—the evacuation at the end of 1964 brought the crisis in the eastern Congo to an end for the white captives. Yet some had died, and many suffered, as illustrated by the story of Didier Welvaert and Lucien Welvaert. Didier Welvaert, a soldier, had been reported killed in action in or around Stanleyville during operation *Dragon Rouge*. Lucien Welvaert was reported to be returning alive and well. Lucien's family, including his father, mother, wife, daughter, and six month-old son, turned up at Melsbroek air base northeast of Brussels alongside other families welcoming men back, ecstatic to see Lucien return safely home. When Lucien did not come off the plane, his family started asking his buddies if they had "seen Lucien," leading to strange looks and awkward, fumbling answers. It turned out there had been a mix-up. It was true that a soldier named Welvaert had survived, but it was Didier, not Lucien. The accounts and photos in *Le Soir* of the reactions of Lucien's family upon hearing the news were heartrending.[82]

Dragon Rouge and *Dragon Noir* did not lead to any soul-searching. They were quick operations that ended when the captives were freed and returned home. What were the underlying grievances stoking rebellion in the former colony? What role had Belgians played in contributing to the ongoing violence there? The focus in the press was not on such questions, rather on developing a narrative of a heroic rescue carried out in the face of violence perpetrated by rebels and bandits.[83] The *paras* who executed *Dragon Rouge* in late November returned to a hero's welcome at the beginning of December. Again the dynasty was associated with the colony as news photographs showed Baudouin greeting returnees and decorating officers.[84] Press photos showed the crowds that turned out in Brussels for a ticker tape parade as the return dominated front pages; "A Nation feels her heart beat," read one. There was "a veritable tide of human beings," a "sea of men, women, and children" present to welcome troops as they paraded through central Brussels, from porte de Schaerbeek down rue Royale to place Poelaert.[85] "The crowd, breaking the roadblocks, carry the paras in triumph," read another headline.[86] Although it had been a controversial operation that did nothing to alleviate international condemnation of Belgian meddling, politicians and the country rallied around the action. As *Le Soir* put it, "This responsibility, our government had to take it. It took it. Parliament, the emanation of the country, approved it without ambiguity, the opposition joining the majority in a unanimous movement."[87] Many Congolese, by contrast, sought to be evacuated, but without success, bringing to mind today film footage from the later U.S. evacuation of its

South Vietnamese embassy in 1975, or of how, even later, Rwandans were left to their fate during the 1994 genocide while European troops evacuated white people.[88] By 1965, there had already been a steep decline in the number of Belgians living in the Congo, and henceforth it was to be much more rare to see news about the former colony or Belgian-Zairian relations make the front page of newspapers. Exceptions to this trend, such as they were, may have stood out to readers as much for the subject being reported as for their infrequency.[89]

The importance of the 1950s

The decade of the 1950s, which was bookended by Baudouin's accession to the throne and an ignominious end to colonial rule, had a disproportionately large impact on memories and perceptions of the colonial past. Many commentators and scholars have over the years criticized Belgians for their supposed amnesia about colonial history, arguing that if they knew anything about it, it was only about two episodes: of the alternately heroic or atrocious Leopoldian years (1885-1908), and of the Congo crisis (1960-1965), the latter with its own attendant traumas and atrocities. Hein Vanhee and Geert Castryck write that, "The period of the actual Belgian Congo (1908-1960) is largely *terra incognita* for the wider public."[90] This misses a major truth, which is that Belgians for long knew quite a bit about the colony of the 1950s, even if much of what they had taken in about those years was absorbed subconsciously. The abundant images, stories, propaganda, and memories of the 1950s formed much of the basis for post-1960 Belgian views of colonialism and the nation's actions in central Africa, fundamentally influencing Belgians and their culture.

There are reasons why this particular decade was so important in framing views of the colonial past, the first being its economic successes. In short, the Belgian Congo's economy boomed in the 1950s, including raw materials production, especially the mining, transport, and refining of tin, copper, and uranium ores, and diamonds.[91] After World War II, Belgium instituted the *plan décennal*, or ten-year plan (starting 1949), to coordinate infrastructure investments, one version of several development plans put in motion by Europe's colonial powers after the war.[92] Infrastructure was synonymous with the civilizing mission in the Belgian colonial imaginary. This association dated back to at least the 1890-1898 building of the Matadi-Leopoldville railway. That project had been spearheaded by Albert Thys, for whom a monument was unveiled in 1948 in his native home of Dalhem to mark the railway's half-centenary, which coincidentally fell on the eve of the *plan décennal*'s implementation. That scheme led to planned investments into health facilities, roads, airfields, electricity, agriculture, schooling, and housing, among other areas, making the 1950s the apex of colonial state investment into infrastructure.[93] World War II had proved the importance of the colonies, especially their raw materials resources, and, as noted earlier, Belgium's sovereignty during the war had depended on monies from the Congo that helped fund the government in exile in London.[94] The Korean War that followed jacked up primary materials prices, only further stimulating interest and investment in overseas territories across the European colonial empires. Compared to the Great Depression era, defeat, Nazi occupation, and tough World War II years in the colony, the post-war era in the Congo seemed marvelous.

Former colonists who returned home beginning in the second half of 1960, and their children whom they brought with them—some to step foot on Belgian soil for the first time—carried the golden age of the 1950s fresh in their minds. This contrasted sharply with the shock and atrocities of independence. After 1960, most former colonials—that is, Belgians who had lived and worked in the colony and then returned to Europe—were necessarily people who had lived in central Africa during the 1945-1960 boom years because the white population there had grown so rapidly after World War II: from 23,643 in 1945 to 39,006 in 1950, to 88,913 by 1959, a 276 percent increase in fewer than fifteen years.[95] What is more, their initial departures for the Congo between 1945-1960 had been preceded by years of pro-colonial propaganda designed to instill pride in empire, meaning they arrived to Africa with all they had learned beforehand about the positive effects of Belgian activity, how it was intimately linked with Leopoldian rule, how whites were superior to blacks, and so forth. All other things being equal, returnees brought with them this positive vision of their country's colonial action, which they then by and large carried forward with them into the post-1960 era. Those who were youngsters from 1945-1960 generally held an even stronger positive view, and because of their young age, they typically sustained this view far into the future. "As sociological studies demonstrate, people tend to remember the events that were salient during their adolescence and early adulthood." This meant that decades later, as late as the Congo's fiftieth anniversary of independence, an older generation preserved positive memories of the colonial era. As one study put it, it was no surprise that decades later, in 2010, "older Belgians [expressed] more positive representations of the colonial past than young adults," the latter of whose formative years did not overlap with the height of the colonial era.[96]

Albert Thys (1849-1915)[97]
Location: Dalhem, rue du Général Thys[98]
Sculptor: Charles Samuel
Inauguration: 30 May 1948[99]
Funded/built by: Gilbert Périer and others

Albert Thys was a key figure in the world of colonial affairs in the CFS and then
in the Belgian Congo after 1908. He was particularly influential because of
his role in the building of the Matadi-Leopoldville railway, and because of his
behemoth colonial enterprise, the Compagnie du Congo pour le Commerce et
l'Industrie. He was a native of Dalhem, a small town in eastern Wallonia located
between Liege, Maastricht, and Aachen. He died in 1915 in Brussels.

The modest memorial to Thys in Dalhem was put up across from his birth
home, on the former place du Marché, which was renamed rue du Général Thys
in his honor. The bust is by artist Charles Samuel and dates back to 1915. It was
donated for the 1948 memorial by Gilbert Périer, who was not only a grand-
son of Thys but also a prominent businessman who at one point was director
general of the national airline Sabena.[100] Planning for the Dalhem memorial
started in 1947 so that it would be up in time to mark the fiftieth anniversary

of the 1898 opening of the Matadi-
Leopoldville railway. The monument's
1948 inauguration suggests how colonial monuments, in their own small
way, served as points of unification
for Belgians around the colonial idea.
During the colonial period, in official
colonial discourse, it was not "French-
speaking Belgians" or "Dutch-speaking
Belgians" who went to the Congo,
rather simply *Belgians*. As Léon Anciaux, Thys' biographer for the *BCB* put
it, at the opening ceremonies, former
Minister of Colonies Paul Charles said
of Thys that, "il apportait l'hommage
de la Belgique toute entière: 'Grand ré-
alisateur, grand cœur et grand Belge!'"
(he bore the tribute of the whole of
Belgium: "A great implementer, a big
heart, and a great Belgian!")[101]

Monument to Albert Thys, Dalhem, 2003

During the state rule period in the Congo, Thys was honored in various other ways. Another, larger statue to his memory was unveiled in Brussels in 1927. The Tervuren Museum for years displayed another bust of Thys, which like the one in Dalhem also dated back to 1915, and was also by Charles Samuel. Samuel was the same artist who created a number of sculptures for Tervuren, including the well known *Vuakusu Batetela défendant une femme contre un Arabe*. (Vuakusu Batetela defending a woman from an Arab.) In addition, there is a Thyslaan in Tongeren, in Flanders, and there was a monument built to Thys in the Congo, where a town near the lower Congo took the name Thysville, today called Mbanza-Ngungu. The town of Dalhem itself opened a small "Musée Général Thys" in 1961, which continues to highlight the achievements of its famous native son.[102]

Another reason the 1950s had Belgians looking back at colonial times of yore through rose-tinted glasses is because of the contrasting, terrible experience of what preceded those years, namely World War II and its immediate aftermath. The war had led to extended tours of duty for functionaries in the colony, hardships, difficult working conditions, and rising tensions among Congolese, as witnessed by the 1944 Force publique mutiny at Luluabourg. In Belgium, the Nazi occupation was devastating. Future Inforcongo photographer Henri Goldstein (1920-2014) was imprisoned for years during the war in multiple camps in Germany, later recounting that there were "times when he lived like a beast or a savage."[103] Going to work for Inforcongo after the liberation, "He arrived in Africa still extremely thin and bearing the physical traces of the war."[104] His arrival to a peaceful, more prosperous colonial situation could only have struck him as a major improvement. Or consider what renowned historian and anthropologist Jan Vansina (1929-2017) said about living through occupation: "We grew up in the fear and clamor of war (…) I was used to the sound of incoming artillery by the time I was seven or eight. Then the war broke out. (…) I remember dinners consisting of a single potato." The reader of Vansina's memoir, from which this quote is taken, should be unsurprised he dealt so well with the privations he endured after he left home for the colony in the early 1950s for an extended research stay among the Kuba.[105] With the occupation and post-war strife of the 1940s ingrained on many minds, memories of a prosperous Congo in the 1950s were especially sweet.

The 1950s also signified the high water mark of awareness of the overseas empire, be it through travel there, classroom lessons, exhibitions of empire, or returning missionaries spreading the word about their work.[106] That same decade also represented a colonial-era peak of recognition of Congolese art.[107] There was more production of colonial films and photos during the decade than ever before as the Ministry of Colonies' information office—Inforcongo—stepped up its efforts to promote and defend Belgian overseas rule both at home and abroad. The Leopoldville administration's *Congopresse* photo agency, created in 1947, produced volumes of visual documentation that were sent to the Ministry of Colonies in Brussels for editing and dissemination. The administration largely controlled images that circulated about colonial rule, and it was only after the Congo's independence that non-governmental press agencies really began to photograph and film on the ground there. The number of Belgians who traveled to the Congo was never large as authorities exercised tight controls not only over the movement of Africans, mentioned earlier, but also over the mobility of whites.[108] In addition to administrative controls over travel and settling in the colony, it was expensive to send journalists there, and because the Ministry of Colonies provided copy for press releases, film clips, and photographs to news outlets at virtually no cost, this was further disincentive for independent journalism.[109] This led to in retrospect odd situations such as the socialist and in theory anti-colonialist newspaper *Le Peuple* running photographs of colonial scenes shot by photographer Henri Goldstein, who worked for Inforcongo.[110] For news outlets, the Ministry of Colonies made it worth their while *not* to expend their limited resources to send journalists all the way to the Congo, with one result being that newspaper articles, television reports, and other press accounts reflected the official pro-colonial line.[111] This also meant that independent news sources did not build up their own archives of images, for example photographs of everyday life in the colony, or of Congolese political activity, and so forth.

Florence Gillet and Anne Cornet have traced how a long-established colonialist imaginary was sustained in photography through to the end of the colonial era. Photographs juxtaposed colonizer and colonized and in doing so contrasted the former's civilization, dominance, and normalcy with the latter's savagery, submissiveness, and exoticism.[112] Official photos showed little about travel to and from Africa in order to omit the subject of distance and the emotional and physical distress it could cause. They also avoided indelicate topics such as sickness, old age, or *métissage*, that is mixed-raced unions and their issue. Instead official photography underlined harmony between blacks and whites, peace and order, work and productivity, accomplishments in the fields of medicine and education, and the comforts of city living in the colony's (white) urban areas. This also pertained to motion pictures, discussed in chapter 4.

Continuities across 1960

Although the Congo crisis shocked, there were many continuities across the "divide" of 1960. Certain things continued as if the Congo had never achieved independence, meaning that in important ways decolonization did not "happen" around 1960 in Belgium, at least culturally. In the days leading up to the Congo's independence, a cartoon in *De Standaard* showed a worker taking down a street sign that read "Koloniën Straat." In real life, Koloniën Straat, or the rue des Colonies, kept its name, and the street signs remained.

Street sign for rue des Colonies/ Koloniënstraat, 9 May 2018

"Preparations for June 30th," De Standaard, *22 June 1960*

Pro-empire commemorations continued year after year as former colonial settlers, CFS and other military veterans, and pro-colonial enthusiasts kept holding annual celebrations of empire, often at one of the numerous colonialist monuments that remained in place across the country. Over time, a number of such markers had been or were to be moved, but one could count on one hand the number of them ever taken down, either before or after 1960. Some monuments almost vanished into obscurity on their own, for instance the statue to Camille Coquilhat in a dark corner of Antwerp's Koning Albertpark behind a pond and surrounded by thick foliage, both of which made it largely unapproachable.[113] But this can be overstated, and we should not forget that monuments "concretize particular historical interpretations; in time, such memory grows as natural to the eye as the landscape in which it stands."[114] Memorials large and small, even such a modest one as a marker to colonial

Colonial pioneers
Location: Seraing, former *maison communale*
Inauguration: unknown
Funded/built by: unknown

•CRISMER Victor•
1-10-1866
MATADI
11-4-1894
·—·
HUBIN Nicolas
28-8-1876
MONGA (UBANGI)
28-4-1903
·—·
LAMY Ferdinand
30-8-1857
MATADI
21-6-1892
·—·
LAUBENTHAL Jean
4-11-1877
STANLEYVILLE
30-5-1905
·—·
LENOIR Ernest
5-7-1867
LUSAMBO (SANKURU)
20-1-1901

Plaque to colonial pioneers, Seraing, 2018

This simple plaque sits high up on the northeastern side of the former *maison communale* in Seraing, a city at the center of nineteenth-century industry in eastern Wallonia, especially steel production. The plaque memorializes five men—Victor Crismer, Nicolas Hubin, Ferdinand Lamy, Jean Laubenthal, and Ernest Lenoir—all of whom perished in the Congo before 1908, that is to say during the "heroic" period of Leopoldian rule.

Victor-Oswald Crismer was an accountant who died at the colonial port city of Matadi at the age of 27.[115] Lamy was a mechanic and locomotive fitter who joined the Compagnie du Chemin de fer du Congo in May 1892, at the time of the building of the Matadi-Leopoldville railroad. Lamy died along the railway route just a month and a half after arriving to the Congo, joining the many hundreds of European, African, and Asian workers who perished during its construction.[116] One can gather from the plaque itself that these five individuals spanned a generation of young men from Seraing, each of whom found their way to central Africa for one reason or another, with Ferdinand Lamy (b. 30 August 1857) being born more than twenty years before Jean Laubenthal (b. 4 November 1877). Collectively, their deaths spanned some 13 years, from 1892 to 1905, and all died young, between the ages of 26 and 34. Most perished in different places: Crismer and Lamy in the port of Matadi, Lenoir in Lusambo in central Congo, Hubin in northern Congo on the Ubangi, and Laubenthal at Stanleyville (Kisangani). Other than these scant facts, the historical record speaks little to us across the years about these five early agents of colonialism.

pioneers in Seraing, remained in place, and by doing so framed people's everyday lives throughout the post-1960 era.

The removal of a monument to Baron Francis Dhanis, dismantled completely in 1954, is revealing in its rarity. Dhanis was born in 1861 to a Belgian mother and Irish mother in London and spent his formative years in Scotland. Following higher education in Belgium he joined the military, then the CFS Force publique, and he eventually played a role so significant in the Congo "Arab wars" of the early 1890s that he was made a baron. His 1894 return to Antwerp following those campaigns was triumphal, and he instantly became a well-known figure, his story to be retold for years as a heroic example of the civilizing mission. Dhanis returned to the Congo twice, most notably to play a key role in the suppression of a Force publique revolt in 1897. Back in Belgium, he died in November 1909, of septicemia, only 47 years old. After his death, friends and admirers mobilized to memorialize him, including renaming an Antwerp street Baron D'Hanislaan, a moniker it retains to this day. The Club africain d'Anvers-Cercle d'Études coloniales assembled a Comité exécutif du Monument Dhanis to build a large monument to him in a prominent site in front of Sint-Michielskerk on the Zuiderlei, called Amerikalei after 1918.[117] The work, by sculptor Frans Joris, was financed by public subscription, and the committee needed just a few months to pull together the funds to build it.[118] The large monument was inaugurated on 12 October 1913, proclaiming "Voor de menscheid" (For humanity). Dhanis, top and center, was depicted in uniform in a triumphant pose, holding a rifle aloft in his right hand in a semi-bellicose gesture. An African woman behind and to his left held up an infant in supplication, while the figure of an Arab in a turban, surrendering, is to be seen cowed before him, to his right. The scene was encircled by exotic plants.[119] The monument was dismantled on 21 May 1954, and moved to the grounds of the nearby Colonial University in Middleheim (Antwerp), where it remained, apparently in pieces.[120] Why? It had nothing to do with anti-colonial sentiment or a reconsideration of Dhanis' history, rather it was simply due to construction for road expansion in order to accommodate increased traffic on Amerikalei, a major artery.

Coincidentally there was yet another public tribute to Dhanis that was removed, this one after 1960. The Grand'Poste in downtown Brussels for decades displayed an 1896 painting honoring Dhanis by J. Emmanuel Van den Bussche, located in the building's entrance hallway.[121] The tableau showed Dhanis arriving back to Antwerp after the Arab wars, with Governor-General Théophile Wahis presenting him to a gathered crowd, and Leopold II's representative tendering him the title of baron. In the painting, Dhanis was followed by two Arab chiefs whom he had defeated and brought with him

The 1908 annexation of the Congo
Location: Antwerp, Stadspark, on Rubenslei
Sculptors: Jules Baetes and Jan Kerckx[122]
Architect: Emile Van Averbeke
Inauguration: 1911
Funded/built by: Antwerp Chamber of Commerce

Monument to 1908 annexation of the Congo, Antwerp, 2013

This tall and slender four-sided bronze and granite memorial in Antwerp's Stadspark, topped by a sculpture of an outstretched Mercury, draws the viewer's eyes upward toward the sky. Two of its four sides bear different plaques but the same inscription, one in French, the other in Dutch: "In the presence of His Majesty King Leopold II the Chamber of Commerce of Antwerp celebrates the annexation of the Congo to Belgium. 6 June 1909." The northwestern side bears a plaque showing Leopold II in profile, while a plaque on the southeastern side shows a caduceus, symbolizing commerce. The monument also bears the coat of arms of the city of Antwerp as well as a bronze star.[123]

The inscriptions in bronze refer to a celebration of the Congo's annexation that took place on 6 June 1909, so just several months after Leopold II turned the Congo over to Belgium, and just six months before his death in December 1909. The annexation monument shares several characteristics with other colonial memorials, such as being made of granite and bronze, its inclusion of the Congo star, and its commemoration of Leopold II. At the same time it is highly unusual in that rather than commemorating military men or calling attention to colonial "pioneers," it is a memorial to commerce. Very few other monuments in the country find their origins in commercial facets of Belgian colonialism, perhaps only those to Albert Thys in Brussels and Dalhem, and perhaps also a Schaerbeek memorial to Ernest Cambier, a founder of the Compagnie du Congo pour le Commerce et l'Industrie. That Antwerp boasts a historical marker to imperial commerce makes sense because the city benefited from colonialism; not from Leopold II's largesse in the realm of urban construction, but as a port. Antwerp was throughout the colonial era the main entry and exit point for Congo imports and exports, with major consequences. By 1897, for instance, the port had bypassed London as the world's largest ivory market, importing and reselling hundreds of thousands of kilos of elephant tusks each year.

upon his return, and two Congolese children bore the fruits of their country. It was a representation on canvas of the civilizing mission, the victory over slavery, a connection with the dynasty, and the promise of the benefits to be had through the exploitation of the Congo's natural resources, all in one scene.[124] The defeated Arabs and the Congolese children, and the absence of adult African men and women who might resist, suggested there were no more threats in the Congo; the country was now open for business. The painting hung for decades in the Grand'Poste, an imposing structure built in 1892 and located at the place de la Monnaie in central Brussels. Then the building was gone: torn down beginning in 1966, the Grand'Poste was replaced by the uninspiring Centre Monnaie (1971), an administrative and commercial building.[125] The removal of first the Antwerp monument and then the Grand'Poste tableau left surprisingly few commemorative traces in public space of this key figure. Beginning in 1958, Dhanis' profile figured among several others on a large memorial plaque in the Tervuren Congo museum, and there are streets named after him not only in Antwerp but also in Sint-Niklaas, Tervuren, and Etterbeek. But there is no large, public monument to Dhanis, despite him having been hailed for decades as one of the greatest figures of Leopoldian and Belgian overseas action.

The removal of the memorials to Dhanis are exceptions that prove the rule, namely that colonial monuments were not taken down, which revealed a lack of questioning of the country's colonial history. Indeed, people generally maintained an overwhelmingly positive view of their action in central African during the colonial era as the dominant post-1960 narrative remained one in which Belgians had "done good" in a part of the world that had been terribly backward before their arrival. One journalist, reviewing publications by the Tervuren Museum in the 1960s, discussed how museum director Lucien Cahen was extending the museum publishing's ambit to embrace works of history, including previously unpublished manuscripts, for instance diaries by Belgian explorers and colonial administrators. He lamented the current situation, that of the Congo of 1965, asking the reader to think "about the pitiful situation where lies the country that the pioneers brought out of savagery."[126]

Literature and colonialism

Just as decolonization did not "happen" in the realm of monuments, when it comes to literature, to consider 1960 as some kind of sharp dividing line makes limited sense. Works produced before Congo's independence did not simply disappear—take Léon Debertry's *Kitawala* (1953) as one example, or even more significant, Gerard Walschap's *Oproer in Congo* (1953).[127] As its title suggests, Walschap's award-winning 1953 book, based largely on a 1951 visit to the Belgian colony, hardly painted a rosy picture of the colonial situation. Nonetheless, it was well-received and continued to receive praise well into the post-colonial era. Such "colonial" works of literature remained available even if, as scholar Philippe Delisle states, some became more difficult to find after 1960, including *Tintin au Congo*.[128] Other "colonial" books and publications were being written at the time of the Congo's independence, but only appeared afterward, and of course the experiences upon which people drew for their writing in the years after 1960 often straddled the political divide that that year represents. What is more, poetry, fiction, *bandes dessinées*, novels, and other literary creations are never exclusively "colonial" because innumerable influences inform their production and reception, for instance international and global exchanges that led "colonial" issues to become immixed with related ones, for instance immigration and multi-culturalism.[129] All this said, it is clear that "colonial" works held a marginal position in the realm of Flemish- and French-language Belgian literature.

Even if well-known works with colonial connections such as *Tintin in the Congo* became harder to obtain, or perhaps dropped in popularity, they remained in circulation and did not disappear overnight. The same is true of Georges Simenon's few works that touch on African issues, his "African Trio." Simenon is best known for his Maigret detective novels. But this prolific writer, among Belgium's best-known and probably its most translated, also wrote what are known as his *romans durs*, those that do not follow inspector Maigret. Among these are *Le Coup de Lune* (1933), *45° à l'ombre* (1936), and *Le blanc à lunettes* (1937), all three of which connect to Africa and colonial themes. Simenon was not writing to promote overseas colonialism. Indeed, he harbored serious doubts about it, and sometimes wrote frankly and unflatteringly about the "colonial situation." For instance, in *Le blanc à lunettes*, he clearly lays out how sexual relations between whites and blacks were a commonplace in the Congo, which Belgians frowned on at the time.

With Congo's independence, "Flemish literature on the Congo underwent a drastic change. The rioting, which broke out after independence clearly made a big impression on writers."[130] Some chose to ignore the horrible loss that had occurred, burying the trauma under positive depictions of life in the Congo before 1960.[131] In contrast, a number of other works that emerged soon after the *dipenda* (independence) used the violence of the period as backdrop for considerations of the experience of loss; these include Jan van den Weghe's *Djiki-Djiki* (1972), Paul Brondeel's *Ik blanke kaffir* (1970), and André Claeys' *Het duistere rijk* (1963) and *Zonen van Cham* (1964).[132] As noted, pre-1960 works influenced by colonialism continued to circulate, for instance *Lijmen* by Willem Elsschot, in which Elsschot uses the protagonist's reference to colonial business to comment on the domestic situation within Belgium. There is also the work of pro-Flemish poet Gaston Burssens (1896-1965), who was anything but a "colonial" writer, but some of whose texts made subtle connections with overseas expansion, such as when Burssens used the CFS and the Belgian Congo as a metaphor for oppression, thereby tying an aspect of colonialism into debates on the oppression of Flemish.[133] Many other works published soon after independence revealed a Eurocentric bias and the open wounds of the shock of 1960, for example Daisy Ver Boven's *De rode aarde die aan onze harten kleeft* (1962). "Most authors were eyewitnesses who were caught up in the violence themselves. In their novels the blacks are drawn in a very negative light while the whites are seen as the innocent and defenceless victims of raw racial hatred."[134]

Perhaps the best known author who drew on his colonial experiences wrote in Dutch, the late Jef Geeraerts. Like fellow writer André Claeys, Geeraerts was a former colonial administration, and he stands out because of the complexity and shock value of his novels. Geeraerts' autobiographical cycle *Gangreen*, beginning with *Black Venus* (1967), was based on his experiences circa 1956-1960, and revealed the depravity and degeneration of colonial rule. Geeraerts' protagonist, channeling the author's own experiences, is oversexed and sodden with drink through much of the novel's action. The novel manages to criticize religion in all sorts of ways, refuting the image Belgium's colonial action as civilizing, Catholic, and uplifting supposedly benighted Congolese.[135] Geeraerts shares in the trauma of decolonization and what followed in *Ik ben maar een neger* (1962) and *Het verhaal van Matsombo* (1966), depicting among other scenes the brutal murder of a Flemish priest in a street in Bumba. But he also has as protagonist Grégoire Désiré Matsombo, an African who criticizes blacks and whites, and both Belgian colonial rule and African independent rule that followed. Geeraerts elevates Matsombo to the position of protagonist, but also mocks him by making him appear vain and shallow.[136] These early works by Geeraerts made a big splash, with *Gangrene* at first winning a major national prize before the controversy over it provoked the government to seize and investigate the novel.[137]

Conclusion

For several years after the Congo's independence in 1960, people in Belgium followed events in central Africa closely as the end of empire unfolded as a trauma. Dutch and French speakers were united in their shock at the turn of events in the former colony. The great extent to which the Congo crisis was covered in the press and shook the nation revealed that there was a significant awareness of colonial affairs, and that a certain "colonial culture" had developed to a perhaps surprising degree by 1960. Belgian identity had never been profoundly marked by an avid colonialist spirit, but both Dutch- and French-speaking Belgians had grown to take pride in what were commonly believed to be incredible achievements in central Africa that had brought Christianity, infrastructure, modern technologies, and civilization to backward, benighted peoples. This came to an end beginning on 30 June 1960. Of course, we do not know how Belgian identity would have changed had things turned out differently, that is if the Congo had remained a colony after 1960. Perhaps the export of the country's language disputes to central Africa would have accelerated. Contrariwise, it might be the case that the colony's loss eliminated a common project around which Flemish and French speakers would have continued to unite, in a fashion. What is clear is that a common thread ran through memories of empire in both of the country's main language communities after 1960: the experience of the 1950s. That decade came to have an outsized influence on people's memories as Belgians of all backgrounds looked back on a golden age that preceded the ignominious end of the colonial endeavor.

Chapter 3
Quiescence, 1967-1985

"He left suddenly by the steamer one day; and it was discovered afterwards that the bulk of the collection (...) had been crated and shipped back with his belongings to the United States, no doubt to be the nucleus of the gallery of primitive art he often spoke of starting. The richest products of the forest."[1] — V. S. Naipaul, *A Bend in the River* (1979)

There was much silence about the colonial past in Belgium from the late 1960s into the early 1980s, for several reasons. The turbulence of the post-independence Congo crisis died down by the second half of the 1960s. Because only a small number of Belgians henceforth lived in or traveled to central Africa, there were now many fewer of them there to attract the attention of people back home. Unlike in other former colonial states in Europe, there was no great influx of postcolonial migrants, and the number of Congolese living in Belgium remained small. Many of the few who did live in Belgium were there only temporarily, and they seldom called attention to colonial issues. What is more, other major issues garnered greater attention during this time period, including the devastating 1967 fire at the Horta-designed *Innovation* store on rue Neuve in central Brussels that killed 322 people. On the political front, there was the 1978 scuttling of the Egmont Pact, a reform that had been agreed to the previous year regarding the federalization of the country and relations between its two main communities. The year 1978 also witnessed the emergence of the extremist right-wing Vlaams Blok, and the split of the last of the major cross-linguistic political parties, the Belgian Socialist Party, into French- and Dutch-speaking parties. From 1982 to 1985, the *tueurs du Brabant wallon* grabbed headlines by murdering 28 people and wounding dozens more in numerous attacks, many of them in open public, at supermarkets.[2] The May 1985 Heysel stadium disaster saw dozens killed and hundreds injured, shocking the nation and football fans worldwide. The perennial language dispute between Flanders and Wallonia achieved new intensity, witnessed in the 1968 division of the University of Leuven in two, and the building of an entirely new francophone campus at Louvain-la-Neuve near Ottignies. The split was conspicuous and acrimonious. It was said that because of an inability to cooperate, Leuven's library holdings were simply divided in half, arbitrarily: books with even call numbers went to one campus, odd-numbered books went to the other. On the international front, this was the period of détente, yet east-west Cold War tensions continued to loom large, and politically and culturally, the influence of the United States only continued to grow in Belgium, as it did elsewhere in Western Europe, evidenced by the opening of new McDonald's fast food outlets.

Crucial was the fact that despite regional problems such as the shutting down of the country's last coal mines, Belgium as a whole flourished economically from the late 1960s into the early 1970s, although growth was concentrated in the north. Decolonization affected the country's economy only slightly. It is often asserted that Belgium and other colonial powers like France and Britain "got rich" by exploiting Africa's peoples and natural resources. It is true that many individuals, investors, and companies reaped great profits from the Belgian Congo. Even so, even at the height of Belgian investment in and extraction from the colony, its economy depended on the Congo in no great way.[3] Thus, after 1960, "Contrary to some pessimistic predictions, Belgium emerged from a precipitous and dramatic decolonisation in remarkably good shape. (…) The loss of its colony in no way cast a shadow over the country's golden sixties."[4] Economically, the Congo's loss was a case of the dog that did not bark in the night, and aside from those few who were directly affected, people in the metropole did not on the whole sense the loss of its overseas territories in their pocketbooks.

What Belgians did feel was a serious economic crisis beginning around 1973, which brought an end to the "golden years" of sustained post-war economic growth, the so-called *trente glorieuses* from 1945-1975.[5] The crisis of the 1970s absorbed a great deal of psychic energy. Also worrisome was the acceleration of de-industrialization, although this was mainly of regional significance, as Wallonia suffered more from this structural shift that led to rising unemployment, denoted by the closing of the country's last deep coal mine in 1984. Economic troubles notwithstanding, life in Belgium was marked by a high level of security and steadiness. One study of the 1920s-1990s era identifies the period 1961-1993 as being seen by Belgians as the time during which they felt the least threatened, suggesting stability.[6]

The country's relations with the Congo entered a new era as of 1965, after Mobutu secured his grip on power. This brought the turbulent immediate post-independence years to an end but posed new challenges for the former colonial power as it had to learn to deal with the sometimes mercurial ruler of its erstwhile colony.

Language and religion after empire's end

Although the Congo and the colonial experience were hardly front and center in Belgian life from the late 1960s to the mid-1980s, there were significant changes taking place at the nexus of culture and the colonial past. First was the continued debate over the future of Belgium itself, centered on the language issue. Whereas the linguistic struggle had reignited after World War I, after World War II—the second conflict in three decades to raise the specter of Flemish collaborationism with the occupying power—there was a certain clamp down on Flemish nationalist demands. Yet by the 1960s, the language question was again open for debate.[7] One might take as emblematic how the Tervuren Museum emerged in the press in the mid-1960s not in regard to any questioning of the colonial past, but rather in the context of the language debate. There were reports of francophone discrimination, even abuse, toward Flemish speakers on staff at the museum, and the press questioned how many workers there spoke Dutch or French, a thorny issue because the museum was a national institution, meaning a balance among those speakers was needed.[8]

Indeed, of all cultural issues in play, it was linguistic and regional questions that predominated during this period. The country's language frontier had been fixed by 1963, and in 1970 the parliament enacted state reforms establishing three cultural communities: French-speaking, Dutch-speaking, and German-speaking. By 1980, the idea of federalization had been introduced. Linguistic disunion led to a greater political division of the country, which then only reinforced the linguistic and culture divisions between north and south. Long-term migration across the north-south language border slowed to a crawl, and by 1984 "only 2.83 per cent of internal migration between communes involved migration between Flanders and Wallonia."[9] For long, the country had had no "national" newspapers, and after 1960 each region received its own broadcasting company for television and radio, speeding the two regions along increasingly divergent paths, especially since the 1960s represented the dawn of the golden age of television. Already by that decade, 55 to 60 percent of Belgians watched television pretty much each evening.[10] There was no national mass media, no "national media space" that could act to unify the country's two halves.[11] There was limited social interaction between French- and Dutch-speakers and the number of "mixed marriages" was small.[12] During the 1970s, the nation's two main communities formally adopted their own symbols, each with its own distinguished heritage: in Flanders the *Vlaamse Leeuw*, or Flemish lion, and for Wallonia, the *coq hardi*.

Until recently, almost no one probed the possible links between the political and cultural breakup of Belgium and the country's loss of the Congo in 1960.[13] It is difficult to trace direct, causal connections between a political development like the Congo's independence and cultural shifts such as the growing divide between a country's language communities. Still, it is clear that losing the colony in 1960 meant the forfeiture of a shared "Belgian" project and a source of national pride. Insofar as colonialism was a common project, imperialism had been a nation-building effort—ironically not of the Congo, but of Belgium. "It is often said that the Belgian colonization of the Congo was the last national project to transcend the linguistic and ideological differences among Belgian citizens, and that, when the Congo was decolonized in 1960, the loss of this national project stimulated Belgium's political reforms toward federalization."[14] Pedro Monaville suggests in a study of francophone (former) colonists that "the failure of the idea of nation" in Belgium was for them closely identified with the failure of the Belgian colonial project.[15] Whether the relationship is causal or coincidental, we know that the loss of the colony in 1960 was followed by the slow-motion breakup of Belgium that by the early twenty-first century threatened the kingdom's demise.[16] Following South Sudan's emergence as the world's newest state, in 2011, a *New York Times* "top ten" list of states most likely to break up was headed by Mali, followed by Belgium and its former colonial possession, the Democratic Republic of the Congo, in that order.[17]

Another critical development from the 1960s onward that overlapped with post-colonial culture, politics, and the language divide was the Catholic Church's collapse in the country. The Church had long been an organizing and unifying force, and overseas colonialism had boosted its influence by giving it a privileged zone of action that helped reinforce the institution's role in everyday lives in the metropole. Consider what writer Lieve Joris wrote about her family, including one uncle who departed for the Congo as a missionary in the 1920s: "At the time, in all Flemish families, there was an uncle in the missions. The suffering caused by his absence was largely compensated by the novelty of the world in which the family entered: missionaries on leave brought back stories of the bush and came to eat on Sundays, leaving dark spots of red wine on the damask tablecloth and the whole house permeated with thick cigar smoke."[18] After 1960, there was a marked and essentially continuous decline in such missionaries to the Congo or elsewhere. In 1939, there had been 4,930 Belgian missionaries worldwide, around 10 percent of the global total, three fourths of whom were at work in the colony. Although Belgium could still boast as many as 8,411 missionaries worldwide in 1964, this had dropped to 6,283 by 1974, and then to only 4,511 by 1982, the majority of them, as in the past, being Flemish.[19] Whereas historians long overestimated the real extent of secularization in post-French Revolutionary Europe, by the late 1960s, secularization had definitely begun to take its toll, sapping the Church of its former influence.[20] Already by 1967 only 43 percent of Belgian Catholics reported regularly attending church services, and this percentage dropped to only 30 percent by 1976. This paralleled a secularization of politics in the country. The declining influence of the Church could even be seen in even such small measures as the disappearance of Catholic missionaries from *bandes dessinées* beginning in the 1960s.[21] Whether the connection between the Congo's political independence and the weakening of the Catholic Church in Belgium was coincidental or causal is unclear, but surely decolonization did not buttress the Church's influence in the former metropole.

The Tervuren Museum of the Congo

One cultural and colonialist institution of enduring significance was Tervuren's Congo museum. The museum, which had been a state institution under the Ministry of Colonies before 1960, was placed in a uniquely awkward situation following the Congo's independence. Despite something of a diversification of its ambit in the 1950s, as of July 1960, the Tervuren Museum was an institution whose raison d'être, the Belgian Congo, had ceased to exist, calling into question its very existence. After 30 June 1960, it was placed under the Ministry of Foreign Affairs, which absorbed much of the portfolio of the former colonial ministry. At museum director Lucien Cahen's insistence, the institution was quickly relocated to fall within the Ministry of National Education as part of its Administration de la Recherche scientifique.[22] It was out of necessity that it was renamed: formerly the Musée royal du Congo belge, it now became the Musée royal de l'Afrique centrale in an attempt to become a museum of "Africa" by trying on a new identity as an institution focused on the continent more generally.

Commentators have harshly criticized the museum for not changing after 1960, but this overstates the reality. There is no doubt the Tervuren Museum maintained a pro-colonialist bent for decades, most prominently in its *salle d'honneur* honoring colonial pioneers, which included busts of major colonial figures as well as a wall inscribed with the 1,500-plus names of all Belgians who died in the Congo before 1908—with no names of any Africans who died during the same time period, of which there were likely millions. It is not unusual for a country to remember "its own" victims before turning to the commemoration of others. Public commemoration in Europe after World War II, for instance, started with each country remembering its own who died in the conflict. The difference here is that there has never been a public monument in Belgium to the African victims of colonialism, even now more than a century removed from the CFS era.

Nonetheless, the museum did change over time. The accusation that it remained constantly unchanging appeared in multiple critiques of the museum, many of which seemed to be largely based on single visits to it rather than research into its practices and existence over time. Lucien Cahen, museum director from 1958 to 1977, oversaw the renovation of exhibits in several rooms during his tenure.[23] Even if the museum retained a colonialist spirit that could give a visitor an impression of rigidity, it continued to acquire new pieces for its collections, and curators removed other items from display, altered permanent exhibits, and organized temporary expositions, by the end of the century including ones that involved Congolese artists. In fact, when the museum would eventually close for extensive renovations beginning in December 2013, there would be just one room that had remain unchanged since the museum's 1910 opening, the "Crocodile Room," so called because of the large display of stuffed crocodiles at its center.

Still, and as noted, it is true that in many ways the Tervuren Museum plodded along after 1960, celebrating empire, or at least memories of it, and focusing on European realizations in central Africa through a Eurocentric approach rather than an African one. This was certainly true during the immediate post-independence years. One June 1962 exhibit was of works of "Congolese inspiration" by Claude Lyr (Claude Vanderhaeghe), who had spent eight months in the Belgian Congo (1955-1956).[24] According to one press account, the exhibit was meant to highlight how "our artists" discovered the Congo.[25] Another exposition the same year, from 15 September to 30 October, displayed works of African subjects painted by Belgian artist André Hallet, who had died in Rwanda in 1959.[26] One exhibit "dedicated to our two first kings and Belgian expansion" took place in 1965, that year being the centenary of Leopold I's death and of his son's ascension to the throne.[27] The year 1966 marked the fiftieth anniversary of Belgium's World War I victory at Tabora in east Africa, which the Tervuren Museum celebrated with a special exposition from 17 May to 31 July, created in conjunction with the Cercle Royal des Anciens Officiers des Campagnes d'Afrique (CRAOCA), a colonial veterans group.[28] Specific attendance figures for these exhibits are hard to come by, but annual attendance remained strong: 157,000 visitors in 1965, 172,000 in 1966, and 198,000 in 1967.[29]

The museum's Eurocentric focus was sustained into the late 1960s and well beyond. The 1967 exposition "Tervuren 1897" coincided with the seventieth anniversary of Leopold II's 1897 colonial exposition, which had led to the museum's founding. The focus in 1967 was not on the Congo as much as it was on Europeans, the Art Nouveau movement, and the "école de Tervuren" or Tervuren school of painting that had flourished some one hundred years earlier, in the 1860s and 1870s. Commentary on the 1967 event harkened back to Leopold II's creation of the museum, revealing the favorable view of the king that endured.[30] This Eurocentric focus was typical: in the post-1960 years, attention to central Africa and the colonial past, including critiques, remained firmly centered on the action of Europeans, especially elites such as military officers, or members of the royal family. Both the French- and Dutch-language press covered the "Tervuren 1897" show, for which the Museum took in 40,356 visitors, making it successful if not wildly so.[31]

Even if administrators had wished to more fully "decolonize" the Tervuren Museum by, say, gutting it completely and remaking its exhibits from scratch, the museum building itself remained a colonial relic, a massive colonialist palace on the outskirts of the country's capital. The institution's very edifice exuded an imperialist aura, projecting the country's colonialist past into the present. Because Leopold II had been so closely associated with the Congo and the museum by the time the institution's new building was inaugurated in 1910, Leopold's "double-L" monogram that graced both the edifice's interior and exterior reminded the visitor of colonialism. This representation of colonialism in architecture, the woven fabric of urban space, was to be found in many other places in and around Brussels; possibly even in architect Henry Van de Velde's home, La Nouvelle Maison, also in Tervuren. Debora Silverman has argued that this nautically-themed home's shape "resembled a ship's deck and prow," which evoked overseas voyages and, perhaps by extension, imperialist expansion. Silverman has made a creative argument that in this and other subtle ways the Congo became incorporated into Belgian art and architecture, dating back to the fin-de-siècle and the Art Nouveau movement.[32] Silverman has suggested ways in which Congolese influences insinuated themselves into designs by artist and architect Victor Horta, even into interiors of houses in the form stained glass, furniture, and interior design.[33]

In any case the Tervuren Museum was not gutted, and therefore the pro-colonial exhibits and innumerable objects of Africana on display sustained colonialist attitudes. To be clear, the museum's collections resulted from exploration, armed conquest, and foreign, colonial rule. The very building inaugurated in 1910 itself was a result of the massive numbers of objects that flowed to Europe beginning in the 1880s and 1890s, so many that the original *palais des colonies* (still nearby the current building) could not possibly contain them all. (Neither could the new building opened in 1910; it never displayed but a tiny fraction of the museum's holdings.)

Despite the "loss" of the Congo in 1960, Tervuren remained the country's most-visited museum. Consider attendance figures for one year, 1968, when there were 194,000 visitors, of whom 24 percent were schoolchildren.[34] Those 194,000 visitors represented just more than two percent of the country's entire population. This might not sound like much, but consider that in 2017, the most visited museum in the entire United States, the Smithsonian Air and Space Museum, welcomed some 7 million visitors, similarly equivalent to just more than two percent of the country's population. What is more, attendance at Tervuren *increased* into the 1970s and 1980s, attaining an average of more than 215,000 annual visitors, suggesting some sort of enduring interest in colonial issues, Africa, or both.[35] In 1979, for instance, visits included 967 student groups and 44,370 total students (23 percent of all visitors), and 985 other groups including 36,770 visitors in groups (19 percent of total). That year there were 111,460 individual visitors (58 percent of total), 192,600 total visitors, and 824 guided visits.[36]

In short, many years after Belgium no longer had a colony, the country's main museum to empire remained the starting point when it came to people learning about, exploring, and getting to know central Africa and, by extension, their country's colonialist past. As museum director Guido Gryseels put it in 2010, "For most children Tervuren still serves as their very first encounter with black Africa."[37] Or as author and *bande dessinée* illustrator Jean-François Charles (b. 1952) put it, "We've all made a school trip to Tervuren. (...) For us, it's the first encounter with Africa."[38] The institution's influence can be measured beyond mere attendance figures. Artist Hergé, for example, had included influences from the Tervuren Museum in his creations, such as the character in *Tintin au Congo* who dresses up as an *homme-léopard*, a member of the secret aniota society. This was apparently based on Hergé's knowledge of Paul Wissaert's sculpture *L'homme-léopard* (1913) on display at Tervuren.[39] At the same time, many visitors in the post-1960 era likely missed overt messages in the museum about the colonial past. Children in particular were likely more fascinated by the stuffed animals and other such displays than wordy displays about history and dusty statues of old dead white men.[40]

Contested expertise on Africa

Regardless visitors' reactions, the continued collection of Africana and its display at Tervuren and elsewhere were means by which Belgians sustained their authority as experts on Congolese artwork and culture. By 1960, the country's collectors and dealers had become some of the world's foremost specialists on the plastic arts of the Congo and neighboring regions. One example is Marie-Louise Bastin, a collector and expert on Chokwe art who authored numerous scholarly studies, assisted with expositions, and acted as expert witness for investigations into the illegal African art trade.[41] A factor underpinning Belgium's position in this regard was wealth. The colonial administration had pursued a policy of preventing "poor whites" from moving to the colony, and it was costly both to travel to central Africa and to purchase African artwork on the art market. This meant that collectors during and after the colonial era were, all other things being equal, well to do. After 1960, Belgians continued to live in one of the world's wealthiest countries, measured either in absolute terms or in terms of national income per person, providing the means to collect, study, preserve, and display expensive artwork.[42] Congolese were in a different situation. In 1962, Alphonse Moto recognized that African artists such as himself depended upon sales to white collectors, because African would-be collectors simply did not have the means that Europeans did.[43] Sidney Littlefield Kasfir puts it bluntly: "formally trained artists in Africa must survive in the same economic and political climate as street and workshop artists, so although their patrons are drawn from the elite sectors of society and their work is shown in galleries, museums, or cultural centres, there are not usually enough of these in African cities."[44] The only groups that challenged Belgians as top specialists in this domain were French and U.S. experts and dealers, not Congolese. When it came to art, little changed with the de jure independence of the Congo, and Belgians made sense of empire's end by understanding it as a political change rather than a cultural shift.

Tervuren was an important site where Belgians asserted their expertise by continuing to possess and exhibit what was arguably the world's grandest collection of Africana and Congolese artwork. But so too were the country's many private collections, including missionary ones, an uncountable number of which had come into being by 1960. If as many as 100,000 objects of Africana had been taken from the Congo before 1914, one can only imagine how many more were extracted before 1960.[45] After Congo's independence, Belgian and other collectors continued to work on the ground, as much as it was feasible, depending on circumstances. An example is Pierre Dartevelle, who continued to acquire art and other objects into the 1970s, including statuettes and masks.[46] It is likely many other items collected by Europeans during the colonial era but that remained in the Congo after independence found their way to the international market. V. S. Naipaul suggested as much in *A Bend in the River* (1979), quoted in this chapter's epigraph. In Naipaul's novel, the fictional Father Huisman, a Belgian missionary still at work in the Congo after 1960, had assembled a large collection of African masks. Following his murder at the hands of unknown assailants, an American takes possession of the items in his collection and ships them out of the country, "the richest products of the forest."[47]

Some private citizens maintained African art collections, whom organizers of temporary exhibits in Belgium could call on to provide items for display, while many former colonials held smaller, more personal collections.

> Il est bien rare en effet le décor familier d'un Européen ayant exercé son activité en Afrique qui ne témoigne de ces séjours ou de ces mémoires: c'est l'un ou l'autre objet, statue, masque, pièce de métal ou de bois, vannerie, poterie, qui vient signaler ou rappeler l'existence d'une expérience africaine. (The household decor of a European who carried out work in Africa that does not bear witness to those stays in Africa or to those memories is very rare indeed; normally it's one object or another—a statue, a mask, a piece of metal or wood, a basket, a pot—that signals or recalls the existence of an African experience.)[48]

Significant parts of the country's vast store of Africana were "mobilized" after 1960 by means of exhibits, bringing to light a reservoir of artefacts, objects, and art pieces that otherwise would have remained off limits to the general public. Important art exhibitions took place in Brussels in 1970 and 1979, in Liege in 1979, and again in Brussels in 1983. In 1986, the bank Crédit communal sponsored an exhibit of Kuba textiles in its *galerie* at Passage 44 in the capital.[49] When organizers worked to bring these and other exhibits together, they were able to call on a long list of collectors from either side of the country's language frontier.[50] When the 350 Africans living in the city of Tournai decided to put on a show in 1974 so that their fellow citizens could get to know their culture better, they called on the Tervuren Museum's resources, and also on works held privately by former colonials.[51] One of the greatest private collectors was Jef Vander Straete, and when Mobutu Sese Seko commissioned art expert Joseph Cornet to produce a book on Congolese art, Cornet drew on Vander Straete's collection, not on the many thousands of items at the Tervuren Museum, let alone those in collections in central Africa.[52] In sum, the Tervuren Museum did not hold a monopoly on the possession and display of African art in the post-colonial era.

The very presence of such extensive collections of artwork in Belgium became tricky after the Congo's independence, and the self-conception Belgians maintained as leading experts on Congolese art did not go uncontested. In fact, a years-long struggle between the former colonial power and Mobutu over the Congo's patrimony held in Belgium reached a boiling point in the late 1970s. The struggle was more than just about relocating objects: also at stake was who had the authority to determine the "authenticity" of African art.

Thus, Tervuren's continued success as a destination for schoolchildren and others was tempered by a minor crisis from the late 1960s into the 1970s that surfaced when changing politics in the Congo clashed with persistent colonialist attitudes in Belgium. As early as the 1960 Brussels roundtable negotiations leading up to independence, Congolese representatives had argued for the turnover of their patrimony held in Belgium. The mid-1960s then witnessed an intensification of the *contentieux belgo-congolais*, that is the debates over unresolved financial problems between Belgium and the Congo, which escalated following Congolese nationalizations of Belgian-owned companies beginning in 1967. The debates filled many pages of Belgian newspapers as Mobutu's government asserted its claims, for instance over items held at Tervuren, and even the museum building itself. In 1967, when a major traveling exhibit of artifacts from the Tervuren Museum launched with a show at the Walker Art Center in Minneapolis, the Zairian ambassador to the U.S. characterized it as a scandal.[53] Mobutu's subsequent demands that such African artwork be returned led to protracted negotiations into the 1970s. The demands were part and parcel of Mobutu's "authenticity movement" that included renaming his country Zaire and discouraging European names.[54] Mobutu himself discarded his given name, Joseph-Désiré Mobutu, to become Mobutu Sese Seko Kuku Ngbendu Wa Za Banga. A ban was introduced on Western business suits in favor of the abacost, from *à bas le costume*, "down with the [Western] suit." Mobutu adopted his trademark cane and leopard-skin cap, the leopard being redolent of traditional African authority.

The controversy over Congolese patrimony in Belgium and the strained bilateral relations that followed affected displays of Africana beyond Tervuren. Organizers exhibited a heightened sensitivity to the situation at the 1971 *Arts Primitifs/Primitieve Kunst* exhibit at the Théatre National in Brussels and for a 1972 exposition of art from the Congo at Spa's Musée des Beaux-Arts.[55]

Planners of one mid-1970s exposition of African art in the capital lessened the presence of items from certain African countries, including the Congo, because of the perceived "dangers of reactions of the countries of origin of the pieces."[56] Although Mobutu's increasingly vocal demands for the repatriation of Congo's artistic patrimony held in Europe made Belgian curators and experts careful not offend, they did not cause those people to question their self-perception as owners of, and experts on, Congolese culture.

Tervuren curators, including director Lucien Cahen, strongly resisted demands for the return of Zaire's patrimony.[57] Drawn-out negotiations led to an agreement on a limited return of a comparatively small number of pieces of art and artifacts, to take place in stages. A first transfer took place in 1976, a second the following year, and then a third in 1981.[58] In total, 1,042 objects were returned from Belgium (Tervuren) to the Institut des Musées nationaux du Congo (Zaïre) (Institute of National Museums of the Congo (Zaire)), or IMNC/Z. Yet this total, itself a relatively small number, even overstates the significance of the return because 869 of the 1,042 items originated from the Congo's own Institut pour la Recherche Scientifique en Afrique Centrale. Those 869 items had been sent from the colony to the metropole in the late 1950s, but only temporarily, and had remained there at the moment the colony gained its independence. They were only now being sent back, and begrudgingly so, some two decades later. Moreover, there was no transfer of titles along with the objects, which meant that technically, Tervuren never completely surrendered them.[59] It bears noting that Belgium was a major market for African art and already had accrued an incalculably vast number of objects from central Africa over many decades—about a century by the time the third transfer took place in 1981, meaning the total number of objects returned represented a trifle.[60] Their return allowed Belgians to depict themselves as protectors of African cultural heritage, perhaps even as far as having bestowed upon Africans their own culture. When objects from the IMNC/Z emerged onto the international art market, including items from the transfers in the 1970s and 1980s, this only justified the self-perception among Belgians that they were true protectors of African culture, the only people with the interest, expertise, and means to appreciate and preserve the Congolese artistic patrimony. So, although Belgians begrudgingly returned some items, the manner in which the tussle with Mobutu concluded only affirmed them as protectors of and experts on Congolese art, suggesting little had changed from the colonial era, even into the last years of the twentieth century. The conflict raised many issues, but among them were not any probing questions about the colonial past, meaning the episode was a missed opportunity for a more "complete" decolonization.

Other institutions and collectors

Because the Tervuren Museum was never an institution specifically of African artwork, this provided an opening for other museums to showcase the work of Congolese artists and artisans. The Etnografisch Museum in Antwerp remained a repository of knowledge about African (and other) artwork and craftsmanship, and it hosted exhibits, for example "Face of the Spirits: Masks from the Zaire Basin," organized by then-director Frank Herreman in 1993. The museum became a go-to place for some. When Frans Olbrechts, who was Tervuren Museum director and a major collector of Africana, died, some of his collection was deeded to the Etnografisch Museum, with other objects going to the Norbertine Fathers and the Abbey of Averbode.[61]

By the early twenty-first century, Brussels ranked as one of the top global markets for sub-Saharan African art, rivaled only by Paris and New York.[62] Still today, there are numerous high-end African art dealers in and around the Grand Sablon (Grote Zavel), in particular on the Impasse Saint-Jacques and along rue Ernest Allard and rue des Minimes, and these represent only the "apex of the pyramid." Because Belgian colonials, like their French and British counterparts, brought the colony "back home" with them when they returned to Europe—in the form of Africana, musical instruments, so-called fetishes, and other such material culture—there are art dealers, collectors, and individuals across the country in possession of Africana of various kinds. "À elles seules, les réserves que renferment les musées comptent des centaines de milliers d'objets. Que dire des greniers, des murs, des manteaux de cheminée, des encoignures de l'habitat colonial en Europe ou ailleurs?" (What museums held in their storerooms alone included hundreds of thousands of objects, which is not even to speak of the attics, fireplace mantles, and corners of "colonial" homes in Europe or elsewhere.)[63] "Tribal objects that reached Belgium much earlier, in colonial times, still surface in the provinces—at flea markets, in antique shops, or at local auctions—and quickly find their way to the Grote Zavel dealers in the capital, through various channels and networks."[64] In the capital alone, one can find African art at many places aside from the shops around the Grote Zavel, for instance at the flea market at the place du Jeu de Balle. Ongoing trade has only swelled African art arriving to and being sold in or from Belgium.

Artwork also ended up in numerous convents or monasteries, in what were sometimes called "Africa rooms." As noted, missionaries often sent items back to their mission houses, and objects also came from elsewhere, for example when (as noted) Tervuren Museum director Olbrechts passed away and donated part of his collection of Africana to the Norbertine Fathers

African masks and statuettes for sale, place du Jeu de Balle, Brussels, 2018

and the Abbey of Averbode.[65] Missionary orders had used their collections now and then during the colonial era for teaching purposes, at other times creating exhibits or "missie-expos" to raise awareness of and money for their proselytization. Such displays fell out of fashion after 1960; many Africa rooms were taken down, and in some cases objects were sold off. This happened to such an extent that the Centrum voor Religieuze Kunst en Cultuur led an effort in 2005 to better preserve such collections.[66] Yet even when sold, items were not "lost," rather they more often than not ended up on the art market.

It is difficult to determine the number of visitors to Africa rooms or to temporary exhibits of African art, let alone their reactions. But even if such audiences were comparatively small, such exhibits were both rehearsals and (re)assertions of Belgian know-how about Congolese art; an expertise rooted in the colonial era that, as we have seen, was sustained, even strengthened into the post-1960 period. Collectors who sometimes contributed to these exhibits, or who kept their items exclusively for themselves, came from across Belgium and from both of its main linguistic communities, suggesting this was a national feature that bridged the Dutch-French language divide. The continued collecting, storage, and display of Africana across the nation's regions implicitly validated the country's colonial history.

Debora Silverman asserts that African influences were to be seen not only in the presence of Congolese material culture, but also in Belgian artwork, sometimes in the most subtle of ways. Silverman argues that direct influences growing out of Leopoldian rule fed into artistic production, in particular the Art Nouveau movement for which Belgium is so well known. As she puts it, "Belgian Art Nouveau now looks very different to me that it did before (...) and the specifically Congo style of the 1890s and its coherence as a distinctively imperial form of modernism can now be identified." She claims that in Henry Van de Velde's work, "elephants are anywhere and everywhere in the rooms he designed, and in every medium of expression." The "expressive form of the elephant itself," she writes, "colonized Van de Velde's creative consciousness." The "whiplash" style of Art Nouveau "provides visual equivalents of two foundational elements of the CFS regime: the rugged, relentless, and sinuous coils of the Congo's wild rubber vines (...) and the imperial *chicotte*, the long flogging whip at the center of Leopold's rule."[67] How the whiplash style was suggestive of the *chicotte* and not everyday horse whips common to turn-of-the-century Belgium is unclear. All the same, the whiplash style and other aspects of the Art Nouveau movement became iconic, adorning all sorts of things from posters to city buses, perhaps representing another way the imperial experience continued to filter through into the former metropole's visual culture.

Memories of Leopold and the colony

If people's perceptions of Leopold II changed significantly in the decades after his death, during the 1960s and 1970s he remained a respectable if seldom-invoked figure.[68] The favorable view that former colonials held toward him varied little from the general population's views, although former colonials differed in their unusual preoccupation with African affairs and the colonial past.[69] For the sixtieth anniversary of Leopold II's 1909 death, an exposition at the Musée de la Dynastie highlighted the king and what Belgium owed him thanks to his ambitious urban building projects in Brussels and elsewhere. One reviewer of the exposition lauded the king as "clairvoyant."[70] Liane Ranieri's 1973 book *Léopold II: Urbaniste* drew generally positive conclusions about the monarch's building projects (including the Tervuren Museum), which were only amplified by reviews of the book in the press.[71] Defenders of Leopold II and the colonial past were not hard to find, so much so that if someone publicly questioned the positive role of Belgium in central Africa, one could expect a quick retort. When missionary Père Aelvoet wrote to

Force publique[72]
Location: Schaerbeek, square Riga
Sculptor: Willy Kreitz
Architect: Alphonse de Roeck
Inauguration: 7 March 1970
Funded/built by: Union Royale des Fraternelles Coloniales (URFRACOL); a special stamp issued by Ministère des Postes et des Télégraphes; privation donations[73]

Schaerbeek's "Monument to the Troops of the African Campaigns" was built at a cost of an estimated 700,000 to 1 million francs. The monument comprises a curved stone façade bearing the words "Troops of the Campaigns of Africa 1885 1960" and the names of three battles, along with the years of war: Redjaf 1890-1898, Tabora 1914-1918, and Saïo, 1940-1945. To the left is the simplified outline head of a white, European soldier wearing a pith helmet; on the right is a black, African soldier's head in profile, recognizable in part because topped by a fez, typical of a Force publique soldier. The middle of the monument shows two hands grasped together, their placement between the figures of the white and black soldiers suggestive of a bond between Belgians and Congolese. Set in a circle around the monument are nine stones with the names of different war theaters inscribed in them: Abyssinie, Nigerie, Moyen-orient, Italie, Birmanie, Lindi, Kasongo, Usoke, and Mahenge. Inscriptions on the reverse side in French and Flemish read, "Je tiens à rendre ici un particulier hommage à la Force publique qui a accompli sa lourde mission avec un courage et un dévouement sans défaillance.

Schaerbeek Force publique monument, 2018

Discours prononcé par S.M. le Roi Baudouin Ier le 30 juin 1960 à Léopoldville." (I must here pay particular homage to the Force publique which accomplished its weighty mission with courage and with dedication without fail. Speech given by His Majesty King Baudouin I the 30th of June 1960 at Leopoldville.)

The monument was erected in 1970 at the initiative of the group URFRACOL, a colonial interest group that came into being in 1958 by the fusion of la Fraternelle des Anciens de la Campagne d'Abyssinie and l'Union des Fraternelles des Corps expéditionnaires du Congo Belge. It later embraced additional veterans groups as well as former members of the Force Publique, almost all of them war volunteers.[74] It was inaugurated in 1970 by King Baudouin's brother, at the time the Prince de Liège, later to become Albert II. Also present were the Minister of Cooperation and Development, the Governor of Brabant, the Ambassador of the Congo, the president of UFRACOL, and the mayor of Schaerbeek. The event involved two military detachments, the laying of a wreath, the playing of both Belgian and Congolese national anthems, and a parade by schoolchildren.[75]

The monument is one of very few such colonial markers built after 1960. It also is unique in that it celebrates the Force publique in more general terms as opposed to its white officers only. It is furthermore unusual in that it commemorates not only the campaigns of the 1890s but also World War I and World War II.

The monument is a significant site of remembrance and commemoration. Former colonials place wreaths and flowers on the monument at least once, sometimes twice a year.[76] In 2016, there was a ceremony held there to commemorate the centenary of the 1916 Battle of Tabora.[77] In recent years the site has become a spot for members of the Congolese community to gather in order to call attention to the Force publique, which was staffed overwhelmingly by black African soldiers. In 2008, Congolese called for recognition of the role played by Congolese soldiers, and for the soldat inconnu Congolais, the unknown Congolese soldier.[78]

Belgium's African territories played important but forgotten roles in both world wars. During World War I, for example, almost all production from Congo's nascent copper mining industry in Katanga went to Britain to help meet that ally's wartime production needs.[79] During World War II, the Congo provided the Belgian government in exile funds to keep it afloat, essentially helping sustain the metropole's sovereignty as an independent state. Yet many assertions of the Congo's important role in actual fighting during the two wars have been overstated. The Force publique saw limited fighting in Cameroon and German East Africa during World War I. During World War II, units of the Force publique were stationed in Nigeria and other British-controlled colonial territories and also served in limited capacities in Italian East Africa, Madagascar, and Burma.

La Libre Belgique about an article in the missionary publication *Wereldwijd*, asserting that that the piece had failed to account for the fact that it was the Congolese themselves who had paid for colonial development, a fierce article in reply criticized Aelvoet, saying that it had been Belgium that had invested an incredible amount of resources in the Congo, even taking on Congolese debt.[80] The reply pointed to the construction of the Tervuren Museum as a great way to show this outlay of resources, since it had been paid for by Leopold's private money rather than the Belgian state or the Congolese people. Of course, the response failed to point out that the king had made a fortune by means of an exploitative regime of oppressive, foreign rule.[81] Aelvoet's interlocutor, like other Belgians, continued to hold Leopold II in high regard and to believe their country had given everything to the Congo, costing Belgium much in the process. Former colonials continued to publicly honor the colonial project, for example by laying wreaths of flowers at the equestrian statue of Leopold II in Brussels' place du Trône.[82] In 1970, a rare new imperialistic monument was unveiled, this one "aux troupes des campagnes d'Afrique" (to the troops of the African campaigns) in Schaerbeek. Inaugurated in the presence of the Prince de Liège, the future Albert II, the Schaerbeek memorial celebrated Belgian colonial troops' victories in Africa during World Wars I and II, and afterward served as a site of commemoration for former colonial soldiers, both European and Congolese.[83]

Against the grain

Counter-narratives to the inherited rosy interpretation of Belgium's colonial action did emerge in the 1970s and early 1980s. One such alternative view was conveyed in Hugo Claus' play *Het leven en de werken van Leopold II*, which opened at the Nederlandse Comedie in Amsterdam in November 1970, directed by the playwright himself. Claus was already a well-known and successful author and playwright; when *Het leven en de werken van Leopold II* opened, another of Claus' plays, *Vrijdag*, was already being staged with success in Brussels at the Théâtre Royal Flamand (KVS, Koninklijke Vlaamse Schouwburg, or Royal Flemish Theater). *Het leven en de werken van Leopold II* was by far the most political of the author's works, and its reception was less than enthusiastic.[84] The production was less a critique of the king's colonial actions and more an overall negative assessment of the monarch, calling attention to his romantic liaisons, his disdain for his own people, and his diplomatic shenanigans with France, England, and the U.S.[85] It had a second run in 1972-1973 at Arena, directed this time not by Claus but by J. Tummers, but with even less success. Although the play did not have a great impact, it represented an outstanding critique of Leopold II, and as such also an assault on the dynasty. At the very least it was an indirect attack on the country's history of overseas rule. This was perhaps particularly the case when one remembers that the king at the time the play opened, Baudouin, had always had such high praise for his great-uncle and his role in colonialism. As Claus expressed a certain appreciation for the king after a cordial meeting with him years later, in 1984: "If you had treated one of my ancestors in the way in which I did so in [*Het leven en de werken van*] *Leopold II*, I would not want to meet the person who did that."[86]

Some other critical notes were to be heard during this era, for example in some school history textbooks.[87] Julien Weverbergh's *Leopold II van Saksen Coburgs allergrootste zaak* made plain that the foundations of Belgian colonialism in the Congo were those laid by Leopold II, based on sordid exploitation. Weverbergh broke with tradition by including caricatures of the sovereign, testimonies of abuse, and criticisms by socialist Emile Vandervelde and others.[88] Another Flemish-language textbook in its 12th edition in 1980 interjected more ambivalent notes about the king's colonial administration.

> In deze domeinen [Kroondomein] liet hij de opbrengst van rubber en ivoor vergroten door de inlanders tot dwangarbeid te verplichten, waarbij zelfs lijfstraffen, uitbranding van dorpen en terechtstellingen te pas kwamen. (In these domains [the Crown domain] he increased the yields of rubber and ivory by compelling the indigenous inhabitants into forced labor, whereby corporal punishment, burning of villages, and even executions were used.)[89]

But such critical notes were muted and few and far between well into the 1980s.[90]

Higher education and research

Authors of recent studies of how the empire "came back home" often set up a dichotomy between those who were zealots of empire and those who were more indifferent to it, which has tended to obscure subtle ways in which overseas colonialism affected Europe more generally, both during and after the colonial era.[91] One such way was how overseas empire left traces in Europe's human and intellectual capital. In the Belgian case, there were innumerable ways in which the hard sciences had developed in tandem with colonialism, for example scientists studying how certain plants from central Africa might combat illness.[92] Even if the colony was "lost" in 1960, this did not bring such scientific research to a halt.[93] Other fields like anthropology and museology had been shaped by the colonial relationship with central Africa, and this carried forward after 1960.[94] Institutions like the Tervuren Museum, the Prins Leopold Instituut voor Tropische Geneeskunde te Antwerpen, even the Jardin Botanique National de Belgique or the Jardin colonial de Laeken: all of these owed much of their existence and holdings to colonial rule and the exchanges with the Congo that followed.[95] None disappeared in 1960.[96] In these ways the colony fed into the development of the sciences and modern technologies in Belgium and had knock on effects, many immeasurable, well into the post-colony era.

The drop off of funding dedicated to research on the Congo did not mean the end of research and expertise about sub-Saharan Africa in Belgium, as many have asserted over the years. A great deal of human capital had accumulated before 1960, which continued to pay dividends for Belgium, even if research on central African subjects waned. There continued to be some if albeit low-key interest at universities, including at ULB and Leuven University (divided in 1968 into the Flemish-language Katholieke Universiteit Leuven, now KU Leuven, and the Université catholique de Louvain in Louvain-la-Neuve).[97] Students produced more than 237 *mémoires de licence* (master's theses) on the Congo and aspects of colonial history between 1960 and 2004.[98] The Tervuren Museum, despite funding challenges, remained an important center and publisher of research, as reflected in its journal *Africa-Tervuren*, whose articles dealt with topics as varied as African musicology, history, demography, ethnography, and art. During the colonial era the museum sometimes hid or held back information from researchers "in order to conform to official doctrine, which was supposed to support the colonial consciousness."[99] The degree to which this tendency persisted after 1960 has yet to be studied. Still, into the post-colonial era *Africa-Tervuren* published original, unpublished primary sources from the colonial era, and scholars could visit and draw on the institution's Africana and other objects, archives, photographs, and materials to contribute to knowledge about the Congo and its neighboring regions.[100] As one of the leading figures of this production put it, "les scientifiques belges ont joué un rôle d'avant-garde dans la collecte, la publication et l'interprétation critique des sources africaines, orales ou écrites." (Belgian scientists have played a leading role in the collection, publication, and critical interpretation of African sources, both oral and written.)[101] Research groups pushed scholarship forward, for instance CRISP (Centre de recherche et d'information socio-politiques), which led the way with studies and documents on Congo's independence as early as 1959. This fed into the development of the Centre d'Études et de Documentation africaines in 1971 that later became l'Institut africain-CEDAF/Africa Institute-ASDOC in 1992, whose *Les Cahiers du CEDAF-ASDOC Studies* (1971-1992) and *Cahiers africains-Afrika Studies* series (1993-present) produced a wealth of quality studies on current issues, for example in the fields of economics or African history. Another group was ARSOM/KAOW (the Royal Academy for Overseas Sciences), undeniably linked to the monarchy and the colonial status quo before 1960, but a significant supporter of research and scholarship afterward as well.

Rather than the post-1960 situation being one where research into Africa dropped off completely and Belgian expertise disappeared, it was instead a case of a missed opportunity. Belgium had become a major center of knowledge about the Congo and its neighboring regions by 1960, but this was not followed up afterward by funding and institutional support that could have capitalized on the situation. Instead, the proliferation of African studies programs in the United States and elsewhere in the 1960s found no echo in Belgium. The study of Africa and African history in Belgium declined from a certain height, becoming comparatively lamentable.[102] The country lacked centralized, well-funded initiatives to coordinate African expertise, contributing to a big drop in research from the 1960s into the 1970s, and beyond.[103] As one contemporary put it,

La sclérose des milieux universitaires et l'aveuglement des responsables politiques poussèrent la majorité des spécialistes belges de l'Afrique à émigrer vers d'autres pays, principalement les Etats-Unis ou la France, où l'on était capable d'apprécier leur valeur.
(The sclerosis in Belgian academia and the blindness of political leaders pushed the majority of Belgian specialists on Africa to emigrate to other countries, mainly the United States or France, where people were able to appreciate their worth.)

This was followed by a sharp drop from 1978 that resulted from serious budget cuts, so much so that one scholar wrote in 1983 that, "les possibilités de travail se réduisent à un rythme croissant qui les approche aujourd'hui du néant." (the possibilities for work decreased at a growing pace that makes them today approach nil.)[104] This decline suggests again how Belgian involvement in Africa, even at its height, was always and above all about Belgians, not Congolese, despite rhetoric about colonialism being an altruistic undertaking to better supposedly backward and benighted peoples. Just as the great attention paid to Baudouin's 1955 visit to the colony was more about the royal family than about the Congo, education about central Africa declined as precipitously as did the physical Belgian presence there.[105] Once the Belgians were "out" starting in 1960, people in the former metropole ceased caring much about investment in the Congo, which was reflected in the drop in research support.

And even if research continued and human capital built up before 1960 translated into important advances, those in the field of historiography had little effect on culture more broadly, even the nuanced work of the most preeminent scholars in the field, namely Jean Stengers, Jan Vansina, and Jean-Luc Vellut. Although these three "built an international reputation as leading scholars in their fields," Geert Castryck writes, "within the Belgian context there seemed to be no popular interest in their findings."[106] What was taught in primary and secondary education continued to convey an overwhelmingly positive and slapdash view of the colonial past.[107] Leopold II, wholly rehabilitated by the 1950s, continued to be lauded in history textbooks into the 1970s.[108] According to one, he was "the best and noblest defender of the black peoples in distant Africa."[109] In this way, one must question the degree to which higher education and university-level research projects filtered into the country's culture.

Indeed, aside from the occasional discordant assertion, writers of school textbooks generally revealed that they had interiorized a wholly positive interpretation of Belgium's colonization, another hangover from the last years of colonialism that had the effect of miseducating a whole generation, very few of whom now (in the 1970s and 1980s) had any direct colonial experience.[110] An example is how textbook authors often reproduced an August 1889 letter from Leopold II to Prime Minister Auguste Beernaert as a primary source to develop their discussion of the CFS period. Leopold wrote to Beernaert that,

> Ayant travaillé uniquement pour mon pays, mon cœur souhaite qu'il profite de mon labeur et de mes sacrifices, non seulement pendant ma courte existence, mais de longues années après moi. Je veux, s'il y consent, le faire mon héritier du Congo...
> (Having worked only for my country, my heart's wish is that it benefits from my labor and my sacrifices, not only during my brief life, but for many years after me. If Belgium agrees to it, I want to have it inherit the Congo from me.)[111]

This letter casts the king in an altruistic and benevolent light, especially as it glosses over key points, one being that in 1889, the Congo was far from under Leopold's control, meaning it was not his to bequeath to anyone. A second point omitted is how it was rather easy for the king to offer the colony to Belgium in 1889 because at that time, the Congo was more albatross than treasure. Leopold had exhausted his personal fortune financing the exploration, occupation, and conquest of "his" territories, and they had yet to produce the vast sums they eventually would from ivory and rubber. What is more, citing the letter elided the fact that Leopold put in motion a plan to borrow vast sums from Belgium in support of his own private efforts, a kind of "down payment" on his eventual turnover of the colony.[112]

"Schoolbooks continued to give the colonialist mythology on Belgian heroism, until Congo disappeared from history courses altogether."[113] Yet just because this "colonialist mythology" disappeared from courses due to a drop in interest in the colonial past, the imprint of the lessons remained—in people's minds—as did the books themselves, becoming reference points to maintain a positive view of the colonial past. One website on the celebration of a 2014 commemoration ceremony at the De Bruyne-Lippens monument in Blankenberge, for instance, made reference to a 1962 schoolbook for twelve year olds that praised the two men as heroes.[114] However much Belgians furthered knowledge about Africa, when it came to the layman's knowledge about the colonial past or Africa's history, the work of specialists simply did not filter down to those who wrote textbooks, suggesting in a sense a failure of higher education and the teaching of colonial and African history in Belgium after 1960.[115]

Belgium and Zaire

Whatever the colonial past and conceptions of it among Dutch- and French-speaking Belgians, from the mid-1980s the country's citizens faced a corrupt Zairian regime that was in decline. Turbulence, evacuations, and nationalizations of Belgian-owned industries sapped Belgians of the desire to stay or invest anew in central Africa. The number living there by the 1970s was small, some 18,000 by 1976, which was an eighty percent decline since 1959, and about as many as had been living there in 1930. The Congo had assumed such a reduced position in Belgian life that looking around at Belgian culture at the time, one could be forgiven for thinking the country did not even have a colonial past.[116]

Belgium's relations with Mobutu's regime faced tough times. The period immediately after Mobutu took power in 1965 was one of good Belgian-Congolese relations, particularly in contrast to the four-plus years of tumult that preceded his accession. Yet new issues came up that complicated those relations, including negotiations on the future of the mining giant Union Minière du Haut-Katanga (UMHK). In 1966, Mobutu nationalized UMHK—it was renamed Gécamines—which strained relations. From this point forward, Belgium's dealings with Mobutu to the early 1990s were to be "cyclothymic," or bipolar, as Guy Vanthemsche has put it; that is, relations between the two countries were marked by a "succession of euphoric and depressive episodes."[117] If many in the Belgian establishment had first believed they could mold their former colony, Mobutu's 1965 coup and his strengthening grip on power in the months that followed disabused them of that notion. By the time of the first visit by a member of the royal family to the Congo since independence, that of the Prince de Liège (the future Albert II) in 1969, the establishment had come to view the former colony as a truly different country entirely.[118] The king still saw his role as special: Between 1955 and 1986, "il est clair que Baudouin n'a pas cessé de considérer le Congo comme un territoire que son grand-oncle lui laissait en héritage." (it is clear that Baudouin [had] not stopped considering the Congo as a territory that his great-uncle left for him as an inheritance.)[119] The king's 1970 trip to the Congo with Queen Fabiola to mark the Congo's tenth anniversary of independence was a delicate dance: Belgian authorities wanted to affirm Congo's advances and maintain good relations while Mobutu sought to bolster his prestige and hold on power.[120]

Events in the 1970s sowed greater divisions between former colonial master and subject. As discussed, the *contentieux belgo-congolais*, Mobutu's *authenticité* movement (or Zairianisation), including the nationalization of businesses, put off many Belgians. The two Shaba invasions of 1977 and 1978, when French paratroopers and a Belgian airlift, along with Moroccan troops, propped up Mobutu's rule, hinted that the central African giant was teetering. This situation was reflected in the unsympathetic portrayal of the "Big Man" in V. S. Naipaul's novel *A Bend in the River* (1979), which showed the country in a sad state. As optimism about African independence had faded by the 1980s, so too in Belgium was there disappointment, specifically with the Mobutu regime, its blatant corruption, and its failure to deliver for the Congolese people, about whom many former colonials and missionaries truly cared.[121] The less that Zaire mattered to Belgium, the more important Belgium became for Mobutu and Zaire, due to its development aid, investment funds, cooperation efforts, coordination on military affairs, and how Belgium could act as a bridge between the central African regime and Western nations. After Belgium had more or less gotten over the trauma of the Congo crisis, by the 1970s-80s, in a strange twist, it was Mobutu and Zairian elites who started to use the colonial past more and more for their own purposes.[122]

Émile Wangermée (1855-1924)

Location: Tienen (Tirlemont), Wolmarkt 14

Inauguration: 1924

Funded/built by: Section régionale des Journées coloniales de
Tirlemont[123]

Wangermée was a career military man whose initial training was in engineer-
ing and fortifications. Leopold II brought him into the CFS administration as an
Inspecteur d'État, under Governor-General Wahis. Like many other military men
who entered Leopold's colonial service, Wangermée enjoyed rapid promotion.
He did not leave for the Congo until spring 1893, but already by 1897 had been
promoted to Vice Governor-General of the Congo, and then served as Governor-
General from 1901-1903. Soon after the advent of the Belgian state rule period
in 1908, he became Governor of the province of Katanga, which was created in
1910. With only perhaps a few dozen Europeans in Katanga in 1910, its European population grew significantly as it became a great mining capital, exploiting Katanga's vast mineral resources. Katanga and its capital were almost more
of a southern African colony than a part of the Belgian Congo, and it attracted

Plaque on birth home of Émile Wangermée, Tienen, 2018

numerous English speakers from British-dominated southern Africa. English was the lingua franca for many years. Indeed, Katanga was so remote from the main colonial state, Wangermée reported directly to the Minister of Colonies rather than to the Governor-General in Boma, meaning that in practice Katanga was almost an independent colony under Wangermée's administration.[124] Wangermée did little to counter this tendency toward decentralization. When later he was hailed as founder of the capital of Katanga, Elisabethville, many in the province did so in praise of his tendency to boost the province's autonomy. This promotion of decentralization had consequences, such as when Katanga seceded from the Congo in July 1960, thereby deepening and prolonging the Congo crisis.

The plaque to Wangermée is located on his birth home, an 18th Century dwelling in Tienen. It is plain and straightforward, without adornment: "In this house was born on 14 March 1855 General Émile Wangermée, Vice Governor of the Belgian Congo, Governor of Katanga, Founder of Elisabethville." That its inscription is in French in this Dutch-speaking town is one small testament to the longstanding francophone dominance of the country. It is one of several plaques in Belgium placed on the birth homes of well known and lesser known colonial figures, including ones to Joseph and Lieven Van de Velde (Ghent, 1888),[125] Zoe Cote (Nismes, ca. 1930),[126] Jules Laplume (Salm, 1931),[127] Louis Royaux (Boisseilles, ca. 1933),[128] Gustave Dryepondt (Bruges, 1939),[129] Florent Gorin (Mons, 1939),[130] Philippe Molitor (Villance, 1956),[131] and Émile Storms (Wetteren).[132] In addition to the plaque in Tienen, a street in Etterbeek was named after Wangermée and a monument was put up to him on 4 January 1931 in Elisabethville (Lubumbashi). Moreover, a large funerary memorial was put up in the Ixelles cemetery, at the inauguration of which, on 25 January 1925, several people spoke.[133]

Wangermée's colonial career illustrates two fundamental aspects of Leopold II's CFS: that it was a colonial regime of conquest, and that its creation in 1885 in no way signaled Europeans' actual control over the vast lands and many peoples of the Congo. Wangermée did not depart for the Congo until spring 1893, nearly eight years after the summer 1885 declaration of the CFS. His first term of service saw him dedicating his time and energies to the building of defenses in the lower Congo to protect the capital, at the time still at Boma. In the years that followed he was involved with Francis Dhanis in suppressing the Batetela rebellion of troops in 1897 as well as the revolt in 1900 of African worker-soldiers at Shinkakasa. Also noteworthy is the fact that Wangermée's son Georges Wangermée followed him into colonial service, a rare second generation colonial soldier and administrator.

Albert Thys (1849-1915)
Location: Brussels, Parc du Cinquantenaire (Jubelpark)
Sculptor: Franz Huygelen
Inauguration: 30 January 1927[134]

Albert Thys was an important figure of the Leopoldian era and arguably the
most influential and powerful of the king's collaborators, even if Thys eventually broke with his sovereign over the latter's Congo policies.[135] Another of the
king's agents, Welsh-American explorer Henry Morton Stanley, early on stated
that cataracts and rapids between Kinshasa and Matadi nearer the Atlantic
prevented imports from moving inland from the coast, and from traffic moving
in the opposite direction, from Congo's interior to the Atlantic. Stanley believed
a railway to circumvent the falls was necessary, saying that without one, "the
Congo is not worth a penny." It was Thys who became the leading figure behind
the building of what came to be known as the Matadi-Leopoldville railway,
construction on which lasted from 1890-1898 and cost hundreds of lives. Thys
had founded the Compagnie du Congo pour le Commerce et l'Industrie (CCCI) in
the late 1880s as a device to build the railway, and the company continued on
afterward, becoming a massive colonial enterprise.

In its own subtle way, the Thys monument in Brussels serves to nationalize
the history of the CFS. A similar process happened by means of memorials to

Detail of monument to Albert Thys, 2018

Monument to Albert Thys, Brussels, 2018

Belgians who died during the building of the Matadi-Leopoldville railway, such as Ferdinand Lamy (Seraing) and Joseph-Émile Villers (Bonlez). As discussed elsewhere in this book, memorials to those who died in the Congo before 1908 "nationalized" the colonial history of the CFS, which had been almost as much an international undertaking as it had been a Belgian one. It is true that Thys was the leading figure in the building of the Matadi-Leopoldville railway, and that Belgians died during its construction. But these monuments obscure the fact that not only did Africans provide the bulk of the labor—hundreds of them perished—but also hundreds of non-Belgians worked on it, too: between 1890 and 1898, Italy alone sent more than 600 men to work on the line's construction.[136]

The Brussels monument to Thys is located at the western entrance of the Parc du Cinquantenaire, a short walk from the Monument du Congo in the same park. It is made up of a statue of two women atop a base, on the front of which is a profile of Thys, in bronze, with his name, and the years of his birth and death. The statue of the two women tells a story. One of them, a black African, bears an overflowing cornucopia out of which falls produce, symbolizing the colony's riches. She is being guided by a female spirit, a white woman, suggesting the latter's superior knowledge and know-how. The black woman's upward-looking gaze and smile suggest her (the Congo's) contentment and a happy, better future. The white female figure remains clothed whereas the African woman is bare breasted, the latter providing a whiff of savagery in an otherwise peaceable scene, as nakedness suggested to Europeans backwardness, barbarity, and at the same time subject status.[137] One publication describes the figure of the white woman:

Deux minuscules ailerons symboliquement plantés sur son crâne coiffé à l'antique, et un caducée qu'elle élève de la main droite, accentuent le mouvement de cette noble figure, qui compose, avec celle de la négresse, un groupe d'une heureuse silhouette.
(Two miniscule little wings set on a head coiffed in an antique style, and a caduceus that she raises with her right hand accentuates the movement of this noble figure, which composes, with that of the black woman, a beautifully-shaped form.)[138]

This marker, like the nearby Colonial Monument and the Leopold II place du Trône equestrian statue, became a site where veterans and other groups would come and place flowers during the country's annual *journées coloniales*.[139]

Arthur Pétillon (1855-1909)
Location: Etterbeek
Inauguration: 1976

An entrance to the Pétillon metro stop, Brussels, 2018

The Pétillon metro station is on the Brussels metro line number 5 in Etterbeek, parallel with rue Major Pétillon and between the avenue des Volontaires and the boulevard Louis Schmidt. Its placement in space is arguably "colonial": the station is close to the many streets named after CFS military officers and other colonial figures that can be found on the other side of boulevard Louis Schmidt, and one of Pétillon's adjacent stations is Thieffry, named after aviator Edmond Thieffry, whose claim to fame was being the first to pilot an air voyage to the Congo. Indeed, there are at least six metro or bus or tram stops in the Brussels region named after men associated with European colonialism in central Africa, namely Livingstone, Léopold II, Pétillon, Thieffry, Thys, and Vétérans coloniaux.

Arthur Pétillon was actually born in Péruwelz, but he died in Etterbeek. He was an early colonial pioneer, answering Leopold II's call and entering into service in 1890, for a term of four years. He remained active in public life after returning to Belgium, for instance founding the "Villa coloniale" in Watermael, and joining the city council of Etterbeek.[140] A street there was named after him by a royal decree of 19 June 1931.[141]

The degree to which the station evokes Arthur Pétillon and the CFS for everyday travelers is questionable. Some surely make the mistake of thinking either the metro station or the street named after him (or both) were actually named after Léo Pétillon, a prominent official who served as the penultimate Governor-General of the Belgian Congo, and then briefly as the Minister of the Belgian Congo and of Ruanda-Urundi at the very end of the colonial period. What is more, according to one commentator, "pour la plupart des utilisateurs de la STIB, ces personnages n'évoquent rien de plus qu'un arrêt sur leur itinéraire quoti-dien." (for most riders on the STIB, these figures evoke nothing more than a stop on their daily route.)[142]

Physical traces

Whatever Leopold II's building plans and the role his Congo profits played in them, the colonial era left significant marks on Brussels. When it comes to city planning and architecture, the capital is often remembered for "Brus-selization," that is the indiscriminate, some say abusive tearing down of historic buildings during the 1960s and 1970s to build new thoroughfares and developments. Only more recently have people come to appreciate the degree to which overseas imperialism reshaped the capital. Someone walking the streets of downtown Brussels any time after 1960 could take in numerous former "colonial" buildings. At the place Royale is the location of the former Ministry of Colonies as well as Hôtel Coudenberg, site of the first *cercle colonial*, or local club bringing together colonial enthusiasts and veterans. Leaving the place Royale and continuing up the rue de Namur, one passes the former seat of Leopold's Association Internationale Africaine, and turning left down rue Brederode, one walks past the *pavillon norvégien*, complete with the CFS star, before arriving at the place du Trône, where one can not only consider the grand equestrian statue of Leopold II but also gaze over at the *écuries de la reine*, which housed the CFS' administrative services for several years. Just across the city's inner ring road from the place du Trône is the former Banque Lambert, today the ING building. Walking southeast from that point, one arrives at the porte de Namur and the Matonge neighborhood entrance—in 2018 rebaptized "square Patrice Lumumba"—near which one can find still today the headquarters of the UROME pro-colonial interest group. Other traces are to be found elsewhere, such as the beautiful decorative adornments of banana and other exotic trees at the top of the former G.K.F. (Gérard Koninckx Frères) building at the corner of rue Dansaert and place du Vieux Marché aux Grains.

Similar such bits and pieces are to be found in other cities as well, most notably Ostend, upon which Leopold II lavished his Congo profits. A smaller example is the entrance of the former arms manufacturer Lambert-Sévart at

Former G.K.F. building, Brussels, 2013

16-18 rue Grandgagnage in Liege, where one can find a panel illustration above the entrance door with a typical colonial "export" scene: a white colonial in pith helmet brings goods to a distant shore, complete with palm trees on the beach, and a shipping boat unloading offshore in the background. In this case the good is a firearm, which the European merchant is showing to a dark-skinned man in a turban.[143]

Another "trace" of the colonial era that endured in Belgium, also woven into the very urban fabric of the country itself, was of course the numerous monuments, memorials, and plaques that remembered colonialism and its founder, Leopold II. Even if interest in the Congo declined as Belgians left that country, the colonial past continued to be present in the former metropole in bronze and stone. A monument to Edmond Thieffry in Etterbeek, for example, commemorates the aviator who made the first air voyage to the Congo. One of Mechelen's main avenues is graced by an imposing colonial monument that recognizes those who "gave their lives for civilization."[144] The city of Mons alone has three colonialist monuments: one celebrating geologist Jules Cornet; another to the pioneers of the Leopoldian era; and one to Leopold II himself. There are today at least fifteen public monuments to Leopold II: four in Brussels (Duden Park in Forest, place du Trône, Vorstsquare in Auderghem, and in the Jardin du Roi off avenue Louise); one each in Arlon, Ekeren, Genval, Ghent, Halle, Hasselt, Mons, Namur Tervuren; and two in Ostend.

Edmond Thieffry (1892-1929)[145]
Location: Etterbeek, avenue Boileau
Sculptor: César Battaille
Inauguration: 10 July 1932

Monument to Edmond Thieffry, Etterbeek, 2018

Etterbeek native son Edmond Thieffry was not only a flying ace of World War I, he was also the first person to successfully make a flight from Belgium to the Congo, which he accomplished in 1925. The statue to him in Etterbeek, unveiled on 10 July 1932, is a tall monument topped by a bust of Thieffry in uniform. The inscription "À Edmond Thieffry, Pilote Aviateur," does not call attention to his connection to the colony, but a large map in bronze showing his famous flight trajectory from Belgium to the Congo does. In addition, the inscription on the monument's base calls attention both to his World War I exploits and his successful flight from Belgium to the colony. Thieffry became passionate about Africa, and died and was buried in the Congo following a 1929 air accident. Etterbeek also named the rue Aviateur Thieffry after him, and when a nearby metro stop opened in September 1976, it also took his name.

Jules Cornet (1865-1929)

Location: Mons (Bergen), avenue Frère Orban

Sculptor: Harry Elström (sometimes Elstrøm)

Architect: Georges Pepermans

Inauguration: 1953

Funded/built by: Association des ingénieurs de la faculté polytechnique de Mons[146]

A tall bronze bust of Cornet is at the center of a triptych of sorts, flanked by panels with plaques on them. The one on the left represents two African women carrying baskets on their heads, perhaps containing rock ore, and a crouched colonial in pith helmet and shorts. The bronze relief on the right depicts digging and refining operations, showing two figures working at a mine. A close-by explanatory plaque by the city of Mons—in French, Flemish, and English—emphasizes Cornet's local origin and his prospecting work in the Congo, in particular in Katanga.[147] Below Cornet's figure on the front of monument is the simple inscription: "Jules Cornet 1865-1929". On the reverse a plaque reads, in French: "Au professeur Jules Cornet 1865-1929, Fondateur de la geologie du Congo. L'Association des ingénieurs de la faculté polytechnique de Mons." (To professor Jules Cornet 1865-1929, founder of geology in the Congo. The Association of Engineers of the Polytechnic Faculty of Mons.) It goes on to quote Cornet: "'On a vu, par les considerations que nous venons d'exposer, quelle masse énorme de minerais de fer et de cuivre doit receler le sol de la partie méridionale du bassin du Congo.' Jules Cornet, adjoint à l'Expedition Bia-Franqui 1891-1893 (extrait de son mémoire de 1894, en conclusion)." ("We have seen, by the accounts that I just presented, what enormous mass of iron and copper ores the southern part

Monument to Jules Cornet, Mons, 2018

of the Congo [river] basin must harbor underground." Jules Cornet, deputy to the Bia-Franqui expedition 1891-1893 (concluding excerpt from his 1894 memoir.))

Cornet not only prospected in the Congo and was the main discoverer of Katanga's vast copper ores, he also was a professor at the École des Mines in Mons. That the Mons memorial to Cornet is not merely one to a local son or to mining is indicated not only by its references to the Bia-Franqui excursion and the Congo, but also by the fact that its inauguration took place on the sixtieth anniversary of the Bia-Franqui expedition's conclusion, as opposed to, say, the year he took up teaching at the École des Mines. At the same time, the monument clearly also celebrates Cornet's work as a geologist in Belgium, and therefore can be considered a hybrid monument celebrating colonialism, Mons as a mining center, and the Borinage as a mining region.[148]

Colonial pioneers
Location: Mechelen (Malines), Schuttersvest
Sculptor: Lode Eyckermans
Architect: Van Meerbeeck
Inauguration: 1953
Funded/built by: public subscription; Koloniale Kring van Mechelen; Ministry of Colonies

Mechelen's monument to the city's colonial pioneers is among the more visually striking of such memorials in the former metropole. Whereas many other towns contented themselves with modest commemorative plaques, some of which were placed in rather isolated locations, the city of Mechelen opted for a large, African-themed sculpture in a prominent, open site at an intersection along the Schuttersvest on the city's inner ring road.

Mechelen memorial to colonial pioneers, 2013

The statue is made entirely of carved stone. Two African heads top the monument, one of which represents a man, the other of which depicts a woman who is clearly Mangbetu. The heads are at the top of a stout column on which the names of local colonial pioneers are superimposed upon a map of the Congo. A number of other engravings are included on the column as well, including of elephants.[149] Although the base of the monument is today covered with bushes, old photographs show that the whole monument rests upon a large star, one of the iconic symbols of the CFS.[150] The memorial's main engraving that runs above the names carved into the column reads, "Zij gaven hun leven voor de beschaving," (They gave their lives for civilization.) The statue thus calls attention to the country's civilizing mission in Africa while commemorating the 31 locals who died there before 1908.

Archival documents about the Mechelen memorial reveal how such monuments were funded in the 1950s. The local Koloniale Kring van Mechelen of pro-colonial enthusiasts and colonial veterans organized an "Oprichting Monument aan de Mechelse Pioniers van Congo Opgedragen" (Establishment of a Monument Dedicated to Mechelen's Pioneers of the Congo) to raise money for the statue. Like many other such efforts in the 1950s, the group did its own fundraising, solicited funds from the public, and also received a subsidy from the Ministry of Colonies. In all, the Koloniale Kring van Mechelen provided 30,000 francs from its regular budget and 10,155 francs from special funds just for the monument; 35,245 francs were raised by public subscription; 25,000 francs came from the national organization the Journées Coloniales/Koloniale Dagen; and the Ministry of Colonies provided 15,000 francs.[151]

Mechelen native Guillaume (Willem) Van Kerckhoven is among those honored on the monument. Indeed, the year it was inaugurated, 1953, marked the centenary of Van Kerckhoven's birth in the city, which also renamed a nearby street after him.[152] Van Kerckhoven was an early and dedicated agent of Leopold II's colonial enterprise, embarking for the Congo as early as February 1883, more than two years before the European powers and the United States recognized the CFS as Leopold II's colony.

Van Kerckhoven became notorious for his frequent resort to extreme violence, including burning entire villages, destroying crops in their fields, killing large numbers of people, and waging war on locals to confiscate their ivory.[153] Irishman Roger Casement—whom the British Parliament later commissioned to inquire into the Congo atrocities, and who wrote a damning report—ran into Van Kerckhoven on a Congo steamer in 1887, by which time the Belgian had become a CFS officer. According to Casement, Van Kerckhoven explained to the Irishman how he paid his black soldiers "per human head they brought him during the course of any military operations he conducted."[154] Adam Hochschild suggests

Van Kerckhoven might have been one inspiration for the character of Kurtz in Conrad's *Heart of Darkness*, the successful European ivory raider who went up river in the Congo and became unhinged.[155] According to his biographer in the *BCB*, by contrast, Van Kerckhoven was "un des plus brillants officiers et des meilleurs administrateurs que la Belgique ait envoyés en Afrique." (one of the most brilliant officers and best administrators that Belgium sent to Africa.)[156]

Van Kerckhoven undertook numerous missions in furtherance of Leopold II's quest to acquire as much territory as possible. One historian describes the officer's 1891 expedition to the Nile as "a straightforward military operation for exclusively political ends (...) No one was to be rescued from savage clutches, there were no unknown rivers to be mapped, nor was there the slightest scientific or anthropological pretext."[157] The expedition ended for Van Kerckhoven on 10 August 1892. That day he and his men came under attack, and Van Kerckhoven's gun, which was being carried by his "boy" who was following behind him, discharged, shooting Van Kerckhoven in the back and killing him instantly. Exactly what caused the mishap remains unclear, and perhaps it was an accident, as the standard accounts have it. But perhaps the killing was deliberate, a case of fragging *avant la lettre*. After all, Van Kerckhoven was well known as a brutal officer who pushed his men to the limits, and on 10 August 1892, his leadership had once again placed his men in danger as they came under fire by local resistance fighters. In any case, the shot ended Van Kerckhoven's life, at 39 years of age.

The argument here is not that these are major monuments that garnered great attention, be it in the 1970s, or 1980s, or still today. As one colonial association publication put it, "One cannot say that on the days consecrated to the memory [of colonials] that there are large crowds around the statues that recall the commitment of the elders in black Africa, which most often for the pioneers came at the price of their life. And let us not talk about other days of the year, and a fortiori not of the simple passersby for whom in a general way they are but vestiges of a past that no longer concerns them."[158] Some scholars of monuments exaggerate their importance, and one could do so in the case of Belgium by focusing on the number of such memorials, because there are hundreds of them. In Belgium, as in many other European countries, there is a surfeit of monuments in general, many if not most of which are passed by on a daily basis without eliciting much thought. Belgians are today likely generally unaware of the myriad memorials that are colonial in the country, even local ones. As one person said about local son Edmond Hanssens, a collaborator of Leopold II from the first hour, a statue of whom stands in the city hall of Veurne (Furnes), and for whom a city street was named: "Hardly any person from Veurne knows who Edmond Hanssens was."[159] What is more, as discussed in chapter 6, recent attacks on colonial monuments have awakened only limited debate in the country.

As obscure as some such memorials might be, they are important indicators, both because they were never taken down and because they did, in their own way, frame people's everyday lives, not only perpetuating a colonialist framework for viewing the world, but making it permanent, almost natural. Outsiders or younger Belgians looking at the large De Bruyne-Lippens monument on Blankenberge's boardwalk, or the depiction of those two colonial heroes on the right-hand side of Colonial Monument in the Parc du Cinquantenaire, must see unfamiliar and dated vestiges of colonialism. But during the first few decades after independence, these monuments' depictions of De Bruyne and Lippens likely reinforced messages of Arab viciousness that people had learned over the years as schoolchildren.[160] The hundreds of thousands of Belgian adults and school children who visited the Tervuren Museum had a chance to pass through the memorial hall, where are inscribed the names of all 1,508 Belgians who died in Africa serving Leopold II, that is from 1876-1908. There are no African names.

Colonial monuments acted as sites of commemoration and remembering throughout the decades after 1960, for example the Leopold II statue in Namur, from which as late as 2003 a "Cérémonie nationale d'hommage au drapeau de Tabora" (National ceremony of homage to the flag of Tabora) began.[161] No colonial monument attracted the kind of crowds seen each year at the IJzertoren in Diksmuide in remembrance of fallen soldiers, which also serves as a manifestation of Flemish identity. Some colonial markers drew crowds comparable in size if not larger than those gathered annually at the *monument à l'Aigle blessé* in Waterloo, a destination for some who support Wallonia's independence. One example of a well-attended colonial commemoration occurred in 1984, in Hasselt. The Monument Leopold II in that city, inaugurated in 1952, was honored in 1984 by the Koloniale Vereniging van Limburg, which that year marked its fiftieth anniversary. The event was an elaborate commemoration that in addition to celebrating the 48 Limburgers who died in the Congo before 1908 (i.e., during the Leopoldian period), also included an unveiling of a new plaque to remember 44 Limburgers who died on African soil during the Congo crisis. The commemoration was not an obscure happening hosted by oddball colonial veterans. It was reported on in the mainstream press and drew members of the national and local establishment, including Hasselt mayor Paul Meyers. Resonant of commemorations at such monuments between 1908-1960, the day began with a church service and a mass celebrated by two former missionaries.

The day's tribute involved the national army, including officers and soldiers who paraded for the ceremony. Events took place not only at church and at the memorial itself, but also at the city hall and the city's cultural center.[162] One might say this was an isolated event, because the commemoration in 1984 was special, it being the Koloniale Vereniging van Limburg's fiftieth anniversary, and involving as it did the unveiling of an addition to the monument. All the same, "each year in the month of June a ceremony takes place with a laying of flowers on the monument, organized by the KKVL, the Koninklijke Koloniale Vereniging van Limburg (Royal Colonial Society of Limburg)."[163] The Hasselt monument and many others, such as the place du Trône monument—where one can at times find wreaths of flowers laid there in Leopold II's honor—continued to serve as places of gathering and remembrance for former colonials.[164]

Leopold II (1835-1909)
Location: Namur, place Wiertz
Sculptor: Victor Demanet
Inauguration: 28 October 1928; re-inaugurated 26 October 1958
Funded/built by: Namur Chamber of Commerce;[165] Cercle Colonial Namurois; Ministry of Colonies[166]

This statue is location in Namur, which, according to one colonial-era report was Belgium's "third most colonial city."[167] It was unveiled in autumn 1928, in a prominent position in the centrally-located place d'Armes.[168] Destroyed on 18 August 1944 by German bombs, it was rebuilt and re-inaugurated in 1958, and it stands today in the middle of the roundabout known as place Wiertz.[169]

The monument reads "LEOPOLD II" in large letters on the stela, with two inscriptions on the lowest part of the base, where it connects with the stela: on the lower right side, "Victor Demanet 1928"; and on the back lower side, "Fondeur Compie des Bronzes, Brux."[170] The re-edification of the monument was largely the work of the Cercle Colonial Namurois, which was subsidized in the 1950s by the Ministry of Colonies.[171]

Although in appearance, including its inscription, this statue to Leopold II is not intrinsically "colonial," it became so during the colonial period, and remained so after 1960.[172] During the Belgian state rule era, pro-colonialists honored the empire at the statue, including at its 1928 inauguration, even though the driving force behind its erection was the city's chamber of commerce. After the monument was destroyed during World War II, it was a local colonialist

Statue of Leopold II in Namur, 2018

association that mobilized to put it back up.[173] In subsequent years colonial devotees came to the memorial to honor the king and his colonial legacy, for example when the Cercle royal namurois des anciens d'Afrique (Royal Namur Club of Veterans of Africa) chose the site as the starting point for a celebration and procession in 2003.[174] As one commentator put it rather poetically, the Namur statue to the country's second king, "has become the privileged site of those nostalgic for Leopold II who, every year in June or July, come and voice their militaristic incantations and other colonialist fantasies. It's the High Mass of the sword and the aspergillum."[175]

Like many statues to Leopold II, the one in Namur has been defaced and vandalized numerous times in recent years, and similar to others, it also has been cleaned and restored each time.[176] In this way, colonial devotees and anti-colonialists have worked in tandem to associate this otherwise ostensibly non-colonial monument with the country's history of rule in central Africa.

Leopold II (1835-1909) and colonial pioneers
Location: Hasselt, Congostraat and Kolonel Dusartplein
Sculptor: Raf Mailleux
Architects: Arthur Lippens and Leon Moors
Inauguration: August 1953[177]
Funded/built by: Koloniale dagen van Limburg

This is a monument both to Leopold II and to his local "Limburgse medewerk-ers."[178] The main section, located below a bust of Leopold II, reads "Hulde aan Z.M. Koning Leopold II en aan al zijn Limburgse Medewerkers," (Homage to His Majesty King Leopold II and to all his Limburg collaborators,) and then on a smaller plaque below, "1960 Zaïre 1965 In Memoriam Limburgse Slachtoffers."

(1960 Zaire 1965 In Memoriam Limburg Victims) There is a stone on the ground in front that plays a part of the monument, and which reads: "Deze praalsteen bevat aarde opgenomen te Leopoldstad op de graven van Beckers M.N.E. uit Bilzen E.P. Jehoel uit Eksel." (This monument contains earth taken at Leo-poldville from the graves of Beckers M.N.E. from Bilzen E.P. Jehoel from Eksel.) There are two smaller plaques, on either side of Leopold II: one on the left says "De Beschaving," "Civilization," the one on the right, "De Bevrijding," "Liberation." A ceremony in 1984 honored the 44 Limburgers who died from 1960 to 1965. In 2018, an explanatory text was added to the memorial.

Hasselt colonial monument, 2003

Jules Volont (1863-1894)[179]
Location: Thisnes, on monument to war dead,
behind église Saint-Martin
Inauguration: July 1939
Funded/built by: commune of Thisnes

It might be the case that Volont—like some other young men who signed up for service with the CFS—was seeking adventure through military action with the Force publique. Growing up, Volont worked at a local sugar refinery, where his father was a director. He left in 1884 to enlist in the military before joining the Force publique five years later. Volont departed for the Congo in January 1890, just days after his twenty-seventh birthday, and once there he became a deputy to Francis Dhanis during one of Dhanis' expeditions to get local chiefs to sign treaties recognizing Leopold II's authority. Volont was tasked with exploring the area of the Lunda people, in what is today southwestern Congo and northern Angola, in order to persuade local chiefs to sign treaties. One such signing, with a Chinje chief, saw Volont put in charge of a post at Kapenda-Kamulëmba, in an area that was eventually ceded to Portugal to become part of its colony of Angola.[180] This demonstrates that the 1885 declaration of the CFS did not mean Europeans were masters over the Congo in its entirety. Well into the 1890s Leopold II's armed forces were still exploring, negotiating control over, occupying, and conquering many regions of what would eventually become the colony.

His first term in the Congo successfully concluded by early 1893, the now thirty year-old Volont returned to Belgium, only to depart again for central Africa

Monument to war dead, église Saint-Martin, Thisnes, 2018

in September of that same year. Back in the Congo, Volont took charge of a camp at Niangara, but then had to be replaced after he fell seriously ill. He died of dysentery on 26 May 1894.

Several men who perished in Leopold II's colony were not honored with a stand-alone memorial or plaque, but rather, like Volont, by means of adding a name to an existing monument. This was true also for J.-J. Pennequin on a monument in Willemeau, as for a few others on existing monuments in Ath, Battice, Gosselies, Hemiksem, Neufvilles, and Wierde. The July 1939 unveiling of the memorial inscription to Volont in his hometown of Thisnes was described as a patriotic inauguration of "une plaque commémorative apposée sur le monument des anciens combattants." (a commemorative plaque affixed to the monument to veterans.) A speech by F. Germeau, president of the local chapter of the Journées coloniales from nearby Waremme, highlighted Volont's dedication, saying he died "in Africa, victim of his devotion to the colonial cause." The inscription honoring Volont was added to a monument to soldiers who perished in 1914-1918, which would eventually include an inscription for those who died in 1940-1945 as well. Volont's part of the memorial makes reference to the "campagne du Kwango," or Kwango campaign. This might lead a casual observer to believe Volont died in battle, whereas he died of illness.

Conclusion

The years 1967-1985 were an era of quiescence as regards the presence of the "colonial" in Belgian culture. Although the overseas empire had been lost, in many ways decolonization did not "happen," be it in the realm of claimed Belgian expertise on Congolese culture and art, or the presence of Congolese material culture in museums and on mantelpieces, or in the continued existence of hundreds of pro-colonial memorials in cities and towns across the country, many of which continued to serve as sites of remembrance and commemoration celebrating the country's imperialist record. The emergence of a few discordant notes here and there, including Mobutu's demand for the restitution of Congo's artistic patrimony, hardly upended Belgians' deep-seated belief in the virtue of their past actions. Ideas planted during the colonial era were long-lived, obviating any need to question the past. For example, after the dust settled on the Congo crisis, any questioning of why Belgium had been in the Congo in the first place already had an answer: for the liberation of backward Africans from the pernicious Arab slave trade. This notion had been planted in myriad ways during the colonial era, and it continued to be the go-to answer, sustained by the narratives conveyed by public monuments, or read in school textbooks little affected by more advanced research on the colonial past. For some specific groups, such as erstwhile colonials or African art experts, there was a great deal of continuity: former colonials sustained memories and narratives upholding the goodness of past colonial actions, and art dealers and collectors in many ways carried on as usual. But for many Belgians, this period witnessed a diminishment of the place of the "colonial" in everyday culture. As the Congo crisis receded in time; as the number of Belgians in the former colony declined; as Mobutu's dictatorship somewhat stabilized the situation in central Africa; and as more immediate issues loomed larger: Belgians maintained positive if somewhat fading memories of their country's history of involvement in Africa. At moments, the Belgian-Congolese relationship was foregrounded, for instance when the *contentieux belgo-congolais* made headlines, or when, on a more personal level, individuals visited the Tervuren Museum. But otherwise, this period of quiescence witnessed a diminishment of the presence of the "colonial" in the country's culture.

Chapter 4

Commemoration and Nostalgia, 1985-1994

> "Brussels still has a *Square de Léopoldville*, as if the city wished to
> forget that the name of the capital city in the Congo was changed
> to Kinshasa in 1966."[1] — Idesbald Goddeeris, 2015

Numerous developments predominated over colonial issues in the decade from 1985 to 1994, perhaps foremost the Chernobyl disaster in April 1986 that literally shrouded much of Europe with fears of radioactive contamination. The national football team, the Red Devils, with Jean-Marie Pfaff as goal keeper, placed fourth at the World Cup in Mexico that same spring and summer, losing to eventual winner Argentina after two goals by Diego Maradona. Sandra Kim's win in the horrible yet wonderful Eurovision song contest filled the country's airwaves and television sets with the refrain "J'aime, j'aime la vie." Foreign, especially U.S. films continued to dominate the box office, for instance Stanley Kubrick's *Full Metal Jacket* (1987) or the French *Au Revoir les Enfants* (1987), although there were domestic successes, most notably *Hector* (1987) by Stijn Coninx. Spain and Portugal's bids to join the European Economic Community created controversy because of fears it would lower prices on agricultural products. One shocking event was the *Herald of Free Enterprise* disaster near Zeebrugge in March 1987: because the ferry's bow doors were left open, it flooded and capsized right after its launch, killing 193. Four years later, another calamity grabbed the headiness, namely the July 1991 assassination of socialist politician and sometimes-minister André Cools.

Internationally, the continued influence of the United States was key, and the 1980s were dominated by the presidency of Ronald Reagan, who visited Belgium for NATO meetings twice, in November 1985 and March 1988. Longer-term issues included continuing economic challenges (especially in the francophone south), the ongoing Cold War (with Belgium host to NATO and SHAPE headquarters), and discontent and even resistance to immigration, which continued to be dominated by Europeans and North Africans. Most significant was the 1989 fall of Berlin Wall, which captivated people across the globe.

In regards to Belgian culture, Mobutu's Congo, and the colonial experience, the years 1985-1994 marked an important transition period. By the 1985
centenary of the declaration of the CFS, more than a generation had passed
since the Congo's independence, meaning many adults by the late 1980s had
no first-hand experience with colonialism. Moreover, Belgium's missionary
presence in the Congo diminished to the point that there were only some
4,500 missionaries still there in 1982, and the country's "economic presence
in central Africa noticeably declined in the 1970s and 1980s until it had all
but disappeared."[2] Stephaan Marysse estimates that by 1993 a mere 3,000
jobs in Belgium depended on Belgian-Congolese economic connections.[3]
The country's relations with Mobutu continued to fluctuate. Baudouin's
special connection to the Congo and Mobutu, such as it was—relations
between the two had soured by the 1980s—vanished upon the monarch's
sudden death in 1993.

Commemoration

There was a resurgence of the "colonial" in Belgian culture in 1985 in seeming
inverse proportion to the decline in direct cultural and other connections
between the country and its former colony. That year marked two major
anniversaries, both of which raised public consciousness of the colonial past,
if rather ephemerally. The year 1985 was the centenary of the declaration of
Leopold II's CFS, and it also was the year the Congo celebrated a quarter
century of independence, for which Baudouin and Fabiola once again traveled
to central Africa. Such visits were tricky events because of the bipolar relations
between the two countries.[4] Aside from Baudouin's historical and personal
connection that underpinned them, the visits did permit Belgium to try and
maintain good relations with the central African dictator, and they offered
Mobutu opportunities to boost his prestige at home. Other events took
place much closer to home, including at the Tervuren Museum, such as the
exposition "Leopold II et Tervueren" that had run already in the fall of 1984,
from 6 September to 28 October.[5] The colonial veterans group UROME put
on its own exhibition during the centenary year, and academics also revisited
the colonial past. An exhibition and accompanying book, *Cent ans de regards
belges*, "explored 100 years of images taken from books, photography, film,
cartoons, the plastic arts, school textbooks, lithographs and postal stamps.
In visiting it, the public became aware of the impregnation of Belgian society
by these images, charged with stereotypes and with racism, and gained the
intellectual tools needed to analyse them and distance themselves from them."[6]

Reading about the Congo experience

That the anniversary year of 1985 elicited greater reflection on the country's colonial past is evidenced by the publication of numerous books on colonial life and the colonial past, both academic studies and books intended for a more popular audience.[7] Scholars and others diverge in their interpretations of Belgian "colonial" writings and literature inspired by Africa or the colonial past. On the one hand, literature developing colonial themes occupied little space in the large Dutch-language and even larger francophone literary worlds. A recent survey of Dutch-language literature, for example, concludes the Congo had little affect on Belgian literature after 1960, and two scholars recently declared that, "from a Flemish and Walloon perspective, Congo literature is not widely known and even less studied. Academic interest in Dutch or French literary texts on the Congo is almost non-existent in spite of the fact that the Congo played such an important role in twentieth century Belgian history."[8] On the other hand, recent scholarship on "colonial" or "Congo" literature, in Dutch, French, or in translation, suggests a growing attention in the past twenty years in Belgium and abroad to Belgian colonial literature, much of it focused on works produced during the colonial period itself.[9]

The years from around 1985 to the 1990s produced significant written work drawing on the country's colonial experience, some of it quite nostalgic. Former colonials André Verwilghen, Roger Depoorter, Fernand Lekime, and Gérard Jacques, among others, published studies or memoirs of their years living and working in the Congo, stressing accomplishments and everything that was lost with independence.[10] The 1980s witnessed the production of numerous *bandes dessinées* of *inspiration africaine*, much more so than during the period 1962-1982. Comics often depicted a "bad" colonialist and inherently condemned colonialism, reflecting a more current and acceptable post-colonial view circa 1982-1992. That conditions in Zaire degraded so significantly during the 1980s could cut either way: one could praise colonialism in contrast, or one might criticize past foreign rule as the taproot of contemporaneous woes. Authors and illustrators of *bandes dessinées* of the 1990s were "post-colonial" in that they were of a younger generation with no direct connection to the colonial era, even if comics in the 1970s, 1980s, and 1990s still played on people's attraction to exoticism. Many titles published during the 1980s were in fact not new in that they had originally seen the light of day in weekly or other publications in the 1960s, and were therefore only reprints or reissues of earlier creations.[11]

The Congo, or the colonial experience, found its way subtly into other works of literature. Hugo Claus' great novel *Het verdriet van België* (*The Sorrow of Belgium*) is best known for breaking taboos by grappling with issues of collaboration during World War II. But the colonial experience runs like a thin thread throughout the novel: the novel's main character Louis Seynaeve talks about "Hottentots"; he uses blacks from the Congo as a reference point; and he dreams with his friend Vlieghe about leaving everything behind to become a missionary in the Congo.[12] Many elements of Jef Geeraerts' detective or crime fiction that made him famous in more recent years represented continuities from his colonial-themed works, including misogyny and the dichotomy between the noble savage and a stifling, corrupt civilization.[13] Jean-Louis Lippert's difficult to classify, non-linear novel *Dialogue des oiseaux du phare: Maïak I* (1998) is not about the Congo per se, but it allows him to comment on Belgium and its collective memory about the former colony.[14] Like many others who produced novels and travelogues about the Congo in the 1980s and 1990s, Lippert was born in the colony, in Stanleyville, in the last years of Belgian sovereignty there.

New colonial memoirs, travel narratives, and novels that appeared around the anniversary year of 1985 drew on past connections to the Congo, for example the debut novel *Afscheid van Rumangabo* (1984) by Henriëtte Claessens (Henriette Heuten) about officer's wives whose rather boring lives in the Congo are upturned by the tumultuous events of 1959-1960.[15] Missionary Guido Tireliren, who had returned to the Congo after its independence, wrote three novels about the country that appeared in the years leading up to the CFS centenary: *Uit stenen geboren* (1979), *Levende stenen* (1982) and *Aiwa's tocht* (1984). In them he explored Africans being caught between tradition and modernity "to demonstrate the need for change and development from a black perspective."[16] Lieve Joris wrote *Terug naar Kongo*, based on her trip through the Congo in 1985. Despite its title, "Back to Congo" is not about a return trip Joris made, because she was born in Belgium in 1953 and grew up there. Rather, the title refers to Joris' voyage "back" to where her uncle had been a missionary starting in the interwar years. Joris' sympathy for all those with whom she comes into contact in Zaire, and her open-mindedness toward the Congo and its cultures, makes her depiction of the country's decrepit state that much more arresting. Hilde Eynikel's *Onze Kongo: Portret van een koloniale samenleving* that appeared in 1984 in Dutch, and in French translation as *Congo Belge: Portrait d'une société coloniale*, reached a wide, admiring audience that, according to one reviewer, was due to "the craze that has suddenly been expressed for colonial history." According to the same reviewer, Eynikel's nostalgic book reinforced rose-tinted visions of the colony and the stability of colonial rule that had been sown in colonial-era school texts.[17] By contrast, Marcus Leroy told of the depressing, cynical corruption that a development worker has to deal with in an African country—modeled on the Congo—in his debut Flemish-language novel *Afrika retour* (1993).[18]

It is hard not to perceive a certain creeping nostalgia in much literature that appeared in the mid-1980s, as the country appeared to have moved past the trauma of decolonization and begun to look back on the "good ol' days" of the preceding years. Many such visions were, once again, framed by the positive imagery and recollections of the golden age of the 1950s, which lived on in myriad form. The figure of the good missionary, for example, which had largely disappeared from *bandes dessinées* in the 1960s, reappeared.[19] It is remarkable the extent to which official images and other pro-empire propaganda continued to circulate and frame views on the colonial past.[20] There was also the massive legacy of printed materials, studies, books, travel accounts, essays, scientific articles, novels, and other such documents inherited from the colonial era. Bibliographer Th. Heyse's work on the interwar era identified 1,520 titles published on agriculture and livestock breeding, 703 works on ethnography and indigenous art, 506 on geology, 376 in the field of medical sciences, 202 for languages, in addition to works in other fields.[21] One study estimated that between 100,000 and 150,000 publications of all kinds were produced during the colonial era regarding the Congo and/or Ruanda-Urundi, even if surely many of them were seldom consulted or read after 1960, or by experts only.[22]

If the significance of colonial-era academic studies was limited in shaping culture, not so films and still images, which continued to be recycled and reused, defining the realms of possibility of knowledge about the past. There had already been a pre-1960 "recycling of images," where colonialist photographs were republished again and again, some of them over many years. Photographs that first appeared in *Le Congo illustré* in the 1890s found their way onto postcards years later.[23] *Clichés* by photographer Fernand Demeuse, for instance, which first appeared in *Le Congo illustré*, were reprinted on postcards by Edouard Nels printing company years later, and the Keystone View Company recycled photos from Underwood & Underwood stereographs into the 1930s.[24]

Such "recycling" continued, giving a long life to Inforcongo propaganda and the work of official photographers like Henri Goldstein. As noted, the paucity of direct, on-the-ground journalism in the 1950s and a deference toward official—and low cost, or even free—photography and film meant Belgian news organizations had not developed a photo archive of the colonial era, and they continued to lean on official imagery to illustrate stories about central Africa for decades after 1960. A 1985 article about the Congo in *Le Soir*, the leading Brussels francophone daily, drew on official government

Inforcongo photos from the 1950s showing Joseph Kasavubu, the independent Congo's first president, walking the streets of Brussels in 1959, as well as a staged propaganda photo showing whites and blacks living in harmony in the Congo.[25] Such articles in *Le Soir* and other newspapers were not exposés about official pro-colonial photography, rather they used the photographs uncritically, and the reader surely took them as unmediated representations of the reality of the time the articles were addressing, rather than official, sometimes even staged pro-empire propaganda photographs, which is what they were. Another example of the recycling of colonial-era imagers is how in 1988, the Institut Saint-Stanislas in Brussels brought out from storage Jean Draps' 30-meter-long painting from the 1958 Brussels World's Fair and put it on display to mark the thirtieth anniversary of the exposition.[26] Such uncritical displays reinforced official colonial-era views by reiterating colonialist tropes and messages without questioning them.

Televised nostalgia

As was true for the recycling of colonial-era snapshots, so was it true for films, which were recycled for decades. Most colonial motion pictures dated back to the 1950s, a decade that represented not only the zenith of colonial rule but also the apex of Belgian pro-colonial propaganda, and a colonial-era height of technical mastery of filmmaking. In 1984, the RTBF (Radio Télévision Belge Francophone) program "L'Ecran témoin" rebroadcast André Cauvin's 1955 film *Bwana Kitoko*, a pro-colonial production about Baudouin's 1955 voyage to the colony.[27] As with photographs published in *Le Soir*, RTBF was not analyzing the film, rather rebroadcasting it for uncritical consumption. The positive portrayal of the king and his successful 1955 trip to the colony—showing masses of adoring Congolese greeting their smiling sovereign—can only have served to reinforce extant notions of the colonial past that held Belgian rule as having been a positive, necessary thing.

The rebroadcast of *Bwana Kitoko* is but one example of the many French- and Dutch-language television productions on colonialism that appeared in the years surrounding the centenary of the CFS and a quarter century of Congolese independence. How many saw these shows is unclear, but it is worth noting that television viewing was commonplace by the 1980s. Whereas the period of Belgian state rule in the Congo overlapped with the golden age of movies, the post-1960 era was the golden age of television. Sales of television sets in Belgium, which had increased from 45,000 in 1955 to 700,000 by 1960, jumped to 1,000,000 by 1962, and never looked back.[28] *Boula Matari* was one program shown in the lead up to the anniversary: it was a six-part television series by Joseph Buron and Michel Stameschkine shown on RTBF's Télé 2 channel over a month-long period in January-February 1984. As one account put it, "*Boula Matari* shows in the whole the essential and positive role of the three colonial powers: the administration, the missions, and the large companies." Another criticized the series for not focusing enough on the events of 1960. Although the program was overall positive in its treatment of colonialism, some former colonials admitted abuses on camera, such as the use of the *chicotte*.[29] Still, the series surely had a limited impact. First, the time slot and day of the week when it was shown put it in direct competition with the popular Thursday evening film on the main francophone channel, RTBF 1.[30] Second, a lack of news coverage in both the Flemish- and French-language press suggests the series did not garner a great deal of attention, despite a debate that RTBF held at the end of the last episode.

Two years later, an extended Flemish-language television series on Leopoldian and Belgian colonialism appeared, called *Als een wereld zo groot waar uw vlag staat geplant* (A world so vast, where the flag is planted), a production of Jan Neckers and Pieter Raes. It was shown on BRT (Belgische Radio- en Televisieomroep, today's VRT, Vlaamse Radio- en Televisieomroep) from February to April 1986, and was accompanied by a book (with Vita Foutry) of the same name, as well as radio broadcasts.[31] The series took a chronological and thematic approach, considering the Leopoldian era before examining the Belgian state-rule period, and considering Belgian colonials, Congolese, the colony's three "pillars," and the Force publique. Although the series recycled official images from the colonial period as well as photographs taken by Belgians (as opposed to Africans), thus presenting a Eurocentric view, it did not shy away from controversy. For example, the series made clear—and this during the 1980s, with growing controversy over the white South African regime—that Belgians had established a kind of apartheid regime in the Congo.[32] To judge by the lack of reaction in the press, the series was anything but controversial with the Dutch-speaking public.

Mid-decade productions were followed by occasional series in the second half of the 1980s. In 1988, RTBF launched the four-part series "Chroniques congolaises" by director André Huet, as part of its "Inédits" program. This was a "series of four programs where the Belgian colonial era in Zaire was reconstructed on the basis of archival materials, family photos, and amateur films."[33] The idea was to present everyday life in the colony as it had been experienced by whites by drawing on home videos, providing "a leap through time" to discover "another Congo, the one of everyday reality." As with imagery from the colonial era, however, this was misleading, since the everyday reality the series pieced together was that of white settlers, not daily life for the vast majority of the population of the Congo. The series did not ignore the negative aspects of Belgium's colonial past, talking of "the rubber scandal," the *chicotte*, and "les mains coupées," but overall the series emphasized a sense of adventure and admiration for those Belgians who ventured to central Africa.[34] In 1989, the French community commercial television station RTL-TVI ran the program "Congo: Une colonisation en noir et blanc," in conjunction with the newspaper *Le Soir*.[35] The program included the son of a Belgian colonist (a planter), a Belgian historian, and Congolese professors, journalists, and a lawyer, among others. The program and corresponding coverage in *Le Soir* did not shy away from atrocities, suggesting that if younger people in the 1980s had perhaps not learned much about their colonial past, they were anything but shielded from it, and this years before the publication of Adam Hochschild's book *King Leopold's Ghost*, which was said to have stunned many Belgians.[36]

Exhibiting Africana

The Palais des Beaux-Arts in Brussels got in on the act of displaying African art by mounting its own exhibit, "Utotombo, les merveilles des arts africains," from 25 March to 5 June 1988. The Palais des Beaux-Arts had not hosted such an exposition for decades, the last one having been an exhibit of the art of black Africa more than a half century earlier, in 1930.[37] For the 1988 show, the Musée des Beaux Arts worked with nearly 60 collectors divided pretty much evenly across the country's language communities, half of them of Dutch-speaking background, the other half French.[38] One headline described the show as, "African treasures from Belgian collections."[39] As these objects had not been seen by the public—because held in private collections—one reporter assured that any visitors to the show were guaranteed a true feeling of discovery.[40] Indeed, one of the two main goals of the show was to reveal the depth and value of African artwork held privately in the country, the other being to contribute to the country's commitment to African artwork.[41] As one commentator put it, "Most of these [private collections of African art in the country] attest to the Belgian collector's profound taste for African objects, even a passion often confused with a trade, a way of living."[42]

All told, the exhibit included some 300 objects, and the positive reception by the public, including specialists, suggests the show was a success.[43] Whether the exposition had profound effects on non-specialists was another question. One collector who visited, Lancelot Entwistle, praised the show but lamented to one of its organizers, "Too bad that the general public appreciated it so little."[44] Perhaps this was due in part to the view that continued to prevail that African artwork was not art strictly speaking. As even one reviewer of the Utotombo exhibit put it, "rien ne devrait être plus éloigné de l'esprit africain que la notion de l'art pour l'art." (Nothing should be further distant from the African mind than the notion of art for art's sake.)[45]

Visual imagery in bronze and stone

Colonialist visual imagery appeared in many forms during the colonial period, as we have seen, and many of these endured into and were reproduced in the post-colonial era. As discussed, photographic and film productions were significant, as were historical accounts and school textbooks, insofar as the latter covered the colonial past at all. Of all forms of colonialist imagery, none was literally more substantial, or as enduring, as colonial monuments in bronze, granite, and other such permanent materials. These physical memorials sustained many narratives, in public space, across the period after 1960.

There are many characteristics that these colonial monuments share, perhaps the most prominent one being that they almost all honor men; unsurprising insofar as the country's colonial rule was an almost wholly male affair. With rare exceptions, such as Joanna (Jeanne) Crauwels, whose name is inscribed on a Borgerhout plaque to colonial pioneers, no women are honored in colonial monuments. This is unsurprising, considering that until recent decades, the role of women in Belgian public life was greatly limited. Women as a group were not allowed to vote in national parliamentary elections until 1949, and no woman served as a government minister in Belgium until 1965, when Marguerite De Riemaecker-Legot became Minister for Family and Housing.[46] One can only speculate what role public commemorative statues of the colonial era played, however minor, in reinforcing patriarchy and retarding women's entrance into Belgian public life.

Colonial memorials did not honor male figures involved in colonialism generally, rather they highlighted the role of military men. There are several historical markers that memorialize missionaries, for instance statues to Constant De Deken (Wilrijk, 1904), Victor Roelens (Ardooie, 1952), and Désiré Pellens (Neerpelt, 2002), and a bas-relief in Nossegem to Jean Lenselaer, who died in the Congo in 1962.[47] Aside from memorials to Leopold II, there are very few to colonial administrators, and few to figures from the world of business such as Albert Thys, for whom two monuments were erected, one in Brussels (1927) and one in his native town of Dalhem (1948). Other non-military men, such as Gustave Dryepondt, who is memorialized in his home town of Bruges, are additional exceptions that prove the rule, namely that memorials focus on military figures: colonel Chaltin and captain Crespel (Ixelles), Jules Van Dorpe (Deinze), Baron Dhanis (Antwerp), officer Pierre Van Damme (Arlon), general Émile Storms (Brussels); the list goes on. What is more, and as discussed below, a whole series of streets were renamed after colonial "pioneers" to commemorate those who served Leopold II before 1908, the vast majority of them military men. For many, such an emphasis might be surprising considering how Belgium was a neutral country from its independence in 1830, and a victim rather than an instigator of militaristic aggression in Europe. This makes Belgian colonial memorials all the more revealing: what they disclose is that the country's rule in central Africa was founded upon military conquest and was sustained over the years through the use of force and the threat of the use of force. This military theme reflects both the violent nature of colonial conquest and the era in which most memorials were built, which was from the late 1800s through the 1930s, a time marked by greater nationalism and military violence in Western Europe than in more recent decades.

Another characteristic common to most colonial memorials in Belgium is that they focus on the CFS period and Leopold II and emphasize the so-called civilizing mission, a key justification repeatedly avowed in order to legitimize foreign, Belgian rule in the far distant lands of central Africa. Indeed, no "colonial" figure is commemorated more often in bronze and stone in Belgium than Leopold II. It should not surprise us that the CFS period was so emphasized, because Belgians used that era—and the figure of Leopold II as a genius founder of the empire—to defend Belgian rule in the twentieth century. Moreover, many if not most colonial memorials were put up by colonial veterans groups, local government, and colonial interest groups—in particular the Ligue du souvenir congolais—with subsidies from the Ministry of Colonies. All of these had a direct interest in rehabilitating Leopold II and building the legitimacy of colonial rule by rooting it in a purportedly honorable national past of colonialism; either because they (for instance colonial veterans) were directly implicated in the actions of the CFS period, or because they (for instance civil servants within the Ministry of Colonies) were involved in ongoing colonial rule.

Also worth noting is the geographic distribution of colonial monuments. It is difficult if not impossible to provide a conclusive picture of the location of all Belgian colonial memorials, for several reasons. There are differing interpretations as to what constitutes a "colonial" memorial, and also of what comprises a memorial. Several monuments have been torn down, others were built only recently, and the existence of still others is hard to verify because they have left only the briefest of mentions in colonial archives, period publications, or otherwise. Casting a wide net, this author has identified references to more than 300 memorials, inscriptions, renamed streets, and other public historical markers with a colonialist connection in Belgium. But to be more specific and more accurate, this author compiled a list of 154 colonial memorials by tracking them down and confirming their existence, either through research in the archives and contemporary periodicals, or by visiting them, or both. Included in the following breakdown are memorials more strictly speaking—busts, statues, monuments, plaques, and names inscribed on monuments—that are located in the open for the public to see, and that have a significant colonial connection.[48] Half of them (78, 50.7 percent) are to be found in the francophone southern half of the country and nearly a third in Flanders (49, 31.8 percent). Just more than one in six (27, 17.5 percent) are located in the Brussels-Capital region, including both Bruxelles-Ville and the communes of the capital. This breakdown suggests the importance (and size) of the country's capital, which played a disproportionate role providing men; by contrast, Antwerp, Belgium's largest port, and its surrounding areas contain just seven such monuments, or 4.5 percent of the total. The preponderance of these historical markers being located in Wallonia would seem to reflect both the dominance of the country's francophone population in the colonial endeavor and the military emphasis that many colonial monuments bear; more missionaries came from the Dutch-speaking north of the country than from the south, but memorials focus less on missionary figures than on officers and soldiers.

Street names

Still today, at least 170 streets and squares in Belgium either honor CFS officers, colonial administrators, missionaries, or Leopold II, or through their name make some other direct connection to the colonial past.[49] The practice of naming or re-naming roadways with monikers inspired by overseas imperialism is hardly exclusive to Belgium. In the case of France, Robert Aldrich has identified hundreds of such streets in Paris alone.[50] In Belgium, roads named after colonial figures and the like are to be found across the country, from Taborastraat in Knokke-Heist to rue Général Molitor in Arlon to Leopold II-laan in De Panne to place Achille Salée in Spa. At least forty are located in the Brussels region, seventy-six in the Dutch-speaking north, and fifty-four in the francophone south. Some variant of "rue de Tabora" exists in at least five of the country's cities, celebrating the country's World War I victory in German East Africa. Several other thorough-

Street sign, Anderlecht, 2018

Street sign, Etterbeek, 2002

Street sign, Brussels, 2018

Street sign, Deinze, 2018

fares also take their name from geography, for instance Katangabinnenhof and Kasaibinnenhof (Tervuren), and Afrikalaan and rue Africaine or Afrikastraat (Ghent, Tervuren, Ostend, Saint-Gilles). As noted in this chapter's epigraph, a public square in Brussels still bears the appellation square de Léopoldville, meaning it honors a city name that no longer exists. That said, most "colonial" street names are tributes to individuals, all of them male. Without exception, every single road in the country named after someone from the country's colonial past honors a man.

Many of those honored with a street bearing their name are also memorialized in bronze and stone, either near the street in question, or elsewhere, and sometimes both. These include Ernest Cambier (a street in Ath and both street and monument in Schaerbeek), Camille Coquilhat (streets in Antwerp and Etterbeek and a statue in Antwerp), Constant De Deken (streets in Antwerp and Etterbeek and a monument in Wilrijk), Victor Roelens (both a street and statue in Ardooie), and Émile Storms (street in Florennes; memorials in Brussels and Wetteren), among others. A few names adorn several of the country's avenues, for example famed figures De Bruyne or Lippens, whose names, collectively, appear a total of seven times, or Francis Dhanis, for whom four streets are named. The one individual who reappears most often in this way is Leopold II, for whom at least 22 streets, avenues, or boulevards are named. Even so, there is one historical entity that dethrones even the king: the Congo. There are still today at least twenty-seven streets named Kongostraat or rue du Congo or some variant thereof in Belgium.

The count of "colonial" streets above includes those named after Leopold II, who although known for several reasons was and is undoubtedly a colonial fig-ure. One person not included in the analysis here, even though he was a colonial personage in his own right, is Jules Jacques de Dixmude, for whom numerous streets are named in Belgium and to whom several monuments were erected, some of them clearly colonialist in nature. But roads bearing Jacques' name are not counted here because his main claim to fame was his actions during World War I, which included preventing the town of Diksmuide from falling into Ger-man hands. Nevertheless, his military career was first made in the CFS, where he led expeditions and conquered territory. Thus, the celebration of him in Belgium was paradoxical: he was remembered mainly for his actions defending Belgium from invasion, but also to a significant degree because of his actions invading another country. For example, after being tasked with occupying one region during a three-year tour from 1895 to 1898, and after people there in the village of Inongo cut down all-important rubber vines, Jacques wrote to the local chief of post:

We have to beat them into complete subjection or into complete extermina-tion. (…) Warn the people of Inongo a very last time and carry out your plan to take them to the woods as quickly as possible (…) gather them in the village with a good club and address yourself to the proprietor of the first shack: here is a basket, go and fill it with rubber. (…) If you have not returned within ten days with a basket of 5 kilos of rubber, I will burn down the shacks. And you will burn it as promised. (…) Warn them that if they chop down one more rub-ber vine I will exterminate them to the last one.[51]

The Eurocentrism underpinning Belgian remembrances of Jacques de Dixmude pervades celebrations of colonial figures in street names in the country. Al-though Belgians were quick to celebrate their confreres, and their colony, not so those Africans who struggled for its independence. In fact, until the summer of 2018, there was not a single street named after a Congolese figure from the colonial era: no rue Paul Panda Farnana, no Lumumbastraat, no rue Simon Kim-bangu. Only in 2018 did Brussels name a square after Patrice Lumumba, at the Porte de Namur, at the entrance to the Matonge neighborhood.

Louis-Napoleon Chaltin (1857-1933)
Location: Ixelles (Elsene), square du Solbosch[52]
Sculptor: Arthur Dupagne
Inauguration: 1933; 1946-1947 (moved)

Memorial to Louis-Napoleon Chaltin, Ixelles, 2009

The bronze bust by Arthur Dupagne shows Chaltin in uniform, bearing several medals. The monument's inscription is headed by a large star, evocative of the CFS, and says, simply: "Au Colonel Chaltin, 1857-1933, Vainqueur de Redjaf 1897." (To Colonel Chaltin, 1857-1933, Victor of Redjaf 1897.) On the base it reads "Hommage des coloniaux." (Homage from colonials.) The original monument to Chaltin was probably put up sometime after his death in Uccle in 1933, originally placed in the Union Coloniale Belge.[53] It was transferred to the square du Solbosch and inaugurated at that site around 1946-1947, on the instigation of the group the Vétérans coloniaux, and specifically one of its leading organizers, Emmanuel Muller.[54] There is another large monument to Chaltin in Namur, a street named after him in Uccle, and he was honored in the Tervuren Museum *salle de mémorial* on a tall plaque commemorating the *campagnes anti-esclavagistes*. The latter is titled "Campagnes antiesclavagistes/Veldtochten tegen de Slavenhandel, 1891-1899" (Anti-slavery campaigns, 1891-1899) and was inaugurated in 1959. It pictures Chaltin along with other key figures of the era as well as Leopold II.

Louis Crespel (1838-1878)[55]
Location: Ixelles (Elsene), square du Solbosch
Sculptor: unknown
Inauguration: ca. 1885
Funded/built by: friends of Crespel from Ixelles

The monument to Louis Crespel moved around almost as much as Crespel did. Today it is located in the Brussels-area commune of Ixelles, on the square du Solbosch, near a statue to Colonel Louis-Napoleon Chaltin. This is its fourth location to date. The monument was initially erected at the chevet of the Saint Boniface church in Ixelles.[56] It was subsequently relocated to the place de Londres before moving again to the gardens of the nearby église Sainte-Croix before finding its way after World War II to the square du Solbosch. The year of its inauguration, 1885, was the same year the CFS was declared, which might very well make Crespel's memorial the country's first "colonial" monument in the land.

Memorial to Crespel, Ixelles, 2018

It is hard to tell today, but this monument to Crespel was designed as a fountain. It takes the form of a rectangular column topped with a basin with four lion heads, from which the water flowed into the basin at the base of the column, today filled with soil and plants. Bronze plaques with inscriptions adorn three of the fountain's four sides, a fourth plaque having been removed years ago. The inscriptions on the three extant plaques are straightforward, giving biographical background, information on who built the monument, and the reason why Crespel was worthy of commemoration:

- Né à Tournai le 4 Décembre 1838, Décédé à Zanzibar le 24 janvier 1878. (Born in Tournai the 4th of December 1838, Died in Zanzibar the 24th of January 1878.)
- À L. Crespel ses amis d'Ixelles (To L. Crespel, his friends from Ixelles.)
- Le Capitaine CRESPEL Chef de la 1ʳᵉ expédition belge en Afrique centrale (Captain Crespel, Leader of the 1st Belgian expedition to central Africa.)

The fourth plaque that was removed bore the CFS motto, "Travail et progrès" (Work and progress).[57]

Crespel was indeed one of the very first to enter into the service of Leopold II, joining the AIA on 14 July 1877, and he was remembered as being the first Belgian to die in central Africa in the process. This marker now in the square du Solbosch has for more than a century touted him as having been led the maiden Belgian expedition to central Africa. But in truth Crespel never made it there, instead perishing on the island of Zanzibar on 25 January 1878, having never made it to the continent itself, let alone to the area that became the Congo.[58]

Gustave Dryepondt (1866-1932)
Location: Bruges, Wollestraat, facing Belfry of Bruges
Sculptor: Victor Demanet
Inauguration: 15 October 1939[59]
Funded/built by: Comité Exécutif du Mémorial Docteur G. Dryepondt

This commemorative plaque adorns the birth home of Gustave Dryepondt, whom Paul Crockaert, Minister of Colonies from 1931-1932, called "a fanatic of colonization in Africa."[60] Dryepondt first left for the Congo in 1890, where he was to have accompanied Guillaume Van Kerckhoven on an expedition. Having fallen ill very soon after his departure on the expedition, Dryepondt returned to Leopoldville to recover, and then stayed there to tend to the many whites who

Plaque honoring Gustave Dryepondt, Bruges, 2018[62]

became sick and managed to make it to Leopoldville for treatment and convalescence. His first term in the Congo lasted until 1893, and after returning to Europe he played a big role promoting the colonial idea, including authoring numerous pro-colonial publications. Dryepondt returned to the Congo to work for the Compagnie de Kasai from 1903-1907, and afterward held other positions with private colonial companies while continuing to promote colonialism.[61] In addition to the plaque in Bruges, a street is named after him in Etterbeek, where he died, in 1932.

Dryepondt's memorial is conspicuous for a couple reasons. First, the Bruges plaque honoring him as a "colonial pioneer" is rare in that Dryepondt was a doctor, whereas most men commemorated for their role in Leopold's overseas venture were military figures. Second, Dryepondt was unusual in that he was a *Belgian* doctor in the Congo; most there at the time were Italian. In fact, the CFS and then the Belgian Congo were

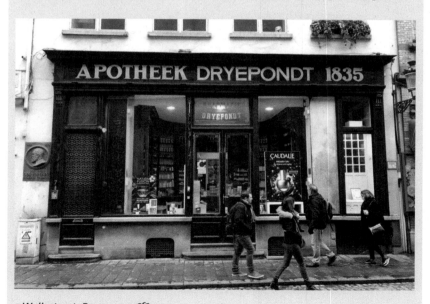

7 Wollestraat, Bruges, 2018[63]

so heavily dependent on Italian doctors that the outbreak of World War I elicited anxiety among colonial officials, who feared that mobilization would lead to a shortage of doctors as Italians returned to Europe for their military service.

One issue Dryepondt weighed in on as author and colonial expert was the question of *métis*, that is, the place and fate of children of mixed parentage in the colony. Until the end of his life, Dryepondt pushed for the "Africanization" of *métis*, which opposed him to others who argued for their "racialization"— treating them as a distinct, third race—and still others who, although fewer in number, advocated "Europeanization," that is, incorporating *métis* into the white, European community. Dryepondt advocated against the creation of a separate legal category for these "children of empire," believing instead that *métis* who were raised by whites would blend into and "disappear" into the white community, while those raised by Congolese would blend into African communities. Dryepondt also argued against state intervention, stating that mixed-race children should by and large be allowed to stay with their mothers, which would have meant in practice almost all of them being raised by their African relatives. Had his views prevailed, the fate of *métis* in the Belgian Congo and then after 1960 likely would have been quite different. As it was, the colonial state eventually did intervene, albeit not uniformly, and not everywhere. In practice, few Belgian fathers recognized their mixed-raced children, and many were taken away from their mothers and placed in orphanages, with terrible consequences, as Belgians are only in very recent years coming to more fully realize.[64]

Jules Van Dorpe (1856-1902) and
Ernest J. B. Van Risseghem (1866-1896)[65]
Location: Deinze (Deynze), Ricardplein
Sculptor: Louis-Pierre (Lodewijk) Van Biesbroeck
Inauguration: 1908

This rectangular, plinth-like monument of stone bears a bronze medallion with the image of local son Jules Van Dorpe. The main inscription on its front reads, "Aan Komdt Jules VAN DORPE / Hoofdcommissaris van den congostaat / het leger / de congostaat / zyn medeburgers / 1856–1902." (To Commandant Jules Van Dorpe / Congo State High Commissioner / the Army / the Congo State / his fellow citizens / 1856–1902.)[66] The memorial is topped by the form of a Corinthian capital, with a Congo star in the middle, atop of which sits a crowned coat of arms. On the reverse of the coat of arms is inscribed the year "1908," which was both the year of the memorial's inauguration and, coincidentally, the end

Monument to Jules Van Dorpe and
E. J. B. Van Risseghem, Deinze, 2018

date of Leopoldian rule in the Congo. One photo of the inauguration shows a massive crowd gathered to honor Van Dorpe's memory.[67]

On either side of the memorial are reliefs in stone depicting a shield and a collection of dangerous-looking weapons. The inclusion of weapons not only hints at the danger and even barbarity of Africa, it is also indicative of Van Dorpe's African career. Van Dorpe first made his mark coordinating the back-and-forth movement of goods between the coast and Leopoldville in the era before the Matadi-Leopoldville railway link was operational, thus making him an expert in logistics. But in essence, Van Dorpe was a military man. Like many other soldiers and officers who found their way into CFS service, he enjoyed quick promotion, surely more rapid than anything he would have been able to achieve had he remained in Europe.[68] Eventually Van Dorpe was promoted commander of the Force publique from 1895-1898, even as he continued his logistics and transportation work.[69] Van Dorpe is also remarkable because he brought his wife, Augustine Swinnens, with him for his fourth and final term in the Congo, beginning in 1898, making her one of a very small number of white, European women to travel to the CFS, if not the very first. Van Dorpe returned to Belgium in 1901, and died about a year later, in France, due to illness likely brought on by his long service in the tropics.

In short, Van Dorpe was a central figure implicated in the early history of European exploitation of the Congo under Leopold II, who has now been honored and remembered in stone and bronze in his hometown of Deinze for more than a century. One would not know from merely looking at it, but the Van Dorpe memorial has changed significantly in the years since it was first unveiled. Old postcards show its original form, which included a nearly naked life-sized African man seated just in front of the monument, holding a staff and flag. Apparently, during World War I occupying German authorities removed the African figure and melted it down.[70] The statue's location also changed: Originally situated in Deinze's Neerleiplein—renamed Kongoplein at the time of the statue's

inauguration—it was moved in 1930 because of construction, and then again
to its current location in 2008-09.[71] That it was not simply mothballed at either
point suggests the enduring importance of the monument to locals.

Deinze's monument also attests to lasting belief during the colonial era, even
at the very local level, in the "civilizing mission." As late as 1958, the Kongo-
lese Herdenkingsbond added an inscription to honor local son Ernest J. B. Van
Risseghem, a commercial clerk who died at Boma in 1896. The inscription is
unadorned except for one star, evoking the CFS flag, and reads, "Hulde aan de
pionier van het Afrikaans beschavingswerk."(Homage to the pioneer of the civilizing work in Africa.) That same year, while the country celebrated the empire
at the Brussels World's Fair, Deinze continued to embrace the longstanding
notion that overseas conquest and rule in Africa was about bringing European
civilization to backwards peoples, meaning the civilizing mission remained
respectable and defended right up until the very end of the colonial era. What is
more, it is only in very recent years that the memorial has come in for criticism,
for instance during a small gathering in 2008, part of a growing wave of questioning of colonial markers in Belgium.[72]

The manner of depicting Africa and Africans presents another similarity
in colonialist public sculpture. Many artists chose to depict "Africa" either as
a woman or as a woman with a child. This can be seen in the Thys monument
in Brussels, the colonial memorial in the city hall of Mons, and even in minor
and out-of-the-way plaques like one to P. A. Druart in Quaregnon. Such
depictions make Africa appear attractive and unthreatening, and also reveal
a paternalism that was a hallmark of Belgian colonial policy. Many sculptors
chose to depict Africans as nearly or completely naked, for instance Arthur
Dupagne's *Tireur a l'arc*, on public display in Etterbeek since 1962. As noted
earlier, nakedness in depictions of colonial subjects suggested savagery,
backwardness, and a lack of civilization, which implied a need for intervention,
which justified foreign rule and exploitation.

Montois who died in the Congo before 1908
Location: Mons (Bergen), entryway of Mons city hall
Sculptor: A. Regnier
Inauguration: 14 October 1930
Funded/built by: Schoolchildren of Mons and Mons City Council

This bas-relief in bronze is located in the entranceway of the hôtel de ville
de Mons alongside other plaques of equal size: one to Canadians for World
War I, one to World War I dead (which was destroyed by Germans during

Commemorative plaque for Mons pioneers, 2018

World War II), one to the United States, and one to an Irish regiment's dead, also for World War I.[73] The colonial monument is "in memory of the *Montois* who died for civilization before 1908."[74] As with other such interwar memorials, the main dates on the monument, 1876 and 1908, were chosen to designate the era of Leopoldian rule: 1876 was the year of the Brussels Geographical Conference that Leopold II organized, and 1908 marked the handover of his CFS to Belgium.

In several ways, the image is similar to the plaque to P. A. Druart in nearby Quaregnon, also signed by A. Regnier. An African woman, standing, plucks a cocoa pod from a tree and places it in a basket held by an African boy, perhaps her son. Except for a small rope loincloth, the woman is nude, and the boy is completely naked, turned slightly toward his mother so that his posterior faces the viewer. Walking among them is a sheep, and in the background are the leaves of the cocoa plants.

The large plaque lists the names of nineteen men, their dates of birth, and their dates and places of death. Among them are several who died of illness:

- Felix Ladam (b. 1864 – d. 1892, Bangasso). Ladam arrived to Boma on 7 March 1892 and died just 143 days later at Bangasso of acute hepatitis.[75]
- Joseph Piron (b. 1869 – d. 1894, Lukungu). Piron, a carpenter, left for the Congo in 1892 and died in October 1894 of hematuric fever.[76]
- Like many others, Georges Henri Alexandre Bricusse was a military man (1st regiment of the *chasseurs à cheval* in 1883, then the École militaire starting in 1888) who entered into service of the CFS. He departed for Africa on 5 March 1894, first heading a post at Engwettra before becoming an adjutant to Captain Vander Minnen, and then commander at the station of Djabir by 3 July 1895. He died of typhomalarial fever on 24 August 1896.

- Octave Siret (b. 1863 – d. 1896, Yassaka). Siret arrived to the colonial capital of Boma on 29 October 1896, and died of malaria on 28 December of the same year, just 60 days into his service.[77]
- Théophile Bernard (b. 1865 – d. 1907, Coquilhatville). Bernard entered into CFS service as a doctor, 2nd class, in 1897. Stationed successively over three tours of duty in Boma, Libenge, and Lisala, he died in Equateur District of dysentery on 2 November 1907.[78]
- Bertrand de Fuisseaux (b. 1875 – d. 1898). Fuisseaux served about one year in the CFS, from September 1897 until his death in October 1898. He had fallen ill and was to return to Europe, but he died of fever on the *S.S. Stanley* near Coquilhatville (Mbandaka). He was 23 years old.[79]
- Georges Collet (b. 1871 – d. 1895, Piani-Lombe). Collet is an exception that proves the rule that most colonial pioneers died of illnesses like dysentery and malaria. In his first term in the Congo, Collet played a significant role in the anti-slavery campaigns, and at one point helped exhume and rebury the corpses of heroes De Bruyne and Lippens. During his second term, beginning in June 1895, he fought as part of the effort to put down the Luluabourg revolt, during which he was caught in an ambush and killed.[80]

Tireur à l'arc
Location: Etterbeek (Brussels), place du Quatre Août
Sculptor: Arthur Dupagne
Inauguration: 1962[81]
Funded/built by: donation of Dupagne family

Tireur à l'arc is by Belgian sculptor Arthur Dupagne, who was born ten years after the 1885 declaration of the CFS and who died in 1961, meaning his lifespan corresponded closely with the era of his country's formal rule in Africa. Along with Thomas Vinçotte (1850-1925), Charles Samuel (1862-1938/39), and Arsène Matton (1873-1953), Dupagne crafted in stone and metal some of the most iconic images of Belgian colonialism. Although these men were first and foremost artists, their work underpinned their country's African rule in multiple ways. Not only did their art almost invariably project a positive image of European action in Africa, its very existence underscored Belgian superiority and colonial control. Their craft implied Europeans being in a position of observer, with the means, time, and resources to scrutinize the foreign "Other," that is, Congolese; to know their forms and ways of living; and to reproduce them, on European terms. In this way such "colonial" or Congo-inspired art asserted the European over the African; the artist over his subject matter; the master over its subject. Simulta-

Tireur à l'arc *by Arthur Dupagne, Etterbeek, 2018*

neously, the work of Dupagne and other sculptors reveals how imperialism was never a one-way relationship of power and influence where Europeans reshaped foreign cultures. Just as empire changed the cultures of the Congo, so did Africa and Africans insinuate major cultural influences into European artistic production and consumption, as seen in Dupagne's legacy.

Although just one among many Belgians inspired by African influences, one biographer averred Dupagne was "le plus remarquable des sculpteurs belges qui ont puisé leur inspiration en Afrique." (the most remarkable of the Belgian sculptors who drew their inspiration from Africa) Hired by the mining giant Forminière, he spent eight years in the Congo, beginning in 1927. After leaving that line of work in 1935 he became a full-time artist, and when he returned to the colony, which he did several times, it was as an artist on his own, not as a colonial company employee.[82] When Dupagne died in Woluwe-St-Pierre in 1961 he left behind an impressive body of work including hundreds of preliminary studies, commemorative medallions, and finished sculptures. These works included numerous statues representing African figures as well as monuments commemorating colonialism, including ones to Louis-Napoléon Chaltin (bust, Ixelles), Leopold II (bust, Halle), Lucien Bia (bust, Liege), and the anti-slavery campaigns of 1892-1894 (medallions, Tervuren Museum). Dupagne was also commissioned to produce memorial sculptures to be installed in the colony, and the results included the monument to commemorate the 1890-1898 *bataille du rail* or "railway battle"—the building of the Matadi-Leopoldville railway—on the 50th anniversary of its completion (1948), and the very large if squat statue of Stanley erected on Mont Stanley in Matadi (1956). Although Dupagne's work endures in Belgium, his two monumental efforts in the colony fell victim to Mobutu-era attacks, torn down in the second half of the 1960s. The Stanley statue remained fallen, destitute and toppled in Kinshasa, as seen in Sven Augustijnen's film *Spectres*.[83]

Above all—and as one might gather from the muscular expectation of release conveyed in *Le tireur à l'arc*—Dupagne was captivated by African bodies. This can be seen throughout his œuvre, and arguably became more accentuated over time, as suggested by the highly stylized nude figures of the *couple bantou* or Bantu couple that the sculptor created for the 1958 Brussels World's Fair main Congo pavilion. Dupagne's fascination with the "African form" is clear in *Le tireur à l'arc*, where a nameless African archer crouches down, aiming his bow, perpetually caught at the tense and critical moment before he releases an arrow.

Not only does its namelessness highlight the anonymity of the archer, so does the location of the *tireur à l'arc* in space in Etterbeek. The unspecified *tireur à l'arc* is located just a short walk from several other colonial sites, including the monument to aviator Edmond Thieffry, metro stops named after Thieffry and Arthur Pétillon, and streets named after colonial figures including Thieffry, Pierre Ponthier, and Francis Dhanis. These men, all white Europeans, are named. The person (or persons) after whom *Le tireur à l'arc* is modeled remains unnamed: he is relegated to being merely a "type," a generic, anonymous African. By contrast, European figures from the colonial era are named.[84]

P. A. Druart (1862/68-1898)
Location: Quaregnon, Grand'Place
Sculptor: A. Regnier
Inauguration: 21 September 1936
Funded/built by: the commune of Quaregnon and the Cercle Africain Borain[85]

This monument to native son Druart is a metal bas-relief located to the left of the entrance to the town hall of Quaregnon, near Mons. The memorial shows an almost-nude female African figure standing in front of palm trees holding a medallion bearing Druart's profile. It declares, "Mort en Afrique au service de la civilization." (Died in Africa in the service of civilization.) The plaque must have been moved from its initial location, since its inauguration in 1936 predated the building on which it is currently located, the former city hall, since construction on the building did not begin until October 1937.[86]

Druart entered the Belgian military in 1891 before joining the CFS military, the Force publique, in 1897. He left for the Congo on the 6th of August of that same year and arrived to his posting at Bomokandi in September. He was dead by the following February, a victim of acute gastroenteritis.[87]

Considering Druart's short career in Leopold's colony, one might take the memorial as representative less of the "civilizing mission" and more of interwar

Plaque to P. A. Druart, Quaregnon, 2018

nationalism and the energetic activity of local colonial interest groups to mobilize the country in favor of the colonial project. The Cercle Africain Borain was a particularly active group of former colonials who erected numerous memorials in the Borinage region. Indeed, the inauguration date for Druart's memorial was chosen to coincide with the fourth anniversary of the Cercle Africain Borain.

Like many other memorials, Quaregnon's to Druart prominently foregrounds the idea that Belgian colonial actions were about bringing civilization to Africa. The memorial is also typical in that it includes a depiction of a nude African woman. In numerous depictions in bronze and stone, African women, often nude, personify "Africa," including memorials in Etterbeek, Brussels (Thys), Charleroi (hôtel de ville), Ixelles, and Mons, among others.

Another similarity across colonial monuments was a shared narrative of heroic Leopoldian—and through association Belgian—action in the Congo, founded on the struggle against the "east coast Arab slave trader" preying on hapless African victims. Those whom the Belgians called Arabs were in reality mainly Zanzibari or Arab-Swahili traders from Africa's eastern coast, many of whom had been living and trading in central Africa long before the arrival of any Europeans. Belgians consistently depicted Arab-Swahili and Zanzibaris as foreign, Arab, and perhaps most importantly, Muslim intruders. The language used by Van Kerckhoven biographer R. Cambier in the *BCB* reflects this negative views of Arabs: Cambier wrote that Van Kerckhoven had to "clear [*nettoyer*] the country of the Arabs who had established themselves there." The use of the verb *nettoyer*, which also means "to clean," implied an association of Arabs with dirt, even filth.[88] Or consider the example of Belgian sculptor Charles Samuel's *Vuakusu Batetela défendant une femme contre un Arabe*, created for the 1897 Tervuren colonial exposition, and that went on permanent display at the Tervuren Museum beginning in 1898. Samuel's sculpture is art, which allowed the artist to work free of constraints of needing to seek historical truth. But the fact that the sculpture was framed within an

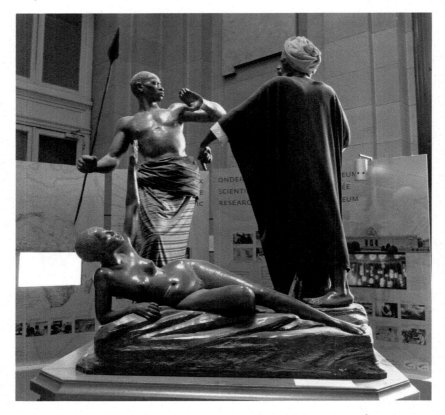

Vuakusu Batetela défendant une femme contre un Arabe, C. Samuel, 1897[89]

official scientific establishment, and for decades, lent the piece an authority it otherwise likely would not have enjoyed, for instance if it had instead been placed in an art gallery or a private institution.[90] The viewer saw the Arab as threatening and Africans in need of defending.

The ruthless Arab slave trader became iconic, reproduced in various media and innumerable times across the colonial era, which carried over into the post-1960 years. Arsène Matton's statue *L'esclavage*, for instance, was one of a number of statues adorning the entrance rotunda of the Tervuren Congo museum that justified colonialism to visitors. In *L'esclavage*, an Arab slave trader, recognizable because of his robes and turban, holds a whip, which he uses to threaten a defenseless, nude, defeated African woman who kneels submissively before him and over a child, who appears to be dead.

The anti-Arab theme appeared again and again, including in sculptor Thomas Vinçotte's "Colonial Monument" in the Cinquantenaire Park in Brussels.

Arsène Matton, L'esclavage, 1920.

Belgian colonialism in the Congo
Location: Brussels, Parc du Cinquantenaire (Jubelpark)
Sculptor: Thomas Vinçotte
Architect: Ernest Acker
Inauguration: 11 May 1921
Funded/built by: Oswald Allard; the Belgian state; the city of Brussels;
public subscription

This large memorial, often simply called the "Monument du Congo," was envisioned as early as 1909, the year Leopold II died. Work on it began in 1911, but
then World War I and the failing health of sculptor Thomas Vinçotte caused
delays. It was only finished and inaugurated in 1921.[91]

Vinçotte's work depicts scenes telling several stories united by the theme of
the beneficence of Belgian action. The scene on the left tells the story of the
heroic Belgian colonial soldier trampling a defeated "Arab" underfoot. The image
is purportedly of Francis Dhanis, the national hero of the so-called Arab wars of
the 1890s. The inscription below the scene declares: "L'Héroïsme Militaire belge
anéantit l'Arabe esclavagiste / De Belgische Militaire heldenmoed verdelgt den
Arabische slavendryver." (Belgian military heroism destroys the Arab slave driver.)[92] The scene transubstantiates the violence of the colonial wars of the CFS
period, transforming them from European, Christian conquests of Africa—which
led to enslavement, just under a different name—to the liberation of Africans
from purported foreign (Arab) Muslim slavery. The scene on the right shows one
military officer tending to another in dire straits, along with an inscription that
states, "The Belgian soldier devotes himself to his mortally wounded superior
officer." The figures represent De Bruyne and Lippens, the protagonists of the
large monument honoring them in Blankenberge, and two men well-known in
Belgium by the time of Vinçotte's monument's inauguration for their duty and
sacrifice during the Arab wars.[93] The imagery in both side scenes sustained an
idea that circulated widely in Belgium during the colonial era (and beyond),
that foreign Muslim Arab slavers in the Congo were vicious; an image repeated
endlessly, for example, in school textbooks that emphasized how De Bruyne and
Lippens had been "lâchement assassinés par les Arabes esclavagistes." (cow-
ardly murdered by the Arab slavers.)[94]

The relief sculptures the form the monument's central frieze represent Belgians in the Congo: the figure of a missionary appears, as do explorers, and a
seated figure to the left appears to be an administrator or superior; some suggest the latter evokes Leopold II. Above the central frieze is inscribed a quote
attributed to Leopold II. "I undertook the work of the Congo in the interest
of civilization and for the good of Belgium, 3 June 1906." A reclining, perhaps

Colonial Monument, Brussels, 2018

nude African male figure representing the Congo River appears in a scene at the base of the monument, on the water's edge, along with a crocodile. Atop the monument, and above the inscription "La race noire accueillie par la Belgique" (Belgium welcomes the black race), Belgium is embodied by the figure of a woman "welcoming the black race," the latter represented by an African woman and child. In short, the monument claims the Congo was "open" for Belgian involvement and praises Belgian colonial veterans of the first hour—missionaries, soldiers, functionaries—whose sacrifice and devotion made it all possible.

Over the decades, the Monument du Congo served as site of pro-colonial remembrances, and more recently also one of protest. Innumerable commemorations took place there during the colonial era, from its 1921 inauguration to the annual laying of wreaths before the memorial on special anniversaries.[95] Veterans and enthusiasts expressed the near-sacredness of their belief in the colonial endeavor, such as when in 1937 Minister of Colonies Edmond Rubbens, a Catholic, stated that Vinçotte's Monument du Congo was "like an altar" at which he and others could come to acclaim Leopold II.[96] Commemorations did not stop with the Congo's independence in 1960, nor with the contemporaneous general disavowal of imperialism. Indeed, former colonials have continued to celebrate the colonial past at the site into the twenty-first century.[97]

During the last years of the twentieth century, however, some began to take issue with the monument, specifically its reference to the Arab slave trade. The growing controversy was related to another development, namely the authori-

*Close-up of Colonial
Monument, 2002*

*Close-up of Colonial
Monument, 2013*

ties' decision to transfer control of a nearby park building—built in an "Oriental" style for an 1880 Cinquantenaire exhibition—to Saudi Arabia beginning in 1967. That building became the Grande Mosquée de Bruxelles, which accommodated some of the capital's significant and growing Muslim population. In the late 1980s, critics including Doryad Azefzaf, the imam of the Grande Mosquée, the Jordanian and Saudi Arabian ambassadors, and the Arab League complained about the inscription on the Colonial Monument, which sits just 150 meters from the mosque.[98] They disputed what they saw as a blanket characterization of Arabs as having been slavers. In 1988 or 1989, the terms "l'Arabe" and "Arabische" were officially removed by being carefully chiseled out. This in turn raised objections from former colonials, leading to a dispute in the press between former colonials (including of the CRAOCA) and city officials, the former suspecting the latter of having ordered the removal of the words. Some former colonials even publicly protested on 5 October 1991. The result: the inscription was restored by the early 1990s, and some time in the following decade the entire monument was restored.

One attempt to address grievances against the Colonial Monument was by putting up a visitor's guide—in French, Dutch, English, and German—that placed the memorial in context. This guide, which was in place in front of the monument in 2002-03 at least, added a note of caution about the monument's imperialist spirit while also capturing what it depicted: "The Congo Monument (1911-1921) is revealing of the colonial spirit of its time, called into question by History. At the lower level, a young black, represents the Congo River. He is surrounded by two groups: to the right, the Belgian soldier devotes himself to his superior, who is mortally wounded; to the left, the Belgian soldier annihilates the slave trade. On the central section, the African continent, henceforth open to civilization, advances towards a group of soldiers who surround Leopold II. Above, Belgium welcoming the black race is represented in the guise of a superb young woman."[99] This explanatory plaque was subsequently removed; perhaps as early as 2005 multiple attacks again chiseled out first "l'Arabe" and then also "Arabische," leaving both words gouged out of the memorial's façade.[100] In 2009, an explanatory note added to the monument stated it was being renovated at the cost of more than 90,000 Euros.[101] In 2011, Écolo member of the Brussels parliament Ahmed Mouhssin protested the monument.[102] In 2013, Rudi Vervoort, head of the Brussels-Capital region, announced the decision that there would be no further restoration of the chiseled-out words, and they remained unrestored as of 2018.[103]

That protests have focused on the monument's characterization of Arabs and not its depiction of Belgian actions against black Africans is revealing. This is suggestive of the degree to which the scale of Moroccan and Arab immigration into Belgium outdistanced that of sub-Saharan Africans, including Congolese. Protests targeting the monument's depiction of Africa and Africans have only just begun in the second decade of the twenty-first century, and have gone hand in hand with similar protests at monuments elsewhere in Brussels and around the country, for instance at the Leopold II statue in Mons.

Belgian independence
Location: Brussels, Parc du Cinquantenaire (Jubelpark)
Sculptors: Thomas Vinçotte, Jules Lagae, Julien Dillens[104]
Architect: Charles Girault
Inauguration: 27 September 1905
Funded/built by: Leopold II

The Arc du Cinquantenaire is a mixed memorial subtly weaving colonialism into the city fabric of Brussels to create a nexus of capital, nation, and empire in the Parc du Cinquantenaire, located just east of the city center. The year of its inauguration, 1905, marked the seventy-fifth anniversary of the country's independence and the fortieth anniversary of Leopold II's accession to the throne. Although the king was a renowned builder and urban designer, the Arc du Cinquantenaire was the first true monument the long-reigning monarch left to the city, and it was unveiled just four years before his death in 1909 at the age of seventy-five.[105]

Numerous historians, journalists, and others have accused Leopold II of using Congo "blood money" for his urban rebuilding projects during his 44 year-long reign. The extensive work that was undertaken during the latter half of the nineteenth century has been said to have transformed Brussels "into a permanent work-site."[106] Colin Blane says that Brussels, "would have been a very different city without its Congo connection," pointing to the avenue de Tervuren and avenue Louise as being "laid out with money raised from Belgium's adventures in the Congo basin."[107] Many critics readily point to the layout of Belgium's capital and its urban infrastructure, including the Arc du Cinquantenaire, as an enduring legacy of the country's history of colonial oppression.

The colonial past is interwoven into the urban landscape of Brussels and other cities, especially Ostend. But when one places the urban changes undertaken by Leopold II in context, a more nuanced picture emerges.[108] A distinction must be made between building during the period from 1865 to 1896, and that which took place from 1896 up until the king's death.[109] In fact, as early as 1863—that is, before he even became king, two decades before he lay claim to the Congo, and three decades before the Congo began to turn a profit—Leopold presented an extended list of building projects to the Belgian government, "most of which were to be implemented during his years as king."[110] The CFS was declared twenty years after Leopold II's ascent to the Belgian throne in 1865, and in its first years, Leopold's colony was unprofitable. It was not until 1895 that the first shipments of Congo rubber began to reach Europe, and not until 1896 that the Congo budget balanced for the first time.[111] Not until around 1898 did exports of rubber take off, reaching a peak around 1903.[112] Long before then, efforts were underway to remake the capital. Work to bridge over the Senne River began in 1867. Architect Joseph Poelaert's colossal Palais du Justice was planned as early as 1862—during Leopold I's reign—and was constructed from 1866-1883.[113] Leopold II directed the creation of the Jardin du Roi in 1873 and paid for its yearly upkeep.[114] The king helped direct the laying out of the Parc du Cinquantenaire, which was begun in 1875 in order to be ready by 1880, which was the fiftieth anniversary of Belgian independence. Leopold also acquired land in Tervuren from 1880-1895, and made available some monies for the Palais Royal restoration as early as 1891. According to one admiring biographer, Leopold's "reign was characterized by the continuous execution of great public works which mark an epoch in the history of Belgian architecture and economic development."[115]

What is more, all of these rebuilding efforts were not sui generis, rather they fit into a pattern of late nineteenth century urban rebuilding in western Europe. Paris under Napoleon III underwent "Haussmannization," which displaced large numbers of Parisians to achieve greater social control through the building of wider, supposedly barricade-proof avenues, which largely transformed Paris into its present-day, familiar form.[116] Napoleon III "fashioned a monumental city that won acclaim in his own time, became a model for city designers throughout the world, and has continued to excite admiration for nearly a century."[117] Vienna in the decades after the revolutions of 1848 underwent a somewhat similar transformation as the old military training grounds, fortifications, and defense system of the city were given up to urban development, creating the *Ringstraße*.[118] Thus Leopold II's rebuilding efforts from the 1860s can be considered part of a broader wave of urban renewal.

All the same there is no doubt that Leopold diverted large sums from his Congo profits to finance urban projects. After it was damaged by a fire, Leopold had the Royal Palace at Laeken, just outside of the capital, rebuilt and expanded after 1890.[119] In addition, such funds went to pay for Leopold's reconstruction of the Royal Palace in Brussels, beginning in 1904, and the Arc du Cinquantenaire.

The Parc du Cinquantenaire, first laid out in 1880, had previously been a military training ground for the Belgian army.[120] Organizers failed to build an arch for the Brussels Exhibition of 1880, and a wooden façade was put up in its place. Being only a temporary structure, it rotted. Both in 1888 and 1897, when other expositions were held on the grounds, a stone arch was not built due to financial obstacles, and once again a temporary wooden facade had to suffice.[121] It was not until Leopold II came up with the funds himself that the Arc du Cinquantenaire was finally built in 1904-1905. Its unveiling took place at a moment at which Leopold II was under tremendous pressure because of international and finally domestic criticism of his misrule. One contemporaneous article attacked his profit making in the Congo, saying, "Leopold says that the results are civilization. The missionaries say they are hell. *But everybody admits that they are profitable.*"[122] So, Leopold recruited front men from the financial community to conceal his plan to pay for the entire monument out of funds he had acquired through his "investments" in the Congo.

When unveiled, the Arc du Cinquantenaire formed a massive gateway from the center of Brussels out the avenue de Tervuren to the hamlet of Tervuren and the colonial edifices being built there according to the king's grandiose plans. Overall the style of the Arc du Cinquantenaire is in Louis XIV mode. The structure is 42 meters high, 58 meters wide, and 20 meters deep. The arch is itself divided into three equal bays, separated by Ionic columns, and topped by a triumphant chariot of four horses, in bronze, by Vinçotte and Lagae.[123] Although some have tied the bronze figures to the exploitation of Katanga's copper ore deposits, it was only after the Leopoldian era that copper mining took off.[124]

The symbolism of the figures set in stone presents a vision of the future for Brussels and Belgium. The figures facing the old city center represent architecture, sculpture, painting, music, engraving, and poetry, all inheritances of the city's past. The figures on the opposite and outward side represent science and industry, agriculture, mechanics, commerce, and the navy.[125] It seems to suggest

The Arc du Cinquantenaire, Brussels, 2018

Leopold was asking his subjects to embrace the new century. The representation of the navy points to the fact that Leopold envisioned them as a sea-going,
expansive people, with an empire. Confined in Europe and with borders guaranteed through neutrality, Belgium had no chance for expansion on the Continent.
The only possibilities lay outside Europe, in the Congo. As Leopold said in 1888,
"If the nation [*patrie*] remains our headquarters, the world must be our objective."[126]

   Although today many might not connect the Arc du Cinquantenaire to
Leopold II and his colonial rule, contemporaries associated the monumental
arch with the king and the Congo. The year of the Arc du Cinquantenaire's
inauguration, socialist political leader Emile Vandervelde implied that one
day people might refer to such monumental constructions as "les arcades des
mains coupées," that is "the arcades of the severed hands."[127] When debat-
ing where to put an equestrian statue honoring Leopold II, which eventually
ended up in 1926 in the place du Trône, multiple people suggested it should
be placed atop the Arc du Cinquantenaire.[128] What is more, the triumphant
Arc led out of Brussels to a figuratively larger and imperial world in the
suburb of Tervuren, where Leopold was building the Tervuren Museum of
the Congo, meaning the Arc du Cinquantenaire served as a gateway to draw
Bruxellois into a larger world, and a wider frame of mind. Leopold indicated
his intention in remarks: "The extremity of the Parc du Cinquantenaire is one
of the most important points for the appearance of the capital. (…) If you do
not invite the public greatly and from afar to enter into our museums which

are outside the center, they will not go there."[129] Contemporaries and people over the years perceived the Arc as linking the capital to Tervuren. Writing in a 1913 volume of *The Town Planning Review*, Patrick Abercrombie made the connection:

> The situation of this monumental arch is justified in more ways than one; not only does it complete the vista from the town side, but it indicates as an arch should, the continuation of the route out of the city. This is the new Avenue de Tervueren, which leads through the Forest of Soignes to the old Park of Tervueren, where the late King placed the Congo Museum.[130]

And as another writer put it the following year,

> In the royal park of Tervueren, seven miles distant from Brussels, [Leopold II] built a magnificent museum, and laid the foundation of a colonial school, in which Belgians and natives of every country were to be instructed (…) Through the great forest of Tervueren he caused a wide avenue seven miles long to be built, leading to the gate of his Colonial Museum. At the commencement of that avenue at the Cinquantenaire Museum at Brussels, he built a glorious Arch of Triumph.[131]

> The association endured. One journalist writing on the sixtieth anniversary of the 1897 colonial fair in Tervuren praised Leopold II, and went so far as to call the creation of the Congo museum "an extension of the Cinquantenaire complex."[132]

After 1960 public statuary continued to honor those Belgians who had fought in the anti-slavery campaigns against east African slavers, the most prominent example being the De Bruyne-Lippens monument in Blankenberge by Guillaume Charlier. The monument honors native son and sergeant Henri De Bruyne and his commanding officer Lieutenant Joseph Lippens. Their story became a staple of colonial histories and was told and retold over generations as a source of inspiration. Both men were taken hostage during fighting against slavers, and when De Bruyne had a chance to escape he decided against it, eventually falling victim to his captors, murdered just as Lippens was, both of their bodies mutilated.

The heroic De Bruyne-Lippens tale substantiated colonial rule, demonized Arabs, and cast "Africa" as feminine and dependant by means of its figures of an African woman and child clinging to the flag that the two men bear, as if hanging onto hope. The monument's main engraving, in French and Dutch,

Henri De Bruyne (1868-1892) and Joseph Lippens (1855-1892)
Location: Blankenberge, Zeedijk
Sculptor: Guillaume Charlier
Inauguration: 9 September 1900; re-inaugurated 10 September 1922
Funded/built by: Komiteit standbeeld De Bruyne (former colonials) and public
subscription

A monument in Blankenberge to native son Sergeant Henri De Bruyne and his
superior officer Lieutenant Joseph Lippens commemorates the two men and
the *anti-esclavagiste* campaigns of the 1890s.

De Bruyne and Lippens became two of the best known figures of the history
of the nation's involvement in the Congo and the story of their deaths "became
a legend in Belgium, a symbol of European courage in the face of Arab and
African savagery."[133] Lippens embarked for the CFS in 1887, De Bruyne two
years later. During the course of the 1892-1894 war between the CFS and the
so-called Arabs in eastern Congo, the Swahili-Zanzibari leader Sefu took Lippens and De Bruyne hostage. During negotiations in the fall of 1892, De Bruyne
was presented with the opportunity to escape to a group of the Force publique.
Given the choice, he refused to abandon his superior officer, who not only was
still being held hostage but had been struck by illness, including multiple bouts
of dysentery, smallpox, and stomach ailments, complicated by hepatitis.[134] A
couple weeks later some of Sefu's men killed the two and mutilated their bodies
by cutting off their hands, which they sent to Sefu.

This monument was built on the initiative of former colonials who grouped
together as the Komiteit standbeeld De Bruyne.[135] Funded by public subscription, it was inaugurated on 9 September 1900.[136] During World War I, the
occupying Germans took the statue and melted it down for the metal. It was
brought back after the war, and added to it was a bronze statue depicting a sup-
plicating woman with child. The ensemble was re-inaugurated twenty-two years
after it had first been put up, on 10 September 1922.

The monument is located on the Zeedijk or boardwalk overlooking the sea,
near the end of the main street to the beach, Kerkstraat. Not only does its
prominent location mean that innumerable sightseers have stopped to look
at it over the decades, it also was the subject of numerous postcard printings,
and it has continued to serve as a site of commemoration. In 2014, for instance,
a military celebration took place with speeches and the laying of flowers,
celebrating the two men as heroes of the fight against Arab slave trading in the
Congo.[137]

More than most, the memorial is a text that not only can be but was meant
to be "read"; it tells a story. The monument comprises an obelisk with the fig-

The De Bruyne-Lippens Monument, Blankenberge, 2018

ures of De Bruyne and Lippens in front of it, together holding a flag. Figures of
an African woman clutching the flag, and a child, are at their feet.

The gold-lettered, all-caps inscription above the two men reads, "De Bruyne
and Lippens, died as heroes for civilization." The two side inscriptions provide
details: "Lippens, Lieutenant in the train regiment, murdered at Kassongo on
the 12th of October 1892 by an envoy of sultan Sefu. [Henri] August de Bruyne,
sergeant in the second line regiment, killed together with his superior Lippens,
for whom he had sacrificed his liberty." The inscription at the back provides the
lesson in obedience, solidarity, and sacrifice: "De Bruyne gives to the world a
sublime example of military solidarity in refusing freedom in order not to abandon his superior." Scenes on three profile bronze plaques portray the last days of
the two men's lives: one, it is said, depicting the last conversation with Lippens
(although to this author it appears like De Bruyne standing on a riverbank,
declining the option of fleeing to friendly forces); the other two the killing of Lippens and the murder of De Bruyne, respectively.

There was discussion of removing the statue, in 1977, but the city council
refused, and in fact by royal decree (20 March, 1980) it gained protected status
as a monument of historical value.[138] An explanatory plaque in Dutch, French,
German, and English was added in recent years.[139]

There are multiple facets to the story told on the Blankenberge boardwalk, a
story that conveys several themes, some of which are shared with other perma-

The murder of De Bruyne

The murder of Lippens

nent colonial markers. Both men are military figures. Although both fought in support of Leopold's armed takeover of the Congo, the real enemies depicted are not Africans but so-called Arab slave traders, clearly identified on the panels as turbaned figures. This echoed what was to be a longstanding belief about Belgian rule in the Congo, namely that it was a fight against barbarous Arabs, which justified the Belgian presence. As one onlooker described De Bruyne and Lippens to this author during a May 2018 visit to the Zeedijk, "Those were the good guys." The memorial also shows how the narrative of Belgian involvement in Africa was often gendered in depictions in the metropole. The men are to be seen standing strong and holding firm, whereas the poor, nude African woman at their feet lies almost prostrate, in supplication, not only apparently help-less but with a child to boot. Another theme, this one less frequently seen, is comradeship and class reconciliation, with De Bruyne's dedication showing the loyalty of the lower classes.[140] The statue has the two side-by-side, one draping his arm over the other's shoulder.

   The monument's importance is underlined by its location and longevity and the fact that not only was it restored after its destruction at the hands of Germany during World War I, it was even amplified or elaborated upon with the addition of the woman and child for the 1922 re-inauguration. Native son De Bruyne not only was commemorated in bronze on the Zeedijk, his portrait also hung for years in Blankenberge's *salle du conseil communal*.[141] The two were celebrated not merely in this coastal city but elsewhere, too, such as on the Cinquantenaire Park's Colonial Monument and in print, including in *bandes dessinées* and school textbooks, even into the post-independence era.[142]

says the two men "died as heroes for civilization," and friezes on the monu-ment's three other sides depict Lippens' last moments and the men's heroic deaths at the hands of their captors. The violent episode was a ready-made morality play about heroism, duty, self-sacrifice, and dedication to country and the *mission civilisatrice*. The monument's prominent placement on the boardwalk of Blakenberge, a coastal tourist destination, means uncountable locals and others have walked by and observed the monument since its 1900 unveiling.

   Just as in the 1970s so in the 1980s were there undertones of dissent from the accepted, heroic narrative of the colonial past.[143] Former diplomat Jules Marchal's works on E. D. Morel and Leopold II's CFS appeared in print, under the pseudonym A. M. Delathuy.[144] Marchal's works were devastating in how they catalogued massive abuses under the CFS, although they were heavy on long quotations from the archives, making them tough reading that was thin on historical analysis. More importantly, they were published by a little-known publishing house, first in Dutch before being translated into French. Another significant academic volume to appear around the anniversary year 1985 was Daniel Vangroenweghe's *Rood Rubber: Leopold II en zijn Kongo*.[145] This was a rare work in its clear depiction of extensive atrocities during Leopold II's rule, yet its impact was muted: on the one hand, academics were already aware of the "red rubber" era, making Vangroenweghe's work to them unsurprising; on the other, former colonials generally dismissed the book as a biased polemic filled with overblown accusations. Even an impartial review described Vangroenweghe as "resolutely in the camp of

Postcard of De Bruyne-Lippens Monument, Blankenberge, ca. 1938

enemies of Leopold II," and said that the work's biggest fault was its tone: "one of an indictment conceived in light of present-day moral conceptions, without taking into account the mentalities of the era in which the events took place."[146] In the end, it remained underappreciated.

Conclusion

Major developments around 1993-1994 transformed those years into the end of an era. The first event was the sudden and unexpected death of the country's monarch, Baudouin, of heart failure in July 1993 at the age of only 62. His reign had lasted 42 years, meaning a majority of Belgians alive at the time of his death had known no one else as their king. Moreover, Baudouin was the last surviving monarch to have ruled over the Congo, because his father, Leopold III, and his uncle, Prince Charles, Count of Flanders—who ruled as regent from 1944-1950— had both died a decade earlier. Baudouin had been closely associated with the Congo, had been an actor in and witness to Congo's independence, and had maintained a special relationship with his former colony and its ruler, Mobutu, at least until the very end of his life, at which time Belgian-Congo relations had deteriorated significantly. With the king's death this particular historical link was severed as Baudouin's younger brother, who ascended the throne to become Albert II, had no such special relationship with the former colony.

The year 1993 was also the year of a fourth major state reform, officially transforming the kingdom into a federal state. Also by this time the results of the Cold War's end were truly being felt. In Zaire specifically, Mobutu was in deep trouble. His country's economy was in shambles, corruption was rampant, large swathes of the country lay beyond his government's control, and the bipolar diplomacy between Belgium and the Mobutu regime had reached a nadir. Prime Minister Wilfried Martens' official visit to Zaire in November 1988 was to be the last such visit for nearly 12 years. By May 1990 Belgium had officially suspended cooperation with the Mobutu regime. "At the time of Baudouin's death in 1993, Mobutu was definitively persona non grata in Belgium and his presence was not desired at the funeral."[147] Mobutu could still turn to other allies of course, and in fact he was the first African head of state to visit with newly-installed U.S. president George H. W. Bush, in June 1989. But another Belgian-French intervention in Zaire in September 1991 on the heels of yet another mutiny and uprising showed the tenuousness of the leopard's hold on power. Before long Mobutu had agreed to a power-sharing arrangement as Zaire's economy deteriorated further and as his international backing waned. Within a few short years, Mobutu's regime was in full-blown crisis, and Belgium's relations with the central Africa of the present as well as its own colonial history were to undergo major changes.

Chapter 5
A New Generation, 1994-2010

"Africa was my brother's preserve, his fiefdom, and I'm not
at all concerned with it."[1] — King Albert II, 1999

"There's an entire generation that wasn't brought up with the Congo,
it wasn't mentioned in our history classes and that explains the strong
urge to rediscover this country."[2] — David Van Reybrouck, 2010

"Some made some mistakes. Progress in these distant lands, was it not ultimately a
series of trial and error? But it is to decidedly lack critical thinking and intellectual
honesty to place mistakes above successes."[3] — *Mémoires du Congo et du Ruanda-
Urundi*, a publication of former colonials, 2016

The decade and a half between the 1994 Rwanda genocide and the fiftieth
anniversary of the Congo's independence witnessed renewed attention to central
Africa and the colonial past. As earlier, however, other issues often predominated
during this time, which largely overlapped the reign of Albert II (1993-2013).
In 1998, Enzo Scifo and Franky van der Elst each garnered greater renown by
playing in their fourth World Cup tournament on the national football team,
the Red Devils. Scandals were important, most prominently one surrounding
the botched arrest and imprisonment of serial killer Marc Dutroux, which
rocked the country beginning in 1996.[4] Three years later a dioxin scandal hit
when it was revealed the government had known of the presence of carcinogenic
polychlorinated biphenyls (PCBs) in animal feed, yet covered it up.

The world from the mid-1990s was a post-Cold War world, contributing to a
changed relationship between Mobutu's government and the West, including
Belgium. The new status quo challenged Belgians less to reconsider their
colonial past, and more their future as a united state. The Belgian presence
in Zaire had been reduced to a very low level by the 1990s: by 1993 there were
maybe 2,800 Belgians working and living there, which further declined to
2,500 by 2001, which was on the eve of an evacuation of even more Belgian
citizens from the country. "By the end of the twentieth century, the former
colony's economic significance to Belgium had become quite marginal."[5] Guy
Vanthemsche rightly points out that just as Zaire's political, diplomatic, and
economic significance to Belgium had declined by the early 1990s, so had

the former colonial power significance to Mobutu's Zaire only increased in reverse proportion as Mobutu sought aid and prestige through his Belgian connections. Even though the former colony's everyday significance to Belgium shrank, paradoxically, the colonial past loomed ever larger.

Colonial memories and national identity(ies)

By century's end, Belgium had better come to terms with a longstanding issue, namely World War II and the question of collaboration, which at least opened up space for the consideration of other historical issues. Hugo Claus' *Het verdriet van België* (1983), discussed earlier, made a splash because it broke the taboo of discussing wartime collaboration, a subject on which Belgians had generally remained silent after 1945. An unspoken myth had taken hold that collaboration was widespread among Dutch speakers, but much less so in the country's south and among French speakers. The 1950 referendum on the *Question royale* reinforced this, as many more in Flanders than in French-speaking areas supported the return of a king tainted by suggestions of wartime collaboration with the enemy. What actually happened during the war, of course, was more complex. Some Flemish speakers did collaborate, but many vehemently opposed the occupier, and some joined the resistance. The country's French speakers also resisted Nazi occupation, but there were of course French speakers who collaborated to greater or lesser extents, from prominent cases like Rexist Léon Degrelle, to borderline ones, such as comic strip artist Hergé.[6]

The issue of collaboration had weighed heavily on debates about identity, regionalism, and nationalist demands, especially by Dutch speakers, which was exacerbated when politicians stoked the issue to mobilize voters. Post-1945 negative views of collaborationism among Dutch speakers were tinged by the nagging belief that the associated post-war clampdown was a Trojan horse for the oppression of Flemish spirits. Overall, Belgians on the political right, whatever their native tongue, tended to view collaborators as slightly less morally objectionable, and amnesty for collaborators as more acceptable. The views of many Flemish shifted over time to where some tended to view collaboration less harshly—and supported amnesty more—than their compatriots in the country's southern provinces. The views of the country's francophone minority were more unchanging. One 2017 study concluded that, "French-speakers [were] more uncompromising towards collaboration and amnesty, while Dutch-speakers [were] less judgmental of collaborators during WWII and [were] relatively more favourable to amnesty."[7] Although unresolved, the issue was more out in the open by century's end, allowing for freer discussion of it. Inhabitants of Flanders, who in 1950 held more favorable views of the monarchy, had tended to turn more and more against the country's ruling house, whereas the opposite was true among French speakers, whose allegiance to king and kingdom strengthened.

Questions about collaboration and about the colonial past were inseparable from those surrounding Belgian-ness, an identity that by the turn of the century had diminished to become quite weak.[8] Some people, in particular francophone pro-monarchists, were reticent when it came to talking about the dark chapters of the country's colonial history, fearing that doing so might weaken the monarchy, and thereby Belgium itself. Contrariwise, "the questioning of the country's colonial past (...) enabled certain Flemish nationalists to criticize the role of the monarchy and the influence of the former French-speaking élite."[9] Indeed, exerting Flemish identity meant displacing Francophones from their historically central position; this could include attacks on colonial history because the francophone bourgeoisie and elites had predominated in the Belgian Congo administration and economy. Yet paradoxically, the more one dredged up the colonial past, the more one by necessity had to speak of a "Belgium" and people's shared, national past. This meant the debate over colonialism in the 2000s held the possibility of rekindling the idea of "Belgium."[10]

The turn-of-the-century weeping and gnashing of teeth about the colonial past was not a phenomenon unique to Belgium, rather it is was one manifestation of a larger, paradoxical development, that of a Europe of diminished powers asserting itself by dwelling on its culpability for past misdeeds. Pascal Bruckner argues that self-criticism and apologies for a dastardly past have allowed Europeans to continuously foreground their centrality in history and in the contemporary world, even as Europe's relative power has declined. Speaking as a European, Bruckner asserts that in the case of the loss of empire, "Decolonization has deprived us of our power, our economic influence is constantly decreasing, but in a colossal overestimation we continue to see ourselves as the evil center of gravity on which the universe depends."[11] Belgium, which had enjoyed the ability to "punch above its weight" during the colonial era because of its possession of the massive Congo, could now return to the global stage through a largely cultural move of reflection and repentance. Maybe Belgium, which had been breaking up since 1960, was in part sustained by engaging in a common project; not actual overseas rule, as in the past, but through a special mission of regret coupled with a renewed relationship with central Africa.

But did Belgians truly feel repentance toward their colonial history? After the 1998 publication of Adam Hochschild's *King Leopold's Ghost,* many commentators criticized them for not facing up to that past, especially the atrocities of the Leopoldian era, even though plenty of time had elapsed to allow for a full accounting, occurring as they had some one hundred years in the past. There is, of course, some truth in such accusations. For example, it is astonishing that in 1997, on the centenary of the Tervuren Museum's founding, a new monument honoring Leopold II was inaugurated on the museum grounds, Tom Frantzen's "The Congo, I presume." That said, one must consider the context in which any consideration of the past would have occurred at the time. By the 1980s and 1990s, open divisions within the country made it more difficult to address the colonial past as *one* country.

> The partitioning of Belgium has made it harder for the country to own up to its historical responsibilities toward the Congo and its neighbors. As the national consciousness fades along with the national institutions, so does the national sense of history and responsibility.[12]

Present-day issues impinged on historical reflection as the ongoing split with Mobutu and the continued decline in Zaire remained paramount to many minds. Any former colonial, or any Belgian for that matter, who read Lieve Joris' account of her almost Kafka-esque incarceration and questioning at the end of her 1985 voyage to Zaire in *Terug naar Kongo* would be forgiven for concluding that the Belgians had indeed done a good job during the colonial era, and that decolonization was a loss for both Belgians and Congolese. When the former colony was dealing with such intractable problems, why dwell on issues from the long-distant past?

King Leopold's (and Lumumba's) ghost

A turning point arrived in 1998 when American journalist Adam Hochschild published *King Leopold's Ghost: A Story of Greed, Terror, and Heroism in Colonial Africa*, which was quickly translated into French and Flemish.[13] Reactions were mixed and strong, and the book placed past colonialism front and center in the country. Many admitted that there had been abuses during the Leopoldian regime but countered that Hochschild's book exaggerated its negative aspects. "The book triggered contrasting reactions. (…) Some—in particular the former colonials—expressed indignation, contesting and delegitimizing this version of history and stressing the positive side of colonialism (…) Other Belgians welcomed the book as a revelation (…) In both cases, the emotion—as a response to infamy or unveiled truth—was vividly felt. For both groups, the conflict between the two historical narratives was intertwined with concerns about the meaning of their identity."[14] The book was a sensation that awakened all sorts of reconsiderations of the past.

Why did Hochschild's book have such an impact? Earlier works by Daniel Vangroenweghe and Jules Marchal had detailed the same abuses, as did Martin Ewans' *European Atrocity, African Catastrophe: Leopold II, the Congo Free State, and Its Aftermath*, which appeared not too long after Hochschild's book.[15] In no small part Hochschild's success was due to his engaging writing style. As one reviewer put it, Hochschild achieved "a vivid, novelistic narrative that makes the reader acutely aware of the magnitude of the horror perpetrated by King Leopold and his minions."[16] The book also arrived on the heels of the 1994 Rwanda genocide, Mobutu's 1997 fall, and the soul-searching that these had caused in Belgium. Not only was the country the former colonial power in Rwanda, but its government had withdrawn all of its soldiers from Rwanda on April 10, 1994 (after several casualties), which was followed by the killing of hundreds of thousands of Tutsis and Hutu moderates. The genocide then induced Belgium to disengage from Africa, leading to inaction there.[17] The First Congo War took place 1994-1997, ending with Laurent Kabila's accession to power and Mobutu's exile and death in 1997, followed by the outbreak of a Second Congo War in 1998 and eventually Kabila's mysterious assassination in 2001. News of all this was regularly brought to francophone and Flemish readers by a host of journalists including Eric de Bellefroid at *La Libre Belgique*, Axel Buyse at *De Standaard*, and above all Colette Braeckman, author and journalist at *Le Soir* who for decades relentlessly lived and told of the turmoil in the Congo.[18] Braeckman not only was a journalist and editor for *Le Soir*, she wrote for *Le Monde diplomatique*, published a blog, authored numerous books on central Africa such as *Le Dinosaure: Le Zaïre de Mobutu* (1992), and collaborated on related film projects. As Jean-Luc Vellut put it in 1994, the sum total of such reporting in the country's media, "assures for central Africa an echo and a weight that this region does not find elsewhere in the world."[19] While Congolese continued with their struggles, in Belgium a commission investigated the government's action and inaction during the Rwandan genocide.[20] Even if Belgium during these years was actually less active on the ground in Africa, "the works of the Rwanda commission and what followed from them opened Pandora's Box."[21] At the moment that Hochschild's book appeared, the country was ripe for reconsideration of its past actions in Africa. This had not been the case years earlier, and when Ewans' book appeared in 2002, it could not jolt the public as had Hochschild's retelling of the story of CFS atrocities.[22]

What astounded many readers of *King Leopold's Ghost* was its author's electrifying assertion that 10 million people, or half the population of the

Congo, had perished as a result of Leopoldian rule, a claim Hochschild made even though it was impossible to prove or disprove due to the nature of demographic evidence from the era.[23] Critics ran with the number of 10 million, and it was reiterated repeatedly on television, in the press, in public criticism, and in academic and other publications, so much so that it became a widely-accepted figure despite being contested by academics and others, some arguing with statistics that it was a "totally inflated figure."[24] Only slowly have more careful efforts to treat population figures of the Leopoldian era shifted popular opinion, a task made difficult by the risk that by critiquing Hochschild or his figures, one might be perceived as an apologist for Leopold II.[25]

Another spur to sales of King Leopold's Ghost was Hochschild's use of the term Holocaust, even though colonial rule in Congo was never genocidal.[26] The French title of the book, Les fantômes du roi Léopold: Un holocauste oublié, left little to the imagination, and in the text the author drew parallels between Leopold II, Adolf Hitler, and Joseph Stalin. Hochschild's critics pointed out that although deaths in the CFS might have been genocidal in scale, they were not so in essence or intent, and Hochschild himself later backtracked from his use of the term Holocaust without admitting its misuse. In an opinion piece criticizing the 2005 Tervuren Museum exhibit "Memory of Congo: The Colonial Era," Hochschild took issue with an exhibit that addressed the loss of life during Leopold's regime: "One wall panel at the new museum exhibit raises—and debunks—the charge, 'Genocide in the Congo?' But this is a red herring: No reputable scholar of the Congo uses the word." Yet earlier in the same piece he upheld his linkage of Leopold's regime with Nazi Germany by asking, once again, about the Tervuren Museum's historical silence on the deaths of Africans under the CFS: "It was as if a great museum to Jewish art and culture in Berlin revealed nothing about the Holocaust."[27] Hochschild's book and choice of terms were so influential that the terms "Holocaust" or "Congolese Holocaust" were often and rather carelessly used in subsequent years in innumerable book reviews, news articles, and even academic publications on Belgian colonial history.[28] From such an interpretive standpoint, accusations that Belgians had forgotten their colonial past were particularly troubling because of the ethical implications, following on the imperative to "never forget" the Holocaust. This gave Hochschild's book, in the words of one reviewer, "a particular ethical urgency."[29] Reactions in Belgium showed how by 1998 people in the country were well aware of the Holocaust: its use as a frame of reference resonated strongly. This contrasted with their ignorance about their own colonial past. The debate about Hochschild's book indicated quite a bit about culture, public memory, and colonialism in Belgium, but also much about the great awareness of the Holocaust there and in Europe more generally by century's end.[30]

King Leopold's Ghost was quickly followed by the publication of Ludo de Witte's *De moord op Lumumba* (1999), which caused controversy not because it revealed Belgium's involvement in Lumumba's death; many were aware their country was at least partially responsible for the murder. As Colette Braeckman put it, "depuis quarante ans aussi, entre la Belgique et le Congo la mort du leader congolais fait partie de ces secrets de famille que chacun connaît mais dont, par bienséance, on ne parle pas." (Also, for forty years, between Belgium and the Congo, the death of the Congolese leader was one of the 'family secrets' that everyone knew, but about which one did not speak, out of a sense of propriety.)[31] Some did learn, or were reminded of this responsibility by de Witte's book, but it made a splash by breaking a certain taboo on the subject of Lumumba's death, and by accusing the government of assassination; that is, of deliberate, calculated murder. This is something seen more clearly in the title of the French-language translation that appeared in 2000, *L'Assassinat de Lumumba*. *De moord op Lumumba* was partly a response to Jacques Brassine's successful Ph.D. thesis (ULB), defended in the 1990s, which had largely exonerated Belgium for involvement in Lumumba's death. De Witte's book did not totally reshape public opinion, but it, along with accompanying films and interviews on television, did "reopen old wounds" and awaken dormant emotions.[32]

The attention paid to the period of Leopoldian rule and the era of Congo's independence in *King Leopold's Ghost* and de Witte's book, respectively, is reflective of a trend, namely the overwhelming focus of scholarly and other commentary regarding Belgium's colonialism being centered on the years before 1908 and those from around 1960 to 1965, with little interest in the longer period of Belgian state rule in between. Criticisms of Belgian colonialism and its vestiges in Europe tended to focus on only the most salacious aspects of Leopoldian rule, collapsing Belgian state colonialism into the period of "red rubber."[33] As Benoît Verhaegen rightly put it, we must not "télescoper les périodes en attribuant au colonisateur belge de 1950 les atrocités du système léopoldien," (collapse the two periods together by attributing to the Belgian colonizer of 1950 the atrocities of the Leopoldian system) and he called on people not to conflate colonial rule in the 1950s with Leopoldian atrocities circa the 1890s.[34] There also is the tendency to view the Belgian "system" in isolation without reference to other colonial regimes, or to idealize pre-colonial African societies and cultures. Considering the focus on Leopoldian atrocities and the assassination of Lumumba, colonial history is too often depicted as binary—colonialism bad, Africans good—whereas history is not two-sided but multifaceted.

An explosion of productions

The Rwanda genocide followed by Mobutu's fall and then Hochschild's and de Witte's books in quick succession led to growing attention to central Africa and Belgium's colonial past, which manifested itself in myriad ways.[35] Just five years after the genocide, the francophone theater group Groupov, based in Liege, staged the epic five-hour work *Rwanda 1994*, directed by Jacques Delcuvellerie. The play starred Yolande Mukagasana, who had barely managed to escape the genocide with her life and who lost her entire family, including her three children. Performances first took place at the 1999 Festival d'Avignon and then the following year in Liege, Brussels, and Lille, confronting audiences in two European countries involved in the lead up to and response (or lack thereof) to the genocide to face this recent past. The play was then taken elsewhere, including Rome and Paris, and even Rwanda itself by 2004.[36] *Rwanda 94* combined music, images, theater, fiction, and non-fiction in order to understand the incomprehensible: "le spectacle use de tous les possibles du théâtre pour mieux s'approcher de l'indicible d'un genocide." (the show uses all that is possible in theater to get closer to the unspeakable of a genocide.)[37] It included long sequences of images of massacres. It is worth noting that when he was thinking about the audience for *Rwanda 94*, Delcuvellerie started from the premise that audiences would not know much if anything about central Africa. In his words, "le public n'avait quasiment aucun référent sur l'Afrique centrale, sur l'histoire du Rwanda et sur la complexité extrême de ces sociétés et de leur histoire." (the public had almost no reference regarding central Africa, the history of Rwanda, or regarding the extreme complexity of these societies and their history.)[38]

Other cultural productions followed. Internet sites dedicated to colonial history and issues took off, for instance the website for COBELCO, which was set up in 2000. In April 2000, the play *Bruxelles, ville d'Afrique* by Antoine Pickels, Jacques André, and Virginie Jortay (Groupe Kuru) took the audience through the capital city, tracing its colonial connections, for example in former headquarter buildings of colonial companies. The year 2001 witnessed a number of related expositions: the exhibit "Notre Congo" in Liege; the ExitCongoMuseum exhibit at Tervuren Museum (discussed below); and an exposition about the career of museum director Frans Olbrechts at Antwerp's Ethnographic Museum, curated by Constantine Petridis. These kinds of exhibits were anything but controversial.[39] African suffering, including in Rwanda, was not the only subject. A certain renewed focus on whites who suffered during and after 1960 because of their flight from central Africa also emerged. An example is Flemish public broadcast journalist Peter Verlinden's

Weg uit Congo: Het drama van de kolonialen, which sought to bring to life the drama of the July days of 1960, when settlers in the Congo became "vluchtelingen"—refugees in what had for them become their new home.[40] Reflections on the colonial past and its aftermaths emerged in new film and television productions. As he was to do several times in the 1990s and early 2000s, documentary filmmaker Thierry Michel tapped into a larger francophone audience with a film centered on the Congo after colonialism. His documentary *Mobutu, roi du Zaïre* emphasized the role of the individual by documenting Mobutu's decades of misrule. Michel followed this enthralling figure from Mobutu's 1965 seizure of power through to his death, including footage from surprisingly candid conversations with the dictator.[41] Another Belgian film director, Francis Dujardin, produced the touching *Boma-Tervuren: Le voyage*, about the deaths of Congolese Ekia, Gemba, Kitoukwa, M'Peia, Zao, Sambo, and Mibangé at the 1897 colonial exposition in Tervuren, suggesting that some were not as unaware of this tragic past as many observers of Belgium claimed.[42] In 2000, Haitian director Raoul Peck released *Lumumba*, a tour de force of the tragedy of decolonization that at the same time in its final scenes expressed hope in a post-Mobutu future.[43] VRT's Canvas channel produced the mini-series "Kongo" in 2002, which focused on the life of planters in the colony.[44] Hochschild's book made a reappearance of a sorts in 2004 in the form of Briton Peter Bate's film *Congo: White King, Red Rubber, Black Death*, a British production shown on BBC Four in February 2004. It was brought to Belgium and shown on RTBF and VRT in April of that year, the RTBF version being followed by a debate; the film and debate on RTBF attracted 145,200 and 113,900 viewers, respectively.[45] The film, which depicted a mock trial of Leopold II, followed Hochschild's lead by drawing explicit comparisons between Leopold II and Hitler.[46] Foreign headlines announced "Belgian fury" at the film's showing, but in truth it was the Belgian government more than ordinary people that denounced the film, with Foreign Minister Louis Michel calling it "partisan" and "one-sided."[47] As with the Lumumba commission, discussed below, some Flemish nationalists took advantage of this new flare-up to attack the Belgian state and the monarchy.[48]

Sad chapters of the past also lent art a renewed subject, namely colonialism's last years and the assassination of Patrice Lumumba.[49] Luc Tuymans' reflections on Lumumba's murder were shown in "Mwana Kitoko: Beautiful White Man" from November 21 to December 23, 2000, at the David Zwirner Gallery in New York, and then again in the Belgian pavilion at the 2001 Venice Biennale. His paintings of Baudouin (*Mwana Kitoko*) and Lumumba juxtaposed the leaders and their actions in an almost accusatory way, calling attention to the young king's complicity in the prime minister's downfall and assassination, prefiguring the conclusions of the Lumumba commission that would release its findings the same month the Venice Biennale closed.

The Lumumba Commission

The turn of the century witnessed a minor settling of accounts, which fit a larger pattern of European apologies for past misdeeds, from Germany's apologies and reparations for the Holocaust to French recognition of its role in the same, to repeated European apologies for colonialism. In April 2000, Prime Minister Guy Verhofstadt (VLD, Liberals) apologized for Belgium's role in the Rwanda genocide. Verhofstadt, who had been in charge of a 1996-1997 parliamentary commission of inquiry (in the Senate) on Belgium and the genocide, traveled to Rwanda for its sixth anniversary where he publicly assumed "the responsibility of my country, the Belgian political and military authorities."[50] There were other turn-of-the-century manifestations of a continuing interest in the legacy of colonialism, for example, considerations of what remained of colonialism's successes, forty years after independence.[51] Unlike earlier and later celebrations of Congo's independence, however, there was no visit by the king in 2000, nor even by the prime minister. Instead, Laurent Kabila had to content himself with the company of Foreign Minister Louis Michel. As at other moments, Michel's visit was not without controversy: criticisms of Congo's human rights record and the Yerodia affair—where the Belgian government issued an arrest warrant for the Congolese foreign affairs minister, Abdoulaye Yerodia Ndombasi—made the foreign minister's stopover anything but comfortable.

Verhofstadt's apology was followed by a parliamentary inquiry into Lumumba's murder, sparking a long debate whose presence in public life was accentuated by other developments. As noted, Belgium issued an arrest warrant in 2000 for the Congolese foreign minister; in 2001 the government ordered the trial of four Rwandans for their role in genocide; and in 2004, Congo president Joseph Kabila (Laurent Kabila's son) spoke before the Belgian parliament, and was surprisingly positive about the colonial era, folding the story of white missionaries, colonial functionaries, and CFS pioneers into the history of his country.

But back to 2000. Although there was a "broad national consensus" in favor of the parliamentary commission, it did not arise merely out of a general will to face the past but because of the conjuncture of de Witte's book and the politics of the moment.[52] The spring 1999 dioxin scandal helped lead to the coming to power of the Flemish Liberals or Open VLD (Open Vlaamse

Liberalen en Democraten), under Verhofstadt, who now as prime minister led a coalition of Flemish and francophone liberals, socialists, and greens. This not only had Liberals lead a government for the first time since 1938, it put the Christian Democrats out of power for the first time since 1954; it had been leading figures of the Christian Democrats who had been involved or at least implicated in the events of 1961 in the Congo. Foreign Minister Michel pivoted the nation's foreign policy toward central Africa, saying that, "Belgium has a heavy responsibility regarding the African continent."[53] He recognized the complexity of issues there, but did not let this deter him from engagement, and his April 2000 visit to the Congo was the former colonial power's first official state visit in nearly 12 years.[54] When Belgium took over the rotating presidency of the European Union Council, Verhofstadt's government made plain it would make central Africa a priority.[55]

In short, the parliamentary commission on Lumumba's murder led to an official yet somewhat vague recognizance of the country's role in Lumumba's death.[56] The commission's work has been criticized from many angles, for example for not giving enough credence to oral testimonies. Membership in the commission was comprised of both experts appointed by parliament and political members. A book based on its work that appeared in 2004 did strange work in the sense that in writing it, the commission acted less as independent, impartial historians reconstructing events of the past and more as judge and jury, seeking to prove or disprove Belgium's innocence. In the end it was the political members rather than the experts who pushed for the recognition of Belgium's "moral responsibility."[57] The commission did take strides toward a public and official coming to terms with Lumumba's murder, and although it split the difference between recognizing the country's responsibility and absolving the government of the time, it did conclude Belgium had a "moral responsibility" in Lumumba's death. Another result was an additional apology, one of many emanating from Western countries around the turn of the century, this one in 2002 from Foreign Minister Michel. Less of a blanket apology, Michel recognized the responsibility of certain Belgian "actors" in the 1961 death, and offered his government's sincere regrets.[58] As Gauthier de Villers has pointed out, the apology by Michel, as vague as it was, was applauded by politicians across the political spectrum, and constituted a milestone. "Dans un pays où Patrice Lumumba, transformé en bouc émissaire pour une décolonisation 'cochonnée', fut si exécré et diabolisé, le phénomène est impressionnant." (The phenomenon is stunning in a country where Patrice Lumumba, transformed into a scapegoat for a 'bungled' decolonization, was so execrated and demonized.)[59] By contrast, some politicians were shocked by Michel's speech and continued to believe Lumumba should have been eliminated from the political scene—if not assassinated—because of his politics and what he had done following independence. A group of ex-colonials met with Michel to protest the government's decision to create a "Fondation Lumumba" as a kind of recompense for Belgian responsibility in Lumumba's death.[60]

The Lumumba commission report shows how the colonial past was used at times to influence contemporaneous debates. The fact that the report revealed at the very least neglect on the part of Baudouin to prevent Lumumba's death opened up room for those critical of the monarchy to attack it. Unsurprisingly, there was less support for a positive view of state rule—but not necessarily a negative view of the role of missionaries in the Belgian Congo—among Dutch-speaking Belgians. As *Le Soir* put it,

> au nord du pays, le rapport de la Commission Lumumba entraîne des conséquences imprévues: le fait que la responsabilité du roi Baudouin ait été mise en cause, qu'à l'époque le souverain ait pris des initiatives personnelles sans toujours en informer le gouvernement, est utilisé comme argument par ceux qui souhaiteraient revoir la fonction royale!
> (in the north of the country, the Lumumba Commission report led to unforeseen consequences: the fact that the responsibility of King Baudouin was called into question—that at the time the king took personal initiatives without always informing the government—was used as an argument by those who wished to modify the royal function.)[61]

The anti-monarchist extreme right-wing Vlaams Blok could use de Witte's exposé and what followed to attack the monarchy and the state because de Witte's book implicated Baudouin in the assassination.

Some institutions and individuals continued to hold the line on a positive vision of Belgian colonialist action, in particular former colonials, including those who ran the African museum in Namur. The centrality of the Tervuren Museum meant it had always overshadowed smaller museums of the Congo. Despite the overwhelming focus on Tervuren by journalists, scholars, and commentators, other museums linked Belgium to Africa and the colonial past throughout the twentieth century, including a small institution in Namur, the Musée Africain de Namur, largely organized and run by former colonials.[62] There had been different incarnations of the Namur museum of Africa during the colonial era, after which it continued on as the Musée Colonial de Jambes, before closing in 1977. It re-emerged in the mid-1980s, taking over the *caserne Léopold* in the city, and was inaugurated by Minister of Public Works Louis Olivier in 1985 as the new Musée Africain de Namur.[63] Into the twenty-first century, the Namur museum remained Eurocentric and unabashedly royalist and colonialist, with rooms named after missionaries like Scheutist Father Emeri Cambier and conquerors like Alexis Vrithoff, who fought in the "anti-slavery" campaigns and died in 1892, supposedly cooked and eaten.[64] Former colonials donated much of Namur's collections, and its triumphant displays of weaponry and related objects, many surely seized by force or under the threat of force, indicated a lack of reflection on the origins of the museum's pieces.[65] While the Tervuren Museum was preparing to launch the self-reflective 2005 "Mémoire du Congo" exhibit and looking ahead to a complete renovation, the Musée Africain de Namur was still evoking "la grande épopée africaine," or "great African epic," and still calling Leopold II "le grand roi," and lauding his "genius" and humanitarian actions in Africa.[66] Nonetheless, the museum continued to function and receive some attention in the local press.[67] One other local, rather idiosyncratic museum was one created to celebrate Albert Thys, the Musée du Général Thys in Dalhem, sustained by Georges Defauwes, who wanted to highlight native son Thys' achievements.[68]

Thus there was attention paid to central Africa right around the turn of the century, which during the years of Verhofstadt I (1999-2003) centered around responsibility, the Rwandan genocide, and Lumumba's assassination. As noted, this reawakening to past crimes was not a strictly Belgian phenomenon. Indeed, there was also a certain coming to terms with the 1954-1962 Algerian conflict—which France only recognized as a war in 1999—as well as Germany's recognition of the atrocities and genocide it perpetrated in German Southwest Africa; revelations in Britain about the Mau Mau uprising; and new findings on Australia's sad record with Aborigines. Nevertheless, many recent studies on Belgium and colonial "guilt" treat the Belgian case, as it were, in a vacuum. Too many foreign observers continue to harp on Belgium's supposedly complete lack of coming to terms with the past, as seen in the quote from Michela Wrong that forms part of the epigraph to this book's Introduction.[69] In fact Belgium has come some distance in facing up to its past, especially in comparison to some other former colonial powers. As mentioned, Belgium apologizing for its role in the Rwandan genocide and in Lumumba's death can be seen as part of a larger story of European self-flagellation regarding the supposedly unmitigated destructiveness of Europe's past.[70]

The Tervuren Museum

The Tervuren Museum of the Congo has long had a reputation for being "dusty." As one scholar described his impressions after a visit in 2003, "One could almost think that the Congo is still a Belgian colony."[71] The museum focused on its scientific and educational goals and remained conservative and unreflective regarding the colonial past through the tenure of director Dirk Thys van den Audenaerde (1986-1999).[72] But to argue that it "remained largely untouched for nearly a century," as Debora Silverman puts its, "a virtual petrified forest of imperial triumphalism," oversimplifies a more complex history.[73] A museum and the visitor experience derive only in part from the physical building itself and its permanent displays, and also important are temporary exhibits, the context of the visit, and the visitor him or herself.

Viewed more comprehensively, the Tervuren Museum did change after 1960, albeit not dramatically. As discussed, it did maintain a colonialist spirit and acted as a vehicle praising Leopold II. The *salle de mémorial* remained in place, with its "Mémorial à la mémoire des Belges morts au Congo avant 1908" (Memorial to the Memory of the Belgians who died in the Congo before 1908) that included the names of the hundreds of Belgians who died in central Africa during the Leopoldian era. That room also included busts of famous colonial heroes and vitrines highlighting the fight for the colony, for instance one display case with memorabilia from Émile Storms. The museum continued to depict Congolese as anonymous *types* and the Congo as frozen in time.[74] Nonetheless, and as noted earlier, Lucien Cahen oversaw the renovation of several rooms in the museum between 1958 and 1977, and but a single room remained unchanged after the museum's 1910 inauguration, the so-called Crocodile Room.[75] Director Thys van den Audenaerde took advantage of the institution's vast riches by participating in important itinerant exhibitions, a move that made sense considering the museum itself could only display a tiny fraction of its enormous collections, which numbered in the many millions of items.[76] An example of the kind of shows that resulted was 1995's successful traveling exhibit "Hidden Treasures of the Tervuren Museum."[77] By the last decade of the twentieth century, Tervuren was playing host to painting contests that involved children and events like book launches for works on central Africa, in addition to organizing exhibitions to highlight past as well as contemporary African paintings.[78] It continued as a research center, producing innumerable publications in many fields including archaeology, botany, ethnography, ethnomusicology, geology, history, ichthyology, linguistics, and zoology, among others.[79] And this despite the fact it had suffered severe budget cuts after 1960 and continued with meager funding in the decades thereafter.[80]

Since the turn of the century the museum has taken a number of major steps to address the colonial past, and the museum's role in it, something that cannot be said of many other former colonial museums or other such institutions elsewhere in Europe. Director Guido Gryseels, who took over in

Émile Storms (1846-1918)
Location: Brussels, square de Meeûs[81]
Sculptor: Marnix D'Haveloose[82]

Bust of Émile Storms, Brussels, 2002

This white stone bust of General Émile Storms in Brussels remembers one of the very earliest of Leopold II's "pioneers." Storms was likely one of the oldest of the king's adjutants, being almost of the same generation as Leopold. Storms embarked for central Africa even before the CFS came into existence, taking part in a fourth expedition organized by the Belgian committee of the Association Internationale Africaine (1882-1885), the supposedly neutral committee that Leopold II used as a front organization to set up his own takeover of territories in central Africa. Although Storms' first term in Africa was a successful venture of exploration and conquest, he was recalled home in late 1885 and completed only one more term of work for the CFS before returning to military service in Belgium. Just eleven years' Leopold II's junior, Storms died nine years after him, in 1918, at the age of 72.

The inscription on the square de Meeûs memorial is straightforward: "Au Lt Général Storms 1846-1918, Fonda le Station de M'Pala Mai 1883, Étendit la civilisation sur la région au Tanganika" (To Lt. General Storms 1846-1919, founded the station of M'Pala Mai 1883, extended civilization over the region to Tanganyika). As with so many other such colonial markers, it emphasizes the role that extending "civilization" played in the country's overseas conquest and rule, or at least in the self-conception Belgians developed about them. The bust was originally in bronze, and the square where it was located was originally called the square de l'Industrie, which was renamed square de Meeûs in 1946. The original bronze was removed at night sometime in 1943, during Nazi Germany's occupation of Belgium, probably to be melted down.[83]

Storms was also honored with a display case of memorabilia about him in the *salle de mémorial* in the Tervuren Museum, a bust in that same room, another memorial in his hometown of Wetteren, in addition to having a "rue Général Storms" named in his memory in Florennes. Storms himself left other traces of the colonial era in his home country. Similar to some others who conquered the Congo, Storms became a collector, sending back from his explorations and encounters numerous natural specimens, African objects, even the skulls of vanquished foes.[84] He himself carried home the skull of the Tabwa chief Lusinga, whom he had beheaded in December 1884 after defeating him in a conflict.[85] Storms' widow donated much of his collection to the Congo museum in Tervuren.

2001, set out to gain greater attention for the museum. That year, Boris Wastiau and guest curator and Congolese artist Toma Muteba Luntumbue staged the ExItCongoMuseum exhibit, an "examination of conscience" that reflected on the origins of the institution's collections and the museum itself, even asking how its main building might be considered part of the museum's displays.[86] In 2003, the small-scale self-guided tour "A Historical Stroll" consciously placed several key displays and their items in the context of the time at which they were created in order to give the visitor a sense of the museum's history.[87] There was more open recognition that missionaries had forced Africans to hand over objects, that all sorts of items had been seized in military actions, and that functionaries had been ordered to collect items and send them back to Belgium, which oftentimes included the use of force.[88] The museum's staff foregrounded how the museum's collections were tied to conquest and colonialism in the most intimate of ways, and that the museum would have to change if it was going to remain relevant in a post-colonial world.

The museum only continued "opening up" to a fuller recognition of its own colonial past and the need to incorporate Congolese voices into the institution. Scholars who worked through the museum to organize academic conferences tried to increase collaboration with African researchers by finding travel funding to bring people in from Africa. The museum started new initiatives to reach a broader public, including the country's now much-larger Congolese population. One 2002 children's Africa-inspired art contest involved 1,618 different school classes and drew 38,915 paintings and drawings.[89] The museum organized a yearly Tervuren/Congo fashion show and festival starting in 2007.[90] Most significant was the 2005 exhibit "Memory of the Congo: The Colonial Era," spearheaded by Africanist and historian Jean-Luc Vellut and accompanied by a richly-illustrated edited volume by expert authors. Gryseels was supportive of Vellut's independence when the latter took on the difficult task of organizing the exhibit, which was intended as a broad-ranging reconsideration of central Africa's history.[91]

This support continued in the face of criticism along the way. Gryseels said at the time that he received "a flood of letters from Belgians who are concerned that the exhibition will besmirch the names of all those who dedicated their lives to the Congo's development."[92] Critics on the left desired a more radical confrontation with the era's atrocities, and Adam Hochschild censured the exhibit for what he said was a whitewashing of killing that had occurred on a genocidal scale.[93] Critics on the right, meanwhile, exercised pressure by publicly and privately expressing fears that the exhibit might go too far to discredit the country's past actions overseas.[94] In the end, "Memory of Congo" navigated the rocky waters of public opinion with success, accomplishing a large, more Afro-centric exhibit in a prominent central space in the Tervuren Museum, giving African history its due by explaining European intervention—as significant as it was—as but one stage in a longer history of central Africa. The exhibit reached a large audience, bringing in some 140,000 visitors and garnering in the neighborhood of 400 press articles, in addition to being covered in dozens of radio and television programs.

Monumental memories

That Brussels and other urban areas, mainly Ostend, owed a great deal of their urban fabric to wealth from the Congo was a fact widely known by century's end.[95] The site of most traces was Brussels, and people including Antoine Tshitungu, Lucas Catherine, Erik Nobels, and the group CADTM (Comité pour l'annulation de la dette du tiers monde) had begun giving occasional guided tours of those colonial sites, for example the "Congolese" neighborhood of Matonge.[96] Catherine even published a short book to take the reader on a "Walk in the Congo" by means of a colonial "tour" of Brussels.[97] The book is explicitly anti-colonial, falling into the unhelpful good-bad dichotomous interpretation of history that has attracted so many. As John Darwin has commented, some scholars "convey the impression that writing against empire is an act of great courage: as if its agents lie in wait to exact their revenge or an enraged 'imperialist' public will inflict martyrdom on them."[98] In other work Lucas Catherine has fallen into another trap that many others have fallen into, namely confusing all of Leopold II's architectural achievements in Belgium with his Congo profits, as discussed earlier.[99] Many traces of empire are very small-scale, such as the colonial bric-a-brac for sale in various stores and markets, for instance at Eric Van Ghendt's stand of *antiquités* in the Grand Sablon, where colonial-themed books and a sign urging to "Achetez Congo" have been on display for purchase.[100] Many such traces have changed over time, from antiques changing hands to the disappearance of the bar "Congo belge," at 8, rue Ropsy Chaudron. Chéri Samba's mural *Porte de Namur, Porte de l'Amour* at Chaussée de Wavre and Chaussée d'Ixelles at the entrance to the Matonge neighborhood was taken down for some time, before being returned. All this said, many if not most of these are locations that virtually no one would recognize as prima facie "colonial" sites today.

By the start of the twenty-first century, Belgians had done nothing to put up monuments recognizing the "dark" aspects of their colonial past, nor had they deliberately torn down monuments that celebrated colonialism. Indeed, the country actually added colonialist memorials after 1960, such as the 1970 Schaerbeek Force publique monument, plaques honoring the former Belgian African administration inaugurated on the Musée de la Dynastie in Brussels (today the Musée BELvue), and the Tervuren memorial honoring Leopold II by Tom Frantzen, "The Congo, I presume," unveiled in 1997. One can compare this to France, which removed its last rue Pétain in 2013. In Spain, a "Law of Historical Memory" helped drive a removal of statues to Francisco Franco and a renaming of streets in that country, and in 2018 its socialist government revived plans to deal with the Valle de los Caídos, the massive memorial to Franco, José Antonio Primo de Rivera, and the quasi-fascist dictatorship that ruled the country 1939-1975. As noted, some Belgian pro-colonialist memorials have moved or disappeared completely, although not for ideological reasons but because of construction, for instance Antwerp's memorial to Dhanis on the Amerikalei in front of Sint-Michielskerk. First relocated to the Colonial University in Antwerp, in recent years it reappeared in a small museum in Sint-Niklaas, southwest of Antwerp.[101] Another example is the commemorative stone to Alphonse Lange dating to 1898 that was moved to a park in Wenduyne after the cemetery in which it was located was eliminated. A memorial to Hubert Lothaire was at some point relocated from Rochefort's hôtel de ville to a nearby park. Such examples of moved or vanished monuments are rare. Many colonial-era monuments have in fact been restored. Gent's well-known "Moorken" to brothers Jozef and Lieven Van de Velde was restored around 2004, as was the Colonial monument in the Parc du Cinquantenaire around 2006 and the Leopold II place du Trône equestrian statue in 2005, the latter in time for Belgium's 175th anniversary celebrations.[102]

Following the appearance of Hochschild and de Witte's books and the showing of Bate's film on television, attacks on public representations of colonialism in Belgium spiked. Beginning as early as 2001, there were multiple attempts to protest memorials honoring empire, particularly those to Leopold II, and

Alphonse Louis Lange (1865-1897)
Location: Wenduyne (De Haan), Lange Park
Sculptor: Hippolyte Le Roy
Inauguration: 1898, re-inaugurated 1936[103]
Funded/built by: friends of Alphonse Lange

Monument to Alphonse Louis Lange, Wenduyne, 2018

A commemorative stone to Alphonse Lange, originally from Liege, and who fought in the anti-slavery campaigns, was put up on 21 August 1898, just 12 months after he died.[104] It later was moved to a park in Wenduyne today named "Lange Park" after the cemetery in which it was originally located was removed, sometime around 1930.[105] Today it sits in the park that bears his name right on the edge of Leopold II-laan and almost directly across from the Wenduine Molen.[106]

Lange fought in the anti-Arab campaigns under the command of Francis Dhanis and alongside other figures later memorialized in Belgium, including Aristide Doorme and Pierre Ponthier. Lange also explored the Ruzizi River and established two posts there. Struck by dysentery, he returned to Belgium on 29 July 1897 and died one month later, in Wenduyne.[107]

The monument calls attention to the fact that he was wounded in fighting in October 1893, during the same fighting that saw Pierre Ponthier suffer a mortal wound. The stone is inscribed with the names of locations of battles, Lange's rank, that he was an officer of the Force publique, and the places and dates of his birth and death. The bronze on the monument shows Lange in profile, wearing a kepi and uniform, bearing several medals.

Jozef (Joseph) Van de Velde (1855-1882) and
Lieven Van de Velde (1850-1888)
Location: Ghent, Citadel Park
Sculptor: Louis Mast[108]
Inauguration: 1888

*Monument to Jozef and Lieven Van de
Velde, Ghent, 2018*[110]

The brothers Van de Velde from Ghent were both explorers, and both died in the Congo. Their native city's monument to them can be found today in Citadel Park, and is known colloquially as "Het Moorken." It was inaugurated in 1888, the same year in which Lieven died.[109] A stone medallion attached to a rough-hewn boulder shows the two brothers in profile, and the whole is topped by a bronze sculpture of an African boy, Sakala, whom Lieven brought with him to Belgium for a time. The profile portrait of the men was originally enwreathed with a bronze garland, and there were various items set at the foot of the memorial, including a shield and two spears. Apparently these were removed (stolen) during World War I, presumably to be melted down, a fate that befell a number of other monuments as well.[111]

The Van de Velde brothers were honored in multiple ways, and the city of Ghent boasts several other memorials to the colonial era. A street was named after them, Gebroeders Vandeveldestraat, and the City of Ghent put up a plaque honoring them on their birth home, a house that was later demolished. There were busts of both brothers to be found in the MRAC (1887, 1888, by Jul. Lagae, cast by J. Petermann, Brussels). In Ghent, there is also a memorial to the city's *vétérans coloniaux*—those who died in the Congo before 1908—which was inaugurated on 29 June 1936. It is a large star-shaped sculpture set in the ground, which includes numerous names, including those of the Van de Velde brothers.[112] A close-by monument to Leopold II by statuary Géo Verbanck, from Ghent, was inaugurated 24 September 1955. The latter was put up by "la Foire de Gand" on the occasion of the 10th trade fair in Ghent, at whose inauguration were present

Monuments to colonial pioneers and Leopold II, Ghent, 2018

a representative of the king in addition to Minister of Colonies Auguste Buisseret.[113] Both are located at Acht Mei Plein, northeast of Citadel Park, where in
2018 there was a substantial explanatory plaque in French, Dutch, and English.[114]

Hubert Lothaire (1865-1929)
Location: Rochefort
Inauguration: 16 September 1934[115]

Lothaire was a leading military figure in the CFS. Although his campaigning
was extensive, he is best known for the arrest and execution of Charles Stokes
in 1894-1895 and the controversy that ensued.[116] Stokes was an Irish-born
merchant from Britain who became an arms trader in central Africa. Lothaire
believed Stokes to be a trafficker in arms who was aiding the Arab-Swahili forces
with which the CFS was struggling, and so he had him arrested. After a brief trial, Stokes was found guilty and executed by hanging. This provoked the "Stokes
Affair," a major diplomatic incident that only further tarnished Leopold II's repu-

Memorial to Hubert Lothaire in Rochefort, 2003

Lothaire's funerary monument in Ixelles, 2002

tation in Britain. The CFS actually brought Lothaire to trial in the capital, Boma, as a result. He was acquitted, a decision affirmed afterward by a Belgian court.

Lothaire's acquittal paved the way for his complete rehabilitation, in the eyes of his compatriots at least. A few years following his death in 1929, a commemorative plaque in honor of him was inaugurated, with fanfare, at Rochefort's city hall.[117] It bore a quotation from Albert I that honored him while harkening back to an essential justification for Belgium's takeover of the Congo: "Je rends un profond hommage à la mémoire de ce colonial de haute valeur, à ce chef militaire intrépide qui prit une part décisive à la destruction de la puissance des Arabes, trafiquants d'esclaves." (I pay a profound tribute to the memory of this colonial of great worth, to this intrepid military leader who took a decisive part in the destruction of the Arabs, traffickers in slaves.)[118] This quote and a similar if not identical bronze of Lothaire in profile also figure on a funerary monument on Lothaire's tomb in the cemetery of Ixelles, the Brussels commune where he died.[119] The memorial in Rochefort was later moved from the hôtel de ville to a nearby park, perhaps because of wartime damage to the city hall, considering that much of the small town was destroyed during the Second World War. The plaque remained on display into the twenty-first century, attached to a large rock.

there were efforts to rename streets named after him. In 2004 the local chapter of the Flemish left-liberal party Spirit asked the city of Halle to remove a monument to Leopold II in the city park "because mass murderers do not deserve a monument."[120] That same year a dramatic attack sawed a hand off of an African figure on Ostend's large memorial to Leopold II. The activist group De Stoeten Ostendenoare published a photo of the severed hand on the internet, saying they would return it if a corrective plaque was affixed to the monument explaining where the money came from to build it and for the development of Ostend: from Congolese.[121] This act of vandalism—or of correction, depending on your view—was promoted on the internet, including in Pieter De Vos' celebratory short film *Sikitiko: The King's Hand*.[122]

Leopold II (1835-1909)
Location: Ostend, at the "Drie Gapers" archways on the Zeedijk
Sculptor: Alfred Courtens
Architect: Antoine Courtens
Inauguration: 19 July 1931

Leopold II monument, showing memorial plaques to Aristide Doorme (left) and colonial pioneers (right), Ostend, 2018

Postcard of Leopold II monument, Ostend, ca. 1940s

Depiction of European and Africans, including one with severed hand, Ostend monument to Leopold II, 2018

This large monument inaugurated in 1931 by Albert I and Queen Elisabeth celebrates Leopold II as benefactor and protector of both the Congo and the coastal fishing community of Ostend.[123] It is flanked on either side by a plaque bearing the names of Ostend colonial pioneers and by a memorial to Aristide Doorme (1863-1905). The latter calls Doorme a "Hero of the campaigns against the Arabs and the Batetela," referencing the 1892-1894 anti-slavery campaigns and the 1897 Batetela revolt.

The Leopold II monument itself has been vandalized multiple times and restored each time, with one exception: in 2004, the group De Stoeten Ostendenoare protested the monument's complete lack of contextualization by cutting off the hand of one of the Congolese figures. Initially unnoticed, the group had to call attention to their own vandalism, which was later highlighted in the 2010 short film *Sikitiko: The King's Hand*.[124] Despite pleas

from associations of former colonials, the city council decided against restoration of the hand and in favor of adding an explanatory sign, which was later
replaced with a revised plaque. The newer plaque explains how the ensemble is
a "typical example of colonial art," and points out the fact that the king's many
investments in the city of Ostend were largely financed by his Congo profits. It
also references the 2004 attack that left one of the figures without a hand and
calls attention to the nearby plaque to Doorme and its colonialist rhetoric about
the anti-slavery wars that "was used at the time, and sometimes still is, as justification for colonization."[125] The monument came under renewed scrutiny amid
the mounting attention to the colonial past at the time of the December 2018
reopening of the Tervuren AfricaMuseum.[126]

Leopold II (1835-1909)
Location: Halle, Koning Albert I Park
Sculptor: Arthur Dupagne
Architect: Guy Lefebvre
Inauguration: 28 June 1953
Funded/built by: Cercle Colonial de Hal and the Ministry of Colonies, among
other sources[127]

This modest memorial in Halle is one of at least fifteen public monuments in
the country to Leopold II, the others being four in the Brussels-Capital area, two

Halle city park monument to Leopold II, 2002

Halle city park monument to Leopold II, with explanatory plaque, 2018

in Ostend, and one each in Ekeren, Mons, Tervuren, Ghent, Arlon, Namur, Genval, and Hasselt.

In 1948, the Cercle Colonial de Hal (1920-1966) formed an honorary committee composed of a number of prominent former colonials in order to build a monument to the memory of the colonial work of Leopold II. Orders were placed with sculptor Arthur Dupagne to cast a bust and with architect Guy Lefebvre to design a monument with a map of the Belgian Congo on it. It was inaugurated on 28 June 1953 during that year's "colonial day." Unveiled in the Albertpark in Halle, it faced a memorial to Baron Jacques de Dixmude and local colonial pioneers that had been inaugurated 20 years earlier.

The monument is of stone and metal, the latter being a large bronze bust on its front side, alongside a simple inscription of the king's name and the inauguration date. Its reverse bears an outline map of the Congo and the words "ARBEID EN VOORUITGANG" and "TRAVAIL ET PROGRÈS"—"WORK AND PROGRESS," the slogan of the CFS.[128]

As with others to Leopold II, the memorial in Halle has become a focal point of criticism of the king's colonial reign. In 2004, a politician for Spirit Halle asked for it to be taken down because, as he put it, "mass murderers do not deserve a monument."[129] A compromise solution was an explanatory plaque, which was added in 2009, and which recognizes that harm was done to the Congo.[130] It reads, in Dutch:

The "civilizing work" of Leopold II, the slogan for which was "Work and Progress," was supposed to bring the Congolese people prosperity. The colonial rule of Leopold II, who ruled from 1885 to 1908 as king-sovereign over the former International Congo Free State, was then already intensely criticized. The rubber and ivory trade that was largely in the hands of the king took a heavy toll on Congolese lives.

The compromise explanatory plaque has not satisfied everyone. When this author last visited the monument, in May 2018, it had been defaced with spray paint that read *suceur de bite,* "cocksucker."[131]

Colonial pioneers of Halle
Location: Halle (Hal), city park
Sculptor: Dole Ledel
Architect: Mario Knauer
Inauguration: 29 May 1932[132]

At the top of this cylindrical stone monument is a carved profile representing Jacques de Dixmude. On its side is a standing African figure, who looks up and back over his shoulder, almost lovingly, at the bald, mustachioed, and large head of Jacques that seems to hover above and just behind him. Like many African figures on Belgian colonial monuments, this nameless African figure appears to be nearly, or perhaps even completely naked. He stands in front of a short plant carved into the stone and carries what appear to be bananas or some other tropical produce, which sculptor Ledel seems to have conveniently used to cover his mid-section. As the figure appears to be African yet the stone color is quite light, almost white, some have labeled the monument "De witte neger" (The white negro).[133]

Also inscribed on the monument's sides are the names of Jacques de Dixmude, Albrecht (Albert) Ardevelde, Victor Baetens, and Felix Steens, labeled as "pionniers de l'œuvre colonial / pioniers van het koloniaal werk." (pioneers of the colonial work.) The site is a centrally-located and sometimes busy city park in Halle between the train station and downtown.[134] The day-long inauguration festivities at its unveiling provide an example of how these markers were national productions that acted to unify the French- and Dutch-speaking people of the country.[135]

Other native sons of Halle who also died in the Congo are not honored on the memorial, including missionary Jean-Baptiste Brichaux, who went by the name Frère Mathieu, and Louis Nelis. Brichaux died in 1944, so after the monument's inauguration.[136] Nelis died in Leopoldville in 1919, thus years before the monument's unveiling, but after 1908, meaning Nelis was not a "colonial pioneer" of the first hour. One local native who was a colonial pioneer yet who is not

Statue to colonial pioneers, Halle, 2018

honored on the Halle marker is Ernest Courtois, one of the very first Belgians to travel to the Congo. Courtois was a pharmacist who departed for central Africa on 1 August 1883, nearly two years before the CFS even came into being. Assigned to go on the Hanssens expedition of 1884, Courtois fell ill and died of hematuria during the night of 25-26 June, 1884, near Basoko.[137]

When this author last visited the sculpture in May 2018, it looked as if someone had recently put red paint on the African figure's head and perhaps elsewhere, and that it had been cleaned. Traces of the red substance remained.

Different groups have taken additional actions at other monuments. The activist group CADTM has pushed for the removal of a plaque commemorating Liege's dead that pro-empire enthusiasts, including colonial veterans groups, installed in 1934. Those who have advocated for removal have argued that such historical markers are fundamentally untruthful:

Des citoyens, et notamment des jeunes, entrant dans le hall de l'hôtel de ville de la ville de Liège, ou allant de la rue du Trône vers la place Royale à Bruxelles, passent devant la plaque saluant l'œuvre coloniale ou devant la statue équestre de Léopold II. Des citoyens passent devant la statue de Léopold II érigée à Ostende en front de mer. Ils voient un Léopold II majestueux avec, en contrebas, des Congolais tendant leurs mains reconnaissantes. Seul commentaire: le rôle civilisateur de Léopold II pour libérer les Congolais de la traite des esclaves... Il est urgent de rétablir la vérité historique et d'arrêter de mentir à nos enfants, de mentir aux citoyens belges, d'arrêter d'insulter la mémoire des victimes, des descendants des victimes et des descendants des Congolais qui ont subi dans leur chair, dans leur dignité, une domination absolument terrible.

(Citizens, and notably young people, entering into the foyer of the city hall of Liege, or going from the rue du Trône toward the place Royale in Brussels, passing before the plaque saluting the colonial work or before the equestrian statue of Leopold II. Citizens passing in front of the statue of Leopold II erected in Ostend that faces the sea. They see a majestic Leopold II with, below him, Congolese reaching up their hands, gratefully. The only interpretation [possible]: the civilizing role of Leopold II to liberate the Congolese from the slave trade… It is urgent to reestablish the historical truth and to stop lying to our children, lying to Belgian citizens, to stop insulting the memory of the victims, the descendents of the victims, and the descendents of the Congolese who suffered, in their flesh, in their dignity, an absolutely terrible domination.)[138]

City councilor Messaouad Barkat's October 2006 speech asking for the removal of the plaque in Liege's historic hôtel de ville met with strong resistance.[139] Around the same time, protestors doused a statue of Belgium's second king in Ekeren with red paint, which was repeated at least once, in November 2009; someone set up a Facebook page calling for its removal.[140] In 2008, wearing a shirt that read "Leopold 2 – serial killer," artist Théophile de Giraud climbed up on top of the Leopold II equestrian statue at the place du Trône and doused it with red paint.[141] One June 27, 2010, someone draped, "un collier fait de mains coupées," (a necklace of [knitted] hands,) over the same statue.[142] De Stoeten Ostendenoare in 2013 attacked the bust of Leopold II in the Prinses Clementinaplein in Ostend with a red smoke bomb.[143] When this author visited the bust in 2018, it bore marks of someone having tried to cut off Leopold II's nose with a power saw.[144]

Leopold II (1835-1909)

Location: Brussels, place du Trône

Sculptors: Thomas Vinçotte, Frans Huygelen

Architect: François Malfait

Inauguration: 15 November 1926

Funded/built by: Baron Carton de Wiart; Albert I; Princess Stéphanie; public subscription

This statue is probably the country's most prominent monument to Leopold II.[145] It comprises a large bronze equestrian statue on a stone base prominently situated in the place du Trône, right next to the Royal Palace and on the city's inner ring road.

As unpopular as Belgium's second king was by the end of his reign, within days of his death on 17 December 1909 a committee had formed to build a monument in his memory.[146] The effort was officially announced in the *Moniteur* of 31 May 1914, and a national committee was put together. King Albert I gave 100,000 francs, and Princess Stéphanie, one of Leopold II's daughters,

Equestrian statue of Leopold II, Brussels, 2018

another 20,000. Other major donors included members of the aristocracy and military and prominent political figures. Mining company Union Minière de Haut-Katanga (UMHK), which of course owed its very existence to the deceased sovereign, provided the materials for the statue from the Belgian Congo itself for a bronze alloy of copper, tin, and perhaps pewter.[147] Several colonial companies gave large sums, including the Banque d'Outre-mer (10,000 francs) and the UMHK (3,000 francs).[148] All told, the public fundraising campaign was oversubscribed, collecting 625,000 francs by August 1914.[149] The statue was inaugurated in a large ceremony on 15 November 1926, Saint Leopold's Day, and also Belgium's Fête de la Dynastie.[150] Still, some in the public jeered and made fun of the statue, suggesting Leopold's enduring unpopularity.[151]

The place du Trône monument was conceived, funded, and inaugurated as a national commemoration, but because of Leopold II's prominent role in overseas colonialism, it unavoidably celebrated the country's colonialism as well. Yet in appearance, the monument is not colonial, with a simple inscription that reads "REGI BELGARUM, 1865-1909, PATRIA MEMOR," which could be translated as "the homeland remembers" or "the native city remembers." (Leopold was born in Brussels.) Even if its appearance suggests no colonial connection, its placement in public space connects it to overseas expansionism and the civilizing mission. A bird's eye view of the statue's position reveals that it mirrors the placement of the statue of Godefroid de Bouillon—another equestrian statue, the first in Brussels—on the opposite, western side of the Royal Palace. Moreover, numerous parallels connect Leopold II and Godefroid across the eight centuries that separate them in time. Godefroid (ca. 1060-1100)—who some say was from Brabant—was a knight, lord, and eventually a duke, while Leopold II, who was from Brabant, was Duke of Brabant before ascending the royal throne. Like Leopold II, Godefroid led a crusade to fight against Arabs overseas, in his case not in the Congo but in the Levant, and both men tried to expand the realm of Christendom, whatever their motivations. As Leopold II became *roi-souverain* of an overseas colony, the CFS, so did Godefroid become ruler of his own overseas kingdom, in Jerusalem.[152]

The place du Trône monument became iconic, reproduced in many forms over the years and becoming a symbol of Leopold II and empire. Because the fundraising for the memorial was oversubscribed, surplus monies were used to cast a similarly-sized statue that was put up in the Belgian Congo capital of Leopoldville (Kinshasa). Other duplicates were produced as well, including a smaller-sized reproduction in bronze in Elisabethville (Lubumbashi).[153] The monument's image or silhouette could be seen in innumerable photographic reproductions, which found their way into various publications over many years.[154]

Like a number of other prominent colonial monuments, the place du Trône statue is a destination to pay tribute to Leopold II and Belgian colonialism that in more recent years has become a site of protest. The monument was a site of pilgrimage for colonials throughout the state rule years, offering opportunities to laud the civilizing mission and sustain a positive image of a rehabilitated monarch.[155] In 1960, after his dismissal as head of the Armée nationale congolaise, General Émile Janssens made a scene in front of the monument: almost immediately upon his return to Brussels, he visited the statue, placed a bouquet of flowers before it, and was widely quoted as having said, in reference to Congo's new leaders, "Sire, ils vous l'ont cochonné." (Sire, they have botched it up.)[156]

As at the Cinquantenaire Park Monument du Congo, pilgrimages to the place du Trône statue continued into the twenty-first century.[157] One such commemoration took place after it was cleaned and restored for the country's 175th anniversary of independence in 2005. On 24 June of that year, the shiny, refurbished statue was re-inaugurated in a ceremony organized by the Association des Anciens et Amis de la Force publique du Congo Belge, a group that annually pays hommage at the site.[158]

Numerous protesters have used the monument to contest the country's colonial past. In 2008, artist Théophile de Giraud climbed atop the equestrian statue and dumped red paint on it.[159] In 2010, a group placed a harness of crocheted hands around the horse's neck to call the public's attention to the *mains coupées* of the red rubber era.[160] The monument was further vandalized in 2015 after the city proposed and then cancelled a ceremony to honor the king's contributions to the Brussels area, and then once again in 2018, when someone doused the statue with red liquid.[161] In all these instances, authorities have carefully cleaned and restored the statue so that any casual passerby or tourist would have no idea the monument had been defaced in the past.

Colonial pioneers
Location: Liege, hôtel de ville, *salle des pas perdus*
Sculptor: Théo Derocher[162]
Inauguration: 24 June 1934
Funded/built by: Liege section of the Association des Vétérans coloniaux

Plaque dedicated to colonial pioneers, Liege, 2018

Liege is known as having been the seat of the Prince-Bishopric of Liege and, later, for its role resisting the German onslaught at the start of World War I. Many visitors might not suspect the city also has connections with overseas colonialism in Africa, including having sent dozens of men to explore, fight, and die for Leopold II's colonial venture.

This plaque "Aux 75 Coloniaux Liégeois Morts pour la Civilisation, 1876 — 1908" is located in the *salle des pas perdus* of the city's historic, three hundred year-old city hall.[163] It lists three columns of names of men from the city who died in central Africa before 1908. Similar to other such markers in the country, many of those honored died young and because of illness, for example dysentery, including the two best known among them, Lucien Bia (1852-1892) and Camille Coquilhat (1853-1891). Bia led several early expeditions, including one during which Jules Cornet discovered Katanga's great underground riches, before Bia died of an unspecified illness of the liver. He was also celebrated in other memorials, including busts like the one on display for decades in the Tervuren Museum. Coquilhat was a central figure in the earliest years of European action in central Africa, serving alongside Stanley to explore and set up posts as of 1882, under the banner of the AIA. Coquilhat eventually rose to become Vice Governor-General, a position he held at the time of his death in 1891 of dysentery. He was born in Liege, and his mortal remains were repatriated to Antwerp where a statue by Comte Jacques de Lalaing was put up in 1895 to honor him.

The plaque in Liege was inaugurated during the traditional colonial festivities of the year 1934.[164] Its unveiling was a moment to celebrate not just the colonial enterprise but also the city of Liege, and in his speech Mayor Xavier Neujean not only honored the men but also heaped praise on Wallonia, Liege, and the locals for their pioneering work.[165] There were busts to Baron Jacques de Dixmude and Baron Tombeur de Tabora in the *salle des pas perdus* at some point as well, and a memorial to Colonel Louis Haneuse (1853-1938) was inaugurated in 1939 or 1940 at his tomb in the Liege cemetery.[166] The funerary memorial to Haneuse continues to be a site of pilgrimage where former colonials go to lay wreaths.[167]

In 2006-2007, there were multiple attempts to call attention to the plaque and to open debate about racism, the country's colonial history, and the role of Liege and its citizens in it, one of which was spearheaded by the activist group CADTM. They were unsuccessful and the plaque remained. There was a thorough restoration of the *salle des pas perdus* in 2014, and the decision was made to keep the plaque, and it remains there today.[168]

Leopold II (1835-1909)
Location: Ostend, Prinses Clementinaplein
Sculptor: Thomas Vinçotte
Inauguration: pre-World War II; 1986 in current location[169]

This bronze bust of Leopold II on a marble socle is one of several colonial-related memorials and monuments in Ostend. It was first displayed in Ostend's "second" Kursaal, the large seaside center for theater, concerts, and other entertainment. German occupying forces destroyed the Kursaal during World War II, after which the bust was transferred to the Ostend Historical Museum De Plate, which itself moved locations several times over the years.[170] In February 1986, the memorial was transferred to its current location, in a corner of the central and verdant Prinses Clementinaplein, just a few hundred meters from the large equestrian monument to Leopold II on the city's boardwalk.[171]

The bust at Clementinaplein is suggestive of how memorials to Leopold II have become sites of protest about the colonial past, and also how those protests have gained little traction. One 2008 attack saw the statue doused with red paint on November 15, St. Leopold's Day, and just a few weeks afterward artist Théophile de Giraud mounted the Brussels equestrian statue of the king

Bust of Leopold II, Ostend, 2018

to cover it with red paint. A statement released by the unknown assailants in Ostend criticized the royal family, suggesting the attack was more about the monarchy than colonialism.[172] More recently the bust was attacked with red smoke bombs by the group De Stoeten Ostendenoare, the same activists who severed a hand from an African figure on Ostend's Leopold II equestrian statue. But again, in a statement the attackers suggested anarchist tendencies more than a desire to attack the kingdom's colonial past or the city's reluctance to face up to it.[173] The bronze was subsequently cleaned, but one could still in 2018 detect traces of red paint, and close inspection revealed that someone had taken a power saw to Leopold's nose to remove it from his face. The bust in 2018 was accompanied by an explanatory plaque, although it said nothing about colonialism.[174]

The memorial to Leopold II at the Prinses Clementinaplein also highlights the leading role sculptor Thomas Vinçotte played in the commemoration of Leopold II and Belgian empire. Born in Borgerhout (Antwerp) in 1850, Vinçotte studied at the Academy of Fine Arts in Bruges, then in Paris. He eventually worked at the National Fine Arts School in Antwerp. His bust of Leopold II in the Prinses Clementinaplein is the same as other such bronzes in Auderghem and Parc Duden in Forest, among others. He aslo created the same form of Leopold II but made entirely of ivory that for years graced the *entrée d'honneur* of the Tervuren Museum of the Congo. Aside from these busts, his other major works to Leopold II and the Congo colony are the place du Trône equestrian statue, the Colonial Monument in the Parc du Cinquantenaire, and the sculpture atop the Arc du Cinquantenaire, completed with Jules Lagae.

Justin Malfeyt (1862-1924)
Location: Ostend, Leopold Park
Sculptor: Frans Huygelen
Architect: Paul Jaspar
Inauguration: 1929[175]
Funded/built by: committee[176]

Memorial to Justin Malfeyt, Ostend, 2018

Malfeyt first embarked for Leopold II's CFS in 1891, where he ended up playing a major role suppressing revolts and extending the king's control, particularly in eastern regions of the colony, where he became an administrator. Like many others, Malfeyt then continued in colonial service after Belgium's 1908 takeover of the Congo, becoming Vice Governor General of the Belgian Congo in March 1909. It was during his seventh extended stay in the colony that World War I broke out, and after the victory of Entente colonial forces in eastern Africa, he was named royal commissioner for occupied territories in (former) German East Africa. He returned to Belgium in December 1919, retired two years later, and died in 1924.[177]

At the center of the memorial is a bronze profile of Malfeyt in military uniform with a bronze wreath above it.[178] Originally located further east in the park, it was moved because of the construction of Leopold II-laan, and today stands at the northeast entrance of Parc Léopold.[179] The monument's inscription reads

Justino Malfeyt

MDCCCLX [sic] – MCMXXIV

QVI IN HORRIDIS AFRICAE REGIONIBUS

AUCTORE ET AUSPICE LEOPOLDO II

EGREGIAM OPERAM NAVAVIT

CIVES MEMORES

[The citizens remember

Justin Malfeyt

1860 [sic, b. 1862] – 1924

Who in the rugged regions of Africa

under the authority and auspices of Leopold II

rendered distinguished service]

The reaction to all these attacks has been general indifference and official opposition, even if there have been press accounts including television and radio reports following some of them.[180] The interest group "Mémoires coloniales" has tried to awaken debate on the colonial past, including the financial gain Belgium enjoyed because of the Congo, represented in Leopold II's adornment of the capital and Ostend; with little effect. Mémoires coloniales has managed to broach the subject of possible reparations, but the concept appears to have no traction among the broader public.[181]

It is telling that the various busts and statues that have been attacked have all been restored: the paint scrubbed off in Ekeren and Brussels; graffiti removed from the stele supporting Leopold II's bust in Parc Duden outside Brussels; and so forth. One exception is the hand of the African cut off in Ostend, which has not been replaced, although one can argue this was because of indifference more than anything else. Over four years the short film *Sikitiko*, which called attention to the attack and the monument, garnered only 5,670 views on YouTube.[182] An anti-colonial tour of Brussels run by CADTM in September 2008 gathered a mere 70 people, some of whom were former colonials who had tagged along "soucieux de défendre les aspects positifs de la colonization." (anxious to defend the positive aspects of colonization.)[183] When you consider that there are more than a dozen monuments to Leopold II still standing in cities across Belgium today—not to mention his tomb in the easily-accessible royal crypt in Laeken—the fact that there have not been more defacements is indicative of the apathy on the issue.

One group in Belgian society not indifferent to attacks on colonial monuments is former colonials. By the first decade of the twenty first century, the number of former colonials had declined to around 30,000. Year after year, different organizations of these former colonials organized public commemorative displays at monuments in various cities from Namur to Hasselt to Brussels to honor Leopold II and uphold a positive narrative of the country's past actions in Africa. After the 2004 attack on the monument to Leopold II in Ostend, several pro-colonialists tried, unsuccessfully, to have it repaired. More than five decades after independence, many former colonials remained highly nostalgic, maintained stereotypical "colonialist" views, did

Leopold II (1835-1909)
Location: Ekeren, Markt, next to Sint-Lambertuskerk[184]
Sculptor: Joseph Ducaju[185]
Architect: Eugène Gife
Inauguration: 1873

Statue of Leopold II, Ekeren, 2018

This statue of a young Leopold II, already recognizable with his trademark beard, bears the simple inscription, "Aan Z. M. Leopold II, 7.7.1873." It was the first public statue erected to honor the country's second king, and considering it was put up years before the 1876 Brussels Geographical Conference even took place and more than a decade before the declaration of the CFS, it is no surprise that there is nothing colonial about its appearance. It was originally part of a town water pump, and was put up to mark the king's brief August 1869 visit to Ekeren, just a few years after his ascent to the throne. Although not colonial in origin and form, the Ekeren statue has become "colonial" over time as people have used it as a site to protest the king, vandalizing it several times, including by dousing it with red paint. It has been cleaned and restored each time. In response, the communal government in 2018 took the decision to add an explanatory plaque about the king's role in colonialism, even though the statue is not itself colonialist in appearance or origin.[186]

not question the colonial past, and viewed empire as something that was necessary since whites were dominant and black Congolese inferior and in "need" of colonial rule.[187] The Congo's decline only reinforced their belief that colonialism had been not only good but necessary.[188] Former colonials kept their positive interpretation of history alive by means of letters to newspapers, social media, their own *cercles coloniaux*, and, as noted, ceremonies at public colonialist markers. One association, Mémoires du Congo et du

Ruanda-Urundi and its Dutch-speaking division Afrika Getuigenissen, not only continued to propagate a positive vision of empire, it began recording interviews with Belgians, Congolese, and others to capture memories of the colonial era.[189] A number of *cercles coloniaux* continued to put out their own publications, which, as can be seen in this chapter's epigraph, gestured toward potential excesses but always adhered to a hard line that maintained colonialism was on balance a very positive stage in central Africa's history. As noted, even though the number of former colonials necessarily declined after 1960, the number of associations that made up the pro-colonial "lobby" in Belgium actually grew.[190] Their sometimes public but more often than not behind-the-scenes defense of an upbeat view of the country's history in Africa helped underpin an enduring, largely positive view of Leopold II and Belgian imperialism.

The colonial experience on stage

There was an efflorescence of theatrical productions and collaborations in the first years of the new century. In 2003, director Raven Ruëll dusted off Hugo Claus' *Het leven en de werken van Leopold II* (1970) for a production at the KVS, after which it was taken to Kinshasa and various theaters in both Dutch- and French-speaking Belgium, including to the Molière theater in Matonge and to Ostend by 2013. In 2005, Mark Twain's "King Leopold's Soliloquy" was performed, which touched a nerve; some requested it be banned.[191] The Wallonia-Brussels community established the Centre Wallonie-Bruxelles à Kinshasa with both a theater and a library to foster exchanges and Congolese artistic production.[192] Beginning in 2005 the Festival KVS<>Congo linked Belgium and the Congo through a growing collaboration. KVS members travel to Kinshasa to hold theater workshops, to work with Congolese actors and other artists, and to co-produce performances, making theater a contact point, including at festivals in Brussels and, since 2009, the festival Connexion Kin in Kinshasa. If one considers KVS' connections to the Congo in context, it is clear that productions related to the Congo are just a fraction of what they do. Still, the KVS in many ways was on the forefront of bringing artistic productions regarding the diaspora, Congolese, Congo, and the colonial past to the Belgian public.

A breakthrough was David Van Reybrouck's *Missie*, first performed in 2007. This monologue by white missionary Grégoire Vanneste, who was played by Bruno Vanden Broecke, was drawn from Van Reybrouck's interviews with some fifteen missionaries in Kinshasa, Bukavu, Kamina,

Victor Roelens (1858-1947)

Location: Ardooie, city park

Sculptors: Frans Tinel (sculptor), Vuylsteke (mason)

Architect: Lucien Lattrez

Inauguration: 1952[193]

Statue of Victor Roelens, Ardooie, 2003

Victor Roelens left Belgium for Algeria in 1880 to join Cardinal Lavigerie's White Fathers. He was ordained a priest by Lavigerie in 1884, traveled to eastern Africa in 1891, and from there continued on to the eastern Congo. In east Africa he was for a time a companion of Alphonse Jacques (later Baron Jacques de Dixmude) as well as of Frenchman Captain Leopold Louis Joubert, as those two soldiers combatted slaving in Africa. In 1893, Roelens founded Baudouinville or Bouwdewijnstad (today Kirungu) in eastern Congo, and two years later became the first bishop in the CFS. He was a tireless missionary, spending the vast majority of his life in the Congo. He died there in 1947 at the age of 89.[194]

This bronze statue to Roelens' memory was put up quickly. Indeed, the inscription on the back of the monument reads, "First stone dedicated by Monseigneur Lamiroy, placed by Minister Wigny, 16-9-47," indicating a date little more than a month after Roelens died on 5 August 1947. Today the statue sits in Ardooie's small city park in the center of town. It was originally located in a more prominent position on the Marktplein next to Sint-Martinuskerk, but was moved to its present location in 1998-1999, where it is visible to passersby and drivers moving along Mgr. Roelensstraat, another hometown honor to the churchman.

The statue emphasizes Roelens' work as a founder and missionary, depicting him planting a cross on a globe that bears an outline map of Belgium's African territories. The inscription reads, "Monseigneur Victor Roelens, White Father, Vicar Apostolic of the Upper Congo, First Bishop of the Belgian Congo, Roman

Count, Brilliant Missionary, Ardooie 1858, Badouinville 1947."[195] The transfer
of the statue from the Marktplein to the city park is not the only change, for
the inscription seems to have been re-done at some point over the years, for it
used to read "Z. Exc." for "Zijne Excellentie" and was in relief, whereas now it is
inscribed.[196]

and elsewhere in the Congo, men who collectively had spent many years in
Africa.[197] *Missie* lets the missionaries speak for themselves. Father Grégoire
touches on topics including missionary education, personal choices, the call
to service, travel to and from Belgium, and the rough conditions of living
in the Congo: no electricity, bad roads, corruption, disease, insects, and
sometimes terrible food. The monologue conveys confidence and faith,
while also revealing moments of self-doubt. Criticism from the missionaries
also emerge: about the materialism of life in Belgium; about the attitudes
of NGO workers in Africa; and about the terrible violence of the 1990s
under Laurent Kabila and Rwanda's Paul Kagame, including rape, pillage,
mutilations, and murder.

Overall, *Missie* presented a view of missionary action during and after
the colonial era from the vantage point of missionaries, and as such it was
a sympathetic portrayal of both the *mission civilisatrice* and proselytization
in Africa specifically. What shocks in *Missie* is how, despite years living in
Africa, the missionaries who speak through Father Grégoire tell no stories
of personal, close interactions with Africans. When Grégoire speaks of the
importance of camaraderie and friendship, he refers to friendships with white
European missionaries, not their charges. This is resonant of the analysis of
Bambi Ceuppens, who traced the distance separating not only missionaries
but also administrators and other colonials from those over whom they
ruled.[198] Absent from Vanneste's monologue is any self-questioning about
his fundamental mission, or self-doubt as to the Christian presence in central
Africa, or reflections on the connection between imperialism and missionizing, or praise for African cultures.[199]

Missie was a success that was well-received by both the francophone and
Flemish press. "Het stuk dat vertolkt werd door Bruno Vanden Broecke kreeg
niet alleen een belangrijke prijs, maar werd ook laaiend positief ontvangen
door pers en publiek." (The play, which was performed by Bruno Vanden
Broecke, not only won an important award, but also received wildly positive
responses from the press and the public.)[200] The play garnered Van Reybrouck
the honor of being named laureate by winning the honorary Arkprijs van het
Vrije woord, and the play went on to be performed elsewhere, for instance
as part of the Festival Theaterformen in Braunschweig, Germany, in 2010.[201]

Constant De Deken (1852-1896)
Location: Wilrijk, the Bist
Sculptor: Jean-Marie Hérain
Inauguration: 28 August 1904
Funded/built by: commune of Wilrijk

Statue of Constant De Deken, Wilrijk, 2018

De Deken, born in Wilrijk in 1852, became a Scheutist missionary, embarking for western China in 1881 where he explored and traveled through Tibet with Prince Henri d'Orléans—great grandson of Louis-Philippe of France—and Frenchman Gabriel Bonvalot. After returning to Belgium he was told to go to the Congo, and he made two stays there in the 1890s, during the second of which he died of fever, at Boma, in March 1896.[202]

Within a few short years of De Deken's death, an Antwerp committee made up of local dignitaries organized the funding of a monument to him, which was erected on the Bist, the central square of Wilrijk. The monument was located on the Bist itself for a century before being moved across the street to a new yet very close-by location facing the Bist, just steps from its original location. As in the past, the Bist remains today a central location between the city's main shopping zone, the town hall, the police department, and several banks.

For more than a century the statue was left to explain itself. The bronze sculpture shows De Deken standing and "baptizing a native" who kneels in intense prayer at his feet.[203] The monument's inscription reads, "Father De Deken, Missionary, Explorer in Tibet, Pioneer of the Congo, 1852 1896."

Due to construction work on the Bist and the surrounding streets, the statue was taken down around 2009, and then in 2014 came under fire. Antwerp resident and activist Seckou Ouologuem claimed that the statue's depiction was offensive to many groups in Antwerp and that it should either be removed to a museum, or at the very least accompanied by an explanatory plaque. One journalist claimed that part of the statue's offensiveness was that it depicts De

Deken resting one foot on the back of the African kneeling before him.[204] Quick examination of the statue shows, however, that the foot in question is rest-ing on a tree trunk before which the African kneels. The city council disagreed with protestors, deciding that "the statue would not be hidden," and would be returned to the Bist, now accompanied by an explanatory plaque by the city.[205] The plaque sketches a brief biography of De Deken, mentions the violence of the Leopoldian period, and cryptically, and almost reluctantly admits that the statue "expresses the relationships between Europeans and Africans in the Congo Free State at the time" it was first built.[206]

The positive portrayal of the Belgian missionary in *Missie* reflected not a renewed interest in religion—as the play's protagonist put it, "en Belgique [...] les églises sont vides et les prisons sont pleines." (In Belgium [...] the churches are empty and the prisons are full.)—but a nostalgia for missionaries and their work.[207] Already in 2005, a VRT/RTBF poll to choose "The Greatest Belgian" saw missionary Pater Damiaan (Jozef De Veuster) come in first in the Flemish program and third with RTBF, besting Andreas Vesalius, Hergé, Georges Simenon, and Peter Paul Rubens. A further sign of such fond memories was Annemie Struyf's documentary "In God's Name," which tracked down some of the very last of the Flemish female missionaries.[208] This is not to say *Missie* escaped criticism, because it provoked a public exchange on the historical and ongoing effects of missionary activity. Didier Goyvaerts, a professor at Universiteit Antwerpen and Vrije Universiteit Brussel (VUB), called Van Reybrouck an apologist for missionaries for having too often taken his informants at their word, sometimes quoting them and their justifications verbatim. Goyvaerts insisted missionaries were agents of oppression and domination.[209] Goyvaerts was in turn dressed-down by Hilde Kieboom, president of the Community of Sant'Egidio in Antwerp and columnist for *De Morgen*, whose refutation of Goyvaerts' claims not only praised Van Reybrouck's play but also pointed out a key fact: *Missie*, a piece centered on missionary activity in the Congo, had been written by an atheist and was being well-received by largely non-Catholic and secular audiences.[210]

Recent years have witnessed additional theater performances imbued with colonial themes. KVS has taken its Congo project to Ostend's Theater Aan Zee and in 2010 organized a reading and debate with Adam Hochschild.[211] Rik Van Uffelen and Greet Verstraete brought *King Leopold's Soliloquy* back out at Arsenaal in Mechelen in spring 2010 and at the Theater ann Zee in Ostend in the summer of that year. All this said, if you look at the many cultural outlets in both French- and Dutch-speaking regions, there are many more productions that have nothing to do with the colonial past, which still remain few in number.

Anniversaries and reminiscences

A series of anniversaries followed one after another in the first decade of the third millennium, eliciting a slew of events related to empire's past. The year 2005 marked the 175th anniversary of Belgium's independence and the 120th anniversary of the founding of the CFS. Thierry Michel's documentary *Congo River* appeared the following year. One year later, in 2007, CIVA's (Centre International pour la Ville, l'Architecture et le Paysage) "Congo paysages urbains regards croisés" exposition of 11 young Congolese artists and 3 Belgian artists were part of the 150 artists of the festival Yambi that highlighted the Congo.[212] In 2007 also, the Centre Wallonie-Bruxelles in Paris held its 16th Annual Quinzaine du cinéma francophone festival, which gave the Democratic Republic of the Congo a place of honor.[213] Several partners, including the Tervuren Museum, the Cinematek, and KADOC (Documentatie- en Onderzoekscentrum voor Religie, Cultuur en Samenleving) began a project to preserve the film patrimony of central Africa.[214]

Another anniversary fell in 2008, the year marking the centenary of the turnover of the colony to Belgium, as well as ninety years since the armistice ending World War I and fifty years since the 1958 World's Fair. A show that year which revealed how memory, colonialism, culture, immigration, and politics mixed was the 2008 exhibition by the commune of Ixelles (Brussels) called "Black Paris – Black Brussels," a show that, "reversed the traditional thesis that Europe brought culture to Africa."[215] The exposition drew together a solid array of work from African and other black artists, such as Chéri Samba, as well as Europeans and others who had drawn inspiration from the colonial past or African cultures, including Luc Tuymans. As museum curator Martine Boucher said about the *artistes noirs* represented in the show, "ces artistes s'inscrivent dans notre histoire et font partie intégrante de notre culture." (these artists are part of our history and form an integral part of our culture.)[216] Still, a main reason the show was brought to Ixelles was politics. The show launched in Germany, originally called "Black Paris," and was shown at the Iwalewa-Haus in Bayreuth and the World Cultures Museum in Frankfurt. It grew to include "Black Brussels" after the Musée des Arts derniers and the Mairie de Paris pulled out and organizers needed an additional venue and financial backing.[217] At the time, communal elections were looming in Ixelles, where the Matonge quarter is located, and local officials thought the exhibit might be one way to gain the favor of some voters. Still, the Ixelles exhibit was undoubtedly a success in the eyes of its organizers and received a very favorable reception in the press.[218]

The year of the Black Paris-Black Brussels exhibit was also the centenary of Belgium's takeover of the Congo, and it was marked by a renewed diplomatic crisis leading to a mini-break between Joseph Kabila's government and that of Yves Leterme (CD&V – Christen-Democratisch en Vlaams), another chapter in the perennial up-and-down relationship between the Congo and Belgium.[219] Part of the dispute was the much more direct diplomacy under Foreign Affairs Minister Karel De Gucht in Leterme's government.[220] Belgium had offered assistance to the Congo during the Mobutu era in various ways, including aid through its Office de coopération au développement (OCD). De Gucht baldly stated that if Belgium was to continue sending millions of Euros to the Kabila regime, it had better clean up its act. Accused by some of neo-colonialism for preaching to the Congolese, De Gucht replied that a normal, straightforward approach acknowledging the Congo government's terrible shortcomings was the approach to take. "If that is what neocolonialism is, than I am a neocolonialist," he said.[221]

These anniversary years continued to reverberate among the public at large. The year 2008 led to calls to commemorate the "soldat inconnu congolais," and new calls for reparations from Belgium to the Congo.[222] In 2008, Extra City in Antwerp put on the exhibition "Letter to Leopold." Things had reached such a state that some issues did reach public debate, for example when the 15-21 November 2008 edition of the popular *Télé-Moustique* was dedicated to the issue of reparations and the Belgian colonial past, with on its cover a photoshopped image of Leopold II's statue in the Jardin du Roi being lifted off its socle. The year 2009, which marked a century since Leopold II's death, saw some scholars take advantage of the centenary to present reconsiderations of the king at a March conference that resulted in a publication about Leopold that appeared simultaneously in French and Flemish.[223]

Generational change

By the first decade of the 21st Century, Belgium had done much to confront its colonial "demons," and yet for many people colonial issues were literally more distant—in time—as ever. A key reason behind this, of course, was generational change. This shift had been embodied as early as 1993, when Baudouin's younger brother, Albert II, came to the throne. Unlike for his brother, Africa did not hold a special place in the new king's heart. As Albert put it, quoted in this chapter's epigraph, "Africa was my brother's preserve, his fiefdom, and I'm not at all concerned with it."[224] This was even though Albert was already 26 when the Congo became self-governing, and despite the fact that he had traveled there.

At the dawn of the twenty-first century most people in both Belgium and the Congo had no direct experience of the colonial era. In October 2004, Foreign Affairs Minister De Gucht put it this way: "When the Congo gained independence in 1960, I was six. And 80 percent of the people now living there were not yet born."[225] As author David Van Reybrouck expressed it, quoted in this chapter's epigraph, a younger generation had not learned about the Congo, but was now eager to do so. Those who had grown to adulthood by the 2000s were born well after the loss of the Congo. "The common silence and/or indifference towards this particular episode of the national past underlines once again—but in a different way—the critical importance of the experience that was lived and transmitted by individuals. Except for a specific and limited group of people, the colonial period remains essentially an external reality that does not resonate with their own life."[226] Emblematic of this generational change was the death of Gérard Soete in 2000, the year Raoul Peck's *Lumumba* was released. Soete was one of the men who had disinterred Lumumba's body to dispose of it by cutting it into pieces and dissolving it in acid.

Generational change was at work among academics as well. "Ook weten-schappers zijn verlost van de grote polemiek: zij hebben geen emotionele band meer met Congo en bestuderen de kolonie *an sich*, zonder apologie of maatschappijkritiek." (Also scientists are freed from the great polemic: they no longer have an emotional connection with the Congo and study the colony for what it is, without apology or social criticism.)[227] A younger generation of Belgian scholars were inescapably detached from the Belgian Congo except for distant connections, for instance a forbear who once resided there.[228] A revival of the field of colonial history could be seen in the 2008 symposium "Belgium-Congo: History vs. Memory" hosted by Brussels-based CEGESOMA (Centre d'Études et de Documentation Guerre et Sociétés contemporaines/Studie- en Documentatiecentrum Oorlog en Hedendaagse Maatschappij). Whereas a couple decades earlier, historians working on colonial history were somewhat of an exotic species in Belgium, CEGESOMA in 2008 could draw together Belgian scholars working across a variety of fields, from film (Guido Convents), to history and historiography (Guy Vanthemsche), to Eurafricans and *métis-sage* (Lissia Jeurissen and Bambi Ceuppens), to the Lumumba commission (Emmanuel Gerard), among others, the entire symposium introduced by Foreign Affairs Minister De Gucht.[229] Sustained expertise manifested itself in works such as Filip De Boeck's ethnography of African urban place and its inhabitants, *Kinshasa: Tales of the Invisible City*.[230] One could find renewed efforts to promote Belgium's expertise on central Africa, for example in the recently-formed E-CA-CRE-AC, or "Belgisch Referentiecentrum voor

de expertise in centraal Afrika/Centre belge de référence pour l'expertise
sur l'Afrique centrale." Moreover, the colonial era was now so far removed
from the present that attention had fallen on the post-colonial era, and a
shift in the historiography began to occur, away from preoccupations with
neo-colonialism and colonizing powers' responsibility for the shortfalls of
independent countries like the Congo and toward a reassessment of the
shortcomings of independent African leaders and their governments.[231]

New research has "led to historical works outnumbering popular literature
on the subject," and it is unclear what affect this has had on Belgian culture
more generally. One scholar recently asserted that despite the flurry of publications by historians, their work remains "in the shadows (...) These writings
rarely reach the broader public, due mostly to their specialized subjects, different languages and publication by international publishing houses."[232] Other
scholars assert that students of Belgian colonial history clearly have reacted to
public debates about the past by allowing their research, and conclusions, to be
guided by public interests, and their work in turn has influenced far-reaching
cultural works; examples of the latter being Van Reybrouck's play *Missie* and his
blockbuster *Congo: A History*.[233] Congolese contributions to the historiography
of the Belgian colonial past have increased, for example the work of Osumaka
Likaka and Didier Gondola, both based in the U.S.; Isidore Ndaywel È Nziem
and Jean-Marie Mutamba, based in the Congo; Elikia M'Bokolo, who lives
between Paris and Kinshasa; among others. At independence in 1960, there
had been virtually no African students of higher education. The first history
diplômes de maîtrise (Master's degrees) were awarded only in 1970, and early
histories of central Africa were written by Americans and Europeans.[234] One
could see that a shift had occurred with the publication of Ndaywel È Nziem's
landmark *Histoire du Zaïre: De l'héritage ancien à l'âge contemporain*.[235] Even
at the turn of the century, however, research on the history of the Congo or
Belgian colonialism remained dominated by Europeans and Americans, as one
can see—to take just one example—from the participants at the international
colloquium "Colonial Violence in Congo" that took place at the Tervuren
Museum in 2005, where less than a handful of the more than two dozen
participants were from the Congo or of African heritage.

Colonial past, classroom present

As regards education, little on the colonial past was to be found in school
history curricula by the end of the twentieth century. As Guido Gryseels,
Tervuren Museum director from 2001 to the present, put it, "My generation

was brought up with the view that Belgium brought civilization to Congo, that we did nothing but good out there. I don't think that during my entire education I ever heard a critical word about our colonial past."[236] One scholar of textbooks wrote as recently as 2017 that, "Indeed where Belgian history textbooks do address the colonial past, it is the Catholic mission and the Belgian monarchy that continue [to] symbolise a redemptive liberation from savagery, barbarism, and primitivism."[237] Research suggests young Belgians in the 1990s, 2000s, and early 2010s simply did not know much about Belgium's colonial past. When I explained my research on Belgian colonial history to young people during an extended research stay in Brussels in 2002-2003, they responded by saying they knew basically zero about their country's colonial past.[238]

The lack of attention to atrocities in the Congo in Belgian textbooks is hardly exceptional.[239] Such texts in any country must cover a lot of ground, both in terms of geographic and chronological coverage as well as themes.[240] Many people have criticized Belgium for not coming to terms with its colonial past. One recent study concludes, "The growth in new imperial history or domestic post-colonial studies exploring Belgium's colonial past has not yet influenced the content or design of Belgian history curricula or textbooks."[241] This said, in some recent textbooks, the country's dark colonial chapter is anything but hidden. It is true you can find textbooks, as Guy Vanthemsche has, that still hew to a pro-colonialist, apologist view, such as Jean-Pierre Lefèvre's A la conquête du temps, which declares:

> When the Belgians arrived in the Congo, they found a population that was a victim of bloody rivalries and the slave trade. Belgian civil servants, missionaries, doctors, colonists and engineers civilized the black population step by step. They created modern cities, roads and railroads, harbours and airports, factories and mines, schools and hospitals. This work greatly improved the living conditions of the indigenous people.[242]

Other recent texts provide a broad context in which to contemplate overseas empire-building, and then delve into the Belgian case without shying away from embarrassing topics. In Histoire 3e/6e: Jalons pour mieux comprendre, for example, both atrocities of the Leopoldian era and Belgian failures at the time of decolonization are clearly dealt with, as is the subject of the kingdom's contemporaneous relationship with its former colony, and the post-colonial debate as to Belgium's responsibility (humanitarian, political, or otherwise) in central Africa. Students are presented with both sides of the debate, the textbook concluding that the answer probably lies somewhere between the two extremes of fuller engagement and disengagement.[243] Other textbooks addressed the controversies surrounding imperialism head-on and raised difficult questions, such as one French-language text in use in 2010 that asked whether it was legitimate that European museums keep objects that are part of the African patrimony.[244] By the 2010s, many textbooks provided nuanced views of European imperialism in the Congo and elsewhere, including primary documents from the time depicting atrocities, and incorporating work from Congolese scholars.[245]

Conclusion

By the first decade of the twenty-first century, clear divides had emerged between Belgians who viewed colonialism favorably, those who took the opposite view, and those who were generally or completely indifferent. It is true that many remained either uninformed about, or indifferent to, the country's colonial past, in particular those born after 1960 and recent immigrants and their children. Most Belgians, if they knew much about colonialism, continued to associate the Leopoldian period (1885-1908) with the Belgian state rule period (1908-1960), conflating them if not considering them one and the same.[246] Former colonials generally had a positive view of Belgian actions, which is not surprising considering their personal implication in them. In general, older Belgians, even if not personally implicated, held more favorable views of colonialism, much more so than younger people who, by contrast, more freely associated mutilations, exploitation, and so forth, with Belgian African rule. Older people tended to talk more about development when it came to issues of "exploitation," bringing up the hospitals, roads, and other infrastructure Belgian rule created in the Congo.[247] Some older people dismissed the claims of Hochschild's book as overblown, whereas many young folk took them to heart. At least in the southern, French-speaking part of the country, an opposition developed between two diametrically opposed extremist views of Belgian colonialism, one holding that Leopold II and colonialism were good, the other that Belgian imperialism was wholly bad.[249] Some passed from believing in a "mythe d'un roi génial et bienfaiteur" (myth of a brilliant king-benefactor) to the opposite extreme, believing in a "mythe d'un roi génocidaire." (myth of a genocidal king.)[250]

As controversy grew over Leopold II's CFS regime and colonialism more generally, another dividing line emerged: between the Dutch-speaking and francophone communities. The two populations did share many outlooks on the colonial past. For instance, both looked back on the 1950s with nostalgia as a golden age that preceded the Congo's descent into disorder and corruption. But Flemish cultural productions from the 1980s were on the whole more nostalgic. Flemish writers and television producers tended to emphasize more missionary activity, perhaps unsurprising considering most missionaries came from more Catholic Flanders. Whereas criticisms of colonial conquest and economic exploitation were acceptable, many cultural productions asserted that, in essence, missionaries were "ok," as seen in David Van Reybrouck's *Missie*. The worst abuses of colonialism were connected to Leopold II, his collaborators, and the colonial administration, which had been dominated by the francophone elite. To consider missionaries and the colonial administration as separate endeavors, in a sense, was not entirely historically inaccurate. Although many automatically associate Christian missionizing in sub-Saharan Africa with European conquest and rule, missionaries and colonial military men and administrators often worked more near than with each other. Not only did their actual day-to-day work have them often working at cross purposes, they viewed the world differently. "While missionaries and secular imperialists traveled similar geographical routes around the world, philosophically they moved on different planes."[251] The history of missionaries in the CFS was not one of straightforward collaboration with Leopold's regime. Belgian missionaries were slow to embrace their king's colonial vision, and foreign Protestant missionaries were among the first to bring the abuses of the CFS regime to international attention; Belgian Catholic missionaries were more reluctant to join the chorus of criticism. Post-1908 was a different story as missionaries and the administration worked in open, close coordination. As distance grew from the collaborationist stigma of World War II, and as Flanders' economy came to predominate from the 1960s, some Flemish memoirists, chroniclers, and others tended to accept a rather rosy view of missionary action in the Congo while expressing skepticism about the monarchy and the colonial past more generally, which worked to distance Flanders from the nation-state of Belgium. This also tended, however, to downplay the extreme degree to which Catholic missionaries work hand-in-glove with the Belgian colonial administration after 1908.

Among some older French-speaking Belgians, there was a reluctance to address controversial questions about their nation's colonial past because of how it might weaken the kingdom, a prospect that was more threatening in economically weaker Wallonia. Regionalism in the southern, francophone provinces was much weaker than its Flemish counterpart, unsurprising considering the troubled economy Wallonia suffered during an era of de-industrialization; inhabitants there needed the Kingdom of Belgium more than their Dutch-speaking counterparts in the north did. Now, support for the monarchy was greater in the south than in the north, a major shift from the immediate post-World War II era. At the time of the *Question royale*, Dutch speakers had supported the return of the king more than French speakers. When the 1950 referendum was held, the Flemish vote was 72 percent in favor of King Leopold III's return, whereas 58 percent of French speakers opposed it. By the twenty-first century, francophone Belgians were much more likely to embrace the kingdom's ruling dynasty than their Dutch-speaking confrères.

Chapter 6
2010 and Beyond

"Participer à une chasse au Katanga, c'est fouler la terre telle que Dieu l'a créée. [...] Le jardin de l'Éden? Il est ici, devant vous." (To take part in a hunt in Katanga is to tread upon the earth as God created it. [...] The Garden of Eden? It is here, in front of you.)[1] — *Le Roi du Congo*, 2012

"I live in Elsene, and if I'm sitting on the 95 bus going past Troon, it's disturbing to see the statue of a mounted Leopold II. As a Belgian of Congolese origins, I want to feel at home here, and that's not easy when you see statues of the oppressor of your ancestors."[2] — Tracy Bibo-Tansia, 2017

The year 2010 not only was a year of parliamentary elections, it also marked forty years of federalism in Belgium, dating back to the state reform of 1970, and a half century since the country had been without a colony, which was nearly as long as it had been a colonial power. This anniversary year was not only one in which the Congo and the colonial experience flooded the country's cultural scene, it and those that immediately followed also represented a unique generational conjuncture. Even though the number of former colonials and their children were perforce declining because of the tyranny of mortality, they were still present. And now they found their own inherent interest in colonial affairs paralleled—if not matched—by the curiosity of many younger Belgians, some of whom revisited the colonial past with verve. In contrast, in important ways the colonial past receded not only further in time during this period, but also in terms of its cultural relevance, and this because of younger generations coming to adulthood and recently-arrived immigrants and their children: for the majority of them the colonial experience simply did not resonate.

The fiftieth anniversary of Congo's independence led to an outpouring of reflections on the Congo of the time and of the past, all of which occurred in a context of political upheaval that fostered more positive expressions regarding the country's shared colonial past. The year 2010 witnessed innumerable paintings, films, television events, memoirs, press coverage, commemorations, and other cultural events in Belgium. RTBF produced the documentary series "Congo: 50 ans de l'indépendance—50 ans plus tard," which to judge by viewer letters was well-received by the public, including those of Congolese descent.[3] Colette Braeckman described the torrent of new books as "une véritable fièvre éditoriale" (a bona fide publishing fever).[4] *Le Soir* issued a double-DVD on 27 April containing Raoul Peck's *Lumumba* and Thierry Michel's documentary *Mobutu, roi du Zaïre*. François Ryckmans, journalist and grand-son of Pierre Ryckmans, published *Mémoires noires: Les Congolais racontent le Congo belge*.[5] The exposition "Mayombe: Masters of Magic," which drew on the Congolese collections of KU Leuven—many of the items having been donated by Scheutist Leo Bittremieux, as discussed earlier—was but one such exposition focused on the Congo.[6] In Antwerp, the Zuiderpershuis' "Afrik (In)dépendance 50" festival took place throughout the spring, and the FotoMuseum Antwerpen held the exhibition of Carl De Keyzer's arresting photography, "Congo belge en images."[7] The Afrika Filmfestival in Leuven, which each year put one African country in the spotlight, chose in 2010 to focus on the Congo. Celebrating fifteen years that year, the Afrika Filmfestival was a major forum to highlight African filmmaking, almost universally uncelebrated. Starting from modest roots in Leuven in the mid-1990s, by the second decade of the twenty-first century the film festival, under the leadership of Guido Convents, had become an established annual event with film screenings not only in Leuven and Brussels but in cities across the country.[8]

Even if innumerable images shown in Belgium in 2010 were fresh, for instance in the films shown as part of Afrika Festival, the 2010 festivities also led once more to a "recycling of images." One example is the Cinematek's "Caméra Congo" that showed fifteen films by Ernest Genval, Gérard De Boe and André Cauvin, all colonial-era productions created between 1925 and 1955.[9] Genval, De Boe, and Cauvin had been leading "go-to" directors for colonial authorities, and all three cast Belgian actions in central Africa in a positive light. "Les expositions se suivent, partout en Belgique, pour les 50 ans de l'indépendance de ce qui fut notre colonie," (Expositions follow one after another, throughout Belgium, for the 50 years of the independence of what was our colony) concluded one commentator.[10] David Van Reybrouck said that, "The word Congo used to have very dark connotations but today some of that darkness has lifted. There's even a kind of Congo mania in Belgium."[11] This said, long-term cultural issues preoccupying many people continued to weigh on many minds into the second decade of the century, in particular the kingdom's long-standing language/cultural divide.[12]

As Idesbald Goddeeris has pointed out, domestic political developments around the year 2010 were such that reflections on the colonial past generally refrained from dwelling on negative, let alone scandalous aspects of Belgium's past imperialism. The nationalist, separatist New Flemish Alliance's (N-VA)

Leopold II (1835-1909), P. J. Neuenhaus (d. 1905),
E. C. De Cooman (d. 1905)
Location: Auderghem, square du Souverain
Sculptor: Thomas Vinçotte
Architect: Armand Rambo[13]
Inauguration: 3 August 1930
Funded/built by: commune of Auderghem

Monument to Leopold II,
Auderghem, 2018

The building of this memorial was prompted by the country's centenary (1830-1930), which coincided with efforts by colonial veterans to build memorials in each of the country's communes that had lost at least one of its native sons in Africa during the CFS period. In this case, Auderghem, a commune in the Brussels region, decided to create a small *place*—today's square du Souverain—and a monument to Leopold II and two native sons who had died in the CFS: P. J. Neuenhaus and E. C. De Cooman. The inscription to these two foot soldiers of Leopold's empire reads, in French and Flemish, "Died in the Congo for Civilization." With these words the Auderghem memorial, like so many other such contemporary markers, makes specific reference to the *mission civilisatrice*, thereby justifying Belgian colonialism as an endeavor to bring a superior, European civilization to backward Africans.[14] Still, the commune's commemoration of the king in stone and bronze was actually motivated less for his role in securing a colony and more for what Leopold II did to remake the Brussels area, including being the driving force behind the laying out of roadways, including the boulevard du Souverain along which the square du Souverain is located.[15]

Like other memorials to Leopold II, the bust in Auderghem has served both as a site of pilgrimage, where pro-colonials lay wreaths of flowers to honor the king, and of protest. Some kind of explanatory plaque was placed on the stela at some point not long ago, but it has since been removed, leaving a kind of ugly square spot below the memorial's inscription. A May 2018 visit suggested that someone had colored the king's eyes, and that the bust had recently been cleaned (albeit not completely) after having been doused with red paint.

breakthrough at the polls in successive elections shook the political status quo and raised once again the question as to whether Belgium would split into two countries. At the federal level, the country went without a government for more than 500 days as negotiations dragged on. Anyone wishing to discuss the colonial past, even to criticize it, had to raise with the concept of "Belgium," perhaps thereby reinforcing the nation by discussing a shared past, albeit in a negative sense. But those on the left-wing of politics, including anti-racist organizations, who wanted to attack the colonial past likely recognized that to do so would also be to attack Belgium itself, potentially weakening the country at a critical juncture. Contrariwise, again according to Goddeeris, the N-VA shied away from raising questions about the country's history because of the risk that it would bring up issues of collaboration and World War II, dangerous terrain for Flemish nationalists.[16]

The end result was a series of cultural manifestations centered on the country's colonial experience that manifested confidence, perhaps even some nostalgia, rather than being self-critical or raising unsavory chapters of the past. One can consider *Ligablo, exposition bon marché* at the Royal Library in Brussels as indicative of the many small-scale yet impressive events put together for 2010. Organized by the NGO Coopération par l'Education et la Culture (CEC), *Ligablo* ran from 2010 into 2011 and focused on everyday items from the Congo that marked "the Congolese spirit and imaginary" since that country's independence, including King Baudouin's sword, which was famously stolen from him during a 1960 visit to the colony. "L'intention est de privilégier l'expérience, le contact et l'interpellation du public afin de déclencher une évocation vivante et forte de l'univers populaire congolais." (The intention is to privilege the experience, the contact, and the questioning of the public in order to set off a lively and powerful evocation of the popular Congolese universe.)[17] Even such small-scale exhibits could be intense, as its catalogue suggests, bringing together as it did commentary, albeit brief, from renowned scholars and writers including Valentin-Yves Mudimbe, Antoine Tshitungu Kongolo, and Alain Mabanckou.[18]

The Musée Royal de l'Armée in Brussels got in on the act, breaking what one historian called "un assourdissant silence qui durant des décennies a ignoré la vaillance des soldats congolais" (a deafening silence that for decades ignored the bravery of Congolese soldiers) by putting on the exhibit *Lisolo na Bisu*, or "Le Soldat Congolais." The focus was not on the Force publique per se—attention to which traditionally overwhelmingly emphasized its white officers—but more specifically on the African soldier. This was an attempt to compensate for past neglect, as the enlisted African soldier had been an overlooked subject in past representations of the colonial army down to a 1985 exhibition at the Royal Military Museum.[19] Not just those exhibits but in history books, the classroom, and elsewhere: any focus on the Belgian Congo's military force and its actions had always centered on white officers or on the Force publique as an institution. "Dans les manuels d'histoire ainsi que dans les ouvrages édités par les services d'information des armées coloniales, la bravoure militaire des Africains n'est évoquée qu'à travers les qualités des officiers européens." (In history textbooks as well as in books edited by the information services of the colonial armies, the military bravery of Africans [was] only evoked through the qualities of the European officers.)[20] In the years leading up to 2010 there had been a slow-growing awareness of Congo's role in both world wars, some starting to ask whether Belgium had done enough to compensate Congolese not just for colonialism generally speaking, but specifically for their wartime contributions.[21] Journalist Colette Braeckman, among others, broached the subject of reparations, and a new history by Guy Vanthemsche (VUB) recognized how the Belgian Congo had essentially maintained Belgian sovereignty during World War II.

Lisolo na Bisu was spearheaded by Philippe Jacquij, who worked alongside Pierre Lierneux and Natasja Peeters to take advantage of the museum's collections on the Force publique—some of which had been put on display as early as the 1920s—to create a show for a mere 30,000 Euros. The seven-room exhibit covered the pre-1914 period down to June 30, 1960, its focus squarely on the colonial period. It attracted around 650 people to its June inauguration, and another 15,000 came to see it before it closed at the end of September.[22] Although the show was not massively attended, press coverage, both domestic and foreign, fed into a growing awareness of the Congo's contribution to Belgian war efforts.[23] The growing consciousness of this aspect of the colonial past may have been reinforced by the traveling exposition *Tokopesa Saluti!* (We salute you!), comprising 35 panels showing in chronological fashion the military ties between Belgium and the Congo from 1885 to 2006.[24] *Tokopesa Saluti!* reached not only larger cities like Antwerp but also smaller towns like Zoersel, Zonnebeke, and Rumst. The tour included visits by schoolchildren, even if, being a small traveling exhibit, it sometimes attracted limited numbers of visitors at its stops, for example only some 400 during its showing at Antwerp's Vredescentrum from 3-13 January 2011.[25]

The Palais des Beaux-Arts, whose name was now refashioned as "BOZAR," put on the festival "L'Afrique visionnaire – Visionair Afrika" to commemorate the fiftieth year of "African independences," the plural signaling how the festival focused not just on the former Belgian Congo, but also the dozen-plus other African countries that became independent in 1960. "L'Afrique visionnaire – Visionair Afrika" consisted of exhibitions, film showings, dance and music performances, including the screening of a film by Haitian filmmaker Raoul Peck, and musical performances by Beninoise Angélique Kidjo and Malian Rokia Traoré.[26] The event that anchored the festival was the show "GEO-graphics," directed by British-Ghanaian architect David Adjaye, showing 230 ethnographic masterpieces from private collections from the whole continent of Africa.[27] Although diverse in aims, the events tended to focus on Belgium's erstwhile colony, as could be seen during BOZAR's celebration of Congolese music in July that included Congolese performers Papa Wemba, Ferre Gola, Manuaku Waku, among others. As one commentator put it, "Voor Congolezen is dit alsof Johnny Hallyday, Julien Clerc en Madonna samen op het podium zouden staan." (For Congolese this is as if Johnny Hallyday, Julien Clerc, and Madonna would be on stage together.)[28] The concert received extensive press coverage in numerous newspapers, several evening news programs, radio broadcasts, and various websites.[29] One account, however, warned that the viewing public might miss some of the greater issues in play during the BOZAR festival, from questions about contemporary Belgian-Congo interactions to ones about past relations between the two countries, one wealthy and stable, the other troubled and unstable:

> Impossible donc pour une grande partie du public de comprendre tous les enjeux. Au risque de voir un nouveau fossé se creuser entre une élite ayant les armes pour comprendre ce projet et le grand public, restant figé dans les clichés du passé.
> (Thus impossible for a large part of the public to understand all the issues. At risk of seeing a new chasm open between an elite having the means to understand this project and the broader public, remaining stuck in the clichés of the past.)[30]

At the time of its centenary, the Tervuren Museum, which had been inaugurated by King Albert I on April 30, 1910, remained one of the country's most-visited museums. A large number of those who saw the museum continued to be school children, sustaining a tendency dating back a century. Tervuren held its own celebrations on its centennial—even fireworks—and ran temporary expositions including *100 ans du musée en 100 photos*, "Indépendence cha cha," and an exhibit on the Congo River itself, *Fleuve Congo: 4700 km de nature et culture en effervescence*.[31] The anniversary was accompanied by

Colonial pioneers Dieudonné Palate (1868-1895),
Joseph Hernotte (1862-1891), and Ernest Poskin (1875-1905)
Location: Vezin
Sculptor: Camille Maniquet
Inauguration: 13 September 1937
Funded/built by: commune of Vezin

Memorial to colonial pioneers, Vezin, 2018

In 1929-1930, the pro-colonial interest group the Ligue du souvenir congolais put together a list of all "colonial pioneers" who had served Leopold II in the Congo and who had died in Africa sometime between 1876 and 1908. The former year was that of the Brussels Geographical Conference, taken by many as the start date of the Leopoldian colonial project, and 1908 was the year of Leopold II's turnover of the colony to Belgium. In 1930, the group sent out notices to more than 500 communes, the goal being to put up a memorial of some kind in each and every community from which a pioneer had come.

Vezin, near Andenne, was one such commune, and it answered the call to honor its three native sons who had left the village, gone to the Congo, and died there: Sergent-Major Dieudonné Palate, Sous-Lieutenant Joseph Hernotte, and Sous-Lieutenant Ernest Poskin. Palate arrived to the Congo just in time for the start of the 1892-1894 anti-slavery campaigns, but then found himself fighting rebels following the Force publique revolt at Luluabourg in 1895. He died at their hands,

Close-up of memorial to colonial pioneers, Vezin, 2018

reportedly facing the enemy.[32] Hernotte, another soldier, served two "tours" in the Congo, one from 1887 to April 1890, the second from October 1890 until his death at a post at Bomu in November 1891. Poskin was born in 1879, and although he was not born in Vezin itself, he spent his childhood there. He joined the Belgian military, then left it in 1903 to join the Force publique, leaving Belgium that same year to arrive in Boma in November. He died of illness at the post of Rutshuru on October 25, 1895, just shy of two years in the colony, at the age of 26.[33]

The cemetery at the center of the village was relocated, creating a small, sloped green space, which was rebaptized "place Palate." This is where the colonial monument was erected in 1937. Sculptor Maniquet supposedly carved the monument out of stone from the ancestral church of Vezin.[34] *Vers l'Avenir* hailed the three as "héros coloniaux." As at many other such inaugurations in the early 1930s, the unveiling was a grand event. The streets were filled with people, including the families of those being honored. The king and the Ministry of Colonies sent representatives, who figured alongside dignitaries of the colonial and public world who attended including Baron Tombeur de Tabora, the provincial governor M. Bovesse, Henry de la Lindi, and Father Cambier of the White Fathers. The monument still stands in Vezin in the green space at rue de la Colline and rue de Bourgmestre Orban.[35]

the publication of a richly illustrated volume on the museum's history by Maarten Couttenier.[36] The museum's events garnered extensive attention in the printed press and on television, as did its impeding renovation, announced countless times. All the while, the museum's collections continued to expand, as when, for instance, the institution in 2013 acquired some 2,000 paintings from Bogumil Jewsiewicki.

The year 2010 once again demonstrated that the half-century old hangover of the last years of colonial rule continued to buttress distorted understandings of the past, that is the endurance of a colonial-era imaginary underpinned by official and unofficial photographs of the golden age of the 1950s.[37] An example was *Belgisch-Kongo: 50 Jaar Koloniale Herinneringen* by VRT journalist Peter Verlinden and Sarah Hertsens, one of the slew of publications prepared in time to appear during the anniversary year.[38] The book gives voice among others to Carlo Lamote, a Belgian who moved to the Congo in 1950 to work for Inforcongo. Lamote paints a favorable picture, recalling for example that he and his wife got along well with Congolese. Photographs in the book are intermixed with recollections from the era itself, one contemporary Belgian transplant describing life in the Congo in Panglossian terms: "alles is op zijn best in de beste der werelden." (everything is at its best in the best of worlds.) Many of the photographs in the book are from Inforcongo archives, including images by official photographer Henri Goldstein, and they give a picture of racial harmony and success. No sense of any problems enters the picture, literally, until independence, which the book covers with some photographs of contemporaneous difficulties.

The recycling of images in print was matched by the same on television. VRT marked the 2010 anniversary year by showing the propagandist *Bwana Kitoko* (1955) *again*. As Guido Convents put it, "The avalanche of images that VRT showed in May and June 2010 as part of the fiftieth anniversary of the independence of Congo was peppered with colonial nostalgia and culture. That on June 30 in primetime the inferior colonial documentary and propaganda film *Bwana Kitoko* by Belgian André Cauvin was shown, is incomprehensible."[39] This was only one of many television productions that summer, VRT alone showing a whole series of documentaries and films including a three-part documentary series comprising ULB historian Samuel Tilman's *Kongo: Black heart, white man* about exploitation in the Congo (25 May); Daniel Cattier's *Les Grandes illusions* (1 June); Isabelle Christiaens and Jean-François Bastin's *Le Géant inachevé* (8 June); and "Nonkel pater," focused on missionaries (July-August).[40] There was also "Het laatste koloniale taboe" about Congo's turbulent decolonization, with, once again, Peter Verlinden; Filip De Boeck and Sarah Vanagt's "Cemetery State," a fascinating and somewhat quixotic look at life around Kinshasa's Kintambo cemetery; and Thierry Michel's documentary, *Katanga Business*.[41] VRT's Canvas channel showed Rudi Vranckx's seven-part series "Bonjour Congo," which took him across the Congo, surveying the former colonial possession 50 years on.[42] The French-language RTBF likewise broadcast a whole slew of productions on radio, television and online, many of which depicted rosy

Colonial pioneers
Location: Leuven (Louvain), city cemetery
Inauguration: ca. 1930[43]

Plaque to colonial pioneers, Leuven, 2018

This simple commemorative stone plaque at the entrance to the Leuven city cemetery lists the names of thirty individuals from the city who died in the Congo before 1908. The only symbols on the plaque are two flags placed atop a commemorative wreath: one the city flag of Leuven, the other that of the CFS.

This otherwise unremarkable monument is noteworthy because it exemplifies so many themes of colonial memorials more generally. First, it suggests how colonial monuments could have worked to unify Belgians around a shared object, namely their colonial rule in Africa. The memorial is inscribed in both French and Flemish, referencing "l'œuvre congolaise" or the "congoleesch werk." The presence of both languages is unsurprising since it was put up in Leuven; although in Flanders, the city is a well-known university town where still into the 1930s the language of higher education was overwhelmingly French.[44] Although they were divided by language, the plaque suggests one way in which Belgians might unite before 1960, namely behind their shared Congolese "project."

Another element the Leuven memorial shares with others is that it acted as a site of remembrance. Reports from the 1950s suggest that the memorial had become a focal point for celebrations of the colony, the local Koloniale Kring van

Leuven leading pilgrimages to the memorial during that decade, which included
"un défilé devant le mémorial des pionniers au cimetière de la ville" (a parade
before the memorial to the pioneers in the city cemetery)[45] and "le dépôt de
fleurs devant la pierre commémorative ornée des noms de nos vaillants pionniers morts au Congo." (the placing of flowers before the commemorative stone
adorned with the names of our valiant pioneers who died in the Congo.)[46]

Third, similar to the memorial plaque in Anderlecht, among others, the
Leuven plaque reveals that many if not most Belgians who died in the Congo
during the Leopoldian period died of illness. Of the 30 Leuven pioneers commemorated, half, at least, died of some infirmity. Several died of hematuria,
which probably meant malaria or blackwater fever (Boine, Cappuyns, Henrard,
Poullet, Stassart, Thiry, Van Hove); others died of dysentery (de Wenckstern, Van
Lint, Verdussen); two perished because of fever (Huyghe, Milants); Engels "suc-
combait à la peine" (dying either of grief, or of punishment, or of overwork); and
Verhaeren of an unspecified illness.[47]

Finally, because the Leuven plaque celebrates those who died in the Congo
"before the annexation of the Congo to Belgium (15 November 1908)," it like
so many others explicitly connects back to the Leopoldian era.[48] In this small
way, it legitimized contemporary colonialism (ca. 1930) by rooting it in the one
colonial "tradition" Belgian had, that of the CFS period.

views of colonialism.[49] Critical voices were again muffled. "In the interest
of delicate diplomatic relationships and particularly in order not to offend
the Belgian royal family, the Belgian government actively monitored the
commemoration." Rudi Vranckx's series "minimised or censored nearly
everything that could place Belgian authorities in a bad light."[50]

This longstanding hangover of 1950s colonialist images endured. In
2013, the display "Prestige and African Leadership," which was part of the
permanent displays on the fourth floor of Antwerp's new Museum aan de
Stroom (MAS), looped two propaganda films by Gérard De Boe showing
re-enactments of Congolese leadership ceremonies. De Boe was a filmmaker
who had worked for colonial authorities on contract in the 1950s to produce
colonialist films. The MAS display included clips of his films with zero
explanation or context.[51] One school project put on display in spring 2018 in
the Saint-Josse-ten-Noode city hall included many official photos. This was by
students from the Guy Cudell high school, who created an exposition called
"Noirs Desseins pour Blanches Aspirations? Une histoire belgo-congolaise."
(Black Designs for White Aspirations? A Belgo-Congolese History.) Many
of the photos on display were by René Stalin, a photographer who worked
for Inforcongo.[52]

Perhaps the outpouring of 2010 was a sign of a renewed interest in the former colony, or an embrace of an optimistic view of future Belgian-Congolese relations. But many events and cultural productions did not grow out of popular initiative but rather from deliberate state efforts to improve relations with the recognized government of the Congo. After all, it was the foreign affairs ministry that had asked BOZAR to "conceive and present a cultural programme honouring the 50th anniversary of independence of 17 African nations (one of them the former Belgian Congo)."[53] The Tervuren Museum's wonderful, high-quality book on colonialist films, which included digitized copies of 1950s-era documentaries on several DVDs, is another example.[54] It was initiated by the foreign affairs ministry, with many dozens of copies destined to be sent to the Congo as a gesture of goodwill in order to improve relations with Joseph Kabila's regime.[55]

A discordant note in 2010 was the debate about King Albert II's trip to the former colony to celebrate its independence anniversary, after he received an unexpected invitation to do so from Kabila in January. Albert eventually undertook the visit, accompanied by Queen Paola and former prime minister Yves Leterme.[56] The debate that this visit unleashed revealed francophone Belgians were much more in favor of it whereas Dutch speakers were much more inclined to oppose it.[57] Some Flemish once again took a critical position on the colonial connection in order to criticize the monarchy and thereby the nation-state, whereas French speakers now adhered to the king and country more closely than their northern counterparts.

Perhaps the most remarkable moment in Belgium connected to the fiftieth anniversary of Congo's independence was the publication of David Van Reybrouck's *Congo: Een geschiedenis*. This history of the Congo on a grand scale, with journalistic, historical, and anthropological approaches, became a national sensation that also showed how works of history could reach a popular audience.[58] Van Reybrouck based his magnum opus on the historical literature but also on his experiences in the Congo, including numerous interviews. Van Reybrouck said part of his motivation to write the book was because people's knowledge of the Congo was restricted to the atrocities of the "red rubber" era and the period of decolonization. The book had sold 250,000 copies in Dutch alone by September 2012, an astounding feat considering the size of the Dutch-language communities in Belgium and the Netherlands. By comparison, Hochschild's *King Leopold's Ghost*, which had been translated into a dozen languages, had according to one account sold 600,000 copies by 2013, fifteen years after its initial publication.[59] Moreover, Van Reybrouck's *Congo*, clocking in at more than 700 pages in length, was, as one reviewer put it, "a brick."[60] It was a triumph nonetheless, and won the AKO Literatuurprijs. As Van Reybrouck explained its success,

> À un moment où l'Europe réintègre ses frontières géographiques et voit son influence s'amenuiser dans le monde, le rappel du passé colonial fascine, même si les Européens sont conscients des dégâts que le colonialisme a pu causer.
>
> (At a moment when Europe is reintegrating its geographical borders and sees its influence dwindling in the world, the reminder of the colonial past fascinates [people], even if Europeans are aware of the damage that colonialism could cause.)[61]

There were cultural productions that reached smaller audiences yet that nonetheless suggested not merely the underlying, lasting presence of "the colonial," but also new ways of looking and thinking through it. Stand-up comedian Pie Tshibanda continued to enjoy success, drawing on colonial history for material, as well as his own experience of escaping the Congo to exile in Belgium in the 1990s. In 2011, Brussels-based artist and filmmaker Sven Augustijnen rolled out *Spectres*, a documentary paired with a book and exhibition of the same name, the latter of which displayed photographs and prepared archival materials.[62] It was shown in Brussels from May-July 2011, before being exhibited abroad in Bern and then Amsterdam.[63] The exposition and Augustijnen's film examined how Belgium remained haunted by the assassination of Lumumba.[64] It ended up following Jacques Brassinne, author of a Ph.D. thesis on Lumumba's assassination, to which Ludo de Witte's 1999 book was in large part a reply. Whereas de Witte pinned blame on the Belgian government, especially because of one telex transmission calling for the definitive elimination of the Congolese prime minister, Brassinne's dissertation was much more exculpatory. Some criticized Augustijnen's analysis for mainly focusing on whites, even though he deliberately drew in African voices as well. But in the final analysis, its focus on white Belgians made sense, because the documentary was above all an exploration of the Belgian psyche and the unresolved tensions of the assassination of Lumumba.

Other cultural manifestations were more traditional, including the 2013 BEL-vue museum exhibit "Dr. Livingstone, I presume?" that ended on November 11, 2013, and which attracted more than 35,000 visitors.[65] Colonial history had made such a comeback, it formed the backdrop for crime fiction in Alain Berenboom's *Le roi du Congo*.[66] Set in 1948, Berenboom gets his history right. Mounting tensions suggest the coming of independence. The presence of Russian bad guys presages the Cold War struggle over the Congo that internationalized its independence in 1960. As indicated in this chapter's epigraph, Berenboum even has one character, Doutrement, a long-time resident of the Congo, capture the love many Europeans developed for central Africa, which as discussed earlier, caused nostalgia for the post-World War II years in the colony.

One piece of literature that came under renewed criticism was *Tintin in the Congo*. Mounting calls for a more full reckoning with the past included a 2012 effort to ban the book, led by Bienvenu Mbutu Mondondo, a Congolese national living and studying in Brussels. It received little attention in Belgium and ultimately failed.[67] More recently, *bandes dessinées* like *Africa Dreams: L'Ombre du roi* have come out as means by which to criticize colonialism.[68] All told, the number of novels and comic books dealing with the colonial legacy is small in comparison to the total production of books. One only has to browse through a Brussels bookstore like Filigranes, or one of its shops dedicated to *bandes dessinées* like Brüsel on Blvd. Anspach, or its neighbor MultiBD to realize that colonial themes appear only occasionally in the country's annual publishing output.

The colonial era seems to have had little influence on music in Belgium until arguably just the past several years, when artists of sub-Saharan African descent like Stromae made a big impact on the scene, and when Belgian Congolese hip-hop artists—who are primarily French-speaking, and concentrated in Brussels—began to be noticed.[69] The messages in Belgian-Congolese hip hop music are mixed. Artists were born after the colonial era and seldom know the Congo well, blaming both Belgians and Congolese for the current poor state of affairs in central Africa. The racism they speak out against is that which they encounter in Belgium, not necessarily a colonial phenomenon.

The comparatively small presence of "colonial" *bandes dessinées* and small number of "post-colonial" hip hop artists tells us that potential signs of a great attention to the colonial past in Belgium should be taken with a grain of salt. Some of these were small-scale and/or driven by merely a few actors. For example, December 2011 witnessed the exposition "Visages de Paul Panda Farnana" a retrospective including a film that centered on the Congo's first national activist, who was really a nationalist *avant la lettre*, Paul Panda Farnana. But the event was largely driven by one man, Antoine Tshitungu Kongola, and the video of the exposition had just 267 views on YouTube by 2014, and only 2,074 by mid-February 2019.[70] The numerous attacks on monuments in the first two decades of the twenty-first century have garnered some attention in the mainstream press, but have been carried out by small bands of anarchists, anti-monarchists, and anti-colonialists. For instance, the 2018 attack on a bust of Leopold II in Forest, a commune of Brussels, made the news, but seems to have been carried out by a fringe group.

Leopold II (1835-1909)
Location: Forest (Vorst), Parc Duden (Dudenpark)
Sculptor: Thomas Vinçotte
Inauguration: 11 May 1957[71]
Funded/built by: commune of Forest and the Donation Royale

This bronze bust on a rectangular plinth does not in and of itself call attention to Leopold II's colonial rule. Instead, the statue commemorates the king's role in establishing public parks, including Duden Park, its dedication reading, "To King Leopold II, benefactor of public parks." Nonetheless, this modest memorial is connected to the sovereign's rule in central Africa, and in multiple ways. First, in recent years anti-colonial activists have deliberately targeted the bust, lending it a colonial association despite the intentions of those who put it up in the first place. In early 2018, the group Association Citoyenne pour un Espace public Décolonial (ACED) vandalized the statue the night of January 10-11.[72] And this attack was only the latest of several against this particular statue, as well as against others to the king in the Brussels area. This time, in January 2018, the bust itself was "déboulonné," which can mean literally unbolted and removed, but also "brought down," as a politician might be taken down by scandal. Scrawled in black letters above the monument's original inscription was an accusatory demand for an explanatory text: "CONGO FREE STATE & 'CONGO HORRORS' EXPLANATORY TEXT = NECESSARY HERE." ACED also issued a statement lamenting the commemoration of Leopold in public spaces. In an appeal on Facebook, the mayor of Forest, Marc-Jean Ghyssels, recognized the vandalism as a political act and called for the return of the bust, and for dialogue. The mayor's plea emphasized how the statue celebrated Leopold's role in establishing the park and that the statue belonged to the *patrimoine bruxellois*.[73] Just a few days after having been removed, the bust was discovered not far away. Although it was reported that it was to be restored within a couple months, it was still missing as of May 2018.

   Although some, including mayor Ghyssels apparently, might interpret the Parc Duden bust as a tribute to Leopold II's development of park spaces in the city, the memorial was connected to the colony in fundamental ways from the very beginning. The commune of Forest first built the bust with the permission of and with funds from the Donation Royale, or Royal Trust. Leopold II himself had established the Donation Royale in 1900 to mark the sixty-fifth year of his birth.[74] He did so by bequeathing to the Donation Royale properties and goods from his massive estate that he did not want to see go to his daughters, who had married foreign princes and from whom he was estranged. During his reign's early years the king had been one of the richest people in all of Europe,

Bust of Leopold II, Forest, 2013   *Missing bust of Leopold II, Forest, 2018*

but he spent almost all his fortune on the exploration, conquest, and administration of his CFS colony. That he had managed to not only rebuild his finances but
become even wealthier than ever by 1900 was essentially due to his Congo endeavors. Duden Park itself was bequeathed to Leopold II by its owner, German-
born businessman Guillaume Duden and his wife, before Leopold II made the
park a gift to the Donation Royale, which is what makes it today a park for the
public that remains property of the Donation Royale.[75]

Africa, still on display

As we have seen, there had been the possibility for a more "real" decolonization
in the 1970s and 1980s, with the demand for repatriation of African art and other
objects to the Congo. This would not have been just about the movement of
objects but could have opened up the possibility for a greater questioning of
the former colonial connection, creating opportunities for renewed relations
and changed *mentalités* in Belgium. But it was missed. Only in recent years have
there been low-level shifts, most connected to generational change. Still, the
view continues among many that African art was not really artwork, including
among African art dealers in Brussels.[76] Specialists continued their work, for
example Marc Felix, a leading example of Belgian consultants, writers, experts,

and promoters of Congolese art who continued to be shaped by it, thereby subtly influencing their country's cultural scene. Felix becoming a driver behind the Brussels Non European Art Fair, or BRUNEAF, a major event in the capital each year.[77] The extent to which private collections of African material culture and artwork continued to shape private space in Belgium into the twenty-first century—albeit overwhelmingly among those able to afford collecting—is suggested by what happened to the René and Odette Delenne collection. René and Odette Delenne had begun collecting African artwork after having visited the Congo pavilions at the 1958 Brussels universal exposition. The Cleveland Museum of Art obtained 35 objects from their collection in 2010, and the curator who arranged the acquisition said it would have taken decades to put together any comparable collection by means of purchases on the open market.[78] When put up for auction at Sotheby's in 2015, other items in the René and Odette Delenne collection sold out, fetching three million dollars.[79]

The collections of dealers, collectors, and individuals represented an important reservoir of Congolese art—or a "database" in Jean-Luc Vellut's formulation—whose presence in the former metropole sustained a positive view of the colonial past.[80] Organizing exhibits meant enacting or re-enacting claims of authority in which white Europeans exercised ownership and expertise; only recently have Congolese been involved at any significant level in such expositions. By building collections, preparing exhibitions, evaluating art, and helping set market prices, museum curators, collectors, even missionaries and private citizens from across the country's language divide sustained a shared position of expertise on Congolese art. As Sarah Van Beurden has shown, by the end of the colonial era Belgians had come to exercise a cultural guardianship over traditional Congolese culture.[81] Displaying "authentic" Congolese artifacts and art after 1960 was a subtle way of justifying colonial power and Belgium's colonial action after the fact. The question of authenticity and who possesses the authority to determine or bestow it remains essential to collectors and experts down to today. Baudouin de Grunne, a longtime mayor of the commune of Wezembeek-Oppem, amassed a huge collection of African artwork, including of Tabwa figures, Mitsogho gongs, and Hemba rattles.[82] His assemblage was among the most significant such private collections before it was auctioned off by Sotheby's in 2000. His son, Bernard de Grunne, who is also a collector and expert, asserts on his website:

Questions of authenticity in the arts of Africa, Oceania and Tribal Indonesia are of upmost [sic] concern to new collectors. Bernard de Grunne can offer impartial and scholarly advice in this difficult area thanks to his experience in handling great numbers of undisputed masterpieces in these fields.[83]

Colonial pioneers
Location: Ixelles (Elsene), square de la Croix Rouge
Sculptor: Marcel Rau[84]
Architect: A. Boelens[85]
Inauguration: 8 October 1933
Funded/built by: commune of Ixelles

Memorial to colonial pioneers, Ixelles, 2018

For this memorial by the Brussels commune of Ixelles for "its children who died in the Congo," sculptor Marcel Rau carved a slender statue out of "pierre bleue de Sprimont."[86] Similar to many other colonial monuments in Belgium, a representation of an African woman is central, in this case a striking sculpture of a Mangbetu woman's head. The Mangbetu became almost iconic in Belgium during the colonial period because of their practice of wrapping babies' heads to elongate the skull. Adults, especially women, often accentuated this elongation by using materials, their own hair, or a combination of the two to create a coiffure that extended backward. In Rau's sculpture, the woman's eyes and lips appeared closed, making her appear meditative. One of her hands holds the Congo star, conjuring up the CFS flag, which was blue with one large gold star in the middle. Like all other such images of Africans in stone or bronze in Belgium—and unlike their European colonial counterparts—the woman remains unnamed and anonymous, akin to the *types* of European representations of Africans in the nineteenth and twentieth centuries. In this case this female Mangbetu *type* tops a monument comprised mainly of a single column on which Rau engraved the names of all Ixelles pioneers on several bands that wrap around a column that also bears imagery, including carvings of a mask, an elephant, huts, a tree, a crocodile, a rhinoceros, and a slit drum.[87] The top of the column reads, "Ixelles à ses pionniers coloniaux" (Ixelles to its colonial pioneers), and the front of the monument includes the landmark dates of 1876 and 1908.

The striking profile of the monument made it popular with photographers, and it was reproduced both in specialist colonialist publications and mainstream newspapers.[88] The speech of Ixelles mayor Armand Huysmans at its inauguration reveals the spirit of the time that motivated the building of such monuments:

The commune of Ixelles wanted (…) to participate in this beautiful moment of recognition. Because they were thirty two, those children of Ixelles who left their homes, their families, and their attachments for mysterious regions where the genius of Leopold II had seen into the incredible future. They brought with them there their youth, their enthusiasm, and above all the strong qualities of their race: love for work and an indomitable will (…) nothing would serve to perpetuate their names if we were to one day allow their work to perish. On this site of greenery and flowers, so suitable for reflection (…) we will come often to think of them.

In few words, Huysmans commemorated the local while praising Leopold II, recommitting to the country's larger colonial project, trusting the strengths of the white race, and baptizing the monument a site of remembrance and commemoration.

Such immutability of sensibilities is not unique to the Belgian case. As one scholar has noted, "the world of connoisseurs, collectors, and dealers of what once would have been called primitive art" changed little over the years in post-colonial France.[89] Of course, there is a profound irony in that it was white European dealers, missionaries, and curators deeming African art authentic rather than Africans themselves. For decades after 1960, there was no real end of empire in the realm of art dealership in metropolitan Europe.

Some Africana has become somewhat effaced. Antwerp's Etnografisch Museum founded in 1952 was by the turn of the century in dire straits. When Director Herreman left the museum in 1995, it was not until 2000 that he was he replaced by another Africanist, and there were no Africa-focused exhibits at the museum from 1995-2001. After other changes and moves, the museum was merged with three others, including the Maritime Museum, to create the MAS, which opened in May 2011. Ethnographic objects, including those from the former Belgian Congo, have since then been integrated—one is tempted to say lost—into theme-oriented displays on each of the MAS' several floors. One whole floor covers maritime Antwerp, including some exhibits on colonialism, providing information on Ons Huis, Matadi, and the ivory trade, and showing rubber samples. The colonial era is folded into the history of Antwerp, without mention of colonial-era abuses.[90]

As we have seen, the reservoirs of Congolese artwork in Belgium were periodically mobilized. Dealers, collectors, curators, and academics saw themselves as experts on and guardians of "authentic" African culture. Africana continued to adorn private homes, museum collections, and dealers' galleries. Belgians' refusal to return this Congolese patrimony in any significant way could be construed as an unspoken assertion of the legitimacy of the colonial conquest of the late 1800s and the foreign rule that followed. In this realm, decolonization never happened, or it has only just recently begun.

Race and racism

Racism is experienced in various ways by people of color in Belgium, such as being stopped on the street by police to have one's paper's checked. Belgian Jean Muteba Rahier, son of a white colonial and his African *ménagère*, recounted his experience being the only "black person" in the passport line for Belgians when entering the country in 1994, and the extensive inspection his passport and luggage underwent at the hands of the border police.[91] Rahier's account rings true, as this author has stood in line for an extended period behind a black person of African descent at the Brussels airport, watching other recently-arrived passengers streaming through other lines as the traveler before me was questioned at length.

One aspect of the country's colonial legacy that received virtually zero attention until only very recently was mixed-race couples and their children, either those who ended up in Belgium or the Congo after 1960. One might excuse this inattention if mixed-race children had been excluded from the metropole, but as early as the first years of the twentieth century there were offspring of "colonial" mixed marriages there. An example is Joseph Droeven, Belgium's first "black" soldier, who was the son of a Belgian gunsmith and his Congolese wife, and who fought for Belgium in World War I. The practice of men having *ménagères* in the colony was well known, and not only in official circles, where it was a subject of grave concern lest mixed-race children detract from white prestige or create a group with anti-colonial potential.[92] People in Belgium were aware of sexual relations between whites and blacks in the colony, as illustrated by Georges Simenon's *Le blanc à lunettes* (1937).[93] The reader not only learns that the novel's protagonist, Ferdinand Graux, has a relationship with his 15-year-old African housekeeper Baligi, but that this is known to Graux's family back home, even to his fiancée who remained there. A rather naïve Englishwoman whom Graux meets on a return trip to his plantation in the colony questions him about personal matters, including his sex life:

"You mean to say you've lived five years all by yourself in the Congo and been
true to your fiancée all the time? Don't tell me you've never made love to one of
those pretty little black girls I've heard so much about!"
To which he replied quite coolly:
"I have a housekeeper—like everybody else."
"What does that mean, 'housekeeper'?"
"It means—everything!"
(...)
"What about that girl you're engaged to?"
"She knows, of course. I've told her."[94]

Simenon himself once asked, "Will we be remembered as benefactors (...)
Or for having sown the countryside with small beings of mixed color?"[95] The
central character of David Van Reybrouck's *Missie* bears this out, deriding
the Vatican for its adherence to a policy of celibacy.

Ecoutez, le célibat n'est pas fait pour l'Afrique. [...] Ici, l'évêque de Bukavu
qui vient de mourir, c'était même dans le journal. A la phonie, il y avait
souvent des messages pour lui: 'Monseigneur, votre fille a besoin d'argent
pour un passeport.'
(Listen, celibacy is not made for Africa. [...] Here, the bishop of Bukavu,
who just died... it was even in the newspaper. There were often telegraph
messages for him: "Your Grace, your daughter needs some money for a
passport.")[96]

Estimates of the number of *métis* in the Belgian Congo show that sexual
relations between Europeans and Africans were common, one author putting
the number at 10,000 by 1956, another as high as 20,000 by the end of the
colonial era.[97] Considering that at the height of European settlement there
were only 112,000 whites in the Congo, among them some 89,000 Belgians,
the possibility that there were as many as 20,000 children of mixed-race
descent reveals the great extent to which Europeans and Africans had sexual
intercourse.

Despite its significance, the issue of *métissage* remained taboo, even after
the number of mixed-race children living in Belgium jumped after 1960.

Au moment de l'indépendance du Congo (1960) et du Ruanda-Urundi
(1962), des centaines d'enfants métis résidant dans les missions furent «ra-
patriés» à Bruxelles par avion militaire et confiées à l'A.P.P.M. [Association
pour la Protection des Mulâtres] pour être adoptés par des familles belges.

(At the moment of the independence of the Congo (1960) and of Rwanda and Urundi (1962), hundreds of mixed-race children residing in the missions were 'repatriated' to Brussels by military plane and handed over to the A.P.P.M. [Association pour la Protection des Mulâtres] to be adopted by Belgian families.)[98]

The silence on the issue has only recently begun to lift. Scholar Jean Muteba Rahier explained his origins and difficult childhood in a 2003 autobiographical piece, born as he was in 1959 in the Congo to a European father and an African mother.[99] The 2010 documentary film *Bons baisers de la colonie* raised the subject of mixed-race relatives in Nathalie Borgers' family. Many European fathers left their mixed-race children in Church hands rather than recognize them as their legal children, and it was not until April 2017 that the Catholic Church apologized to *métis* for their poor treatment.[100] That same year appeared *De kinderen van Save* by Sarah Heynssens, the first book-length monograph tracing the fate of mixed-race children from the colony, through abandonment, to placement with nuns at Save, to relocation to Belgium.[101] In short, Belgian memory has only recently been reawakened to the *traumatisme métis* of the colonial era, that is the existence of numerous mixed-race "children of empire," many of whom were uprooted and taken to Belgium at the time of decolonization.[102]

The role of immigration

One reason for the increased attention to race and the colonial past in recent years has been the growth in the country's population of central African or Congolese descent. Immigration was nothing new; Belgium has for long been a country of immigrants. It is telling that in the 1956 Marcinelle mining disaster that killed hundreds (mentioned in chapter 1), 136 of the more than 250 dead were Italian. The rapid increase in the population of Belgians of Congolese descent was a novelty of the late twentieth and early twenty-first centuries. By 1991 there were some 17,451 Congolese nationals living in Belgium, which declined to 14,606 in 1993 before dropping further to 12,130 by 1998.[103] This can be explained. First, significant numbers of asylum seekers from the Congo sought refuge in Belgium in the early 1990s, and many planned to return home if possible. Second, citizenship and census regulations are such that it is difficult to track the non-European origins of the country's citizenry. Still today it is a challenge to get a firm handle on the total number of people living in Belgium of Congolese descent—whether Belgian, Congolese, or otherwise by nationality—because someone from Congo who took Belgian nationality is not counted as Congolese by official records, and Belgium for decades had a liberal nationality law in terms of according citizenship to foreigners. In any case, by the end of the millennium, with the genocide in Rwanda and then the ouster of Mobutu from power, the influx of political and other refugees swelled, many of whom lived marginal existences, for example Paul Rusesabagina, mentioned earlier. By the first years of the twenty-first century, the population of people of Congolese origin living in Belgium had increased dramatically. By 2006 there may have been as many as 40,000 people of Congolese nationality and a total of 70,000 people of Congolese descent residing there.[104]

Still, the combined number of Congolese nationals and people of sub-Saharan African origin remained much smaller than those of other immigrants to the country. If there were in the neighborhood of 12,000-17,500 Congolese in Belgium by the 1990s, already by 1978 there were, according to official statistics, 876,577 total immigrants living in Belgium.[105] By one estimate, by 2008-2012 there were somewhere in the neighborhood of 42,000-45,800 Congolese nationals living in Belgium, not counting other nationals of Congolese descent.[106] In 2007, by comparison, 932,161 of the country's 10,584,534 inhabitants were foreign-born (8.8 percent), of whom foreign-born Congolese comprised less than five percent.[107] As of the 1990s, the Congolese population of France was larger than its counterpart in Belgium, and by 1992, 52 percent of all Congolese living in Europe resided in France against only 29 percent in Belgium.[108] Difficult as it is to believe, Congolese immigration as a percentage of total immigration into Belgium reached a peak *in 1961* at just more than seven percent of total immigration. Since then, Congolese immigration has never amounted to more than five percent of the total. Between 1948 and 2007, total immigrants to Belgium regularly numbered more than 40,000 a year whereas during the same time period the per annum number of Congolese immigrants only once numbered more than 2,500.[109] Or consider how "entre le 1er janvier 1991 et le 1er janvier 2006, la part des personnes nées congolaises est passée de 1,5% à 2,5% de la population totale née étrangère." (between 1 January 1991 and 1 January 2006, the proportion of people born in the Congo passed from 1.5% to 2.5% of the total foreign-born population.)[110]

When debates about multiculturalism arose in Belgium in the 1980s, they focused overwhelmingly on Turks and North Africans, especially Moroccans, Algerians, and Tunisians. Unlike France and Britain, most "post-colonial" migrants to Belgium came not from former colonial territories but from Muslim Mediterranean countries, making its experience hew closer to that

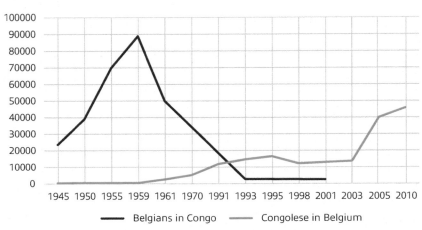

The number of Belgians living in the Congo plotted against the number of Congolese living in Belgium, 1945-2010[111]

of post-empire Germany, where large numbers of mainly Turkish *Gastarbeiter* changed the ethnic makeup of that country. The focus on Maghrebi migrants to Belgium, as opposed to those from central African, led two scholars to call the latter "the forgotten Congolese" in the multicultural debates in Flanders.[112] Since the September 11, 2001, terrorist attacks on the United States, even more attention has turned toward Muslims in Western European countries.[113] The case of Muriel Degauque, a Belgian convert to Islam who blew herself up in Iraq in 2005, made headlines worldwide. (U.S. troops shot and killed her husband and would-be suicide bomber Issam Goris, a Belgian Muslim of Moroccan origin.)[114] The group Sharia4Belgium grabbed headlines by calling for the imposition of Islamic rule in the country. This attention only heightened with the Arab Spring and start of the Syrian civil war in 2011, which has attracted radical Muslims from Europe to fight. "Even peaceful Belgium is now asking just who's living there and what they do when they go abroad."[115] Congolese even complain about the lack of attention to them, and the greater attention paid to other immigrant communities in Belgium. As one person put it, "jullie negeren ons, erger nog; jullie wijzen ons af. Belgen praten altijd maar over Marokkanen en Turken." (you ignore us; even worse: you reject us. Belgians always talk more about Moroccans and Turks.)[116]

A visitor walking the streets of cities like Brussels or Antwerp today, or even smaller cities and towns, clearly sees that Belgium's urban areas are extraordinarily diverse. It is estimated that a quarter of the Belgian population in 2018 has immigrant roots, many of them recent arrivals. What is different today is that many of these have a hard time identifying with either "side" of the Dutch/French language divide, and many also have difficulty seeing the issue of Belgium's colonial past as something that relates to them, or an issue in which they should take interest.[117] There may be only 70,000 or so people of Congolese descent in Belgium, but there are many others of African descent. There are more Congolese than ever in Belgium, yet there are not many Congolese in Belgium. In past years, emigration of Congolese sometimes outpaced immigration.[118] The population of Congolese in Belgium has gotten older and has become more female than male. Nevertheless, they have since the late 1990s become more visible, even if they remain a tiny minority. Since 2001, Matonge en Couleurs has been a celebration of the Congolese community in the Matonge neighborhood of Ixelles to coincide with the end of June and the anniversary of Congolese independence. Beginning in 2007, the "Matonge en Couleurs" in Brussels found a parallel in the Dutch-speaking north when the Congolese community of Antwerp organized the first "Congo in Vlaanderen" festival.[119] This festival, in its eighth edition as of June 2014, has been described as "het enige openluchtevenement in Europa dat jaarlijks de onafhankelijkheid van Congo herdenkt." (the sole open-air event in Europe that annually commemorates the independence of the Congo.)[120] This was a shift from the colonial-era *journées coloniales* to "Congo in Vlaanderen." "Black Paris – Black Brussels," festivals like Congo in Vlaanderen, Matonge en Couleurs in Brussels, and more recently Congolisation—smaller-scale analogues to Congo na Paris—have made the public aware of the important and growing presence of Africans from Congo in the country.[121] Artistic cooperation extends beyond the plastic arts to movie making, theater, art collaborations, and cultural festivals, including the Afrika Filmfestival founded by Guido Convents and Guido Huysmans in 1996 in Leuven that brings African films that do not make mainstream movie theaters to cities big and small across the country's regions.[122]

The most famous Congolese *quartier* in the country is Matonge, in Ixelles, a Brussels commune. For all its reputation as a Congolese neighborhood, perhaps epitomized by Congolese artist Chéri Samba's giant mural *Porte de Namur, Porte de l'Amour*, very few who live there are Congolese. "Barely 5 percent of the inhabitants of the Matonge neighborhood are of African origin, but the neighborhood remains the symbolic heart of the Congolese community [in Belgium]."[123] From the 1960s into the 1980s the Matonge neighborhood was smaller, and was a stop for well-to-do Congolese politicians and others, such as Sûreté head Kalume (with whom Lieve Joris had a run-in during her voyage to the Congo) who traveled regularly to Belgium, sometimes to get tailored clothing made there.[124] Since the political troubles of the 1990s, Matonge has grown as the Congolese population of Belgium has increased.[125] This neighborhood was one of great movement, of people in and

out, and not so much viewed as a residential area, at least not (perhaps) until
the 1990s, when more Congolese started to settle down there and elsewhere
in Belgium.[126] "Dat merk je bijvoorbeeld als het openbaar vervoer staakt:
dan ligt de buurt er verlaten bij." (You notice for example as soon as public
transport service ceases: then the area is deserted.)[127]

Even though the Congolese population is more settled today, this does
not mean that Matonge is a Congolese neighborhood. Instead, it is a diverse
neighborhood known for its Congo connections.[128] Yes, there is a concentra-
tion of Congolese and African shops and restaurants in Matonge, but such
establishments are not exclusive to that neighborhood, and they are not
necessarily frequented most often by Congolese or Africans. As Thierry
Van Pevenage, director of the Maison Africaine in 2010 put it, "Of course
Congolese here know Matonge, but even they don't come here often."[129]
During the *journées zaïroises* of 1988, there were as many Europeans as Africans
there to celebrate, and the ongoing Matonge en Couleurs involves many
besides just Congolese.[130] Going to an area restaurant such as, for example,
Soleil d'Afrique, you are more likely to hear English, Spanish, French, or
some other Western language than any African language.

The identity of Congolese in Belgium is complex. While this author was
traveling from Brussels to Antwerp in November 2013, a young woman of
African descent asked me a question, and we struck up a brief conversation.
When I asked her out of curiosity where she was from, she responded, "The
Congo." Having heard her speaking Flemish, I asked, "Were you born in
the Congo?," to which she replied, "No, I was born in Antwerp." When it
comes to the colonial past and potential claims against Belgium, views on
the colonial past among Congolese living in the country are heterogeneous,
varying in different ways including by generation, as some of these people
lived under colonialism while middle-aged and younger people of Congolese
descent never experienced formal Belgian colonial rule.[131] By the 2010s, many
Congolese living in Belgium and Belgians of Congolese descent have come
into their own, defining who they are and making their own contributions.
In Koli Jean Bofane, author of *Mathématiques congolaises*, has said, "I detest
that publishers set aside special collections for us as if we [African authors]
formed a separate group. (…) Me, I'm Belgian of Congolese origin, my friend
Didier de Lannoy feels himself to be Congolese of Belgian origin, and both
of us write in French. These categorizations are absurd."[132] Immigrants in
general feel rather welcome in Belgium, eight out of ten reporting in a 2009
study that they feel well accepted there, compared even to other European
states where they have lived.[133]

Conclusion

The torrent of events provoked by the fiftieth anniversary of the Congo's independence in 2010 demonstrated that far from being forgotten, the colonial experience was alive if not always well in Belgian culture. Nevertheless, the extent to which the outpouring of events, books, films, exhibits, television shows, and musical performances was a reflection of popular culture in the country is open to debate because many cultural productions were initiated, funded, or carried out by state agencies. What is more, for many people the "colonial" had little resonance; not because they forgot the colonial past, but because they were recent immigrants for whom colonial history and the "colonial experience" were foreign. Many of the now much more numerous non-European immigrants living in Belgium, including people of Congolese descent, continued to experience racism. Racism or racialist thinking represented one longstanding "hangover" of empire that persisted, even into the period after 2010. Another surprisingly enduring hangover was that of official colonial propaganda images, which continued to appear and reappear, even more than half a century after the Congo won self-rule.

Epilogue

"I undertook the work of the Congo in the interest of civilization and for the good of Belgium."[1] — King Leopold II

As work on this book drew to a close in 2018, several developments suggested an accelerated decolonization of *mentalités* in Belgium. These were tinged, however, by other events during the summer and fall of 2018 that highlighted persistent racism, and which acted as a Stygian doppelganger to Belgians' increasingly frank recognition of their colonial heritage.

A younger generation, many with immigrant roots, continued to push for action at colonialist monuments in Belgium. As noted, "anti-colonial" writers like Lucas Catherine already had organized "colonial walks" to highlight colonialism's legacy in the country's built infrastructure. Thierry Demey had produced a lavishly illustrated guide showing how Leopold II had left his mark on Brussels.[2] In 2017, Brussels-based Brazilian artist Daniel Cabral created the project "Tour Leopold II," a tourist map for visitors to use to create a self-guided tour of imperialistic sites in the capital, which also raised awareness of the colonial legacy that surrounded Bruxellois every day.[3] Fringe leftist or quasi-anarchist groups and left-leaning political parties including Ecolo-Groen continued to question the presence of colonialist monuments and street names and to demand new and better explanatory plaques at such sites.[4] Many of these, "rather than targeting a monarch or, more generally, the colonial past, embedded their case in broader actions against racism," a legacy (in part) of the colonial era.[5]

Actions to "decolonize" the country did not escape criticism, in particular from individuals on the political right, some of whom claimed that political activists from Ecolo and other groups were politicizing colonial sites to mobilize electoral support among particular constituencies. Those behind such counter-criticisms presumed that the continued existence of colonial monuments was a neutral status quo; as if the original construction of such permanent markers was apolitical. In fact, erecting colonialist monuments and holding pro-colonial commemorations were political acts that underpinned the Belgian colonial project. Pro-colonialist sentiment had long been the status quo. But any status quo endures not naturally, or merely through inertia, but rather as a result of actions taken to maintain it. In this case, this included

Paul Panda Farnana (1888-1930)
Location: Ixelles (Elsene), rue Jules Bouillon
Inauguration: 21 December 2011

Plaque to Paul Panda Farnana, Ixelles, 2013

Paul Panda Farnana is considered by some to have been the first Congolese intellectual and nationalist, although it is perhaps better to consider him a nationalist *avant la lettre*, since Congolese nationalism hardly existed during his life-
time. Panda came to Belgium at the turn of the century, and went on to study
agronomy, becoming the first Congolese to earn a higher education degree in
Belgium. He went back to the Congo, and it was during a subsequent return
trip to Europe that the outbreak of World War I caught him in the metropole, in
August 1914. Panda joined the Corps des Volontaires Congolais, briefly fought,
and was captured. He spent the remainder of the conflict in a German prisoner
of war camp. Panda remained in Europe after the war and formed the Union
Congolaise to promote African rights, in particular those of Congolese veterans.
He became a forceful advocate, addressing audiences at both the 1920 Congrès
colonial national in Brussels and the London Pan-African Congress of 1921.[6]
Paradoxically, Panda's activism might have induced Belgian colonial authorities
to further tighten what were already strict controls on Congolese, which might
have had the effect of further retarding the development of nationalist sentiment in his home country.[7] He returned to the colony in the late 1920s and died
there, of unknown causes, in 1930.

Panda is largely forgotten in Belgium today. In that sense the 2011 plaque honoring him is not only appropriately hard to find and see—blending as it does into the building to which it is affixed—it also is located on an out-of-the way, run-down building in Ixelles.

literal acts of maintenance including preserving memorials, relocating them as necessary, or restoring them if damaged, in addition to holding events of remembrance. The fate of permanent, public pro-empire markers in Belgium after 1960 confirms James Young's point that monuments represent "the state's memory of itself."[8]

Those seeking greater recognition of Congolese historical figures could claim a victory in 2018 following the inauguration of square Patrice Lumumba in Brussels at the entrance to the Matonge neighborhood. This was not the first public marker recognizing a Congolese figure. As discussed earlier, a monument in the Namur area honors Colonel Chaltin and black soldiers of the CVC, and a marker in Schaerbeek's square Riga memorializes the Force publique. Moreover, as of 2011 there was a plaque in Ixelles to honor Paul Panda Farnana, considered to be the Congo's first nationalist. As to the mortal victims of colonialism, next to the town church in Tervuren were seven tombs for the Congolese who died there during the 1897 colonial exposition. (The graves are symbolic; the seven were buried elsewhere.) Even if there still was no monument to the uncounted African victims of Belgian colonialism, honoring Lumumba by naming a public square after him was a landmark development considering some Belgians still saw him as a violent and radical antagonist who sabotaged the course of history.

Belgium reached another milestone in October 2018 when the city of Ganshoren elected the country's first black mayor, Pierre Kompany, father of footballer Vincent Kompany, who had captained the nation's 2014 World Cup team. According to professor Zana Aziza Etambala, Kompany's election win marked "the undeniable presence of the Congolese here in Belgium (...) I'm especially proud, and so is the whole Congolese community, that a black man was directly elected by Belgians in a city like Ganshoren, which has maybe 100 people of Congolese origin."[9]

For every step Belgians seemed to take toward a fuller reckoning with their colonial past, they took two backwards. In August 2018, press accounts and social media told of an attack on a young black woman at the Pukkelpop music festival. One online account reported that young people at the event had made the Hitler salute and had sung, "Handjes kappen, de Congo is van ons," "Cut hands, the Congo is ours."[10] In September, RTBF weather presenter Cécile Djunga revealed the innumerable racist messages she had received over the preceding months, and implied a connection to people's ignorance of their colonial past. "In Belgium, people do not know anything about colonisation or immigration," she said. "They feel it is all the fault of foreigners. I think in Belgium we have a problem in that we never explained the truth about colonisation, and it should be told in the schools."[11] She underlined that racists would not define her identity, "I am Belgian and now they're going to stop telling me to go back to my country. Because this is my country."[12] The Facebook video post in which she called attention to the abuse garnered more than 2 million views.

One of the most significant events in the country, and one which acted as a catalyst for debate and discussion, was the reopening of the Congo Museum in Tervuren. Re-baptized the AfricaMuseum, the institution reopened almost five years to the day after its December 2013 closure to begin a years-long overhaul under the direction of long-serving museum chief Guido Gryseels.[13] Although unique in its own way, the renovation fit into a bigger picture of "new museums" being created in Europe and elsewhere that highlighted debates about the representation of ethnicity and cultural diversity.[14]

Efforts toward a more profound "decolonization" of the museum and other sites were already underway before the museum's renovation was complete. Younger Belgians, including people of immigrant backgrounds and from the left of the political spectrum, continued to push decolonization along. The 2016 exhibit "Congo Art Works: Popular Painting" was a collaboration between BOZAR and the AfricaMuseum that questioned the long-enduring positive images of colonialism transmitted in official photography, for instance in colonial-era magazines. It was a sign of the times that the exposition was curated by Bambi Ceuppens and Sammy Baloji, both of African heritage.[15] The exhibit took a critical stance not only toward Belgium's history in central Africa, but also toward the actions of Congolese.[16] *Lobi Kuna*, a collaborative experimental film directed by Matthias De Groof and others, opened up the Tervuren Museum—closed for renovations at the time of filming—to re-read the institution as a mausoleum of Congolese culture.[17] Even more significant than the Belgian-Congolese collaboration behind the film was the access Tervuren granted the filmmakers, a risky move by an institution with such historical baggage, and itself a sign of a growing decolonization at the museum.[18]

A slew of events and productions took place in the weeks and days leading up to Tervuren's December 2018 reopening. KU Leuven and BOZAR hosted discussions of the museum's renovation and the state of decolonization in the country. VRT's six-part series "Children of the Colony" became a sensation. Widely reported on in the press, the series included numerous interviews with

Africans who had lived under foreign rule, which confronted the nation with ugly truths about the Belgian state-rule colonial era after 1908: that it was cruel; that Belgians were complicit in the murder of Lumumba; that Belgian rule consisted of a system of racial segregation as oppressive as apartheid; and so forth.

The sequence of high-profile events in 2018 primed the nation for the reopening of the AfricaMuseum, at which time the question of restitution once again raised its head. Calls for the return of Congolese heritage held in Belgium did not take place in a vacuum. French president Emmanuel Macron had commissioned a study of African art in France, and in November 2018 Bénédicte Savoy and Felwine Sarr issued a report calling for the return to African countries of artwork held in France.[19] Savoy and Sarr's report found an echo in the days leading up to the AfricaMuseum's reopening when a group of researchers, foreign leaders, authors, academics, journalists, and others wrote an open letter asking, "What are 300 Congolese skulls doing in Belgium?" They called attention to the mortal remains of Africans in the former metropole, which had been removed from central Africa during the colonial period. One of those skulls was that of the African chief Lusinga, defeated in battle by Émile Storms, who had Lusinga decapitated and his skull prepared so that he could return it to Europe; the skull was one of three Storms brought home with him. After Storms' death his widow handed the skull over, and it ended up in the natural history museum.[20] In December, president of the Democratic Republic of the Congo, Joseph Kabila, gave an interview with *Le Soir* in which he sought the return of Congolese artwork and documents from Belgium.

Despite Tervuren's notoriety and years-long calls by critics for profound changes to it, the 2013-2018 restoration resulted in more continuity rather than a great break with the past, despite considerable self-reflection. Much of the 74 million Euros devoted to the renovation was spent on physical and structural changes rather than redesigning the story that the institution presented to visitors. The museum's main structure was renewed, including the addition of new spaces and the revamping of its underground galleries. The renovation addressed the perennial challenges of controlling the museum's climate and the power of the suns ray's through the addition of new windows and state-of-the art, towering glass walls. Construction also added a remarkable glass-walled welcome center and tunnel entrance.[21] One room from the original 1910 permanent exhibits, the so-called Crocodile Room, remains in its original state, closed off to walk-through visits to make it, "une sorte de musée du musée." (a sort of museum of the museum.)[22] The bust of Leopold II in the original interior *cour d'honneur* was removed and selected statues "de qualité mais très colonials" (of very colonial features) were relegated to a *dépôt des statues* in the bottom-level galleries. Remaining in place are colonial-era and very much colonialist statues by Arsène Matton and Arthur Dupagne in the former *salle d'honneur* rotunda, including Matton's "La Belgique apportant la Civilisation au Congo" (Belgium bringing civilization to the Congo), "La Belgique apportant le Bien-être au Congo" (Belgium bringing welfare to the Congo), and "L'esclavage" (Slavery) (see page 165). The statues are now contextualized with explanatory plaques, and acting as a counterpoint to them is the sculpture "Congo, Nouveau Souffle" (Congo, New Breath), by Congolese artist Aimé Mpané.[23] Also remaining in place is the 1934 wall memorial honoring those Belgians who died in the Congo before 1908, which lists all 1,508 of their names, to which the museum provided two counterpoints. First, the room pays homage to the Congolese victims of foreign rule by means of a contemporary art installation. Second, the museum placed the names of the seven Congolese who died in Tervuren during the 1897 colonial exposition—Ekia, Gemba, Kitoukwa, M'Peia, Zao, Sambo, and Mibangé—on the glass walls of the memorial room, to be cast in shadows onto the interior walls by the sun.

Considering the degree to which the institution is itself a relic, the renovation might have attempted to transform the entire museum into an exhibit about the colonial past. Whether this could have been engineered is another question. Some critics have said it should have been shut down completely, one averring that, "The bravest decision would have been to close the museum."[24] Gryseels hewed to a middle-of-the-road approach by keeping the museum largely as-is while incoporating some African voices. As a result, displays in many areas are fundamentally similar to those in place before, including exhibits on natural resources, insects, and the tropical forest. Rather than making the reopened museum a reflection on the museum and its role in colonialism, it continues to try to be a museum of Africa. Additional continuity is to be seen in the institution's enduring goal of making the museum a destination for school field trips, just as it was during the colonial and post-1960 eras, when the institution's leadership stressed the need to attract visitors, especially schoolchildren and their teachers.[25] The lack of profound transformation was perhaps inevitable. "However radically the interior may have been refashioned to reflect new attitudes to Africa, the grandeur of King Leopold II's design and the fervour of his desire to promote his imperial venture into the continent's heart still overwhelm the visitor."[26] In any case, the refurbishment left little room in the museum for history, which could have invited a more clear-eyed reflection to visitors regarding the country's colonial experience.

* * *

The colonial inheritance was never of primary importance in Belgium after 1960. Although there was a certain sustained interest in the Congo of Mobutu and afterward, and despite significant historical and other work, the degree to which popular culture was shaped and reshaped after 1960 by the country's earlier colonial experience was limited. In many ways, decolonization did not even "happen" starting in 1960. In the realm of artwork, for example, Belgians continued to claim a paramount expertise on Congolese culture, and the African art trade largely continued as "business as usual" for decades, even in the face of strident Congolese demands for restitution and recognition.

To understand the cultural significance of the colonial experience after 1960 is to tease out different, often subtle ways in which it manifested itself. The end of empire may have reinforced shifts already underway, for instance the decline of Catholic Church authority. With the former colony no longer providing a privileged *champ d'action*, the Catholic Church lost one means by which it had sustained its stature. The colonial experience also endured in individual and, to a lesser degree, in collective memory. Many have singled out Belgium for a unique failure in coming to terms with its colonial past and for forgetting about the atrocities of the Leopoldian era, what Adam Hochschild called "The Great Forgetting." But, as one commentator has noted, "So far, no other former colonial power has shown an appetite for looking back with a critical eye."[27] Instead of a "Great Forgetting," there was a repeated cycle of forgetting and remembering. "Successive generations have forgotten the Congo atrocities so that these could be brought to attention again. Time and again, the remembered events are condemned or denied; subsequently they are buried again, rediscovered, condemned, and denied, and so on. (…) The Congo atrocities have never really been forgotten, but, rather, that the memory has relentlessly been unearthed."[28] The presence of the "colonial" and awareness of the colonial past ebbed and flowed after 1960 as people re-discovered their colonial past again and again: in 1985, in 1994-1999, in 2010, and again in 2018. The state played an important role in shaping public memory, from making cuts to funding of the Tervuren Museum after 1960, to restoring vandalized statues of Leopold II, to propelling events in 2010 that marked the fiftieth anniversary of Congo's independence.

Memory varied over time. After the immediate shock and trauma of the Congo crisis had passed, there emerged a great deal of nostalgia for colonialism, especially among former colonials, and in particular because of the outsized influence of the 1950s. In unacknowledged ways, Belgians carried much cultural baggage with them directly into the post-colonial period, in the form of a colonial imaginary inherited from the last decade of their colonial rule, abruptly ended by a sudden and largely unexpected independence. There was an astounding "recycling of images" that continued to shape Belgians' views of their past. Official propaganda from the 1950s had long-enduring effects, giving that decade a long afterlife. With generational change, the passage of time, a succession of anniversaries, and a growth in non-European immigration into the country, younger people especially began to view the colonial past with more skepticism.

Movements of people, including Congolese immigration, were important. The return of significant numbers of Belgians from the Congo beginning in 1960 and the smaller number of Congolese who migrated to the former metropole contributed to an enduring pro-colonialist orientation to public and private memories. This also contributed to, until very recently, meager contestation of the overwhelmingly positive public narrative of the colonial era, including in colonial-era monuments in the metropole. In other contexts, historical memorials have been highly contested, for instance those to the Holocaust in Poland, contested by Jewish, German, and Polish angles.[29] Not so in Belgium, where until very recently there were few Congolese to contest the colonial past, and even fewer in a well-established position from which to do so.

The criticism that Belgians have not faced up to their colonial past also misses the mark insofar as the country does not share one single colonial past. Imperialism was not a history with just two sides, colonizer and colonized. Belgium has long been a country of immigration, and since 1960 even more so, especially of non-European migrants. Many such "new" Belgians view the history of the Leopoldian and Belgian overseas ventures in Africa differently, or with indifference. What is more, citizens of more recent arrival themselves do not represent one block with one view on the past. They originated from a wide variety of European and non-European countries, and have arrived at different times. Gert Oostindie has done a masterful job of showing how different post-colonial immigrants into the Netherlands faced acculturation differently, leading to significantly different colonial and post-colonial migrant experiences, meaning there was no "one" post-colonial immigrant community or viewpoint on that country's past colonialism.[30] There also were successive (and differing) waves of colonial and then post-colonial immigration into Britain.[31] The history of Belgian/Congolese migration paralleled these cases because Congolese immigrants also arrived in different "waves." Despite the much larger presence of Congolese in Belgium after 1960 compared to that of the colonial era, these individuals had little to do with the shaping of culture when it came to the colony and central Africa of the post-colonial period. This represented a continuation of what occurred during the colonial era, when Belgian officialdom generally managed to control depictions of the colony.

What has happened to pro-empire markers left sprinkled across the country, from large cities to small villages, suggests that Flemish and French speakers in Belgium also have remembered the colonial past differently, but not radically so. Any monument's meaning depends on the responses of its viewers.[32] On the whole, the reactions of the country's inhabitants to monuments suggest they remembered their colonial past *as Belgians* through most the post-colony era, although this diminished over time as people in the country's north increasingly remembered them as Dutch speakers, and as French speakers recalled the past evermore as inhabitants of either Brussels or the French-speaking southern community. One caveat: Former colonials, whichever their language, have tended to defend a positive view of *Belgium's* colonial past. Them aside, Flemish speakers have tended toward greater nostalgia for missionary action, whereas French speakers have been more ardent supporters of a positive view of the monarchy and its role in colonialism. "Many francophones have long rebutted criticism of Leopold II's brutal rule of the Congo Free State whereas many Flemings, by contrast, criticize that same rule in order to discredit the monarchy."[33] More than one municipality in Flanders has put up memorials to colonial-era missionaries in recent years. One might infer from the 2018 headline, "Most statues of Leopold II have plaques in Flanders," that Dutch-speaking Belgium had better come to terms with the Leopoldian colonial era.[34] But in fact, those plaques—at monuments honoring the king in Hasselt, Ekeren, Ghent, as well as two in Ostend—are small and rather anodyne; the plaque at the bust of Leopold II in Prinses Clementinaplein in Ostend, to point to one example, makes no mention of colonialism. Thus, the original meanings of pro-colonial memorials tend to shine through more prominently than the messages conveyed by a limited number of explanatory plaques.

"Empire" was much more prominent in Belgian culture after 1960 than previously believed. In many aspects, Flemish and French speakers in the country remembered the colonial past in similar ways, with small but significant differences. Only recently have strident voices emerged challenging the longstanding positive interpretation of the foreign, European domination that reigned in central Africa from the late 1800s down to 1960. The lasting presence of colonial monuments suggests a "colonialist" view toward the past endures in many ways. Just as the experience of empire acted at the margins of Belgian culture post-1960, so have changes to colonialist attitudes and memories of the colonial past taken place at the margins, be it in textbooks, at the Tervuren Museum, at memorials, or in the realms of literature and the arts. This chapter's epigraph, a quote still present on various public monuments in the country, might continue to serve as a byword for the aftereffects of the colonial adventure on Belgian culture.

Appendix

Readers can access a detailed list of monuments in Belgium linked to the country's colonial past at the URL www.lup.be/leopard or via the QR code below.

Notes

Introduction

1. Quoted in V. Rosoux and L. van Ypersele, "The Belgian national past" (2011), p. 53.
2. M. Wrong, "Belgium Confronts Its Heart of Darkness," *The Independent*, 23 February 2005, http://www.independent.co.uk/news/world/europe/belgium-confronts-its-heart-of-darkness-6151923.html. Accessed 3 July 2014.
3. Unless otherwise noted, all translations are my own.
4. Invitation at "Brusselse herdenking voor Leopold II schiet in verkeerde keelgat," *De Morgen*, 15 December 2015, https://www.demorgen.be/binnenland/brusselse-herdenking-voor-leopold-ii-schiet-in-verkeerde-keelgat-bfc0a36d. Accessed 9 August 2018.
5. D. Cullen, "Leopold Must Fall" (2016).
6. N.G., "La statue de Léopold II vandalisée," *La Libre Belgique*, 17 December 2015, http://www.lalibre.be/regions/bruxelles/la-statue-de-leopold-ii-vandalisee-567309273570ed3894a11a01. Accessed 14 June 2018.
7. B. Barnard et al., *How Can One Not Be Interested in Belgian History* (2005).
8. J. Destrée, *Lettre au Roi sur la séparation de la Wallonie et de la Flandre* (1912), p. 6.
9. S. Leys, *The Hall of Uselessness* (2013), p. 212.
10. H. Van Goethem, *Belgium and the Monarchy* (2010), p. 135.
11. See Barnard et al. (2005).
12. Quoted in P. van de Craen, "What, if Anything, Is a Belgian?" (2002), p. 25.
13. Review of Marc Reynebeau, *Een geschiedenis van België* (2003), *Knack*, 15 October 2003.
14. E.g., C. Kesteloot, "Mouvement Wallon et Identité Nationale" (1993), pp. 1-48; M. Reynebeau, *Het klauwen van de leeuw* (1995); M. Van Ginderachter, *Le chant du coq* (2005); idem., "Belgium: Too many pasts, too many memories" (2015), pp. 7-14; L. Wils, *Histoire des nations belges* (1996); idem., *Vlaanderen, België, Groot-Nederland* (1994); idem., "Introduction" (1992), pp. 1-39.
15. Much of the following is drawn from M. Stanard, "The colonial past is never dead" (2016), pp. 151-174.
16. A. Crosby, *Ecological Imperialism* (1986).
17. P. Doolen, "Dutch Imperial Past Returns to Haunt the Netherlands" (2014).
18. D. Fieldhouse, "Can Humpty-Dumpty Be Put Together Again?" (1984), pp. 9-23.
19. J. MacKenzie, *Propaganda and Empire* (1984).
20. A. Thompson, ed., *Writing Imperial Histories* (2013) reflects on the state of scholarship and MacKenzie's legacy. See also M. Farr and S. Barczewski, *The MacKenzie Moment* (2019).
21. E.g. C. Hall and S. Rose, *At Home with the Empire* (2006).
22. P. Blanchard et al., *Colonial Culture in France since the Revolution* (2014).
23. E. Ames et al., *Germany's Colonial Pasts* (2005).

24. G. Oostindie, *Postcolonial Netherlands* (2011).

25. E.g., T. Lumumba-Kasongo, "Zaire's Ties to Belgium" (1992), pp. 23-48.

26. J.-P. Peemans, "Imperial Hangovers" (1980), pp. 257-286; G. Vanthemsche, *Belgium and the Congo, 1885-1980* (2012).

27. Much of the following is based on M. Stanard, "Lumumba's Ghost" (2019).

28. B. Ceuppens, *Congo made in Flanders?* (2003).

29. V. Viaene et al., *Congo in België* (2009).

30. J. MacKenzie, ed., *European Empires and the People* (2011).

31. E. Buettner, *Europe after Empire* (2016).

32. P. Van Schuylenbergh, "Trop-plein de mémoires, vide d'histoire?" (2014), pp. 31-71; G. Vanthemsche, "The Historiography of Belgian Colonialism in the Congo" (2006), pp. 89-119; I. Ndaywel È Nziem, "L'historiographie congolaise" (2006), pp. 237-254.

33. See J.-L. Vellut, *Congo: Ambitions et désenchantements, 1880-1960* (2017), including "Bibliographie de Jean-Luc Vellut," compiled by A. Cornet, P. Van Schuylenbergh, and G. Vanthemsche, pp. 495-503.

34. Van Schuylenbergh (2004), pp. 35-39.

35. E.g., *Zaïre 1885-1985* (1985), and L. Joris, *Mon oncle du Congo* (1990), first published as *Terug naar Congo* (1987) after her voyage there around the centenary.

36. Van Goethem (2010), pp. 180-181; Wils (1996), pp. 215-223, 244-261.

37. See L. Gann and P. Duignan, *The Rulers of Belgian Africa, 1884-1914* (1979).

38. Only 3,615 of 6,991. Vanthemsche (2012), p. 279.

39. J. MacKenzie, "Empire from Above and Below" (2016), pp. 37-48; idem., "Epilogue" (2015), pp. 188-206.

40. C. Wills, *Lovers & Strangers* (2017).

41. On the enormity of Congo's recent travails see J. Stearns, *Dancing in the Glory of Monsters* (2011).

42. P. Rusesabagina, *An Ordinary Man* (2006).

43. A. Hochschild, *King Leopold's Ghost* (1998), pp. 292-306.

44. J. Young, *The Texture of Memory* (1993), p. xi.

45. Hochschild (1998).

46. L. de Witte, *De moord op Lumumba* (1999).

47. I. Goddeeris, "Postcolonial Belgium" (2015), pp. 434-451.

48. The institution in Tervuren has undergone numerous name changes. Upon its 1897 founding it was called the Musée du Congo, which was changed to Musée du Congo belge beginning in 1908, which became the Musée royal du Congo belge. It became the Musée royal de l'Afrique centrale (MRAC) beginning in 1960. This is not even to mention its names rendered into English or Dutch. The name Africa Museum was commonly used by the early twenty-first century, and the institution made it official after re-emerging from its 2013-2018 renovation as the rebranded AfricaMuseum. This book will often refer to it simply as the Tervuren Museum.

49. J. Rahier, "The Ghost of Leopold II" (2003), pp. 58-84; M. Stanard, *Selling the Congo* (2011); M. Couttenier, *Als muren spreken* (2010).

50. Van Schuylenbergh (2004), p. 37.

51. M. Quaghebeur and E. Van Balberghe, *Papier blanc, encre noire* (1992); P. Halen, *Le petit belge avait vu grand* (1993); P. Halen and J. Riesz, *Images de l'Afrique et du Congo/Zaïre dans les lettres françaises de Belgique et alentour* (1993).

52. E.g., S. Cornelis, P. Maréchal, and J.-M. Goris, *Artistes belges dans les territoires d'outre-mer 1884-1962* (1989); B. Jewsiewicki, *Art pictural zaïrois* (1992).

53. D. Van Reybrouck, *Congo* (2010).

54. An earlier, more impressionistic volume is L. Vints, *Kongo made in Belgium* (1984).

55. To refer to *lieux de mémoire* is to draw of course on P. Nora's *Les lieux de mémoire* (1984-1992).

56. Stanard (2011), pp. 167-202.

57. Young (1993), p. 34.

58. Ibid., p. 5.

59. V. Viaene, "Reprise-remise: de Congolese identiteitscrisis van België rond 1908," in Viaene et al. (2009), p. 45.

Belgians and the Colonial Experience before 1960

1. This oft-referenced phrase appears on multiple colonialist memorials. It is a short-ened version of a quote from a 3 June 1906 statement by the king: "J'ai entrepris, il y a plus de vingt ans, l'œuvre du Congo dans l'intérêt de la civilisation et pour le bien de la Belgique." Leopold II made the 1906 statement following the 1904-1905 com-mission of inquiry he had appointed, which had confirmed atrocities in the Congo. *Le Congo: Moniteur colonial illustré* (Brussels), no. 113 (24 June 1906), p. 197.

2. For a succinct account of Leopoldian and Belgian colonialism see G. Vanthem-sche, "The Belgian Colonial Empire (1885/1908-1960)" (2014), pp. 971-997.

3. J.-L. Vellut, "European Medicine in the Congo Free State (1885-1908)" (1997), pp. 67-87; Gann and Duignan (1979); M. Stanard, "Violence and Empire" (2013), pp. 454-467.

4. D. Pavlakis, *British Humanitarianism and the Congo Reform Movement, 1896-1913* (2015).

5. Much of the following is drawn from Stanard, *Selling the Congo* (2011).

6. See Stanard, *Selling the Congo* (2011); on the 1897 exposition, M. Wynants, *Des ducs de Brabant aux villages congolais* (1997). Liege hosted a World's Fair in 1905 at which the colonial presence was limited.

7. Belgians, like other Western countries, put colonial subjects on display in "human zoos," the literature on which is vast. See N. Bancel, et al., *Zoos humains* (2004).

8. P. Van Schuylenbergh, "Découverte et vie des arts plastiques du bassin du Congo dans la Belgique des années 1920-1930" (1995), pp. 1-62; J. Guisset, *Le Congo et l'art belge, 1880-1960* (2003).

9. S. Kasfir, "Visual Cultures" (2013), p. 439.

10. "Histoire du Congo par les monuments" (1985), p. 34.

11. *Le Mouvement antiesclavagiste* (1894), p. 119; "Histoire du Congo par les monu-ments" (1985), p. 34.

12. Author's visit, 23 March 2003.

13. "La Fontaine Ponthier" (2018).

14. "Ponthier, Pierre" (n.d.).

15. M. Coosemans, entry for Ponthier, *Biographie Coloniale Belge/Belgische Koloniale Biografie* I (1948), columns 766-771. *Biographie Coloniale Belge/Belgische Koloniale*

Biografie (later the *Biographie Belge d'Outre-Mer/Belgische Overzeese Biografie*) hereafter *BCB*.

16. G. Vanthemsche, "Van de *Belgische Koloniale Biografie* naar het *Biografisch Woordenboek van Belgen Overzee*" (2011), pp. 215-235.

17. M. Coosemans, entry for Ponthier, *BCB* I (1948), columns 766-771.

18. Around 1.1 million 2018 US Dollars. R. Corbey, "African Art in Brussels" (1999), p. 12.

19. E. Schildkrout and C. Keim, "Objects and agendas: Re-collecting the Congo," in E. Schildkrout and C. Keim, *The Scramble for Art in Central Africa* (1998), p. 23.

20. F. Cattier, *Étude sur la situation de l'État indépendant du Congo* (1906).

21. S. Colard, "Photography in the Colonial Congo (1885-1960)" (2016), p. 35.

22. E.g., A.-M. G., *Le Congo belge illustré ou l'État indépendant du Congo* (1888), p. 29.

23. V. Viaene, "King Leopold's Imperialism and the Origins of the Belgian Colonial Party, 1860-1905" (2008), pp. 741-90.

24. M. Stanard, "Digging-In" (2014), pp. 23-48.

25. Vanthemsche (2012), p. 276.

26. Colard (2016), pp. 71-101.

27. S. Hertmans, *War and Turpentine* (2017).

28. "BRAFA Art Fair" (n.d.).

29. A. de Cock, *Le Congo belge et ses marques postales* (1986); M. Vancraenbroeck, *Les médailles de la presence belge en Afrique centrale 1876-1960* (1996).

30. For other examples of juvenile literature see L. Boudart, "Congo belge et littérature de jeunesse dans l'entre-deux-guerres" (2012).

31. B. Ceuppens, *Congo made in Flanders?* (2003), pp. 295-355.

32. Stanard, *Selling the Congo* (2011), pp. 47-88.

33. T. Verschaffel, "Congo in de Belgische zelfrepresentatie," in Viaene et al. (2009), pp. 63-80.

34. B. Cleys, et al., "België in Congo, Congo in België: Weerslag van de missionering op de religieuze instituten," in Viaene et al. (2009), pp. 147-165.

35. A. Leurquin, "La Distraction de l'objet africain ou l'histoire d'une errance" (1988), pp. 315-329.

36. F. Herreman et al., *Musée d'Ethnographie Anvers* (1991), p. 7; author's visit to Museum aan de Stroom (MAS) with Els de Palmenaere, 13 November 2013.

37. Many of the ideas presented here on Congolese artwork, Africana, and Belgian culture during the colonial era and after 1960 are developed in M. Stanard, "African Art and Post-Colony Belgium" (forthcoming).

38. J.-L. Vellut, "Le Congo dans les esthétiques de l'Occident, l'Occident dans les esthétiques du Congo," in J.-L. Vellut, *Congo: Ambitions et désenchantements, 1880-1960* (2017), pp. 287-308; idem., "La peinture du Congo-Zaïre et la recherche de l'Afrique innocente" (1990), pp. 633-659; G.-D. Périer, "Rendons les Fétiches aux Noirs!" (1930).

39. P. Halen, "Les douze travaux du Congophile" (2000), pp. 139-150; first quote from J. A. Cornet, et al., *60 ans de peinture au Zaïre* (1989), p. 18; P.-P. Fraiture, "Modernity and the Belgian Congo" (2009), p. 50.

40. J. Tollebeek, *Mayombe* (2010). Thank you to Guy Vanthemsche for bringing this work to my attention.

41. S. Van Beurden, *Authentically African* (2015), pp. 34-35.

42. Joris (1990), p. 11.
43. Cornet, et al. (1989), p. 10; B. Wastiau, "The Violence of Collecting: Objects, Images and People from the Colony," paper presentation, "American Historical Association conference", New York, 4 January 2009. My thanks to Boris Wastiau for sharing his paper with me.
44. Vellut, "Le Congo dans les esthétiques de l'Occident" (2017), p. 291.
45. J. Monroe, "Surface Tensions" (2012), pp. 445-475; C. Wintle, "Decolonizing the Smithsonian" (2016), pp. 1492-1520; P. Brocheux and D. Hémery, *Indochina* (2009), pp. 217-249.
46. Folder "1894-1938," Papiers André Van Iseghem, Archives historiques privées, AfricaMuseum.
47. *Bulletin de l'Association des Vétérans coloniaux*, October 1930, no. 11, p. 2, and September 1930, no. 10, p. 11. See also document # 5268.42, "Discours prononcé par M. Detry, Délégué de la Ligue du Souvenir Congolais au Mémorial Congolais à Anderlecht," Papiers Emm. Muller, and invitation from the Vétérans coloniaux to André Van Iseghem, folder "1894-1938," Papiers André Van Iseghem, both Archives historiques privées, AfricaMuseum.
48. A. Lacroix, entry for Declerck, *BCB* II (1951), column 236.
49. A. Lacroix, entry for Fichefet, *BCB* I (1948), column 372.
50. A. Lacroix, entry for Croes, *BCB* II (1951), column 206.
51. A. Lacroix, entry for Verlooy, *BCB* II (1951), column 951.
52. J. Conrad, "An Outpost of Progress" (2013).
53. The *BCB* identifies at least seven Belgians who took their own life before 1908 either in the CFS or shortly after returning from Africa to Europe. The number is likely higher considering the stigma attached to suicide and the limited information available to biographers about causes of death. The rate of 464 per 100,000 was arrived at using those seven and dividing by 1,508, the number of total Belgian deaths compiled by the Ligue du souvenir congolais.
54. P. Curtin, *The Image of Africa* (1964), p. 177.
55. "Conférences et Manifestations coloniales" (1930), n.p.
56. M. Coosemans, entry for Villers, *BCB* III (1952), column 891.
57. A. Engels, entry for de Meulenaer, *BCB* II (1951), columns 694-695.
58. Author's visit, 13 May 2018.
59. A. Lacroix, entry for Crauwels, *BCB* IV (1955), columns 163-164.
60. *L'Illustration congolaise*, no. 179 (1 August 1936), p. 5984; author's visits, 24 November 2002 and 11 May 2018.
61. *Bulletin de l'Association des Vétérans coloniaux*, no. 7 (July 1931), p. 4.
62. A. Lacroix, entry for Collet, *BCB* II (1951), columns 177-178.
63. M. Coosemans, entry for Guéquier, *BCB* VI (1968), column 429.
64. M. Coosemans, entry for Dortu, *BCB* III (1952), column 258.
65. A. Lacroix, entry for Piron, *BCB* II (1951), column 772.
66. Email communication from Léon Nyssen, 20 March 2003, and letter from Alain Noirfalisse, 21 March 2003. Thank you to Mr. Noirfalisse for sharing his photographs of gatherings at the site.
67. See Vanthemsche (2012).
68. M. Conway, *The Sorrows of Belgium* (2012).
69. See V. Dujardin and M. Dumoulin, *L'Union fait-elle toujours la force?* (2008).

70. Vanthemsche (2012), p. 280.

71. Lack of access to archives means the exact reasons for the expulsions are yet to be determined. See M. Stanard, "Revisiting Bula Matari and the Congo Crisis" (2018), p. 11.

72. M. Stanard, "'Boom! Goes the Congo'" (2017).

73. G. Jacquemyns, "Le Congo belge devant l'opinion publique" (1956).

74. B. Verhaegen, "La Colonisation et la décolonisation dans les manuels d'histoire en Belgique" (1992), pp. 333-379.

75. What had been the Ministry of Colonies' Office colonial became the Centre d'information et de documentation du Congo belge et du Ruanda-Urundi (CID) from 1950, later becoming the Office de l'information et des relations publiques pour le Congo belge et le Ruanda-Urundi (Inforcongo) from 1955-1960.

76. M. Stanard, "'Bilan du monde pour un monde plus déshumanisé'" (2005), p. 283.

77. Author's visit, 23 March 2003.

78. "Erection d'un monument au roi Léopold II à Arlon" (1950), p. 40; "Grandiose manifestation coloniale à Arlon" (1951), p. 478.

79. Email communication from Pierre Eppe, 20 March 2003.

80. P. Derom et al., *Les sculptures de Bruxelles* (2002), p. 110.

81. F. Dellicour, entry for Tombeur, *BCB* VI (1968), columns 1022-1026.

82. *Instantanés* (1951), p. 2.

83. "Le salut aux drapeaux des campagnes d'Afrique," *Le Soir*, 24-25 June 1962, p. 8.

84. G. Vanthemsche, "Belgian royals on tour in the Congo (1909-1960)" (2018), pp. 169-190; Buettner (2016), pp. 171-174.

85. [M.] Z. A. Etambala, "«*Bwana Kitoko*» (1955), un film d'André Cauvin" (2010), pp. 142-144.

86. G. Castryck, "Binnenste-buitenland: de Belgische kolonie en de Vlaamse buiten-landberichtgeving," in Viaene et al. (2009), pp. 271-282.

87. B. Metcalf and T. Metcalf, *A Concise History of India* (2002), p. 161.

88. R. Boon, "De Prins-Regent naar Belgisch-Congo en Ruanda-Urundi (29 juni-12 augustus 1947)" (2012), pp. 49-62.

89. See Vanthemsche (2018), pp. 169-190.

90. Stanard (2005), pp. 267-298.

91. G. Vanthemsche, "De belgische socialisten en Congo 1895-1960" (1999), pp. 31-65; S. Hocq, "Baudouin Ier et les visites d'État au Congo" (2012), pp. 2-48.

Reminders and Remainders of Empire, 1960-1967

1. Quoted in "Marred: M. Lumumba's offensive speech in King's presence," *The Guardian*, 1 July 1960, https://www.theguardian.com/world/1960/jul/01/congo. Accessed 12 December 2018.

2. There were reports Lumumba ad libbed these words in his speech during independence day ceremonies, 30 June 1960; the written text of his speech did not include them.

3. Vanthemsche (2012), p. 209.

4. Dujardin and Dumoulin (2008).

5. Ibid., p. 46.

6. "Histoire du Congo par les monuments" (1985) p. 34; "Budgets Coloniaux -- Dépenses des Services d'Europe. Prévisions budgétaires pour l'année 1955", 3 December 1954, and Buisseret to Marquette, 27 June 1956, no. 661/Inf., indicate a Ministry of Colonies subsidy of 140,000 Frs, both at liasse "32A. Subside Monument Léopold II à Mons," portefeuille 59 Infopresse, Archives Africaines, Federal Public Service Foreign Affairs. "Archives Africaines, Federal Public Service Foreign Affairs," hereafter abbreviated AA.

7. "A Mons: L'inauguration du monument à Léopold II," Le Soir, 15 September 1958.

8. On the original location, in addition to the article in Le Soir on its inauguration, see "Les cérémonies du 50e anniversaire de la bataille de Tabora (18-9-56) [sic]" (1966), p. 61.

9. Collectif, Mons 1865-2015 (2015), p. 102.

10. Author's visit, 15 December 2002. Hennuyers refers to someone from the province of Hainaut, of which Mons is the capital.

11. Author's visit, 10 May 2018.

12. "Mons: les mains coupées s'agrippent à la statue de Léopold II," lavenir.net, 13 September 2017, https://www.lavenir.net/cnt/dmf20170913_01054469?pid=3388079. Accessed 15 June 2018.

13. M. Stanard, "Après nous, le déluge" (2019).

14. E. Kets, Kuifje & Tintin kibbelen in Afrika (2009); N. Hunt, "Rewriting the Soul in a Flemish Congo" (2008), pp. 185-215.

15. Stanard, "Revisiting Bula Matari" (2008), pp. 144-168.

16. Buettner (2016), p. 181.

17. J. Rahier, "Métis/Mulâtre" (2003), p. 94.

18. Buettner (2016), pp. 168-171. On Belgian comic strips see P. Delisle, Bande dessinée franco-belge et imaginaire colonial (2008); idem., Spirou, Tintin et Cie, une littérature catholique? (2010). On Tintin see also N. Hunt, "Tintin and the Interruptions of Congolese Comics" (2002), pp. 90-123.

19. J. Rich, " 'Tata otangani, oga njali, mbiambiè!'" (2009).

20. Hergé, Tintin in the Congo (1962).

21. Halen (1993), p. 180, n. 57.

22. L. Monseur, "La Colonisation belge" (1984-1985), p. 143.

23. See Stanard (2005).

24. "Om zich de parlementaire instellingen eigen to maken!," De Standaard, 2 May 1960.

25. Rahier "Métis/Mulâtre" (2003), p. 95.

26. J. Geeraerts, Black Ulysses (1978), p. 17.

27. There has been doubt cast on whether Lumumba actually spoke these words that day. Nevertheless, that there was (and remains) the widespread impression he spoke them suggests perceptions of his resistance to European colonialist narratives. M. Wrong, "The famous things they never said" (2008); T. Turner, Ethnogenèse et nationalisme en Afrique centrale (2000), p. 294.

28. Quoted in J. Meriwether, Proudly We Can Be Africans (2002), p. 170.

29. Author's 29 June 2001 conversation with Ludo de Vleeschauwer, son of Albert de Vleeschauwer; the latter served as Minister of Colonies 1938-1945.

30. I relate this story in Stanard (2016), pp. 151-152.

31. Vanthemsche (2012), p. 202.
32. Buettner (2016), p. 52.
33. "Stèle à un combattant de 1914-1918" (n.d.).
34. Author's visit, 11 May 2018.
35. "U.S. Missionaries Rescued in Congo," *The New York Times*, 25 January 1964.
36. Geeraerts (1978).
37. A. Cornet and F. Gillet, *Congo Belgique 1955-1965* (2010), pp. 129-130.
38. See K. Dunn, *Imagining the Congo* (2003).
39. Buettner (2016), p. 232.
40. Belgium gained Ruanda-Urundi after World War I as League of Nations mandates, which became UN Trust Territories after World War II before gaining independence in 1962. Belgians always focused above all on the Congo.
41. The only comparable case is Germany, which lost is colonies in one fell swoop in 1919. Nonetheless, Germany had possessed multiple overseas territories in Africa, east Asia, and Oceania.
42. L. Namikas, *Battleground Africa* (2013).
43. M. Dumoulin, "L'Enseignement sur l'Afrique a varié avec l'histoire" (2010), p. 26.
44. A. Wigley, "Marketing Cold War Tourism in the Belgian Congo" (2014).
45. Buettner (2016), p. 228.
46. Vanthemsche (2012), p. 208.
47. Ibid., p. 262, drawing on P. Salmon, "Les retours en Belgique induits par la décolonisation" (1994), pp. 191-212.
48. M.-B. Dembour, *Recalling the Belgian Congo* (2000), p. 72; L. Licata and O. Klein, "Regards croisés sur un passé commun" (2005), pp. 244-271.
49. L.-F. Vanderstraeten, entry for Emmanuel Muller, *BCB* VIII (1998), column 315.
50. "Une visite au home des vétérans coloniaux," *Le Soir*, 4 May 1961, p. 4.
51. My thanks to Guy Vanthemsche for this information.
52. D. Thys van den Audenaerde, "In Memoriam, Lucien Cahen" (1982), pp. 3-4.
53. J. Lepersonne, "Lucien Cahen" (1982), p. 9.
54. Much of this discussion is drawn from M. Stanard, "Imperialists without an Empire" (2008), pp. 155-170.
55. See Stanard, *Selling the Congo* (2011).
56. See Stanard (2008).
57. F. Gillet, "Le pélerinage des anciens coloniaux en région bruxelloise" (2008), p. 54.
58. E.g., J. Clément et al., *La colonisation belge* (2004); G. De Weerd, *L'État indépendant du Congo* (2015). My thanks to Guy Vanthemsche for the latter reference.
59. Gillet, "Le pèlerinage" (2008), p. 57.
60. See Hocq (2012).
61. Castryck, "Binnenste-buitenland," in Viaene et al. (2009), p. 275.
62. *Le Peuple*, 17 February 1953, p. 5.
63. See *Le Peuple* series "Kivu 1953," 18 February-3 March 1953.
64. "Voyage du prince Albert et de la princesse Elisabeth au Congo," in A. Gérard, F. Lermingniaux, and C. Masson, *Histoire de Belgique* (Brussels, 1966), located at L. de Heusch, "Ceci n'est pas la Belgique" (2002), p. 20.
65. J. Boittin, *Colonial Metropolis* (2010).

66. Among other works see M. Z. A. Etambala, *Des Écoliers congolais en Belgique 1888-1900* (2011).
67. Author's visit, 10 May 2018.
68. F. Hessel, "Pour l'honneur d'avoir combattu" (2014), pp. 8-11.
69. G. Brosens, *Congo aan de Yser* (2013).
70. The Ministry of Colonies' Office colonial paid 20 francs each to a number of Congolese in Belgium to show up at an exposition to give it an authentic flair. Liasse "205.812.11. Expositions de Quinzaine. 13) Expositions des produits coloniaux. 5) Crédits," portefeuille O.C. 414, AA.
71. J. Vrelust et al., *Antwerp, World Port* (2012), p. 112.
72. Museum aan de Stroom exhibit, 13 November 2013.
73. B. Kagné, "Africains de Belgique, de l'indigène à l'immigré" (2000), p. 65.
74. Vanthemsche (2012), p. 260.
75. S. Demart, "De la distinction au stigmate" (2008), p. 59.
76. Joris (1990), p. 284.
77. Kagné (2000), pp. 62-67.
78. To focus here on Belgians' trauma is not meant to minimize the suffering and pain of Congolese; it is because the subject here is Belgium and its cultures.
79. K. Quanten, *Operatie Rode draak* (2014).
80. *Het Laatste Nieuws*, 26-28 November, 1964; "Les premiers réfugiés de Stan sont arrivés à Bruxelles-National," *Le Soir*, 26 November 1964, front page.
81. *De Standaard*, November 26, 1964; "Les premiers réfugiés de Stan sont arrivés à Bruxelles-National," *Le Soir*, 26 November 1964, front page; Buettner, p. 230.
82. See coverage in *Le Soir*, November 1964.
83. *Le Soir*, 27 November 1964, front page.
84. *Het Laatste Nieuws*, 2 December 1964, p. 3.
85. "«Ticket parade» rue Royale...," *Le Peuple*, 2 December 1964; *Het Laatste Nieuws*, 2 December 1964; quote from *Le Soir*, 2 December 1964, front page.
86. *Le Soir*, 2 December 1964, front page.
87. "Les para-commandos belges sont arrivés juste à temps," *Le Soir*, 25 November 1964, front page.
88. "Des centaines de Congolais ont souhaité sans succès d'être évacués," *Le Soir*, 26 November 1964, p. 7; *Ghosts of Rwanda*, dir. G. Barker (2004).
89. E.g., "Zaire stelt ronde tafel over relaties met België voor," *De Standaard*, 11 April 1986, front page.
90. H. Vanhee and G. Castryck, "Belgische historiogafe [sic] en verbeelding over het koloniale verleden" (2002), p. 308.
91. The colony's economy slowed in the late 1950s, but political developments overtook economic ones.
92. M. Thomas, B. Moore, and L. Butler, *Crises of Empire* (2008); G. Vanthemsche, *Genèse et portée du "plan décennal" du Congo belge (1949–1959)* (1994).
93. It bears noting that all funds for the *plan décennal* were raised in the Congo itself, although this was not widely recognized at the time.
94. See Vanthemsche (2012).
95. Vanthemsche (2012), p. 280.
96. L. Licata and O. Klein, "Holocaust or Benevolent Paternalism?" (2010), p. 48.
97. Léon Anciaux, entry for Thys, *BCB* IV (1955), columns 875-881.

98. Author's visit, 18 May 2003.
99. *La Revue coloniale belge*, 1 July 1948, no. 65; "Histoire du Congo par les monuments" (1985), p. 34.
100. "Thys, Albert," *Connaître la Wallonie* (n.d.).
101. Léon Anciaux, entry for Thys, *BCB* IV (1955), column 881.
102. "Thys, Albert" (n.d.); author's visit, 18 May 2003.
103. Quoted in Colard (2016), p. 115.
104. Ibid.
105. J. Vansina, *Living with Africa* (1994), p. 4; see also J. Vansina, *Through the Day, Through the Night* (2014). Thank you to Guy Vanthemsche for bringing Vansina's boyhood memoir to my attention.
106. S. Van Beurden, "The Value of Culture" (2013), pp. 1-21; Stanard, *Selling the Congo* (2011).
107. Leurquin (1988), pp. 315-329; Van Beurden (2013).
108. M. Stanard, "Belgium, the Congo, and Imperial Immobility" (2014), pp. 87-110.
109. Cornet and Gillet (2010), p. 14.
110. Front page photo by Henri Goldstein, "La Force Publique au Congo," *Le Peuple*, 26 February 1953.
111. See Stanard, *Selling the Congo* (2011).
112. Cornet and Gillet (2010), pp. 15-20.
113. Author's visit, 17 December 2002.
114. Young (1993), p. 34.
115. *Africa-Tervuren*, vols. 1-6 (1955), p. 114.
116. M. Coosemans, entry for Lamy, *BCB* III (1952), column 493.
117. Letter from Ch. Corty and Tielemans of the Comité exécutif du Monument Dhanis (Club africain d'Anvers, Cercle d'études coloniales) to Gov. Gen. Fuchs, 30 August 1913, document(s)/folder(s): R.G. 765, Papiers Félix Fuchs, Archives historiques privées, AfricaMuseum.
118. *Bulletin de la Société d'Etudes d'intérêts coloniaux de Namur*, no. 9 (September 1913), p. 111.
119. *La Tribune congolaise*, 18 October 1913, no. 35; "Histoire du Congo par les monuments" (1985), p. 34; "Anvers – Monument Baron Dhanis" (n.d.).
120. http://www.gva.be/dossiers/-a/leien/1954.asp. Accessed 11 September 2004. In 2013, the statue of Dhanis himself was re-erected on a socle and moved to Sint-Niklaas (where there is also a street named after him) for the exposition Coup de Ville. "Baron Dhanis staat eindelijk in Sint-Niklaas," *Het Nieuwsblad*, 11 September 2013, https://www.nieuwsblad.be/cnt/dmf20130910_00734939. Accessed 13 June 2018.
121. "Qu'est devenu le Commandant Dhanis?," *Le Soir*, 4 September 1966, front page; *L'Illustration congolaise*, no. 187 (1 April 1937), p. 6335.
122. Agentschap Onroerend Erfgoed, "Monument Belgisch-Congo" (2017).
123. Author's visits, 20 October 2002 and 13 May 2018.
124. "Histoire du Congo par les monuments" (1985), p. 33.
125. The painting might have been acquired by the MRAC. "Qu'est devenu le Commandant Dhanis?," *Le Soir*, 4 September 1966, front page.
126. D.D. [likely Désiré Denuit], "Les publications du musée royal de l'Afrique centrale," *Le Soir*, 12 January 1965.

127. L. Debertry, *Kitawala* (1953); G. Walschap, *Oproer in Congo* (1953).
128. P. Delisle, "Le Missionaire dans la bande dessinée franco-belge" (2007), p. 137.
129. See L. Renders, "In Flanders' Fields" (2008), pp. 1-14.
130. L. Renders, "In Black and White" (2009), p. 116.
131. J. Vermeulen, "Ontstaan van de post-koloniale roman in 1959-1970" (1989), pp. 82-89.
132. Renders (2009), p. 116.
133. M. de Ridder, "'Een Congoleesche werpspeer en een brok rubber, die onder's konings neus neergelegd waren'" in Viaene et al. (2009), pp. 203-214.
134. Renders (2009), p. 117.
135. J. Geeraerts, *Gangrene* (1974).
136. Geeraerts (1978); J. Bel, "Political correctness at the dawn of the millennium" (2004), pp. 113-121.
137. Nederlands letterenfonds, "Jef Geeraerts" (n.d.).

Quiescence, 1967-1985

1. V. S. Naipaul, *A Bend in the River* (1979), p. 89.
2. M. Beyen and P. Destatte, *Nouvelle histoire de Belgique 1970-2000* (2009), pp. 89-96.
3. A. Mommen, *The Belgian Economy in the Twentieth Century* (1994), p. 114.
4. Vanthemsche (2012), p. 201.
5. See Beyen and Destatte (2009).
6. R. Hogenraad and T. Grosbois, "A History of Threat in Europe and Belgium (1920-1993)" (1997), pp. 221-244.
7. S. De Mul, "The Holocaust as a Paradigm for the Congo Atrocities" (2012), p. 174.
8. *Le Soir*, 30 March 1967, p. 1; "Zon en schaduw over Vlaanderen" (1965).
9. P. Thomas, "Belgium's North-South Divide and the Walloon Regional Problem" (1990), p. 44.
10. *L'Opinion publique belge* (1971), p. 271.
11. De Mul (2012), p. 174.
12. R. Mnookin, "Ethnic Conflicts" (2007), p. 112.
13. N. Tousignant, "Les Manifestations publiques du Lien colonial entre la Belgique et le Congo belge (1897-1988)" (1995).
14. De Mul (2012), p. 173.
15. P. Monaville, "The Untraceable Colonialist" (2006), pp. 59-66.
16. V. Bragard and S. Planche, "Museum practices and the Belgian colonial past" (2009), pp. 54-64; D. Lesage, "Federalism and Post-Colonialism: About the Belgian Nation-State as Museum," conference paper, "Belgium's Africa: Assessing the Belgian Legacy in and on Africa," Ghent, Belgium, 1999, p. 6.
17. F. Jacobs and P. Khanna, "The New World," *The New York Times* 22 September 2012, http://www.nytimes.com/interactive/2012/09/23/opinion/sunday/the-new-world.html?_r=0. Accessed 25 June 2014.
18. Joris (1990), p. 10.
19. O. Degrijse, "La Belgique et les missions" (1985), p. 7.
20. See the work of H. McLeod, e.g., *Religion and the People of Western Europe 1789-1989* (1997).

21. Delisle (2007), p. 145.
22. *Le Soir*, 10 December 1961, p. 1; Thys van den Audenaerde (1982), p. 3.
23. Thys van den Audenaerde (1982), p. 3.
24. Mobil'Art, "Claude Lyr" (n.d.). Quote from *Le Soir*, 26 June 1962, p. 2.
25. *Le Soir*, 10 June 1962, p. 2.
26. *Le Soir*, 16 September 1962.
27. "Expositions…. temporaires….," *Le Soir*, 26 October 1963.
28. "Exposition de souvenirs de guerre 1914-1918 et 1940-1945 en Afrique Centrale," *Le Phare Dimanche*, 15 May 1966.
29. *Africa-Tervuren*, vol. 24, 1978, 1, p. 4.
30. A.B., "Tervueren 1897," *Le Soir*, 17 June 1967, p. 7.
31. "Succesrijke tentoonstelling School van Tervuren," *De Volksgazet*, 6 June 1967.
32. See also L. Spaas, "The Congo in Brussels" (2007), pp. 51-65.
33. D. Silverman, "Art Nouveau, Art of Darkness" (2011), pp. 139-81; idem., "Art Nouveau, Art of Darkness" (2012), pp. 175-95; idem., "Art Nouveau, Art of Darkness" (2013), pp. 3-61.
34. *Le Soir*, 15 June 1969, p. 1.
35. T. D., "Het Koninklijk Museum van Midden-Afrika te Tervuren: Meest bezocht museum van België," *De Nieuwe Gids*, 17 August 1970; attendance figures from *Africa-Tervuren*, vols. 17-26 (1971-1980).
36. "Statistieken van de bezoeken aan het museum in 1979" (1980), p. 3.
37. G. van der Speeten, "Metamorfose voor hunderdjarig museum," *De Standaard*, 28 April 2010, p. 30.
38. M. Meunier, "Africa Dreams, l'ombre du roi" (2010).
39. Hergé (1962); Halen (1993), pp. 158-181; V. van Bockhaven, "Leopard-men of the Congo in Literature and Popular Imagination" (2009), pp. 79-94.
40. See for example L. Kockerols, "Le Dieu Créateur" (1969).
41. M.-L. Bastin, *Art décoratif Tshokwe* (1961); idem., *La Sculpture Tshokwe* (1982); idem., *Introduction aux arts d'Afrique noire* (1984); D. Hersak, "In Memoriam" (2000), p. 17; anonymous, "Caveat Emptor" (1976), p. 68; L. de Heusch, "Pour Marie-Louise Bastin" (1999), p. 213.
42. Kasfir (2013).
43. Interview with Alphonse Moto, *Le Soir*, 9 August 1962, p. 5.
44. Kasfir (2013), p. 447. Cf. D. Musonda Milundu, "La circulation des objets d'art" (2008), pp. 269-293.
45. E. Schildkrout and C. Keim, *The Scramble for Art in Central Africa* (1998).
46. Corbey (1999), p. 14.
47. Naipaul (1979), p. 124.
48. Vellut, "Le Congo dans les esthétiques de l'Occident" (2017), p. 288.
49. G. Meurant, *Dessin Shoowa* (1986).
50. "Note 2," 28 June 1974, folder "Art africain dans collections belges, 1976," box "1988 25/3-5/6-'88 Utotombo Bruikleen form," Utotombo files, BOZAR archives.
51. F. D., "Une très intéressante exposition d'art africain," *L'Avenir du Tournaisis*, 26 April 1974.
52. J. Cornet, *Art of Africa* (1971); Corbey (1999), pp. 11-16.
53. R. Corbey, *"ExItCongoMuseum"* (2001), p. 27.

54. The country called the Democratic Republic of the Congo at the moment of its independence in 1960 was renamed in 1971 the Republic of Zaire, which it remained until it reverted to its original name in 1997. This book uses the names "Congo" and "Zaire" and related terms like "Zairean" and "Congolese" interchangably for the period 1971-1997.

55. *Arts primitifs/Primitieve Kunst* (1971); "Au Musée de Verviers, Art de l'Afrique centrale," *Le Jour*, 19 September 1972.

56. "Note," from 28 June 1974 meeting, folder "Art Africain dans collections belges, 1976," box "1988 25/3-5/6-'88 Utotombo Bruikleen form," Utotombo files, BOZAR archives.

57. L. Cahen, "La collaboration entre le Musée royal de l'Afrique centrale et les Musées nationaux du Zaïre" (1973), pp. 111-114.

58. A.-M. Bouttiaux, "Des mises en scène de curiosités aux chefs-d'œuvre mis en scène" (1999), pp. 606-608. For a justification for the non-return of items see Cahen (1973), pp. 111-114.

59. Van Beurden (2005).

60. Bouttiaux (1999), pp. 606-608.

61. A. Van Damme-Linseele, "From Mission 'Africa Rooms'" (2008), pp. 38-49.

62. Corbey (1999), pp. 11-16; E. Haentjens, "Waarom Brussel wereldtop is voor Afrikaanse kunst" (2016).

63. Vellut, "Le Congo dans les esthétiques de l'Occident" (2017), p. 291.

64. Corbey (1999), p. 13.

65. Van Damme-Linseele (2008), pp. 38-49.

66. *Lubuka! Lubuka!* (2005); Van Damme-Linseele (2008), pp. 38-49; https://www.crkc.be, Centrum voor Religieuze Kunst en Cultuur (2012).

67. Silverman, "Art Nouveau, Art of Darkness," parts I (2011), II (2012), and III (2013).

68. P.-L. Plasman and S. Planche, "Le «cas» Léopold" (2010), p. 28.

69. See, for example, *Revue belgo-congolais illustrée*, January 1967.

70. A.B., "Léopold II, bâtisseur et urbaniste," *Le Soir*, 7 October 1969.

71. "Leopold de Bouwer," *De Standaard*, 7 December 1973.

72. In addition to the following references see also "Monument commémoratif en l'honneur des Troupes des Campagnes d'Afrique 1885-1960" (2012).

73. Pétré (n.d.), p. 3.

74. "Commune de Schaerbeek/Gemeente Schaarbeek" (n.d.).

75. T.M., "Le Prince Albert inaugure le mémorial aux troupes d'Afrique," *Le Soir*, 8-9 March 1970, p. 2.

76. See http://www.urome.be/, Union royale belge pour les pays d'Outre-Mer – Koninklijke belgische unie voor de overzeese landen.

77. Extensive collection of photos of such commemorations at Craoca-Kkooav-Urfracol Facebook page, https://www.facebook.com/craocakkooavurfracol/. Accessed 8 January 2019.

78. A. Tshitungu Kongolo, "Commémoration du soldat inconnu congolais" (2008).

79. B. Fetter, "If I Had Known that 35 Years Ago" (1999), p. 451.

80. "Père Aelvoet" may be Walter Aelvoet, a White Father missionary who worked in central Africa.

81. "Les Belges au Congo," *La Libre Belgique*, 11 October 1971.

82. "Dans la Grande Ombre du Fondateur," *Revue belgo-congolais illustrée* (15 November 1966), pp. 41-42.

83. T. M., "Le Prince Albert inaugure le mémorial aux troupes d'Afrique," *Le Soir*, 8-9 March 1970; R. Pétré, "Monuments aux morts congolais et Belges de la Force publique" (n.d.).

84. *Le Soir*, 24 November 1970; Y T'Sjoen, "'Koloniseren is een smaak die je moet leren'" (2009), pp. 151-166.

85. P. Simons, "Spektakel van Hugo Claus" (1970-1971).

86. Quoted in *Le Soir*, 28-29 January 1984.

87. Verhaegen (1992), pp. 333-379.

88. J. Weverbergh, *Leopold II van Saksen Coburgs allergrootste zaak* (1971).

89. M. Dierickx, *Geschiedenis van België* (1980), p. 189.

90. S. Grindel, "Colonial and Postcolonial Contexts of History Textbooks" (2017), pp. 259-273; S. Planche, "Le 'Roi colonisateur' à l'école" (2009), pp. 269-284; R. De Keyser, "Belgisch-Kongo in den belgischen Geschichtslehrbüchern" (1982), pp. 152-171.

91. See B. Porter, *The Absent-Minded Imperialists* (2005).

92. M. Ngandu Mutombo, "La dépendance de la Belgique du Congo," paper presentation, "Making Europe: The Global Origins of the Old World," FRIAS, May 2010, cited in C. Dejung, "Making Europe" (2010). See also M. Poncelet, *L'invention des sciences coloniales belges* (2008) and R. Mantels, *Geleerd in de tropen* (2007).

93. See, for example, J.-B. Jadin, "Médecine" (1982), pp. 292-319.

94. M. Couttenier, "Anthropology and Ethnography" (2008), pp. 12-13.

95. On the Institute of Tropical Medicine in Antwerp, R. Baetens, "Het Prins Leopold Instituut voor Tropische Geneeskunde te Antwerpen: een overzicht" (2009), pp. 116-129.

96. An exception is the colonial university in Middleheim, outside Antwerp, which ceased to operate.

97. C. Braeckman, "Depuis 50 ans, l'ULB s'intéresse à l'Afrique," *Le Soir*, 3 March 1988.

98. M. Dumoulin, *Léopold II* (2005), pp. 117-118. See also F. Loriaux and F. Morimont, *Bibliographie historique du Zaïre à l'époque coloniale (1880-1960)* (1996).

99. Van Hoecke and Jacquemin, *Africa Museum Tervuren* (1998), p. 242, quoted in Stanard, *Selling the Congo* (2011), p. 112.

100. E.g., B. Mabintch, "Les Œuvres plastiques africaines comme documents d'Histoire" (1981), pp. 9-17.

101. J.-L. Vellut, "Rénovation du Musée royal de l'Afrique centrale" (2017). I thank Dr. Vellut for sharing this piece with me.

102. On the historiography of Belgian colonialism and central Africa, see I. Goddeeris and S. Kiangu, "Congomania in Academia" (2011), pp. 54-75; Vanthemsche (2006), pp. 89-119; Ndaywel È Nziem (2006), pp. 237-254. One can also consult memoirs of two scholars of central Africa: J.-L. Vellut, "Itinéraires d'un rêveur" (2012), pp. 135-160; and Vansina (1994). Older but still useful is J. Stengers, "Belgian Historiography after 1945" (1979), pp. 161-181.

103. G. de Villers, "La Belgique et l'Afrique centrale: le savant et le politique," paper presentation, "Belgium's Africa," Ghent, 21-23 October 1999.

104. A. Coupez, "Études africaines en Belgique" (1983), p. 17.

105. Castryck, "Binnenste-buitenland," in Viaene et al. (2009), pp. 271-282.

106. G. Castryck, "Whose History is History?" (2006), p. 8.

107. A. de Baets, "Metamorphoses d'une épopée" (1991), pp. 45-57.

108. E.g., J. Seressia and E. Daniel, *Manuel d'histoire de Belgique* (1970), pp. 114-116.

109. A. Blommaert quoted in A. de Baets, *De figuranten van de geschiedenis* (1994), p. 104.

110. Verhaegen (1992), p. 349.

111. Reproduced, for example, in Seressia and Daniel (1970), p. 116, and M. Dierickx, *Geschiedenis van België* (1980), p. 192.

112. N. Ascherson, *The King Incorporated* (1999).

113. Castryck (2006), p. 8.

114. de Baets (1994), p. 104, reproduced without attribution at "Herdenkingsplechtigheid aan het Standbeeld Lippens & De Bruyne te Blankenberge" (n.d.).

115. K. Van Nieuwenhuyse, "Towards a Postcolonial Mindset in a Post-Colonial World?" (2018), pp. 155-176.

116. For one example, see photographs from 1975-1990 in H. Gruyaert and H. Claus, *Made in Belgium* (2000).

117. Vanthemsche (2012), pp. 219-220.

118. Ibid., p. 207.

119. Hocq (2012), p. 47.

120. Ibid., pp. 34-43.

121. C. Braeckman and C. Sokal, "Colonisation," *Le Soir*, 3 April 1989.

122. Y. Benoit, "Les élus zaïrois," *Le Soir* 28 December 1988, pp. 1, 4.

123. *Bulletin de l'Association des Vétérans coloniaux*, no. 6 (June 1931), p. 8.

124. G. Moulaert, entry for Wangermée, *BCB* I (1948), columns 951-956.

125. M. Coosemans, entry for L. Van de Velde, *BCB* III (1952), columns 878-882.

126. "Conférences et Manifestations coloniales," *L'Essor colonial et maritime*, 1930.

127. Author's visit, 2003; M. Coosemans, entry for Laplume, *BCB* I (1948), columns 584-587.

128. *L'Illustration congolaise*, no. 146 (1 November 1933), pp. 4704-4705.

129. Document #2668B, Papiers Henry de la Lindi, Archives historiques privées, AfricaMuseum.

130. *Les Vétérans coloniaux. Bulletin mensuel*, no. 3 (March 1939), p. 3. Also *Bulletin de l'Association des Vétérans coloniaux*, 3 December 1940 (Circulaire #2).

131. "A la mémoire du général Molitor," *La Revue coloniale belge*, no. 261 (November 1956), p. 835.

132. M. Coosemans, entry for Storms, *BCB* I (1948), columns 899-903.

133. *L'Illustration congolaise*, no. 23 (31 January 1925), p. 269.

134. *La Revue coloniale belge*, 1 July 1948.

135. Léon Anciaux, entry for Thys, *BCB* IV (1955), columns 875-881.

136. R. Giordano, "Acteurs et témoins: officiers italiens dans l'État Indépendant du Congo," in J.-L. Vellut, *La mémoire du Congo* (2005), pp. 228-231.

137. P. Levine, "Naked Truths" (2013), pp. 5-25.

138. Author's visit, 9 October 2002; *L'Illustration congolaise*, no. 63 (15 November and 1 December 1926), p. 1200.

139. "Les journées coloniales," *La Nation belge*, 26 June 1933.

140. A. Engels, entry for Pétillon, *BCB* II (1951), column 767.

141. Direction des Monuments et Sites du Ministère de la Région Bruxelles-Capitale, "Rue Major Pétillon" (1993-1995).

142. F. Solvel, "Ces inconnus du métro" (2015).

143. On this oft-repeated scene representing colonial exports, see M. Stanard, "Interwar Pro-Empire Propaganda and European Colonial Culture" (2009), pp. 27-48.

144. Author's visit, 1 December 2013.

145. Author's visits, 5 December 2013 and 7 May 2018.

146. "Cornet, Jules" (n.d.).

147. The guide is one of few at colonial monuments in Belgium, and probably the longest-lasting. It was the same in 2018 as it was in 2002. Author's visits, 15 December 2002 and 10 May 2018.

148. Thank you to Jean-Luc Vellut for this insight.

149. Author's visit, 1 December 2013.

150. "Mechelen – Schuttersvest" (n.d.).

151. F. Mariens and A. Poortman to J. Van den Haute, 10 July 1953, liasse "29A. Subsides 1953. Généralités," portefeuille 59 Infopresse, AA.

152. "Congo en Mechelen" (2009).

153. "Lettres du Congo" (1891), p. 2.

154. Casement quoted in Hochschild (1998), p. 196.

155. Hochschild (1998), p. 197; cf. J. Stengers, "Sur l'aventure congolaise de Joseph Conrad" (1971), pp. 744-761.

156. R. Cambier, entry for Van Kerckhoven, *BCB* I (1948), column 572.

157. D. Levering Lewis, *The Race to Fashoda* (1987), p. 46.

158. H. Fernand, "L'ASAOM se souvient" (2016), p. 40.

159. J. Clauw quoted in M. Maes, "José Clauw op zoek naar Edmond Hanssens," *Nieuwsblad.be*, 2 March 2005, http://www.nieuwsblad.be/article/detail. aspx?articleid=G4JCUOCN. Accessed 11 August 2014. There is also a street in Tervuren named after him.

160. Q. de Becker, "Représentations de la campagne arabe à Bruxelles" (2008), pp. 12-17.

161. Ville de Namur, "Agenda 2003 – June" (n.d.).

162. J. W., "Koloniale Vereniging van Limburg herdacht 50-jarig bestaan," *Het Belang van Limburg*, 4 June 1984, p. 11.

163. "Monument Leopold II (Kolonel Dusartplein)" (2019).

164. For example, "Hommage à Léopold II," *Le Soir*, 20 November 1970, front page; "Koninklijke Koloniale Vereniging van Limburg herdenkt aan monument op Kolonel Dusartplein," *Het Belang Van Limburg*, 19 June 2012, http://www.hbvl.be/cnt/eid145638/extern-koninklijke-koloniale-vereniging-van-limburg-herdenkt. Accessed 11 August 2014.

165. *L'Illustration Congolaise*, no. 86 (1 November 1928), p. 2177.

166. C. Duponcheel to M. le Secrétaire d'Administration, Ministry of Colonies, 31 December 1958, and other documentation, liasse "Cercle colonial namurois," portefeuille 62 Infopresse, AA.

167. *L'Illustration congolaise*, no. 86 (1 November 1928), p. 2177.

168. R. van der Krogt and P. van der Krogt, "Roi Léopold II" (n.d.).

169. *Congo-Namur*, no. 1, 1947, p. 21; *Vers l'Avenir*, 27 October 1958.

170. Author's visits, 16 March 2003 and 10 May 2018.

171. C. Duponcheel to M. le Secrétaire d'Administration, Ministry of Colonies, 31 December 1958, and other documentation, liasse "Cercle colonial namurois," portefeuille 62 Infopresse, AA.

172. M. Stanard, "King Leopold's Bust" (2011).

173. *Congo-Namur*, no. 1 (1947), p. 21; *Vers l'Avenir*, 27 October 1958; C. Duponcheel to M. le Secrétaire d'Administration, Ministry of Colonies, 31 December 1958, liasse "Cercle colonial namurois," portefeuille 62 Infopresse, AA.

174. Schedule of events for Namur, June 2003, Ville de Namur, "Agenda 2003 – June" (n.d.); *CRAOCA. Bulletin Trimestriel*, no. 1 (2000), p. 9.

175. W. Colette, "La statue de Léopold II recouverte de sang à Namur" (2011).

176. Colette (2011).

177. *Inhuldiging van een Gedenkteken als Hulde aan Z.M. Koning Leopold II en aan al zijn Limburgse Medewerkers in Kongo overleden voor voor 10 October 1908* (brochure), located at portefeuille 59 Infopresse, AA; "Monument Leopold II (Kolonel Dusartplein)" (2009).

178. Author's visit and photos, 18 May 2003. See R. Lavendhomme, "Note pour Monsieur le Ministre," n° 948/Inf, 25 November 1954, liasse "32A. Subside Monument Léopold II à Mons," portefeuille 59 Infopresse, AA. "Dans des circonstances analogues, notamment à Hasselt et à Hal, le Département est intervenu par voie de subside dans les frais d'édification du monument envisagé. A Hasselt, où le coût du monument était de l'ordre de 500,000 frs., l'intervention du Département s'est traduite par une participation de 100,000 frs.; cependant qu'à Hal où la dépense prévue n'était que de 300,000 frs., la participation de la Colonie n'a été que de 50,000 frs. Bien que les frais d'érection du monument de Mons soient estimés à 7 ou 800,000 frs, le Service estime qu'une participation de 100,000 frs. serait suffisante."

179. M. Coosemans, entry for Volont, *BCB* I (1948), column 938.

180. "Volont, Jules, Joseph" (1908), pp. 466-467; M. Plancquaert, "Les Yaka" (1971), pp. 132-133.

Commemoration and Nostalgia, 1985-1994

1. I. Goddeeris, "Colonial Streets and Statues" (2015), p. 399.

2. Vanthemsche (2012), p. 226.

3. Cited in ibid., p. 240.

4. Hocq (2012), pp. 2-48.

5. "Evocation du roi Léopold II lors d'une exposition importante, dès jeudi à Tervuren," *La Meuse*, 5 September 1984.

6. S. Cornelis, "Colonial and Postcolonial Exhibitions in Belgium (1885-2005)" (2008), p. 22.

7. E. Ugeux, "Quand le Zaïre s'appelait Congo," *Le Soir*, 20 February 1986, p. 16.

8. T. Hermans, *A Literary History of the Low Countries* (2009); L. Renders and H. Roos, "The Congo in Literature" (2009), p. 9.

9. Renders (2009), pp. 109-122; P.-P. Fraiture, "Belgique-Congo" (2008), pp. 65-81; Prem Poddar et al., *A Historical Companion to Postcolonial Literatures* (2008); C. Sarlet, "Vingt ans après" (1997), pp. 95-110.

10. Sarlet (1997), pp. 95-110.
11. P. Halen, "Le Congo revisité" (1992), pp. 291-304.
12. H. Claus, *The Sorrow of Belgium* (1990).
13. S. Vanacker, "'As Befits Men'" (2000), pp. 241-253.
14. J.-L. Lippert, *Dialogue des oiseaux du phare* (1998); A. Tshitungu Kongolo, "Colonial Memories in Belgian and Congolese Literature" (2002), p. 82.
15. *Afscheid van Rumangabo* (1984); "Relaas van een Kongovrouw," *Het Laatste Nieuws*, 7-8 April 1984.
16. Renders (2009), p. 118.
17. J.-L. Vellut review of H. Eynikel, *Congo belge* (1985), p. 277.
18. See Renders (2009).
19. Delisle (2007), p. 145.
20. Tousignant (1995), p. 16.
21. J.-L. Vellut, "Ressources scientifiques, culturelles et humaines de l'africanisme en Belgique" (1994), p. 130.
22. F. De Moor and J.-P. Jacquemin, '*Notre Congo/Onze Kongo*' (2000), p. 34.
23. C. Geary, *In and Out of Focus* (2002).
24. A. Maxwell, *Colonial Photography and Exhibitions* (1999), pp. 154-55; E. VanderKnyff, "Parlor Illusions" (2007), p. 57.
25. E. Ugeux, "Quand le Zaïre s'appelait Congo," *Le Soir*, 20 February 1986, p. 16.
26. D. Couvreur, "Descendre le fleuve Congo sans quitter la Belgique," *Le Soir*, 15 March 1988.
27. E. Ugeux, "La colonisation belge," *Le Soir*, 27 February 1984, p. 23.
28. T. Symons and J. Houssiau, "The Everyday Things of Life" (2008), p. 45.
29. E. Ugeux, "La colonisation belge," *Le Soir*, 27 February 1984, p. 23.
30. *Le Soir*, 19 January 1984, p. 25.
31. V. Foutry and J. Neckers, *Als een wereld zo groot waar uw vlag staat geplant* (1986).
32. H. Dejonghe, "Hoe leefde Kongo onder drie generaties Belgen?," *De Standaard*, 21 February 1986, p. 10.
33. *De Standaard*, 1 March 1988.
34. D. Legrand, "Vos images, votre histoire," *Le Soir*, 1 March 1988, p. 31.
35. C. Braeckman and C. Sokal, "Colonisation," *Le Soir*, 3 April 1989.
36. Catherine Ferrant, "Au temps béni des colonies," *Le Soir*, 4 April 1989.
37. J. Debbaut et al., *Utotombo* (1988).
38. List of collectors, doc. 15.01.88, file "Utotombo, 25.3-5.6 1988 00/178," box "1988 Utotombo, 25/3-5/6/88," Utotombo files, BOZAR archives; Debbaut et al. (1988).
39. *De Standaard*, 25 March 1988, p. 8.
40. A. Burnet, "Utotombo, les merveilles des arts africains," *Le Soir*, 28 March 1988, p. 22.
41. J. Debbaut to J. W. Mestach, 19 February 1988, file "Utotombo, 25.3-5.6 1988 00/178," box "1988 Utotombo, 25/3-5/6/88," Utotombo files, BOZAR archives.
42. A. Leurquin, "La Distraction de l'objet africain ou l'histoire d'une errance," in Debbaut et al. (1988), p. 315.
43. A. Burnet, "Utotombo, les merveilles des arts africains," *Le Soir*, 28 March 1988, p. 22.
44. Lancelot Entwistle to Dominique Favart, 30 June 1988, file "Utotombo, 25.3-5.6, 1988 00/78," box "1988 Utotombo, 25/3-5/6/88," Utotombo files, BOZAR archives.

45. A. Burnet, "Utotombo, les merveilles des arts africains," *Le Soir*, 28 March 1988, p. 22.

46. See Beyen and Destatte (2009), pp. 139-152.

47. The memorial to Lenselaer still stands, but the bas-relief had been removed by 2018.

48. Excluded are renamed streets and public squares; tombs; and memorials located inside non-public buildings. Thus the many busts, statues, inscriptions, and other memorials inside the former Colonial University in Antwerp and the Tervuren AfricaMuseum are excluded, but included are memorials located inside city halls; the one exception is the bronze bust to Leopold II that was until recently located in the central courtyard of the AfricaMuseum, which is included in the count.

49. In addition to the following references, see Goddeeris (2015), pp. 397-409.

50. R. Aldrich, "Putting the Colonies on the Map" (2002), pp. 211-223.

51. Quoted in D. Vangroenweghe, "The 'Leopold II' concession system exported to French Congo with as example the Mpoko Company" (2006), pp. 323-372, p. 335, n. 18

52. Author's visit, 9 October 2002; also "Histoire du Congo par les monuments" (1985), p. 33.

53. *L'Illustration congolaise*, no. 139 (1 April 1933), p. 4426.

54. Colonel E. Muller to Eugène Flagey, Bourgmestre d'Ixelles, 13 November 1946, document # 5268.84, Box 52.68 Emm. Muller Box #1, Papiers Emm. Muller, Archives historiques privées, AfricaMuseum. *La Revue coloniale belge*, no. 28 (1 December 1946), p. 392, mentions the inauguration of the Chaltin monument.

55. Author's visits, 9 October 2002, 18 December 2009, and 7 May 2018.

56. Direction des Monuments et Sites du Ministère de la Région Bruxelles-Capitale, "Square du Solbosch" (2013-15); J. Lennep, *Statues and Monuments of Brussels pre-1914* (2000), p. 139.

57. "Histoire du Congo par les monuments" (1985), p. 33.

58. G. Malengreau, entry for Crespel, *BCB* III (1952), columns 171-172.

59. Document #2668B, Papiers Henry de la Lindi, Archives historiques privées, AfricaMuseum; *Bulletin de l'Association des Vétérans coloniaux*, 3 December 1940, circulaire #2 states it took place in 1940.

60. Quoted in M. Coosemans, entry for Dryepondt, *BCB* III (1952), columns 265-268.

61. M. Coosemans, entry for Dryepondt, *BCB* III (1952), columns 265-268.

62. Photo courtesy Karen and Todd Timberlake.

63. Photo courtesy Karen and Todd Timberlake.

64. L. Jeurissen, *Quand le métis s'appellait «mulâtre»* (2003), pp. 68-96.

65. W. Jonckheere, "Het Van Dorpe-monument 100 jaar op het Kongoplein" (2008), pp. 3726-3732.

66. Author's visit, 13 May 2018.

67. Omfloerste histories, verhalen nabij de Leie, "Het ontluisterd monument" (2018).

68. See Gann and Duignan (1979).

69. M. L. Comeliau, entry for Van Dorpe, *BCB* III (1952), columns 255-257.

70. "Gedenkzuil Jules Van Dorpe," http://www.standbeelden.be/standbeeld/46, 25 May 2009. Accessed 30 June 2018.

71. Ibid.; S. De Groote, "Ook in Deinze standbeeld met verwijzing naar duister verlden," *Het Nieuwsblad*, 17 August 2017, https://www.nieuwsblad.be/cnt/blsde_03021680. Accessed 30 June 2018.

72. *Het Nieuwsblad*, https://www.nieuwsblad.be/cnt/blsde_03021680. Accessed 30 June 2018.

73. Author's visits, 15 December 2002 and 10 May 2018.

74. *L'Illustration congolaise*, no. 128 (1 May 1932), p. 3993.

75. M. Coosemans, entry for Ladam, *BCB* II (1951), column 559.

76. A. Lacroix, entry for Piron, *BCB* II (1951), column 772.

77. M. Coosemans, entry for Siret, *BCB* II (1951), column 867.

78. L. Van Hoof, entry for Bernard, *BCB* I (1948), columns 122-123.

79. M. Coosemans, entry for Fuisseaux, *BCB* III (1952), column 350.

80. A. Lacroix, entry for Collet, *BCB* II (1951), columns 178-180.

81. Direction des Monuments et Sites du Ministère de la Région Bruxelles-Capitale, "Avenue du Front" (1993-1995).

82. L. P., entry for Dupagne, *BCB* VIIa (1973), columns 126-128.

83. S. Augustijnen, *Spectres* (2011).

84. Stanard, *Selling the Congo* (2011), pp. 117-119.

85. E. Bouillon and W. Dubois, form letter, 28 August 1936, liasse "205.814 R.1.," documents 205.814 and 205.816, portefeuille R61 Office Colonial, AA.

86. "Druart, Porphyre-Augustin," *Connaître la Wallonie* (n.d.).

87. M. Coosemans, entry for Druart, *BCB* V (1958), column 271.

88. R. Cambier, entry for Van Kerckhoven, *BCB* I (1948), columns 566-573.

89. Photograph by Ji-Elle, 3 July 2012, https://commons.wikimedia.org/wiki/File:Charles_Samuel-Vuakusu_Batetela_d%C3%A9fendant_une_femme_contre_un_Arabe_(4).jpg. Accessed 4 September 2018.

90. The same was true of sculptures by British artist Herbert Ward, which also featured in the museum. M. J. Arnoldi, "Where art and ethnology met: The Ward African Collection at the Smithsonian," in Schildkrout and Keim (1998), p. 202.

91. Essential is F. de Callataÿ, "Le Monument du Congo de Thomas Vinçotte (Parc du Cinquantenaire)" (1990), pp. 197-221.

92. "L'Arabe" and "Arabische" are the original words. R. Bats, D. Cluytens, G. Keuster, A. Delannoy, A. Orlans, and J.-J. Symoens, *Le Soir*, 21 August 1989, found at J.-P. Jacquemin, *Racisme, continent obscure* (1991), p. 118.

93. Document(s)/folder(s): R.G. 765 "Exposition 1910, section congolaise, fêtes sportives," Papiers Félix Fuchs, Archives historiques privées, AfricaMuseum.

94. Seressia and Daniel (1970), p. 116.

95. *L'Illustration congolaise*, no. 155 (1 August 1934), p. 5063.

96. Quoted in *Congo: Revue générale de la colonie belge/Algemeen tijdschrift van de belgische kolonie*, vol. 2, no. 1 (June 1937), p. 99.

97. *CRAOCA. Bulletin trimestriel*, no. 3 (2000), p. 7.

98. de Callataÿ (1990), pp. 197-221.

99. Author's visit, September 2002.

100. See de Callataÿ (1990), and Direction des Monuments et Sites du Ministère de la Région Bruxelles-Capitale, "Monument du Congo" (2009-10); Brussels Hoofdstedelijk Parlement, *BIV-BIQ* (2004-05), pp. 38-41.

101. P. Aiyar, *New Old World* (2013), p. 250.
102. F. L., "Une incitation au racisme," *La Dernière Heure*, 17 June 2011, http://www.dhnet.be/regions/bruxelles/une-incitation-au-racisme-51b78048e4b0de6d-b97e9e9c. Accessed 11 August 2014.
103. "Cinquantenaire: l'inscription «L'Arabe esclavagiste» ne reviendra pas sur le Monument du Congo," *Sudinfo.be*, http://www.sudinfo.be/archive/re-cup/830662/article/regions/bruxelles/actualite/2013-10-09/cinquantenaire-l-inscription-l-arabe-esclavagiste-ne-reviendra-pas-sur-le-. Accessed 14 June 2018.
104. H. Hymans, *Les Villes d'art célèbres* (1926), p. 138.
105. L. Ranieri, *Léopold II* (1973), p. 132.
106. P. Puttemans, *Modern Architecture in Belgium* (1976), p. 55.
107. Colin Blane, "Belgian wealth squeezed from Congo," *BBC News*, 18 January 2001, http://news.bbc.co.uk/hi/english/world/from_own_correspondent/newsid_1123000/1123933.stm. Accessed 28 April 2002.
108. See T. Demey, *Léopold II* (2009). Thank you to Guy Vanthemsche for this reference.
109. Ranieri (1973), p. 21.
110. A. Murphy, "Landscapes for Whom?" (2002), p. 195.
111. Ascherson (1999), pp. 187, 192.
112. See B. Emerson, *Leopold II of the Belgians* (1979), p. 235; Ascherson (1999), p. 241.
113. M. Laurent, *L'Architecture et la Sculpture en Belgique* (1928), p. 24.
114. Ranieri (1973), p. 22.
115. L. de Lichtervelde, *Léopold of the Belgians* (1929), p. 311.
116. P. Nord, *Paris Shopkeepers and the Politics of Resentment* (1986), p. 100; P. Hohenberg and L. Lees, *The Making of Urban Europe 1000-1994* (1995), pp. 326-330.
117. D. Pinkney, *Napoleon III and the Rebuilding of Paris* (1958), p. 210.
118. C. Schorske, *Fin-de-Siècle Vienna* (1980), pp. 24-115.
119. C. Weightman and A. Barnes, *Brussels* (1976), p. 192.
120. Ranieri (1973), p. 123; G. Stinglhamber and P. Dresse, *Léopold II au travail* (1945), p. 241.
121. Ranieri (1973), pp. 123-140; Stinglhamber and Dresse (1945), pp. 241-244.
122. R. Park, "A King in Business" *Everybody's Magazine* (1906), p. 632. Emphasis in original.
123. Hymans (1926), p. 138.
124. The Katanga Company dated to 1891. It explored and prospected for minerals and ores. Copper mining was advanced enough under Leopold that UMHK, the dominant copper mining concern, was founded by 1906. See J.-L. Vellut, "Mining in the Belgian Congo," in D. Birmingham and P. Martin, *History of Central Africa* (1983), 126-162, esp. pp. 126-129; and B. Jewsiewicki, "Rural society and the Belgian colonial economy," in Birmingham and Martin (1983), 95-125, esp. pp. 96-99.
125. Hymans (1926), p. 138.
126. Quoted in Ranieri (1973), p. 124.
127. Chambre des Représentants, *Annales parlementaires de la Chambre des représentants*, 28 February 1905, p. 821. My thanks to Guy Vanthemsche for this reference.
128. *Cercle des Intérêts matériels du Quartier de Linthout Nord-Est*, no. 13 (July 1914), p. 3; Houbar and Lagasse to Ruzette, no. 9199, 27 February 1925, folder 235, Fonds du Bourgmestre, Archives de la Ville de Bruxelles.
129. Quoted in Ranieri (1973), p. 125.

130. P. Abercrombie, "Brussels" (1913), p. 267.
131. J. de Courcy MacDonnell, *Belgium, Her Kings, Kingdom and People* (1914), p. 286.
132. A.B., "Tervueren 1897," *Le Soir*, 16 June 1967, p. 7.
133. R. Slade, *King Leopold's Congo* (1962), p. 109.
134. M. Coosemans, entry for J. Lippens, *BCB* II (1951), column 638.
135. Agentschap Onroerend Erfgoed, "Standbeeld Lippens en De Bruyne" (2018).
136. R. Fuks, *Héros et Personnages de chez nous racontés par leur statues* (1986), p. 184.
137. "Herdenkingsplechtigheid aan het Standbeeld Lippens & De Bruyne te Blankenberge," *Kamp Vogelsang*, http://www.kamp-vogelsang.be/interactief/uw_fotos_2014/blankenberge/. Accessed 8 January 2019.
138. Agentschap Onroerend Erfgoed, "Standbeeld Lippens en De Bruyne" (2018).
139. Author's visit, 13 May 2018.
140. My thanks to Jean-Luc Vellut for this insight.
141. M. Coosemans, entry for De Bruyne, *BCB* II (1951), column 113.
142. E.g., Seressia and Daniel (1970), pp. 115-116.
143. Van Schuylenbergh (2014), pp. 42-44.
144. Among others, J. Marchal (as A. M. Delathuy), *E. D. Morel tegen Leopold II en de Kongostaat* (1985); idem., *De Kongostaat van Leopold II, 1876-1900* (1989); idem., *Missie en Staat in Oud-Kongo, 1880-1914* (1992).
145. D. Vangroenweghe, *Rood Rubber* (1985), translated into French as *Du sang sur les lianes* (1986).
146. J. Kestergat, "Léopold II et le Congo. L'historien flamand Daniel Vangroenweghe relance les accusations du 'caoutchouc rouge,'" *La Libre Belgique*, review of Vangroenweghe, *Du sang sur les lianes* (1986).
147. Hocq (2012), p. 47.

A New Generation, 1994-2010

1. Quoted in Hocq (2012), p. 48.
2. Quoted in Mock (2010).
3. "Vielsalm honore ses pionniers," *Mémoires du Congo et du Ruanda-Urundi*, no. 39 (September 2016), p. 44.
4. Beyen and Destatte (2009), pp. 112-115.
5. Vanthemsche (2012), pp. 200, 262-263.
6. The literature on Hergé and collaboration alone is large. See B. Peeters, "A Never Ending Trial" (2002), pp. 261-271.
7. H. Van Goethem, *Belgium and the Monarchy* (2010), pp. 214-15; quote from L. De Guissmé et al., "Attitudes Toward World War II Collaboration in Belgium" (2017), p. 48.
8. Mnookin (2007), p. 111.
9. Rosoux and van Ypersele (2011), p. 52.
10. N. Tousignant, "L'évolution des représentations du passé mis en exergue par le gouvernement belge depuis 1999" (2005).
11. P. Bruckner, *The Tyranny of Guilt* (2010), pp. 35-36.
12. C. Labio, "Preface" (2002), p. 4.

13. Hochschild (1998).

14. Licata and Klein (2010), p. 47.

15. M. Ewans, *European Atrocity, African Catastrophe* (2002).

16. M. Kakutani, "Genocide with Spin Control: Kurtz Wasn't Fiction," *The New York Times*, 1 September 1998, p. 6.

17. Dunn (2003), p. 163.

18. M. Meunier, "Colette Braeckman visiteuse du «Soir»" (2010).

19. Vellut (1994), p. 138.

20. See Stearns (2011).

21. B. Balteau and M. Dumoulin, "Colonisation belge" (2005), p. 74; G. de Villers, "Histoire, justice et politique" (2004), pp. 198-200.

22. Van Schuylenbergh (2014), pp. 45-54.

23. Stanard (2013), p. 463; J.-P. Sanderson, "La démographie du Congo belge sous la colonisation belge" (2010). Thank you to Guy Vanthemsche for this reference.

24. See V. Mock, "Belgium revisits the scene of its colonial shame," *The Independent*, 30 June 2010, http://www.independent.co.uk/news/world/africa/belgium-revisits-the-scene-of-its-colonial-shame-2014055.html. Accessed 17 July 2014; A. Remy, "There was no genocide in the Congo," *The Wall Street Journal*, 20 April 2004.

25. P.-L. Plasman, "Léopold II, roi maudit?" (2009).

26. Stanard (2013), p. 463.

27. A. Hochschild, "A Monument to Denial," *Los Angeles Times*, 2 March 2005.

28. R. Hamilton, "Forgotten Holocaust," *The Washington Post*, 7 January 2001, p. B3; Labio (2002), p. 6; Kakutani (1998), p. 6.

29. De Mul (2012), p. 165.

30. T. Judt, *Postwar* (2005), pp. 803-834.

31. C. Braeckman, "Une soirée spéciale avec documentaire et débat sur La Deux. Patrice Lumumba hante toujours la Belgique," *Le Soir*, 13 May 2000, p. 15.

32. G. Verbeeck, "De Lumumba-commissie" (2007), p. 4; de Villers (2004), p. 197.

33. For example R. Custer, "La mémoire sélective du Congo" (2007).

34. B. Verhaegen, "Carte blanche," *Le Soir*, 12 January 1989.

35. Van Schuylenbergh (2014), pp. 45-71.

36. "Rwanda 94, Extraits de presse" [2014].

37. J.-C. Planche, "*Rwanda 1994*, par le Groupov" (2000).

38. Quoted in Planche (2000).

39. Visit with Els de Palmenaere, 13 November 2013.

40. P. Verlinden, *Weg uit Congo* (2002); R. Van Doorslaer, "De ondergang van de kolonialen" (2003), pp. 161-175.

41. *Mobutu, roi du Zaïre*, dir. T. Michel (1999).

42. *Boma-Tervuren*, dir. F. Dujardin (1999).

43. *Lumumba*, dir. R. Peck (2000).

44. My thanks to Guy Vanthemsche for this information.

45. Dumoulin (2005), p. 31.

46. *Congo*, dir. P. Bate (2004).

47. A. Evans-Pritchard, "Belgian fury at film on Leopold's Congo terror," *The Telegraph*, 7 April 2004, http://www.telegraph.co.uk/news/worldnews/europe/belgium/1458736/Belgian-fury-at-film-on-Leopolds-Congo-terror.html. Accessed 8 August 2014.

48. P. Belien, "King Leopold's Shadow," *The Wall Street Journal*, 8-11 April 2004, p. A7.
49. D. Spears, "Putting the Wrongs of History in Paint," *The New York Times*, 3 February 2010, http://www.nytimes.com/2010/02/07/arts/design/07tuymans. html?pagewanted=all&_r=0. Accessed 25 June 2014.
50. "Belgian apology to Rwanda," *BBC News*, 7 April 2000, http://news.bbc.co.uk/2/ hi/africa/705402.stm. Accessed 17 July 2014.
51. V. Kiesel, "Regards sur un Congo empreint de belgitude. 1960-2000: Empreintes belges au Congo-Kinshasa," *Le Soir*, 24 June 2000.
52. Verbeeck (2007), p. 7.
53. Quoted in V. Rosoux, "Le Mémoire de la colonisation" (2006), p. 161.
54. V. Kiesel, "Louis Michel adopte les conclusions des experts. La Belgique garde l'Afrique à cœur," *Le Soir*, 2 March 2000, p. 7; Colette Braeckman, "L'Afrique, cible de la diplomatie européenne," *Le Soir*, 7 March 2000, p. 7.
55. "Priorité à l'ex-Congo belge," *Le Monde*, 5 July 2001.
56. On the assassination, in addition to de Witte (1999), see E. Gerard and V. Kuklick, *Death in the Congo* (2015).
57. L. De Vos et al., *Lumumba* (2004); B. Ceuppens, "*Lumumba. De complotten? De moord*" (2007), pp. 1-16; P. Raxhon, *Le débat Lumumba* (2002). My thanks to Guy Vanthemsche for helping clarify some of these issues.
58. "Excuses historiques de la Belgique au peuple congolais," *Le Monde*, 5 February 2002.
59. de Villers (2004), p. 216.
60. J. Omasombo Tshonda, "Lumumba, drame san fin et deuil inachevé de la colonisation" (2004), p. 255. There has been little to no follow up on the Fondation Lumumba.
61. C. Braeckman, "Congo. Après la Commission Lumumba: Un nouveau chantier sur la décolonisation s'est ouvert pour les historiens," *Le Soir*, 19 November 2001; idem., "La Belgique confrontée à son passé colonial," *Le Monde diplomatique*, January 2002, http://www.monde-diplomatique.fr/2002/01/BRAECKMAN/8340. Accessed 18 July 2014.
62. K. Arnaut, "Belgian Memories, African Objects" (2001), pp. 29-48.
63. M. Lefert, *Petit Guide du Musée Africain de Namur* (n.d.).
64. Author's visit to the museum, 2003; B. Taithe, "Missionary Militarism?" (2012), p. 140.
65. Author's visit to the museum, 2003; "Historique du Musée Africain de Namur" (2004); J. Toussaint, "Le Musée africain" (2004), pp. 8-9.
66. "Musées – Museums, Namur" (1997); museum brochure "Musée Africain de Namur" (2003).
67. Toussaint (2004), pp. 8-9.
68. Author's visit to the museum and with Georges Defauwes, May 2003.
69. See also M. Misra, "Heart of Smugness," *The Guardian*, 7 August 2002, p. 11.
70. Bruckner (2010).
71. Rahier, "Ghost of Leopold II" (2003), pp. 58-84.
72. Ibid., p. 62.
73. D. Silverman, "Diasporas of Art" (2015), p. 627.
74. Stanard, *Selling the Congo* (2011), pp. 101-121.
75. Thys van den Audenaerde (1982), p. 3.

76. Bouttiaux (1999), pp. 609-610.

77. G. Verswijver and H. Burssens, "Hidden Treasures of the Tervuren Museum" (1995), pp. 22-31.

78. *Naissance de la peinture contemporaine en Afrique centrale, 1930-1970* (1992).

79. I. Gérard, Royal Museum for Central Africa, *Annual Report, 2005-2006* (2007).

80. G. Gryseels et al., "Integrating the Past" (2005), pp. 637-647.

81. Author's visit, 18 September 2002; Fuks (1986), p. 175.

82. http://www.sculpturepublique.be/1050/DHaveloose-GeneralStorms.htm.

83. M. Coosemans, entry for Storms, *BCB* I (1948), columns 899-903.

84. J. Volper, "Of Sculptures & Skulls" (2012), pp. 86-95.

85. See A. Roberts, *A Dance of Assassins* (2013).

86. B. Wastiau, *ExItCongoMuseum* (2000); author's visit, June 2001; quote from Corbey (2001), p. 26.

87. Author's visit, 20 February 2003.

88. G. Duplat, "L'effrayant pillage des œuvres d'art," *La Libre Belgique*, 10 January 2003, http://www.lalibre.be/culture/arts/l-effrayant-pillage-des-oeuvres-d-art-51b87c5be4b0de6db9a8271d. Accessed 10 August 2014; Wastiau, "The Violence of Collecting" (2009).

89. "Dessins d'enfants: Résultats du Concours," *Le Soir*, 7 February 2003; N.C., "Un livre richement illustré sur les peuples et les paysages congolais," *Le Soir*, 20 December 2010.

90. Silverman (2015), p. 633.

91. Author's conversation with J.-L. Vellut, 25 November 2013.

92. C. Da Fonseca-Wollheim and H. Keinon, "Skeletons in the Basement," *The Jerusalem Post*, 21 February 2003, p. 4.

93. A. Hochschild, "In the Heart of Darkness" (2005).

94. Author's conversation with J.-L. Vellut, 25 November 2013.

95. See Blane (2001).

96. C. Braeckman, J.-F. Munster, and O. Mouton, "Les traces du Congo demeurent à Bruxelles," *Le Soir*, 28 April 2010, p. 16; Mock (2010); P. Imbach, "Promenade anti-coloniale à Bruxelles, l'ancienne métropole du Congo" (2008). CADTM is the Committee for the Abolition of Illegitimate Debt, alternately titled the Committee for the Cancellation of Third World Debt. It calls itself an "alterglobalisation movement" and opposes so-called neoliberal practices and ideology. "About CADTM" (2007).

97. L. Catherine, *Wandelen naar Kongo* (2006); idem., *Promenade au Congo* (2010).

98. J. Darwin, *Unfinished Empire* (2012), p. xi.

99. See L. Catherine, *Léopold II* (2004), whose original title in Dutch suggests his views on the king's building projects: *Bouwen met zwart geld: De Grootheidswaanzin van Leopold II* (2002).

100. Author's visits, 2002-2003 and 2013.

101. "Baron Dhanis staat eindelijk in Sint-Niklaas," *Het Nieuwsblad*, 11 September 2013.

102. "Place du Trône – Statue du roi Léopold II" (2007).

103. E. Janssens and A. Cateaux, *Les Belges au Congo* (1911), p. 160; M. Coosemans, entry for Lange, *BCB* II (1951), columns 583-584.

104. Janssens and Cateaux (1911), p. 160.

105. "Histoire du Congo par les monuments" (1985), p. 34; Agentschap Onroerend Erfgoed, "Gedenkteken Alphonse Lange" (2017).
106. Author's visit, 13 May 2018.
107. M. Coosemans, entry for Lange, BCB II (1951), columns 583-584.
108. R. van der Krogt and P. van der Krogt, "Josef en Lieven Vandevelde met Sakala" (n.d.).
109. L. Guébels, entry for J. Van de Velde BCB I (1948), columns 927-929.
110. Photo courtesy Karen and Todd Timberlake.
111. Gent [Stad], "Gent" (n.d.).
112. L'Illustration congolaise, no. 179 (1 August 1936), p. 5977; author's visit, 13 May 2018.
113. "Un monument Léopold II," La Revue coloniale belge, no. 239 (15 September 1955), p. 649.
114. Author's visit, 13 May 2018.
115. Bulletin de l'Association des Vétérans coloniaux, October 1934, p. 2; p. 5 for list of people who gave money for the monument.
116. D. Vangroenweghe, Voor rubber en ivoor (2005). I thank Guy Vanthemsche for bringing this book to my attention.
117. "Histoire du Congo par les monuments" (1985), p. 34.
118. Author's visit, 2003.
119. Author's visit, 2002.
120. "Standbeeld Leopold II mag blijven," Nieuwsblad.be, 29 October 2004, http://www.nieuwsblad.be/article/detail.aspx?articleid=GG39S7NV. Accessed 16 July 2014.
121. "Krijgt Leopold II straks zijn hand terug?," DeRedactie.be, 23 December 2009, http://deredactie.be/cm/vrtnieuws/regio/westvlaanderen/1.674140. Accessed 11 August 2014.
122. Sikitiko, dir. P. De Vos (2010).
123. Bulletin mensuel de l'Association des Vétérans coloniaux, no. 5 (May 1931), p. 3; L'Illustration Congolaise, no. 102 (1 February 1930), p. 2879.
124. See documents at A.V.R.U.G. Afrika-Vereniging van de Universiteit Gent, http://cas1.elis.ugent.be/avrug/erfgoed/sikitiko/sikitiko.htm; M. Lenain to Général Paelinck, 12 April 2005, located at A.V.R.U.G. Afrika-Vereniging van de Universiteit Gent, http://cas1.elis.ugent.be/avrug/erfgoed/pdf/cercle_2.pdf.
125. Author's visit, 13 May 2018.
126. K. De Vos, "De afgehakte handen van Leopold II" (2018).
127. "…à Hal où la dépense prévue n'était que de 300,000 frs., la participation de la Colonie n'a été que de 50,000 frs." R. Lavendhomme, "Note pour Monsieur le Ministre," no. 948/Inf, 25 November 1954, liasse "32A. Subside Monument Léopold II à Mons," portefeuille 59 Infopresse, AA.
128. Author's visit, 15 November 2002.
129. "Standbeeld Leopold II mag blijven," Nieuwsblad.be, 29 October 2004, http://www.nieuwsblad.be/article/detail.aspx?articleid=GG39S7NV. Accessed 16 July 2014.
130. J.-P. Laus, "09.09.09 Halle" [2009].
131. Author's visit, 10 May 2018.
132. See L'Illustration congolaise, no. 129 (1 June 1932), p. 4033; L'Illustration congolaise, no. 130 (1 July 1932), p. 4058.

133. "De witte neger," http://www.standbeelden.be/standbeeld/973, 26 October 2010. Accessed 28 June 2018.

134. Author's visits, 15 November 2002 and 10 May 2018.

135. Stanard, *Selling the Congo* (2011), p. 172.

136. F. Nolan, "Frère Mathieu" [2016].

137. M. Coosemans, entry for Courtois, *BCB* I (1948), columns 272-274.

138. E. Toussaint, "Les crimes de la Belgique coloniale au Congo" (2007).

139. Ibid.

140. "Vandalen bekladden standbeeld Leopold II," *Nieuwsblad.be*, 10 November 2009, http://www.nieuwsblad.be/article/detail.aspx?articleid=PG2HPPGH. Accessed 11 August 2014.

141. "La statue de Lépold II peinte en rouge," *Le Soir*, [9 September 2008], http://portfolio.lesoir.be/v/belgique/leopoldd/. Accessed 11 August 2014.

142. "Collier pour Leopold 2" (2010).

143. E. Fontaine, "De Stoeten Ostendenoare slaat weer toe," *Nieuwsblad.be*, 21 August 2013, http://www.nieuwsblad.be/article/detail.aspx?articleid=BLE FO_20130821_006. Accessed 11 August 2014.

144. Author's visit, 13 May 2018.

145. Unless otherwise noted the following is based on the author's visits in 2003, 2009, 2013, and 2018, and Stanard, "King Leopold's Bust" (2011).

146. *Comité pour l'érection d'un monument commémoratif à la mémoire de notre Regretté Roi* to the mayor of Brussels, 28 December 1909, folder 235, Fonds du Bourgmestre, Archives de la Ville de Bruxelles.

147. Lennep (2000), p. 141.

148. *L'Étoile belge*, 15 March 1914; *Moniteur belge* (12 June 1914), pp. 3729-3733.

149. Lennep (2000), p. 140.

150. *L'Illustration congolaise*, no. 63 (15 November and 1 December 1926), pp. 1216-1217.

151. Lennep (2000), p. 142.

152. Godefroid refused the title "king," believing Jesus to be the king of Jerusalem; Godefroid was the city's ruler nonetheless.

153. *L'Illustration congolaise*, no. 196 (January 1938), p. 6674.

154. E.g., *Le Congo belge et ses Coloniaux* (1953), title page.

155. E.g., Colonel B.E.M. Stinglhamber, "Discours prononcé au pied de la Statue Equestre de Léopold II, le 16 décembre 1934," available at Royal Library of Belgium (Brussels), côte BRIV 395 B41; *L'Essor colonial et maritime* (Brussels), no. 47, 22 November 1936; "Le 50e anniversaire du rattachement du Congo à la Belgique," *La Nouvelle Gazette*, 22 October 1958.

156. "Décès du général Janssens," *Le Soir*, 5 December 1989, https://www.lesoir.be/art/%252Fdeces_t-19891205-Z0265U.html. Accessed 13 December 2018.

157. E.g., *Le Soir*, 20 November 1970, front page; author's visit, 18 December 2009.

158. "Place du Trône – Statue du roi Léopold II" (2007).

159. "Une statue de Léopold II peinte en rouge à Bruxelles," *RTBF.be*, 9 September 2008, http://www.rtbf.be/info/societe/divers/une-statue-de-leopold-ii-peinte-en-rouge-a-bruxelles. Accessed 24 January 2011.

160. "Collier pour Leopold II" (2010).

161. "La statue de Léopold II vandalisée," *La Libre Belgique*, 17 December 2015, http://www.lalibre.be/regions/bruxelles/la-statue-de-leopold-ii-vandalisee-

567309273570ed3894a11a01. Accessed 22 June 2018; "Standbeeld Leopold II overgoten met rode vloeistof" (2018).

162. Association Royale d'Anciens d'Afrique et d'Outre-Mer Liège, "Histoire" (2002).

163. Author's visit, 11 May 2018; "Histoire du Congo par les monuments" (1985), p. 34.

164. *L'Illustration congolaise*, no. 155 (1 August 1934), p. 5058.

165. Email communication, with text of speech, from Sandrine Schlit, 5 December 2013.

166. Association Royale d'Anciens d'Afrique et d'Outre-Mer Liège, "Histoire" (2002); *Bulletin de l'Association des Vétérans coloniaux*, 3 December 1940 (Circulaire #2); "Cimetière Robermont" (n.d.).

167. See various editions of *Mémoires du Congo et du Ruanda-Urundi*.

168. Author's visit, 11 May 2018.

169. City of Ostend, explanatory plaque, author's visit, 13 May 2018.

170. "The Ostende Historical Museum De Plate" (2018).

171. City of Ostend, explanatory plaque, author's visit, 13 May 2018.

172. "Borstbeeld Leopold II besmeurd met verf," *Het Nieuwsblad*, 16 November 2008, https://www.nieuwsblad.be/cnt/b27576385081116. Accessed 19 June 2018.

173. "De Stoeten Ostendenoare slatt weer toe," *Het Nieuwsblad*, 21 August 2013, https://www.nieuwsblad.be/cnt/blefo_20130821_006. Accessed 19 June 2018.

174. Author's visit, 13 May 2018.

175. *L'Illustration congolaise*, no. 97 (1 October 1929), p. 2655.

176. *L'Illustration congolaise*, no. 43 (1 December 1925), p. 655.

177. A. Engels, entry for Malfeyt, *BCB* III (1952), column 588.

178. Author's visit, 13 May 2018.

179. Agentschap Onroerend Erfgoed, "Leopoldpark – Memoraal Justin Malfeyt" (2016).

180. I. Goddeeris, "Congo in onze navel" (2011), p. 46; "Les statues parlent aussi" (2013).

181. C. Laporte, "Faut-il revoir la mémoire coloniale belge?," *La Libre Belgique*, 27 September 2008, http://www.lalibre.be/actu/belgique/faut-il-revoir-la-memoire-coloniale-belge-51b89fb8e4b0de6db9b3b2d0. Accessed 18 July 2014.

182. De Vos (2010).

183. P. Imbach, "Les monuments publics coloniaux, lieux de mémoires contestés" (2008).

184. Author's visit, 13 May 2018.

185. Agentschap Onroerend Erfgoed, "Standbeeld van Leopold II" (2017).

186. A. Sanchez, "Most statues of Leopold II have plaques in Flanders" (2018).

187. D. Van De Mieroop and M. Pagnaer, "Co-Constructing Colonial Dichotomies in Female Former Colonizers' Narratives of the Belgian Congo" (2013), pp. E66-E83.

188. F. Gillet, "Congo rêvé? Congo détruit…" (2008), p. 101.

189. Mémoires du Congo et du Ruanda-Urundi, "Presentation" (n.d.).

190. F. Gillet, "Le pélerinage" (2008), p. 54.

191. Licata and Klein (2010), pp. 45-57.

192. "Centre Wallonie-Bruxelles à Kinshasa" (n.d.). Thank you to Guy Vanthemsche for this reference.

193. Fuks (1986), p. 182.

194. N. Laude, entry for Roelens, *BCB* VI (1968), columns 861-864.

195. Author's visit, 17 May 2003.
196. "Victor Roelens" (n.d.).
197. D. Van Reybrouck, interview, Festival Theaterformen, *Presence of the Colonial Past* (2010), pp. 12-14.
198. Ceuppens (2003), e.g., pp. 51-113.
199. D. Van Reybrouck, *Mission suivi de l'Ame des termites* (2011).
200. J. Bel, "*Congo, de missie en de literatuur*" (2009), p. 124.
201. A. Dirks et al., *Presence of the Colonial Past* (2010).
202. L. Dieu, entry for de Deken, *BCB*, I (1948), columns 289-290.
203. Ibid.; *Le Soir*, 23 April 1904.
204. "Standbeeld Pater De Deken opnieuw onder vuur," *Gazet van Antwerpen*, 2 April 2014, https://www.gva.be/cnt/aid1563565/standbeeld-pater-de-deken-opnieuw-onder-vuur. Accessed 7 June 2018.
205. "Infobord aan standbeeld koloniale pater," *Het Laatste Nieuws*, 22 May 2015, https://www.hln.be/regio/wilrijk/infobord-aan-standbeeld-koloniale-pater~a83b12ac/. Accessed 7 June 2018.
206. Author's visits, 17 May 2003 and 13 May 2018.
207. Van Reybrouck (2011), p. 11.
208. S. Theerlynck, "Voor onze missies, dank u," *De Morgen*, 24 September 2012, p. 24, located at http://www.kuleuven.be/thomas/page/media/view/74000/. Accessed 15 July 2014.
209. D. Goyvaerts, "En nu de echte waarheid over het Belgische missiewerk," *De Morgen*, 2 April 2009, http://www.demorgen.be/dm/nl/2461/Opinie/article/detail/805069/2009/04/02/En-nu-de-echte-waarheid-over-het-Belgische-missiewerk.dhtml. Accessed 14 August 2014.
210. H. Kieboom, "Een apologie voor de missies," *De Morgen*, 3 April 2009 http://www.demorgen.be/dm/nl/2461/Opinie/article/detail/806447/2009/04/03/Een-apologie-voor-de-missies.dhtml. Accessed 15 July 2014.
211. *Knack Extra*, 7 May 2010, p. 49.
212. "Congo – Paysages urbains, regards croisés" (n.d.).
213. Centre Wallonie-Bruxelles, "Dossier de presse" (2007).
214. KADOC is an interfaculty research center and archive at KU Leuven (founded 1976) focusing on the interplay of culture, religion, and society. The Cinematek is the Cinémathèque royale de Belgique in Brussels, which is a motion picture library and archive that conserves and shows films in addition to maintaining other resources for film study.
215. Bragard and Planche (2009), p. 58.
216. M. Boucher et al., *Black Paris – Black Brussels* (2008), p. 99.
217. Email communication from Tobias Wendl, 3 November 2013.
218. Email communication from Martine Boucher, 7 November 2013.
219. C. Braeckman, "Les Belges jouent la montre," *Le Soir*, 13 June 2008.
220. "De Gucht a parlé au nom du gouvernement," *Le Soir*, 24 April 2008.
221. "Als dat neokolonialisme is, dan ben ik een neokolonialist," *Gazet van Antwerpen*, 25 May 2008, http://www.gva.be/cnt/aid721157/als-dat-neokolonialisme-is-dan-ben-ik-een-neokolonialist. Accessed 18 July 2014.
222. P. Imbach, "Commémorons le Soldat inconnu congolais," *Le Soir*, 10 November 2008. Accessed 17 December 2008. The late professor Pilipili Kagabo had in

the 1990s called for reparations to address the debt Belgium owed the Congo. On Kagabo, see S. Bucyalimwe Mararo and E. Murhula A. Nashi, *Histoire, conscience nationale congolaise et africaine* (2015).

223. V. Dujardin et al., *Léopold II. Entre génie et gêne* (2009); idem., *Leopold II. Schaamteloos genie?* (2009).

224. Quoted in Hocq (2012), p. 48.

225. *De Tijd*, 23 October 2004, quoted in Rosoux and van Ypersele (2011), p. 52.

226. Rosoux and van Ypersele (2011), p. 54.

227. Goddeeris (2011), p. 44.

228. See schedules of CEGESOMA "Studiedag voor Jonge Historici" on colonial history, 20 March 2008 and 25 March 2011.

229. "Belgique-Congo: Enjeux d'histoire, enjeux de mémoire" (n.d.).

230. F. De Boeck and M.-F. Plissart, *Kinshasa* (2004).

231. M. Wiener, "The Idea of 'Colonial Legacy' and the Historiography of Empire" (2013), pp. 1-32.

232. Goddeeris and Kiangu (2011), p. 55; Goddeeris (2011), p. 43.

233. Vanhee and Castryck (2002), p. 311.

234. Ndaywel È Nziem (2006), p. 241.

235. I. Ndaywel È Nziem, *Histoire du Zaïre* (1997).

236. Quoted in A. Riding, "Belgium Confronts Its Heart of Darkness," *The New York Times*, 21 September 2002.

237. A. Mycock, "After Empire" (2017), p. 403, referencing A. Van den Braembussche, "The Silence of Belgium" (2002), pp. 34-52.

238. L. Licata, O. Klein, and C. Gurrieri, "Mémoire de bronze, mémoire de caoutchouc: Un regard psychosocial sur les représentations de l'action coloniale belge au Congo," unpublished paper, n.d., p. 10.

239. R. Hamilton, "Forgotten Holocaust," *The Washington Post*, 7 January 2001, p. B3.

240. E.g., J.-L. Jadoulle and J. Georges, *Construire l'histoire* (2008).

241. Mycock (2017), p. 403.

242. J.-P. Lefèvre, *A la conquête du temps* (2002), p. B9, quoted in Vanthemsche (2006), p. 89.

243. B. Boulangé et al., *Histoire 3e/6e* (2013).

244. H. Hasquin and J.-L. Jadoulle, *FuturHist, 5ème secondaire* (2010), pp. 172-73, 39.

245. Hasquin and Jadoulle (2010), pp. 164-69.

246. Licata et al. (n.d.), pp. 17-18.

247. Ibid., p. 11.

248. C. Braeckman, interview with In Koli Jean Bofane, "«L'écrivain est un voleur de sabre»," *Le Soir*, 24 September 2010, p. 39; Licata and Klein (2010), pp. 45-57.

249. Licata, Klein, and Gurrieri (n.d.), pp. 2-4.

250. Interview with Plasman (2009).

251. O. White and J. Daughton, "Introduction," in White and Daughton (2012), p. 12.

2010 and beyond

1. A. Berenboom, *Le roi du Congo* (2012), p. 88.
2. Quoted in A. Hope, "Calls for removal of statues of Leopold II" (2017).
3. Viewer reactions and letters, communicated by RTBF, email from Françoise de Thier, 12 November 2013.
4. C. Braeckman, "Le Congo suscite une véritable fièvre éditoriale," *Le Soir*, 12 June 2010, http://blog.lesoir.be/colette-braeckman/2010/06/12/le-congo-suscite-une-veritable-fievre-editoriale/. Accessed 7 August 2014.
5. F. Ryckmans, *Mémoires noires* (2010). Pierre Ryckmans (1891-1959) was Governor-General of the Belgian Congo (1934-1946) and is not to be confused with the late Sinologist and writer Pierre Ryckmans (1935-2014), pseudonym Simon Leys.
6. Tollebeek (2010).
7. J. Lagae, "Unsettling the 'Colonizing Camera'" (2012), pp. 327-342.
8. See Afrika Filmfestival, https://afrikafilmfestival.be.
9. "Le Congo de papa sur grand écran," *Le Soir*, 6 October 2010, p. 36.
10. J.-C. Vantroyen, "«Indépendence cha cha»," *Le Soir*, 11 June 2010, p. 43.
11. Quoted in Mock (2010).
12. See for example "La blague belge qui ne fait pas rire le gouvernement," *Le Monde*, 21 March 2010; G. Leménager, "«La Belgique peut exploser»," *Le Nouvel Observateur*, 11-17 November 2010, p. 55.
13. Derom et al. (2002), p. 31.
14. Author's visit, 9 May 2018.
15. "Souverain (square du). Vorstsquare" (n.d.).
16. Goddeeris (2015), p. 405.
17. CEC press release, 19 October 2010, www.kbr.be.
18. T. Muteba Luntumbue, *Ligablo* (2010).
19. A. Mobe, "Le Congo, la Belgique et la Grande guerre" (2013); P. Jacquij et al. [n.d.].
20. A. Mobe Fansiama, "En marge d'une exposition au Musée royal de l'Armée de Bruxelles" (2011-2012), p. 62.
21. S. Cornelis, "Revisiter l'histoire, pour 'réparer'" (2008).
22. Author's meeting with Pierre Lierneux, Musée Royale de l'Armée, 5 December 2013.
23. Christian Laporte, "La Force publique, une saga belge et—surtout—congolaise," *La Libre Belgique*, http://www.lalibre.be/actu/belgique/la-force-publique-une-saga-belge-et-sur-tout-congolaise-51b8bea5e4b0de6db9bc006b. Accessed 8 August 2014; Mobe (2013).
24. Kln, "Tokopesa Saluti, 125 Belgisch-Congolees militair verleden," *Het Nieuwsblad*, 5 November 2011, http://www.nieuwsblad.be/article/detail.aspx?articleid=BLK LA_20111105_001. Accessed 8 August 2014.
25. "Expo Tokopesa Saluti," http://www.vredescentrum.be/album/activiteiten/569 (n.d.), and "Expo Tokopesa Saluti," http://www.vredescentrum.be/thema/de-kijker/expo-tokopesa-saluti (n.d.); "Tokopesa Saluti!" (2013).
26. D. Stiers, "L'outil culturel est sous-exploité," *Le Soir*, 9 July 2010, p. 35.

27. J. Van Hove, "Verrassend Afrika bij Bozar," *De Standaard*, 9 June 2010, p. 40.

28. Chantal Hemerijckx quoted in H. Ceelen, "Rumba ritmes in Brusselse Bozar," *De Morgen*, 16 July 2010, p. 27.

29. "Press review 50 ans Congo _ overview artikels," 4 August 2010, BOZAR archives.

30. J.-M. Wynants, "Une cartographie de l'art africain," *Le Soir*, 9 June 2010, p. 41.

31. D. Legrand, "Musée Expos, fête et feu d'artifice au Musée de l'Afrique centrale," *Le Soir*, 20 April 2010.

32. A. Engels, entry for Palate, *BCB* II (1951), columns 751-753.

33. M. Coosemans, entry for Poskin, *BCB* IV (1955), column 721.

34. Le Collège communal, Ville d'Andenne, "Les Guerres" (n.d.).

35. Author's visit, 10 May 2018.

36. M. Couttenier, *Als muren spreken* (2010).

37. It bears noting that Inforcongo photographs, some of which were taken by Congolese Joseph Makula, also had long lives in Congolese homes after the colonial era. See Colard (2016).

38. P. Verlinden and S. Hertsens, *Belgisch-Kongo* (2010).

39. G. Convents, "VRT en 50 jaar Congo" (2010).

40. Eklektik Productions & Off World, *Kongo documentaire reeks in 3 afleveringen [1510-2010]* (2010).

41. "Congo in de Cultuuragenda," *De Standaard*, 24 April 2010, p. 74; *Katanga Business*, dir. T. Michel (2009).

42. "Bonjour Congo" (n.d.).

43. "Conférences et Manifestations coloniales," *L'Essor colonial et maritime*, 1930.

44. Only in 1930 did the University of Ghent became Belgium's first fully Dutch-language institution of higher education.

45. "Programme des manifestations de propagande coloniale 1952-1953" ([1952]), p. 32.

46. E. Vandermotten and Paul Bailly to Minister of Colonies, 20 September 1954, liasse "Koloniale Kring van Leuven en omliggende," portefeuille 62 Inforpresse, AA.

47. See entries for these men in various volumes of the *BCB*.

48. Author's visit, 17 May 2018.

49. F. Ryckmans, "Congo" (n.d.).

50. R. Vanderbeeken, "Documentary as Anti-Movement" (2012), p. 96.

51. Author's visit to MAS with E. de Palmenaere, 13 November 2013.

52. Author's visit, May 2018.

53. S. McFadden, "Good Housekeeping" (2010), pp. 50-51.

54. P. Van Schuylenbergh and M. Z. A. Etambala, *Patrimoine d'Afrique centrale. Archives Films* (2010).

55. Author's conversation with P. Van Schuylenbergh, 21 November 2013.

56. T. Berthemet, "Albert II invité muet des cinquante ans du Congo," *Le Monde*, 29 June 2010.

57. M. Meunier, "Une histoire belge," (2010).

58. D. Van Reybrouck, *Congo* (2012).

59. "King Leopold's Ghost," Wikipedia entry (n.d.).

60. C. Braeckman, O. Mouton, and B. Delvaux, "La tragédie du Congo: l'idéalisme impatient," *Le Soir*, 8 September 2012, p. 30.

61. D. Delas et al., "À propos de *Congo. Une histoire*, de David Van Reybrouck" (2013), p. 128.
62. T. Demos and H. Van Gelder, *In and Out of Brussels* (2012).
63. Vanderbeeken (2012), pp. 94-105.
64. Augustijnen (2011).
65. Author's conversation with curator M. Leduc-Grimaldi, 21 November 2013.
66. Berenboom (2012).
67. R. Langford, "Photography, Belgian colonialism and Hergé's *Tintin au Congo*"(2008), p. 82; J. Vrielink, "Effort to ban Tintin comic book fails in Belgium," *The Guardian*, 14 May 2012, http://www.theguardian.com/law/2012/may/14/effort-ban-tintin-congo-fails. Accessed 25 June 2014.
68. M. Meunier, "Africa Dreams, l'ombre du roi" (2010).
69. J. Mertens et al., "A New Floor for the Silenced?" (2013), p. 93.
70. *Visages de Paul Panda Farnana*, dir. Mona MK/Afrikavision (2011).
71. Derom et al. (2002), p. 90.
72. "Une statue de Léopold II déboulonnée à Forest" (2018).
73. "Le bourgmestre de Forest lance un appel pour retrouver le buste de Léopold II" (2018).
74. Service Public Fédéral Finances, "Donation Royale" (n.d.).
75. "Le Parc Duden" (n.d.).
76. Author's discussion with art gallery dealer, 12 May 2018.
77. Corbey (1999), p. 14.
78. C. Petridis, "René and Odette Delenne" (2011), p. 118; S. Litt, "Cleveland Museum of Art acquires a stellar collection of Congolese art from Odette Delenne of Belgium" (2011).
79. "Auction Results" (2015).
80. Vellut, "Le Congo dans les esthétiques de l'Occident" (2017), p. 298.
81. Van Beurden (2015).
82. "Décès de Baudouin de Grunne: Bourgmestre un demi-siècle," *Le Soir*, 15 December 2011, www.lesoir.be/art/%252Fbourgmestre-un-demi-siecle_t-20111215-01Q561.html. Accessed 13 December 2018.
83. "Bernard De Grunne" (n.d.).
84. "Histoire du Congo par les monuments" (1985), p. 33.
85. Derom et al. (2002), p. 97.
86. *L'Illustration congolaise*, no. 140 (1 May 1933), p. 4472.
87. Author's visits 2002-2018, and *L'Illustration congolaise*, no. 146 (1 November 1933), p. 4706.
88. *L'Illustration congolaise*, no. 151 (1 April 1934), p. 4903; "Aux pionniers ixellois de l'Œuvre coloniale," *Le Soir*, 9 October 1933.
89. Monroe (2012), p. 448.
90. Author's visit to MAS with E. de Palmenaere, 13 November 2013.
91. Rahier, "*Métis/Mulâtre*" (2003), p. 98.
92. A. Lauro, *Coloniaux, ménagères et prostituées* (2005).
93. G. Simenon, *Le blanc à lunettes* (1937).
94. G. Simenon, *African Trio* (1979), p. 20. This passage translated by Stuart Gilbert.
95. Simenon (1979), p. viii.
96. Van Reybrouck (2011), p. 29.

97. Jeurissen (2003), p. 34; A. Budagwa, interview, "Belgique: l'Eglise s'excuse auprès des enfants métis de la colonisation" (2017).

98. Jeurissen (2003), p. 67.

99. Rahier, "*Métis/Mulâtre*" (2003), pp. 85-112.

100. "Belgique," *TV5monde* (2017).

101. S. Heynnsens, *De kinderen van Save* (2017); cf. K. Ghequière and S. Kanobana, *De bastaards van onze kolonie* (2010).

102. "De Belgische staat stal kinderen in kolonies," *Gazet van Antwerpen*, 22 February 2008, http://www.gva.be/cnt/aid680605/de-belgische-staat-stal-kinderen-in-kolonies. Accessed 18 September 2013; Guy Cudell high school student exhibit "Noirs Desseins pour Blanches Aspirations? Une histoire belgo-congolaise" at Saint-Josse-ten-Noode city hall, author's visit, May 2018.

103. Q. Schoonvaere, "Étude de la Migration congolaise et de son Impact sur la Présence congolaise en Belgique" (2010), p. 13; M. Tipo-Tipo, *Migration Sud/ Nord, Levier ou Obstacle?* (1995), pp. 90-91; Kagné (2000), p. 65.

104. Mertens, Goedertier, et al., (2013), p. 91; T. Peters, "'Valt er iets te vieren, misschien?'," *De Tijd*, 29 May 2010, pp. 43-45.

105. J. Pollain, "L'immigration en chiffres" (1980), p. 141.

106. Schoonvaere (2010), p. 13; M. Geelkens, "Matonge, a story of Congolese immigration" (2013), p. 1.

107. Beyen and Destatte (2009), p. 79.

108. S. Demart, "Histoire orale à Matonge (Bruxelles)" (2013), p. 137; M. Lututala, "L'élargissement de l'espace de vie des Africains" (1997), p. 338.

109. Schoonvaere (2010), pp. 29, 28.

110. Ibid., p. 13.

111. Sources: Vanthemsche (2012), pp. 279-280; Schoonvaere (2010), p. 13; Tipo-Tipo, pp. 90-91; Kagné (2000), p. 65.

112. De Mul (2012), p. 174; K. Arnaut et al., *Een Leeuw in een Kooi* (2009).

113. T. Friedman, "The 2 Domes of Belgium," *The New York Times*, 27 January 2002.

114. "Journey of Belgian female 'bomber'" (2005).

115. T. Shultz, "Europe Worries Young People Are Going Abroad to Seek Jihad" (2013).

116. Quoted in H. Renard, "Matonge, Congolese Wijk in Brussel," *Knack*, 7 May 2010, p. 47.

117. Buettner (2016), p. 389.

118. See Schoonvaere (2010).

119. "Onbegrijpelijk: Vlaams-Waals conflict waait naar Congo over," *Gazet van Antwerpen*, 26 June 2008, http://www.gva.be/cnt/aid729747/onbegrijpelijk-vlaams-waals-conflict-waait-naar-congo-over. Accessed 17 July 2014.

120. William, "Neem deel aan de 8ste editie van Congo In Vlaanderen op 28-juni-2014" (2014).

121. P. Blanchard et al., *Le Paris Noir* (2001).

122. See Afrika Filmfestival, https://afrikafilmfestival.be (n.d.); G. Convents, *Images et paix* (2008); idem., *Images et démocratie* (2006); idem., *L'Afrique? Quel cinéma!* (2003); idem., *Préhistoire du cinéma en Afrique 1897-1918* (1986).

123. T. Peters, "'Valt er iets te vieren, misschien?'," *De Tijd*, 29 May 2010, pp. 43-45.

124. Joris (1990), p. 351.

125. Geelkens (2013).
126. Demart (2013), p. 137.
127. Renard (2010), p. 45.
128. Buettner (2016), p. 392.
129. Renard (2010), p. 45.
130. M. Angali, "Les Journées zaïroises ont métissé danse, mode et lutte contre le sida," *Le Soir*, 25 April 1988, p. 9.
131. Licata et al. (n.d.), p. 11.
132. C. Braeckman, interview with In Koli Jean Bofane, "«L'écrivain est un voleur de sabre»," *Le Soir*, 24 September 2010, p. 39.
133. Independant Research Bureau (IRB) Europe, "Présentation des résultats d'une enquête auprès de populations d'origines différentes en Belgique" (2009), p. 31.

Epilogue

1. *Le Congo: Moniteur colonial illustré* (Brussels), no. 113 (24 June 1906), p. 197.
2. Demey (2009).
3. D. Cabral, "Tour Leopold II" (2018).
4. "Ecolo-Groen appelle à changer le nom du square des Vétérans coloniaux à Anderlecht" (2018); U. Petropoulos, "Patrice Lumumba aura sa plaque commémorative à Mons," *lavenir.net*, 7 November 2017, https://www.lavenir.net/cnt/dmf20171107_01081684/patrice-lumumba-aura-sa-plaque-commemorative-a-mons. Accessed 15 June 2018; J. Truyts, "Nieuw infobord bij omstreden standbeeld van Leopold II in Oostende" (2016).
5. Goddeeris (2015), p. 401.
6. On Panda see F. Bontinck, "Mfumu Paul Panda Farnana 1888–1930" (1980), pp. 591–610.
7. I. Ndaywel È Nziem, *Histoire générale du Congo* (1998), pp. 441–43.
8. Young (1993), p. 211.
9. Milan Schreuer, "Belgium Elects Nation's First Black Mayor, a Congolese Immigrant," *The New York Times*, 15 October 2018, https://www.nytimes.com/2018/10/15/world/europe/belgium-pierre-kompany-congo.html. Accessed 23 January 2019.
10. "Racistische koorzangen op Pukkelpop: 'Handjes kappen, de Congo is van ons'," *Gazet van Antwerpen*, 20 August 2018, https://www.gva.be/cnt/dmf20180820_03673431/racistische-koorzangen-op-pukkelpop-handjes-kappen-de-congo-is-van-ons. Accessed 23 January 2019.
11. Daniel Boffey, "Cécile Djunga: 'It hurts – so we must talk about racism in Belgium'," *The Guardian*, 9 September 2018, https://www.theguardian.com/world/2018/sep/09/cecile-djunga-racism-belgium-viral-video-tv-presenter. Accessed 23 January 2019.
12. "Cécile Djunga: Belgian forecaster hits out at race insults," *BBC News*, 6 September 2018, https://www.bbc.com/news/world-europe-45432783. Accessed 23 January 2019.
13. Gryseels et al. (2005), pp. 637-647.

14. C. Ford, "Museums after Empire in Metropolitan and Overseas France" (2010), pp. 625-661.
15. B. Ceuppens and S. Baloji, *Congo Art Works* (2016).
16. S. Lynch, "Art exhibition confronts Belgium's troubled Congo past," *Irish Times*, 1 December 2016, https://www.irishtimes.com/news/world/europe/art-exhibition-confronts-belgium-s-troubled-congo-past-1.2887765. Accessed 23 April 2018.
17. *Lobi Kuna*, dir. M. De Groof et al. (2017).
18. M. De Groof, "Art and Colonial Archives – Discussion around the Film *Lobi Kuna* (2017)," VUB presentation, 15 May 2018.
19. Farah Nayeri, "Museums in France Should Return African Treasures, Report Says," *The New York Times*, 21 November 2018, https://www.nytimes.com/2018/11/21/arts/design/france-museums-africa-savoy-sarr-report.html?module=inline. Accessed 23 January 2019.
20. "Stuur Afrikaanse kunst terug," *De Standaard*, 27 September 2018.
21. Author's visit, 16 May 2018. Photographs available at https://www.instagram.com/africamuseumbe/. Accessed 30 August 2018.
22. Author's discussions with museum staff, November-December 2013, and May 2018; quote from AfricaMuseum, "Visite du Musée 15.05.2018" brochure and map (internal museum document), 15 May 2018.
23. L. Coirier, "Aimé Mpane – Between shadow and light" (2018).
24. A. Dietl interview of T. Luntumbue, "Tervuren ist kein Sonderfall" (2018).
25. AfricaMuseum, "Visite du Musée" brochure and map (2018); author's visit, 16 May 2018. My thanks to Mathilde Leduc-Grimaldi and Guido Gryseels, and especially to Patricia Van Schuylenbergh, who provided a guided tour of the museum under renovation.
26. "The burden of history" (2018), p. 79.
27. Riding, "Belgium Confronts" (2002).
28. Quote from De Mul (2012), pp. 174-175; Ceuppens, "Remembering Elephants" (n.p.).
29. See Young (1993).
30. Oostindie (2011).
31. Buettner (2016); Wills (2017).
32. Young (1993), p. xii.
33. Ceuppens (2017).
34. Sanchez, "Most statues of Leopold II" (2018).

References

Archives

Archives historiques privées, AfricaMuseum, Tervuren
    Papiers André Van Iseghem
    Papiers Emm. Muller
    Papiers Félix Fuchs
    Papiers Henry de la Lindi

Archives Africaines, Federal Public Service Foreign Affairs, Brussels
    portefeuille 59 Infopresse
    portefeuille 62 Infopresse
    portefeuille R61 Office Colonial
    portefeuille O.C. 414

BOZAR archives, Brussels
    Utotombo files

Archives de la Ville de Bruxelles, Brussels
    Fonds du Bourgmestre

Newspapers

L'Avenir du Tournaisis (Tournai)
Het Belang van Limburg (Hasselt)
La Dernière Heure (Brussels)
Gazet van Antwerpen
The Guardian (Manchester/London)
The Independent (London)
The Irish Times (Dublin)
The Jerusalem Post
Le Jour (Verviers)
Het Laatste Nieuws (Brussels)
La Libre Belgique (Brussels)
Los Angeles Times
La Meuse (Liege)
Le Monde (Paris)
De Morgen (Brussels)
La Nation belge (Brussels)
The New York Times

De Nieuwe Gids (Brussels)
Het Nieuwsblad (Brussels)
La Nouvelle Gazette (Charleroi)
Le Peuple (Brussels)
Le Phare Dimanche (Brussels)
Le Soir (Brussels)
De Standaard (Brussels)
The Telegraph (London)
De Tijd (Brussels)
Vers l'Avenir (Namur)
De Volksgazet (Antwerp)
The Wall Street Journal (New York)
The Washington Post

Published sources

Abercrombie, P., "Brussels: A Study in Development and Town Planning: Part III.–The Present Day," *The Town Planning Review*, vol. 3, no. 4, 1913, pp. 259-272.

"About CADTM," *CADTM*, 8 November 2007, http://www.cadtm.org/About-CADTM, (accessed 13 December 2018).

Africa-Tervuren, vols. 1-6 and 17-26, 1955 and 1971-1980.

AfricaMuseum, n.d., https://www.instagram.com/africamuseumbe/, (accessed 30 August 2018).

Afrika Filmfestival, n.d., https://afrikafilmfestival.be/, (accessed 16 December 2018).

"Agenda 2003 – June," Ville de Namur, n.d., http://www.ville.namur.be/agenda/ manifestation/06.html, (accessed 6 May 2003).

Agentschap Onroerend Erfgoed, "Gedenkteken Alphonse Lange," *Inventaris Onroerend Erfgoed*, 2017, https://id.erfgoed.net/erfgoedobjecten/214211, (accessed 8 January 2019).

——, "Leopoldpark – Memoraal Justin Malfeyt," *Inventaris Onroerend Erfgoed*, 2016, https://inventaris.onroerenderfgoed.be/erfgoedobjecten/77716, (accessed 8 January 2019).

——, "Monument Belgisch-Congo," *Inventaris Onroerend Erfgoed*, 2017, https://id.erfgoed. net/erfgoedobjecten/300509, (accessed 8 January 2019).

——, "Standbeeld Lippens en De Bruyne," *Inventaris Onroerend Erfgoed*, 2018, https:// inventaris.onroerenderfgoed.be/erfgoedobjecten/45052, (accessed 8 January 2019).

——, "Standbeeld van Leopold II," *Inventaris Onroerend Erfgoed*, 2017, https://inventaris. onroerenderfgoed.be/erfgoedobjecten/11369, (accessed 8 January 2019).

Aiyar, P., *New Old World: An Indian Journalist Discovers the Changing Face of Europe*, New York, St. Martin's Press, 2013.

Aldrich, R., "Putting the Colonies on the Map: Colonial Names in Paris Streets," in T. Chafer and A. Sackur, (eds.), *Promoting the Colonial Idea: Propaganda and Visions of Empire in France*, London, Palgrave Macmillan, 2002, pp. 211-223.

Ames, E., M. Klotz, and L. Wildenthal (eds.), *Germany's Colonial Pasts*, Lincoln, University of Nebraska Press, 2005.

"Anvers – Monument Baron Dhanis – Antwerpen – Standbeeld Baron Dhanis," *Verzame-laarke.be*, n.d., http://www.verzamelaarke.be/producten/anvers-monument-baron-dhanis-antwerpen-standbeeld-baron-dhanis, (accessed 8 January 2019).

Arnaut, K., "Belgian Memories, African Objects: Colonial Re-Collection at the Musée Africain de Namur (Belgium)," *Ateliers*, vol. 23, 2001, pp. 29-48.

Arnaut, K., et al., *Een Leeuw in een Kooi: de Grenzen van het multiculturele Vlaanderen*, Antwerp, Meulenhoff/Marteau, 2009.

Arts primitifs/Primitieve Kunst, Brussels, n.p., 1971.

Ascherson, N., *The King Incorporated: Leopold the Second and the Congo*, London, Granta Books, 1999 [1963].

Association Royale d'Anciens d'Afrique et d'Outre-Mer Liège, "Histoire," 2002, http://users.skynet.be/araaom/history.html, (accessed 16 July 2018).

"Auction Results: Arts d'Afrique et d'Océanie," *Sotheby's*, 2 December 2015, http://www.sothebys.com/en/auctions/2015/arts-afrique-oceanie-pf1518.html, (accessed 3 August 2017).

A.V.R.U.G. Afrika-Vereniging van de Universiteit Gent, n.d., http://cas1.elis.ugent.be/avrug/erfgoed/sikitiko/sikitiko.htm, (accessed 24 May 2011).

A.V.R.U.G. Afrika-Vereniging van de Universiteit Gent, n.d., http://cas1.elis.ugent.be/avrug/erfgoed/pdf/cercle_2.pdf, (accessed 24 May 2011).

Baetens, R., "Het Prins Leopold Instituut voor Tropische Geneeskunde te Antwerpen: een overzicht," *Studium*, vol. 2, 2009, pp. 116-129.

Balteau, B., and M. Dumoulin, "Colonisation belge: historiographie et mémoire audio-visuelle," *La Revue nouvelle*, nos. 1-2, 2005, pp. 70-80.

Bancel, N., P. Blanchard, G. Goëtsch, E. Deroo, and S. Lemaire (eds.), *Zoos humains: au temps des exhibitions humaines*, Paris, La Découverte, 2004.

Barnard, B., M. Van Berlo, G. van Istendael, T. Judt, M. Reynebeau, and S. de Schaepdrijver, *How Can One Not Be Interested in Belgian History: War, Language and Consensus in Belgium since 1830*, Dublin, Trinity College/Ghent, Academia Press, 2005.

Bastin, M.-L., *Art décoratif Tshokwe*, Lisbon, Companhia de Diamantes de Angola, 1961.

——, *La Sculpture Tshokwe*, Meudon, Alain et Françoise Chaffin, 1982.

——, *Introduction aux arts d'Afrique noire*, Arnouville, Arts d'Afrique noire, 1984.

Bel, J., "*Congo, de missie en de literatuur*: Over David van Reybrouck, J. G. Schoup en Amaat Vyncke," *Tydskrif vir Letterkunde*, vol. 46, no. 1, 2009, pp. 123-138.

——, "Political correctness at the dawn of the millennium: The representation of the native 'other' in colonial literature," in T. Shannon and J. Snapper, (eds.), *Janus at the Millenium: Perspectives on Time in the Culture of the Netherlands*, Lanham, Md., University Press of America, 2004, pp. 113-121.

"Belgian apology to Rwanda," *BBC News*, 7 April 2000, http://news.bbc.co.uk/2/hi/africa/705402.stm, (accessed 17 July 2014).

"Belgique-Congo: Enjeux d'histoire, enjeux de mémoire. Un bilan," *CEGESOMA*, n.d., http://cegesoma.all2all.org/cms/print.php?article=744&pagnbr=8&pagofs=0, (accessed 7 August 2014).

Berenboom, A., *Le roi du Congo*, nouvelle édition, [Paris], Genèse, 2012.

"Bernard De Grunne," n.d., http://www.bernarddegrunne.com/home, (accessed 3 August 2017).

Beyen, M., and P. Destatte, *Nouvelle histoire de Belgique 1970-2000: un autre pays*, Brussels, Le Cri, 2009.

Biographie Belge d'Outre-mer/Belgische Overzeese Biografie, vol. VI, Brussels, ARSOM/ KAOW, 1968.

Biographie Belge d'Outre-mer/Belgische Overzeese Biografie, vol. VIIa, Brussels, ARSOM/ KAOW, 1973.

Biographie Belge d'Outre-mer/Belgische Overzeese Biografie, vol. VIII, Brussels, ARSOM/ KAOW, 1998.

Biographie Coloniale Belge/Belgische Koloniale Biografie, vol. I, Brussels, Institut royal colonial belge/Koninklijk belgisch koloniaal instituut, 1948.

Biographie Coloniale Belge/Belgische Koloniale Biografie, vol. II, Brussels, Institut royal colonial belge/Koninklijk belgisch koloniaal instituut, 1951.

Biographie Coloniale Belge/Belgische Koloniale Biografie, vol. III, Brussels, Institut royal colonial belge/Koninklijk belgisch koloniaal instituut, 1952.

Biographie Coloniale Belge/Belgische Koloniale Biografie, vol. IV, Brussels, Académie royale des sciences coloniales/Koninklijke academie voor koloniale wetenschappen, 1955.

Biographie Coloniale Belge/Belgische Koloniale Biografie, vol. V, Brussels, Académie royale des sciences coloniales/Koninklijke academie voor koloniale wetenschappen, 1958.

Birmingham, D., and P. Martin (eds.), *History of Central Africa: Volume Two*, London, Longman, 1983.

Blanchard, P., S. Lemaire, N. Bancel, and D. Thomas (eds.), *Colonial Culture in France since the Revolution*, trans. A. Pernsteiner, Bloomington, IN, Indiana University Press, 2014.

Blanchard, P., G. Manceron, and E. Deroo (eds.), *Le Paris Noir*, Paris, Hazan, 2001.

Blane, C., "Belgian wealth squeezed from Congo," *BBC News*, 18 January 2001, http:// news.bbc.co.uk/2/hi/programmes/from_our_own_correspondent/1123933.stm, (accessed 6 August 2014).

Boittin, J., *Colonial Metropolis: The Urban Underground of Anti-Imperialism and Feminism in Interwar Paris*, Lincoln, University of Nebraska Press, 2010.

Boma-Tervuren: Le voyage, dir. F. Dujardin (54 minutes), 1999.

"Bonjour Congo," *Canvas*, n.d., https://www.canvas.be/bonjourcongo, (accessed 7 August 2014).

Bontinck, F., "Mfumu Paul Panda Farnana 1888–1930: Premier (?) nationaliste congolais?," in V. Y. Mudimbe, (ed.), *La dépendance de l'Afrique et les moyes d'y remédier*, Paris, Berger-Levrault, 1980, pp. 591–610.

Boon, R., "De Prins-Regent naar Belgisch-Congo en Ruanda-Urundi (29 juni-12 augustus 1947): Context, achtergrond en doelstellingen," *Museum dynasticum*, vol. 24, no. 1, 2012, pp. 49-62.

Boucher, M., C. Leblanc, I. Six, T. Wendl, and B. von Lintig, *Black Paris – Black Brussels: Art et histoire d'une disapora de 1906 à nos jours*, Ixelles, Commune d'Ixelles, 2008.

Boudart, L., "Congo belge et littérature de jeunesse dans l'entre-deux-guerres," *Strenæ*, vol. 3, 22 January 2012, http://strenae.revues.org/606, (accessed 29 October 2013).

Boulangé, B., M. Colle, C. Grétry, D. Jorissens, and D. Leclerq, *Histoire 3e/6e: Jalons pour mieux comprendre*, De Boeck, n.p., 2013.

"Le bourgmestre de Forest lance un appel pour retrouver le buste de Léopold II," *RTBF. be*, 12 January 2018, https://www.rtbf.be/info/regions/detail_le-bourgmestre-de-forest-lance-un-appel-pour-retrouver-le-buste-de-leopold-ii?id=9809888, (accessed 8 June 2018).

Bouttiaux, A.-M., "Des mises en scène de curiosités aux chefs-d'œuvre mis en scène: le Musée royal de l'Afrique à Tervuren: un siècle de collections," *Cahiers d'Études africaines* 155-156, vol. 34, nos. 3-4, 1999, pp. 595-616.

Braeckman, C., "Le Congo suscite une véritable fièvre éditoriale," *Lesoir.be*, 12 June 2010, http://blog.lesoir.be/colette-braeckman/2010/06/12/le-congo-suscite-une-veritable-fievre-editoriale/, (accessed 7 August 2014).

——, "La Belgique confrontée à son passé colonial," *Le Monde diplomatique,* January 2002, http://www.monde-diplomatique.fr/2002/01/BRAECKMAN/8340, (accessed 18 July 2014).

——, *Le Dinosaure: Le Zaïre de Mobutu,* Paris, Fayard, 1992.

"BRAFA Art Fair: Bernard de Grunne Tribal Fine Arts," n.d., http://www.brafa.art/gallery/Bernard-de-Grunne-Tribal-Fine-Arts, (accessed 8 October 2017).

Bragard, V., and S. Planche, "Museum practices and the Belgian colonial past: Questioning the memories of an ambivalent metropole," in D. Thomas, (ed.), *Museums in Postcolonial Europe,* London, Routledge, 2009, pp. 54-64.

Brocheux, P., and D. Hémery, *Indochina: An Ambiguous Colonization, 1858-1954,* trans. L. Lan Dill-Klein, with E. Jennings, N. Taylor, and N. Tousignant, Berkeley, University of California Press, 2009.

Brondeel, P., *Ik blanke kaffer,* Antwerpen, Standaard Uitgeverij, 1970.

Brosens, G., *Congo aan de Yser: de 32 Congolese soldaten van het Belgisch leger in de Eerste Wereldoorlog,* Brussels, Manteau, 2013.

Bruckner, P., *The Tyranny of Guilt: An Essay on Western Masochism,* trans. S. Rendall, Princeton, Princeton University Press, 2010.

Brussels Hoofdstedelijk Parlement, *BIV-BIQ,* no. 46, 2004-05 (16 March 2005), pp. 38-41.

Bucyalimwe Mararo, S., and E. Nashi (eds.), *Histoire, conscience nationale congolaise et africaine: Hommage au Prof. Dr. Gérard Pilipili Kagabo Byata,* Brussels, Scribe, 2015.

Budagwa, A., interview, "Belgique: l'Eglise s'excuse auprès des enfants métis de la colonisation," TV5monde, 26 April 2017, updated 7 March 2018, https://information.tv5monde.com/afrique/belgique-l-eglise-s-excuse-aupres-des-enfants-metis-de-la-colonisation-166570, (accessed 26 June 2018).

Buettner, E., *Europe after Empire: Decolonization, Society, and Culture,* Cambridge, Cambridge University Press, 2016.

Bulletin de l'Association des Vétérans coloniaux, 1930-1940.

Bulletin de la Société d'Etudes d'intérêts coloniaux de Namur, no. 9, September 1913, p. 111.

"The burden of history," *The Economist,* 8 December 2018, p. 79.

Cabral, D., "Tour Leopold II: A Guide to the Colonial Heritage of the Capital of Europe," 2nd edn., 2018.

Cahen, L., "La collaboration entre le Musée royal de l'Afrique centrale et les Musées nationaux du Zaïre: un chapitre de la 'politique scientifique' du Musée de Tervuren," *Africa-Tervuren,* vol. 19, no. 4, 1973, pp. 111-114.

Castryck, G., "Whose History is History? Singularities and Dualities of the Public Debate on Belgian Colonialism," in C. Lévai, (ed.), *Europe and the World in European Historiography,* Pisa, Pisa University Press, 2006, pp. 71-88.

Catherine, L., *Wandelen naar Kongo,* Brussels, Epo, 2006.

——, *Promenade au Congo: Petit guide anticolonial de Belgique,* trans. J. Dever, Brussels, Aden, 2010.

——, *Léopold II: La folie des grandeurs,* Brussels, Luc Pire, 2004.

——, *Bouwen met zwart geld: De Grootheidswaanzin van Leopold II*, Antwerp, Houtekiet, 2002.

Cattier, F., *Étude sur la situation de l'État indépendant du Congo*, Brussels, Vve. F. Larcier/ Paris, A. Pedone, 1906.

"Caveat Emptor," *African Arts*, vol. 9, no. 4, 1976, p. 68.

CEC press release, 19 October 2010, www.kbr.be, (accessed 7 August 2014).

"Centre Wallonie-Bruxelles à Kinshasa," *Wallonie-Bruxelles International.be*, n.d., http:// www.wbi.be/fr/page/centre-wallonie-bruxelles-kinshasa#.W7D-FaOYRjQ, (accessed 8 January 2019).

Centre Wallonie-Bruxelles, "Dossier de presse," 3 September 2007.

Cercle des Intérêts matériels du Quartier de Linthout Nord-Est, no. 13, July 1914, p. 3.

"Les cérémonies du 50e anniversaire de la bataille de Tabora (18-9-56) [sic]," *Revue belgo-congolaise illustrée*, no. 4, October 1966, p. 61.

Ceuppens, B., "Remembering Elephants," *Collateral*, 2017, http://www.collateral-journal. com/index.php?cluster=5, (accessed 3 February 2017).

——, "*Lumumba. De complotten? De moord*. Onderzoeksrapport of historische studie?," *BMGN – Low Countries Historical Review*, vol. 122, no. 3, 2007, pp. 1-16.

——, *Congo made in Flanders? Koloniale Vlaamse visies op "blank" en "zwart" in Belgisch Congo*, Ghent, Academia Press, 2003.

Ceuppens, B. and S. Baloji (eds.), *Congo Art Works: Popular Painting*, Brussels, Racine, 2016.

Chambre des Représentants, *Annales parlementaires de la Chambre des représentants*, 28 February 1905, p. 821.

"Cimetière Robermont," n.d., http://www.lescimetieres.com/Cimetiere3.0/Photos/ ailleurs/robermont/Haneuse.jpg, (unknown access date).

"Cinquantenaire: l'inscription «L'Arabe esclavagiste» ne reviendra pas sur le Monument du Congo," *Sudinfo.be*, n.d., http://www.sudinfo.be/archive/recup/830662/ article/regions/bruxelles/actualite/2013-10-09/cinquantenaire-l-inscription-l-arabe-esclavagiste-ne-reviendra-pas-sur-le-, (accessed 14 June 2018).

Claessens, H., *Afscheid van Rumangabo*, Brecht-Antwerpen, De Roerdomp, 1984.

Claeys, A., *Het duistere rijk*, Leuven: Boekengilde De Clauwaert, 1963.

——, *Zonen van Cham*, Leuven: Boekengilde De Clauwaert, 1964.

Claus, H., *The Sorrow of Belgium*, trans. A. Pomerans, New York, Pantheon Books, 1990.

Claus, H. and H. Gruyaert, *Made in Belgium*, Paris, Delpire, 2000.

Clement, J., A. Lambrighs, M. Lenain, O. Libotte, and P. Piron, *La colonisation belge: une grande aventure*, Brussels, Blanchart/UROME, 2004.

Coirier, L., "Aimé Mpane – Between shadow and light: sculpting and painting humanity," *TL mag*, 30 June 2018, https://tlmagazine.com/aime-mpane-between-shadow-and-light-sculpting-and-painting-humanity/, (accessed 30 August 2018).

Colard, S., "Photography in the Colonial Congo (1885-1960)," PhD Thesis, Columbia University, 2016.

Colette, W., "La statue de Léopold II recouverte de sang à Namur," *La Revue Toudi*, 16 June 2011, http://www.larevuetoudi.org/fr/story/la-statue-de-léopold-ii-recouverte-de-sang-à-namur, (accessed 14 July 2018).

Collectif, *Mons 1865-2015: Ouvrir les murs*, [Liege], Mardaga, 2015.

Le Collège communal, Ville d'Andenne, "Les Guerres," n.d., from "Monument à la gloire des coloniaux," *Bibliotheca Andana*, https://www.bibliotheca-andana. be/?page_id=194075, (accessed 21 February 2018).

"Collier pour Leopold II," *artPlastiekfabrique*, 28 June 2010, https://artplastiekfabrique. wordpress.com/2010/06/28/crochet-pour-leopold-2/, (accessed 22 June 2018).

"Commune de Schaerbeek/Gemeente Schaarbeek, Troupes des campagnes d'Afrique – Troepen der Afrikaanse veldtochten," *Bel-Memorial*, n.d., http://www.bel-memorial. org/cities/bruxelles-brussel/schaerbeek/schaerbeek_mon_troupes_afrique.htm, (accessed 8 January 2019).

"Conférences et Manifestations coloniales," *L'Essor colonial et maritime*, 1930, n.p.

Le Congo: Moniteur colonial illustré, no. 113, 24 June 1906, p. 197.

"Congo – Paysages urbains, regards croisés," *CIVA*, n.d., http://www.civa.be/sub/01. aspx?content=&uc=C01_1_136, (accessed 21 August 2014).

Congo: Revue générale de la colonie belge/Algemeen tijdschrift van de belgische kolonie, vol. 2, no. 1, 1937, p. 99.

Congo: White King, Red Rubber, Black Death, dir. P. Bate (90 minutes), 2004.

Le Congo belge et ses Coloniaux: Livre d'Or/Belgisch Kongo en zijn Kolonialen: Gulden Boek, Léopoldville, Éditions Stanley, 1953.

"Congo en Mechelen. Een andere naam voor de 'Van Kerckhovenstraat'?," 10 July 2009, http://www.mechelenblogt.be/2009/07/congo-en-mechelen-andere-naam-voor-van-kerckhovenstraat, (accessed 21 June 2018).

Congo-Namur, no. 1, 1947, p. 21.

Conway, M., *The Sorrows of Belgium: Liberation and Political Reconstruction, 1944-1947*, Oxford, Oxford University Press, 2012.

Conrad, J., "An Outpost of Progress," in J. Stape, (ed.), *Conrad's Congo: Joseph Conrad's Expedition to the Congo Free State, 1890*, London, Folio Society, 2013, pp. 94-118.

Convents, G., "VRT en 50 jaar Congo: de wansmaak voorbij," *DeWereldMorgen.be*, 6 July 2010, http://www.dewereldmorgen.be/artikels/2010/07/06/vrt-en-50-jaar-congo-de-wansmaak-voorbij, (accessed 15 July 2014).

——, *Images et paix: Les Rwandais et les Burundais face au cinéma et à l'audiovisuel. Une histoire politico-culturelle du Rwanda-Urundi allemand et belge et des Républiques du Rwanda et du Burundi (1896-2008)*, Leuven, Afrika Filmfestival, 2008.

——, *Images et démocratie: Les Congolais face au cinéma et à l'audiovisuel. Une histoire politico-culturelle du Congo des Belges jusqu'à la République démocratique du Congo (1896-2006)*, Kessel-Lo, Afrika Filmfestival, 2006.

——, *L'Afrique? Quel cinéma! Un siècle de propagande coloniale et de films africains*, Antwerp, EPO, 2003.

——, *Préhistoire du cinéma en Afrique 1897-1918: A la recherche des images oubliées*, Brussels, OCIC, 1986.

Corbey, R., "*ExItCongoMuseum*: The Travels of Congolese Art," *Anthropology Today*, vol. 17, no. 3, 2001, pp. 26-28.

——, "African Art in Brussels," *Anthropology Today*, vol. 15, no. 6, 1999, pp. 11-17.

Cornelis, S., "Colonial and Postcolonial Exhibitions in Belgium (1885-2005)," in P. Poddar, R. Patke, and L. Jensen, (eds.), *A Historical Companion to Postcolonial Literatures—Continental Europe and its Empires*, Edinburgh, Edinburgh University Press, 2008, pp. 21-23.

——, "Revisiter l'histoire, pour 'réparer'," 17 March 2008, http://www.uclouvain. be/166330.html, (accessed 3 July 2014).

Cornelis, S., P. Maréchal, and J.-M. Goris, *Artistes belges dans les territoires d'outre-mer 1884-1962*, in *Annalen: Historische wetenschappen*, vol. 13, Tervuren, MRAC, 1989.

Cornet, A. and F. Gillet, *Congo Belgique 1955-1965: Entre propagande et réalité*, Brussels, SOMACEGES/Renaissance du Livre, 2010.

Cornet, J., *Art of Africa: Treasures from the Congo*, trans. B. Thompson, London, Phaidon, 1971.

Cornet, J.-A., R. de Cnodder, I. Dierickx, and W. Toebosch, *60 ans de peinture au Zaïre*, Brussels, Editeurs d'Art Associés, 1989.

"Cornet, Jules – Statue à Mons," n.d., https://www.bestor.be/wiki/index.php/Cornet,_Jules_-_Statue_à_Mons, (accessed 19 June 2018).

Coupez, A., "Études africaines en Belgique," *Africa-Tervuren*, vol. 29, nos. 1-2, 1983, p. 17.

Couttenier, M., *Als muren spreken: Het museum van Tervuren 1910-2010. Si les murs pouvaient parler: Le Musée de Tervuren*, Tervuren, MRAC, 2010.

——, "Anthropology and Ethnography," in P. Poddar, R. Patke, and L. Jensen, (eds.), *A Historical Companion to Postcolonial Literatures—Continental Europe and its Empires*, Edinburgh, Edinburgh University Press, 2008, pp. 12-13.

CRAOCA. Bulletin trimestriel, 2000.

Craoca-Kkooav-Urfracol, n.d., https://www.facebook.com/craocakkooavurfracol/, (accessed 8 January 2019).

"Les crimes de la Belgique coloniale au Congo," *CADTM*, 12 June 2007, http://cadtm. org/spip.php?page=imprimer&id_article=2676, (accessed 11 August 2014).

Crosby, A., *Ecological Imperialism: The Biological Expansion of Europe, 900-1900*, Cambridge, Cambridge University Press, 1986.

Cullen, D., "Leopold Must Fall," *Imperial & Global Forum*, 28 June 2016, https:// imperialglobalexeter.com/2016/06/28/leopold-must-fall/, (accessed 9 August 2018).

Curtin, P., *The Image of Africa: British Ideas and Action, 1780-1850*, vol. 1, Madison, University of Wisconsin Press, 1964.

Custer, R., "La mémoire sélective du Congo," 21 November 2007, http://www.intal.be/ fr/article/la-memoire-selective-du-congo, (accessed 30 September 2013).

"Dans la Grande Ombre du Fondateur," *Revue belgo-congolais illustrée*, 15 November 1966, pp. 41-42.

Darwin, J., *Unfinished Empire: The Global Expansion of Britain*, New York, Bloomsbury, 2012.

de Baets, A., *De figuranten van de geschiedenis: hoe het verleden van andere culturen wordt verbeeld en in herinnering gebracht*, Berchem, EPO, 1994.

——, "Metamorphoses d'une épopée: le Congo dans les manuels d'histoire employés dans nos écoles," in J.-P. Jacquemin, (ed.), *Racisme, continent obscure: Clichés, stéréotypes, phantasmes à propos des Noirs dans le Royaume de Belgique*, Brussels, CEC-Le Noir du Blanc/Wit over Zwart, 1991, pp. 45-57.

Debbaut, J., D. Favart, and G. Van Geertruyen, *Utotombo: L'art d'Afrique noire dans les collections privées belges*, Ghent, Snoeck-Ducaju & Zoom, 1988.

de Becker, Q., "Représentations de la campagne arabe à Bruxelles: Les pionniers belges au Congo de Thomas Vinçotte (1911-1921)," in A. Lauro, (ed.), *Bruxelles et le Congo*, Cahiers de La Fonderie, vol. 38 (2008), pp. 12-17.

Debertry, L., *Kitawala*, Elisabethville, Essor du Congo, 1953.

De Boeck, F., and M.-F. Plissart, *Kinshasa: Récits de la ville invisible*, Tervuren, MRAC, 2004.

de Callataÿ, F., "Le Monument du Congo de Thomas Vinçotte (Parc du Cinquantenaire)," *Bulletin des Musées royaux d'art et d'histoire*, vol. 61, 1990, pp. 197-221.

de Cock, A., *Le Congo belge et ses marques postales*, 2nd edn., reprint, Antwerp, R-Editions, 1986 [1931].

de Courcy MacDonnell, J., *Belgium, Her Kings, Kingdom and People*, Boston, Little, Brown, and Co., 1914.

Degrijse, O., "La Belgique et les missions," *Eglise et mission*, vol. 237, 1985, pp. 3-9.

De Guissmé, L., S. Lastrego, P. Mélotte, and L. Licata, "Attitudes Toward World War II Collaboration in Belgium: Effects on Political Positioning Towards the Amnesty Issue in the Two Main Linguistic Communities," *Psychologica Belgica*, vol. 57, no. 3, 2017, pp. 32-51.

de Heusch, L.,"Ceci n'est pas la Belgique," *Yale French Studies*, vol. 102, 2002, pp. 11-23.

——, "Pour Marie-Louise Bastin," *Africana Studia*, no. 2, 1999, pp. 211-219.

Dejung, C., "Making Europe: The Global Origins of the Old World," *H-Soz-u-Kult*, 27 July 2010, http://hsozkult.geschichte.hu-berlin.de/tagungsberichte/id=3212, (accessed 6 August 2014).

De Keyser, R., "Belgisch-Kongo in den belgischen Geschichtslehrbüchern," in W. Fürnrohr, (ed.)., *Afrika im Geschichtsunterricht europäischer Länder: Von der Koloni-algeschichte zur Geschichte der Dritten Welt*, Munich, n.p., 1982, pp. 152-171.

Delas, D., D. Van Reybrouck, T. Chanda, M. Le Lay, and N. Martin-Granel, "À propos de *Congo. Une histoire*, de David Van Reybrouck," *Association pour l'Étude des Littératures Africaines*, no. 35, 2013, pp. 119-146.

de Lichtervelde, L., *Léopold of the Belgians*, trans. T. Reed and H. Reed, New York, The Century Co., 1929.

Delisle, P., *Spirou, Tintin et Cie, une littérature catholique? Années 1930/Années 1980*, Paris, Karthala, 2010.

——, *Bande dessinée franco-belge et imaginaire colonial: des années 1930 aux années 1980*, Paris, Karthala, 2008.

——, "Le Missionaire dans la bande dessinée franco-belge: une figure imposée?," *Histoire & Missions Chrétiennes*, no. 1, 2007, pp. 131-147.

Demart, S., "Histoire orale à Matonge (Bruxelles): un miroir postcolonial," *Revue européenne des migrations internationales*, vol. 29, no. 1, 2013, pp. 133-155.

——, "De la distinction au stigmate: Matonge, un quartier congolais à Bruxelles," in edited by A. Lauro, (ed.), *Bruxelles et le Congo*, Cahiers de La Fonderie, vol. 38, 2008, pp. 58-62.

Dembour, M.-B., *Recalling the Belgian Congo: Conversations and Introspection*, New York, Berghahn Books, 2000.

Demey, T., *Léopold II: La marque royale sur Bruxelles*, Brussels, Guide Badeaux, 2009.

De Moor, F., and J.-P. Jacquemin,'*Notre Congo/Onze Kongo': La propagande coloniale belge: Fragments pour une étude critique*, Brussels, Coopération Education Culture, 2000.

Demos, T., and H. Van Gelder (eds.), *In and Out of Brussels: Figuring Postcolonial Africa and Europe in the Films of Herman Asselberghs, Sven Augustijnen, Renzo Martens, and Els Opsomer*, Leuven, Leuven University Press, 2012.

De Mul, S., "The Holocaust as a Paradigm for the Congo Atrocities: Adam Hochschild's *King Leopold's Ghost*," in E. Boehmer and S. De Mul, (eds.), *The Postcolonial Low*

Countries: Literature, Colonialism, and Multiculturalism, Lanham, MD, Lexington Books, 2012, pp. 163-184.

Derom, P., V. Everarts, and G. Marquenie, *Les sculptures de Bruxelles: Inventaire des sculptures publiques en ronde-bosse en plein air dans la Région de Bruxelles-Capitale, à l'exception des monuments funéraires, religieux et monuments liés à l'architecture*, Brussels, Patrick Derom Gallery, 2002.

Destrée, J., *Lettre au Roi sur la séparation de la Wallonie et de la Flandre*, Brussels, M. Weissenbruch, 1912.

de Villers, G., "Histoire, justice et politique: À propos de la commission d'enquête sur l'assassinat de Patrice Lumumba, instituée par la Chambre belge des représentants," *Cahiers d'Études africaines*, vol. 44 (1-2), nos. 173-174, 2004, pp. 193-220.

De Vos, K., "De afgehakte handen van Leopold II," *Canvas Curiosa*, 22 November 2018, https://www.canvas.be/canvas-curiosa/de-afgehakte-handen-van-leopold-II, (accessed 23 January 2019).

De Vos, L., E. Gerard, P. Raxhon, and J. Gérard-Libois, *Lumumba: De complotten? De moord*, Leuven, Davidsfonds, 2004.

De Weerd, G., *L'État indépendant du Congo. À la recherche de la vérité historique*, Brussels, Dynamédia, 2015.

de Witte, L., *De moord op Lumumba*, Leuven, Van Halewyck, 1999.

Dierickx, M., *Geschiedenis van België*, 12th edn., Antwerp/Amsterdam, De Nederlandsche Boekhandel, 1980.

Dietl, A., interview of T. Luntumbue, "Tervuren ist kein Sonderfall," *jungle.world*, 13 December 2018, https://jungle.world/artikel/2018/50/tervuren-ist-kein-sonderfall, (accessed 6 January 2019).

Direction des Monuments et Sites du Ministère de la Région Bruxelles-Capitale, "Avenue du Front," *Région de Bruxelles-Capitale, Inventaire du Patrimoine architectural*, 1993-95, http://www.irismonument.be/fr.Etterbeek.Avenue_du_Front.html, (accessed 8 January 2019).

——, "Monument du Congo," *Région de Bruxelles-Capitale, Inventaire du Patrimoine architectural*, 2009-10, http://www.irismonument.be/fr.Bruxelles_Extension_Est. Parc_du_Cinquantenaire.A004.html, (accessed 8 January 2019).

——, "Rue Major Pétillon," *Région de Bruxelles-Capitale, Inventaire du Patrimoine architectural*, 1993-95, http://www.irismonument.be/fr.Etterbeek.Rue_Major_Petillon. html, (accessed 8 January 2019).

——, "Square du Solbosch," *Région de Bruxelles-Capitale, Inventaire du Patrimoine architectural*, 2013-15, http://www.irismonument.be/fr.Ixelles.Square_du_Solbosch. html, (accessed 8 January 2019).

Doolen, P., "Dutch Imperial Past Returns to Haunt the Netherlands," *Imperial & Global Forum*, 7 April 2014, http://imperialglobalexeter.com/2014/04/07/dutch-imperial-past-returns-to-haunt-the-netherlands/, (accessed 30 June 2014).

"Druart, Porphyre-Augustin," *Connaître la Wallonie*, n.d., http://connaitrelawallonie. wallonie.be/fr/lieux-de-memoire/druart-porphyre-augustin#.Wx6Pt4onZhE, (accessed 8 January 2019).

Dujardin, V., and M. Dumoulin, *L'Union fait-elle toujours la force? Nouvelle histoire de Belgique 1950-1970*, Brussels, Le Cri, 2008.

Dujardin, V., V. Rosoux, and T. de Wilde d'Estmael (eds.), *Léopold II. Entre génie et gêne. Politique étrangère et colonisation*, Brussels, Racine, 2009.

Dujardin, V., V. Rosoux, and T. de Wilde d'Estmael (eds.), *Leopold II. Schaamteloos genie? Buitenlandse politiek en kolonisatie*, Tielt, Lannoo, 2009.

Dumoulin, M., "L'Enseignement sur l'Afrique a varié avec l'histoire," *Louvain*, no. 184, 2010, pp. 26-27.

———, *Léopold II: un roi génocidaire?*, Brussels, Académie royale de Belgique, 2005.

Dunn, K., *Imagining the Congo: The International Relations of Identity*, New York, Palgrave Macmillan, 2003.

"Ecolo-Groen appelle à changer le nom du square des Vétérans coloniaux à Anderlecht," *RTBF.be*, 22 August 2018, https://www.rtbf.be/info/regions/detail_ecolo-groen-appelle-a-changer-le-nom-du-square-des-veterans-coloniaux-a-anderlecht?id=9689228, (accessed 11 June 2018).

Eklektik Productions & OffWorld, *Kongo documentaire reeks in 3 afleveringen [1510-2010]: Persdossier*, May 2010.

Elsschot, W., *Lijmen*, Antwerp, n.p., 1924.

Emerson, B., *Leopold II of the Belgians: King of Colonialism*, New York, St. Martin's Press, 1979.

"Erection d'un monument au roi Léopold II à Arlon," *Revue Congolaise Illustrée*, no. 2, February 1950, p. 40.

L'Essor colonial et maritime, no. 47, 22 November 1936.

Etambala, [M.] Z. A., "«*Bwana Kitoko*» (1955), un film d'André Cauvin: Réalités congolaises ou rêveries belges?," in P. Van Schuylenbergh and M. Z. A. Etambala, (eds.), *Patrimoine d'Afrique centrale. Archives films: Congo, Rwanda, Burundi, 1912-1960*, Tervuren, MRAC, 2010, pp. 141-156.

———, *Des Écoliers congolais en Belgique 1888-1900: une page d'histoire oubliée*, Paris, L'Harmattan-RDC, 2011.

L'Étoile belge, 15 March 1914.

Ewans, M., *European Atrocity, African Catastrophe: Leopold II, the Congo Free State and Its Aftermath*, London, RoutledgeCurzon, 2002.

"Expo Tokopesa Saluti," n.d., http://www.vredescentrum.be/album/activiteiten/569, (accessed 8 August 2014).

"Expo Tokopesa Saluti," n.d., http://www.vredescentrum.be/thema/de-kijker/expo-tokopesa-saluti, (accessed 8 August 2014).

Farr, M., and S. Barczewski (eds.), *The MacKenzie Moment: Essays Presented to Professor John M. MacKenzie*, Basingstoke, Palgrave Macmillan, 2019.

Fernand, H. "L'ASAOM se souvient," *Mémoires du Congo et du Ruanda-Urundi*, no. 39, September 2016, p. 40.

Dirks, A., C. Farke, S. Franzmann, S. Kaufmann, F. Kotzias, and Kathrin Veser, *Presence of the Colonial Past: Afrika auf Europas Bühnen*, Hannover, Festival Theaterformen, 2010.

Fetter, B., "If I Had Known that 35 Years Ago: Contextualizing the Copper Mines of Central Africa," *History in Africa*, vol. 26, 1999, pp. 449-452.

Fieldhouse, D., "Can Humpty-Dumpty Be Put Together Again? Imperial History in the 1980s," *Journal of Imperial and Commonwealth History*, vol. 12, no. 2, 1984, pp. 9-23.

"La Fontaine Ponthier," Marche-en-Famenne, 2018, https://www.marche.be/tourisme/les-statues-et-sculptures/la-fontaine-ponthier-8826/, (accessed 15 June 2018).

Ford, C., "Museums after Empire in Metropolitan and Overseas France," *Journal of Modern History*, vol. 82, no. 3, 2010, pp. 625-661.

Foutry, V., and J. Neckers, *Als een wereld zo groot waar uw vlag staat geplant. Kongo 1885-1960*, Brussels, BRT-Instructieve Omroep, 1986.

Fraiture, P.-P., "Modernity and the Belgian Congo," *Tydskrif vir Letterkunde*, vol. 46, no. 1, 2009, pp. 43-57.

——, "Belgique-Congo: Dialogues et Bricolages Intertextuels," in D. Wa Kabwe-Segatti and P. Halen, (eds.), *Du Nègre Bambara au négropolitain: les littératures africaines en contexte transculturel*, Metz, Univeristé Paul Verlaine-Metz, 2008, pp. 65-81.

Fuks, R., *Héros et Personnages de chez nous racontés par leur statues*, Brussels, Meddens, 1986.

G., A.-M., *Le Congo belge illustré ou l'État indépendant du Congo*, Liege, H. Dessain, 1888.

Gann, L., and P. Duignan, *The Rulers of Belgian Africa, 1884-1914*, Princeton, Princeton University Press, 1979.

Geary, C., *In and Out of Focus: Images from Central Africa, 1885-1960*, London, Philip Wilson, 2002.

"Gedenkzuil Jules Van Dorpe," 25 May 2009, http://www.standbeelden.be/standbeeld/46, (accessed 30 June 2018).

Geelkens, M., "Matonge, a story of Congolese immigration," trans. E. Uskalis, *Reflexions, le site de vulgarisation de l'Université de Liège*, 30 September 2013, http://reflexions.ulg.ac.be, p. 1, (accessed 23 June 2014).

Geeraerts, J., *Black Ulysses*, trans. J. Swan and M. Swan, New York, Viking, 1978.

——, *Gangrene*, trans. J. Swan. New York, Viking, 1974.

Gent [Stad], "Gent: Citadelpark, standbeeld gebroeders Jos en Lieven Vandevelde," n.d., https://beeldbank.stad.gent/index.php/image/watch/729a41f4b97c4b938ffc10ef62cb3128e73e2b4d5fa54c2599eae300af79012616355ae4e3135d3646c2e286c680e3d3, (accessed 8 January 2019).

Gerard, E., and B. Kuklick, *Death in the Congo: Murdering Patrice Lumumba*, Cambridge, Mass., Harvard University Press, 2015.

Gérard, I., Royal Museum for Central Africa, *Annual Report, 2005-2006*, Tervuren, MRAC, 2007.

Ghequière, K., and S. Kanobana, *De bastaards van onze kolonie: Verzwegen verhalen van Belgische metissen*, Roeselare, Roularta Books, 2010.

Ghosts of Rwanda, dir. G. Barker, *Frontline* (120 minutes), 1 April 2004.

Gillet, F., "Congo rêvé? Congo détruit... Les anciens coloniaux belges aux prises avec une société en repentir. Enquête sur la face émergée d'un mémoire," *Bijdragen tot de Eigentijdse Geschiedenis-Cahiers d'histoire du temps présent*, no. 19, 2008, pp. 79-133.

——, "Le pélerinage des anciens coloniaux en région bruxelloise," in A. Lauro, (ed.), *Bruxelles et le Congo*, Cahiers de La Fonderie, vol. 38, 2008, pp. 54-57.

Giordano, R., "Acteurs et témoins: officiers italiens dans l'État Indépendant du Congo," in J.-L. Vellut, (ed.), *La mémoire du Congo. Le temps colonial*, Tervuren, MRAC, 2005, pp. 228-231.

Goddeeris, I., "Colonial Streets and Statues: Postcolonial Belgium in the Public Space," *Postcolonial Studies*, vol. 18, no. 4, 2015, pp. 397-409.

——, "Postcolonial Belgium: The Memory of the Congo," *interventions*, vol. 17, no. 3, 2015, pp. 434-451.

——, "Congo in onze navel: de omgang met het koloniale verleden in België en zijn buurlanden," *Ons Erfdeel*, vol. 54, no. 1, 2011, pp. 40-49.

Goddeeris, I., and S. E. Kiangu, "Congomania in Academia: Recent Historical Research on the Belgian Colonial Past," *BMGN – Low Countries Historical Review*, vol. 126, no. 4, 2011, pp. 54-75.

"Grandiose manifestation coloniale à Arlon," *La Revue Coloniale Belge*, 1 July 1951, p. 478.

Grindel, S., "Colonial and Postcolonial Contexts of History Textbooks," in M. Carretero, S. Berger, and M. Grever, (eds.), *Palgrave Handbook of Research in Historical Culture and Education*, London, Palgrave Macmillan, 2017, pp. 259-273.

Gryseels, G., G. Landry, and K. Claessens, "Integrating the Past: Transformation and Renovation of the Royal Museum for Central Africa, Tervuren, Belgium," *European Review*, vol. 13, no. 3, 2005, pp. 637-647.

Guisset, J. (ed.), *Le Congo et l'art belge, 1880-1960*, Tournai, La Renaissance du Livre, 2003.

Haentjens, E., "Waarom Brussel wereldtop is voor Afrikaanse kunst," *Brussel Deze Week/BRUZZ*, 10 March 2016, http://www.bruzz.be/nl/cultuur/waarom-brussel-wereldtop-voor-afrikaanse-kunst, (accessed 3 August 2017).

Halen, P., "Les douze travaux du Congophile: Gaston-Denis Périer et la promotion de l'africanisme en Belgique," *Textyles*, vols. 17-18, 2000, pp. 139-150.

——, *Le petit belge avait vu grand. Une littérature coloniale*, Brussels, Labor, 1993.

——, "Le Congo revisité: Une décennie de bandes dessinées 'belges' (1982-1992)," *Textyles*, vol. 9, 1992, pp. 291-304.

Halen, P., and J. Riesz (eds.), *Images de l'Afrique et du Congo/Zaïre dans les lettres françaises de Belgique et alentour: Actes du colloque international de Louvain-la-Neuve (4-6 février 1993)*, Brussels, Textyles, 1993.

Hall, C., and S. Rose, *At Home with the Empire: Metropolitan Culture and the Imperial World*, Cambridge, Cambridge University Press, 2006.

Hasquin, H., and J.-L. Jadoulle (eds.), *FuturHist, 5ème secondaire: De l'âge industriel à la fin de la Seconde Guerre Mondiale*, n.p., Didier Hatier, 2010.

"Herdenkingsplechtigheid aan het Standbeeld Lippens & De Bruyne te Blankenberge," *Kamp Vogelsang*, n.d., http://www.kamp-vogelsang.be/interactief/uw_fotos_2014/blankenberge/, (accessed 8 January 2019).

Hergé, *Tintin in the Congo*, trans. L.-L. Cooper and M. Turner, Brussels, Casterman, 1962.

Hermans, T. (ed.), *A Literary History of the Low Countries*, Rochester, Camden House, 2009.

Herreman, F., M. Holsbeke, and J. Van Alphen, *Musée d'Ethnographie Anvers*, Brussels, Ludion s.a. Cultura Nostra, 1991.

Hersak, D., "In Memoriam: Marie-Louise Bastin, 1918-2000," *African Arts*, vol. 33, no. 2, 2000, p. 17.

Hertmans, S., *War and Turpentine*, trans. D. McKay, New York, Vintage, 2017.

Hessel, F., "Pour l'honneur d'avoir combattu," *Mémoires du Congo et du Ruanda-Urundi*, no. 30, June 2014, pp. 8-11.

Heynnsens, S., *De kinderen van Save: Een geschiedenis tussen Afrika en België*, Antwerpen, Polis, 2017.

"Histoire du Congo par les monuments," *CRAOCA. Bulletin trimestriel*, no. 2, 1985, p. 34.

"Historique du Musée Africain de Namur," *Musée Africain de Namur*, 2004, www.museeafricainnamur.be/fr/histo.php, (accessed 8 October 2017).

Hochschild, A., "In the Heart of Darkness," *The New York Review of Books*, 6 October 2005.

——, *King Leopold's Ghost: A Story of Greed, Terror, and Heroism in Central Africa*, Boston, Houghton Mifflin, 1998.

Hocq, S., "Baudouin Ier et les visites d'État au Congo: de la découverte à la désillusion, des retrouvailles aux prémices de la rupture (1955-1959-1960-1970-1985)," *Museum dynasticum*, vol. 24, no. 1, 2012, pp. 2-48.

Hohenberg, P., and L. Lees, *The Making of Urban Europe 1000-1994*, Cambridge, Mass., Harvard University Press, 1995.

Hogenraad, R., and T. Grosbois, "A History of Threat in Europe and Belgium (1920-1993)," *Social Indicators Research*, vol. 42, no. 2, 1997, pp. 221-244.

Hope, A., "Calls for removal of statues of Leopold II," *Flanders Today*, 24 August 2017, http://www.flanderstoday.eu/current-affairs/calls-removal-statues-leopold-ii, (accessed 16 March 2018).

http://www.sculpturepublique.be/1050/DHaveloose-GeneralStorms.htm, [*Sculpture publique en Belgique*], n.d, (accessed 8 January 2019).

https://www.crkc.be, Centrum voor Religieuze Kunst en Cultuur, 2012, (accessed 11 January 2019).

Hunt, N., "Rewriting the Soul in a Flemish Congo," *Past and Present*, no. 198, 2008, pp. 185-215.

——, "Tintin and the Interruptions of Congolese Comics," in P. Landau and D. Kaspin, (eds.), *Images and Empires: Visuality in Colonial and Postcolonial Africa*, Berkeley, University of California Press, 2002, pp. 90-123.

Hymans, H., *Les Villes d'art célèbres: Bruxelles*, 2d edn. rev. and enl. by Fernand Donnet, Paris, Librairie Renouard, 1926.

L'Illustration congolaise, 1925-1938.

Imbach, P., "Les monuments publics coloniaux, lieux de mémoires contestés," *CADTM*, 29 September 2008, http://cadtm.org/Les-monuments-publics-coloniaux, (accessed 11 August 2014).

——, "Promenade anti-coloniale à Bruxelles, l'ancienne métropole du Congo," *CADTM*, 17 September 2008, http://www.cadtm.org/Promenade-anti-coloniale-a, (accessed 13 August 2018).

Independant Research Bureau (IRB) Europe, "Présentation des résultats d'une enquête auprès de populations d'origines différentes en Belgique," *Unia*, https://www.unia.be/files/Z_ARCHIEF/Quelle%20perceptions%20les%20minorites%20ethniques%20ont-elles%20de%20la%20Belgique.pdf. November 2009, (accessed 8 January 2019).

Instantanés, No. 12, July 1951, p. 2.

Jacquemin, J.-P. (ed.), *Racisme, continent obscure: clichés, stéréotypes et phantasmes à propos des Noirs dans le Royaume de Belgique*, Brussels, Coopération par l'éducation et la culture, 1991.

Jacquemyns, G., "Le Congo belge devant l'opinion publique," *Institut universitaire d'information sociale et économique «INSOC»*, nos. 2-3, Brussels, Parc Léopold, 1956.

Jacquij, P., P. Lierneux, and N. Peeters, "Lisolo na Bisu, «Our history»: The Congolese soldier of the «Force publique» 1885-1960," n.d., http://www.klm-mra.be/klm-new/engels/boeken/CongoENG/, (accessed 8 August 2014).

Jadin, J.-B., "Médecine," *Vijftigjarig Bestaan van de Academie/Cinquantenaire de l'Académie 1928-1978*, vol. 1, Brussels, KAOW-ARSOM, 1982, pp. 292-319.

Jadoulle, J.-L., and J. Georges (eds.), *Construire l'histoire. Tome 4, Un monde en mutation (de 1919 à nos jours)*, Namur, Didier Hatier, 2008.

Janssens, E., and A. Cateaux, *Les Belges au Congo: Notices biographiques*, vol. 2, Antwerp, J. Van Hille-de-Baker, 1911.

Jeurissen, L., *Quand le métis s'appellait «mulâtre»… Société, droit et pouvoir coloniaux face à la descendance des couples eurafricains dans l'ancien Congo belge*, Cahiers Migrations vol. 29, Louvain-la-Neuve, Bruylant-Academia, 2003.

Jewsiewicki, B. (ed.), *Art pictural zaïrois*, Sillery, Quebec, Septentrion, 1992.

———, "Rural society and the Belgian colonial economy," in D. Birmingham and P. Martin, (eds.), *History of Central Africa: Volume Two*, London, Longman, 1983, pp. 95-125.

Jonckheere, W., "Het Van Dorpe-monument 100 jaar op het Kongoplein," *Contactblad van de Kring voor Geschiedenis en Kunst van Deinze en de Leiestreek* (Deinze), vol. 28, no. 3, 2008, pp. 3726-3732.

Joris, L., *Mon oncle du Congo*, trans. M. Hooghe, Arles, Actes Sud/Babel, 1990.

"Journey of Belgian female 'bomber'," *BBC News*, 2 December 2005, http://news.bbc. co.uk/2/hi/europe/4491334.stm, (accessed 18 July 2014).

Judt, T., *Postwar*, New York, Penguin, 2005.

Kagné, B., "Africains de Belgique, de l'indigène à l'immigré," *Hommes & Migrations*, no. 1228, 2000, pp. 62-67.

Kasfir, S., "Visual Cultures," in J. Parker and R. Reid, (eds.), *The Oxford Handbook of Modern African History*, Oxford, Oxford University Press, 2013, pp. 437-456.

Katanga Business, dir. T. Michel (120 minutes), 2009.

Kesteloot, C., "Mouvement Wallon et Identité Nationale," *Courrier hebdomadaire du CRISP*, no. 1392, 1993, pp. 1-48.

Kets, E., *Kuifje & Tintin kibbelen in Afrika: de Belgische taalstrijd in Congo, Rwanda en Burundi*, Leuven, Acco, 2009.

"King Leopold's Ghost," *Wikipedia.com*, n.d., http://en.wikipedia.org/wiki/King_Leopold's_Ghost, (accessed 8 August 2014).

Knack Extra, 7 May 2010, p. 49.

Kockerols, L., "Le Dieu Créateur," *Vie féminine*, June 1969.

"Krijgt Leopold II straks zijn hand terug?," *DeRedactie.be*, 23 December 2009, http://dere-dactie.be/cm/vrtnieuws/regio/westvlaanderen/1.674140, (accessed 11 August 2014).

Labio, C., "Preface," *Yale French Studies*, no. 102, 2002, pp. 1-8.

Lagae, J., "Unsettling the 'Colonizing Camera': Curatorial Notes on the 'Congo belge en images' project," *Photography & Culture*, vol. 5, no. 3, 2012, pp. 327-342.

Langford, R., "Photography, Belgian colonialism and Hergé's *Tintin au Congo*," *Journal of Romance Studies*, vol. 8, no. 1, 2008, pp. 77-89.

Laurent, M., *L'Architecture et la Sculpture en Belgique*, Paris, G. van Oest, 1928.

Lauro, A., *Coloniaux, ménagères et prostituées: Au Congo belge (1885-1930)*, Loverval, Labor, 2005.

Laus, J.-P., "09.09.09 Halle: nieuwe tekst voor beeld Leopold II," [9 September 2009], http://www.congoforum.be/ndl/nieuwsdetail.asp?subitem=2&newsid=160840& Actualiteit=selected, (accessed 30 June 2018).

Lefert, M., *Petit Guide du Musée Africain de Namur*, Namur, n.p., n.d.

Lefèvre, J.-P., *A la conquête du temps: Histoire au cycle 10-12*, n.p., Ransart/Gai Savoir, 2002.

Leménager, G., "«La Belgique peut exploser»," *Le Nouvel Observateur*, 11-17 November 2010, p. 55.

Lennep, J., *Statues and Monuments of Brussels pre-1914*, trans. L. Rogers, Antwerp, Pandora, 2000.

Lepersonne, J., "Lucien Cahen: Le Directeur de Musée," *Africa-Tervuren*, vol. 28, no. 4, 1982, pp. 7-10.

"Lettres du Congo," *Journal des débats politiques et littéraires*, 27 May 1891, p. 2.

Leurquin, A., "La Distraction de l'objet africain ou l'histoire d'une errance," in J. Debbaut, D. Favart, and G. Van Geertruyen, (eds.), *Utotombo: l'Art d'Afrique noire dans les collections privées belges*, Gand, Snoeck-Ducaju & Zoon, 1988, pp. 315-329.

Levering Lewis, D., *The Race to Fashoda: European Colonialism and African Resistance in the Scramble for Africa*, New York, Weidenfeld & Nicolson, 1987.

Levine, P., "Naked Truths: Bodies, Knowledge, and the Erotics of Colonial Powers," *Journal of British Studies*, vol. 52, no. 1, 2013, pp. 5-25.

Leys, S., *The Hall of Uselessness: Collected Essays*, New York, NYRB, 2013.

Licata, L., and O. Klein, "Holocaust or Benevolent Paternalism? Intergenerational Comparisons on Collective Memories and Emotions about Belgium's Colonial Past," *International Journal of Conflict and Violence*, vol. 4, no. 1, 2010, pp. 45-57.

Licata, L., and O. Klein, "Regards croisés sur un passé commun: anciens colonisés et anciens coloniaux face à l'action belge au Congo," in M. Sanchez-Mazas and L. Licata, (eds.), *L'Autre: Regards psychosociaux*, Saint-Martin d'Hères, Presses universitaires de Grenoble, 2005, pp. 241-277.

Lippert, J.-L., *Dialogue des oiseaux du phare: Maïak I*, Avin, Belgium, Luce Wilquin, 1998.

Litt, S., "Cleveland Museum of Art acquires a stellar collection of Congolese art from Odette Delenne of Belgium," *Cleveland.com*, 3 June 2011, updated 8 June 2011, http://www.cleveland.com/arts/index.ssf/2011/06/cleveland_museum_of_art_acquir_3.html, (accessed 3 August 2017).

Lobi Kuna, dir. M. De Groof, et al. (46 minutes), 2017.

Loriaux, F., F. Morimont, and J.-L. Vellut, *Bibliographie historique du Zaïre à l'époque coloniale (1880-1960). Travaux publiés en 1960-1996*, Louvain-la-Neuve, Centre d'histoire de l'Afrique/Tervuren, MRAC, 1996.

Lubuka! Lubuka!: 'Gevaar in Afrikacollecties – Afrikacollecties in gevaar', Heverlee, CRKC, 2005.

Lumumba, dir. R. Peck (107 minutes), 2000.

Lumumba-Kasongo, T., "Zaire's Ties to Belgium: Persistence and Future Prospects in Political Economy," *Africa Today*, vol. 39, no. 3, 1992, pp. 23-48.

Luntumbue, T., *Ligablo: Exposition bon marché- Goedkope tentoonstelling*, Brussels, Coopération par l'Education et la Culure, 2010.

Lututala, M., "L'élargissement de l'espace de vie des Africains: Comment le «pays des oncles» européens devient aussi celui des neveux africains," *Revue Tiers Monde*, vol. 38, no. 150, 1997, pp. 333-346.

Mabintch, B., "Les Œuvres plastiques africaines comme documents d'Histoire: Le cas des statues royales ndop des Kuba de Zaire," *Africa-Tervuren*, vol. 27, no. 1, 1981, pp. 9-17.

MacKenzie, J., "Empire from Above and Below," in A. Burton and D. Kennedy, (eds.), *How Empire Shaped Us*, London, Bloomsbury, 2016, pp. 37-48.

——, "Epilogue: Analysing 'Echoes of Empire' in Contemporary Context: The Personal Odyssey of an Imperial Historian (1970s-present)," in K. Nicolaïdis, B. Sèbe, and G. Maas, (eds.), *Echoes of Empire: Memory, Identity and Colonial Legacies*, London, I.B. Tauris, 2015, pp. 188-206.

——, (ed.), *European Empires and the People: Popular Responses to Imperialism in France, Britain, the Netherlands, Belgium, Germany and Italy*, Manchester, Manchester University Press, 2011.

——, *Propaganda and Empire: The Manipulation of British Public Opinion, 1880-1960*, Manchester, Manchester University Press, 1984.

Mantels, R., *Geleerd in de tropen: Leuven, Congo & de wetenschap, 1885-1960*, Leuven, Leuven University Press, 2007.

Marchal, J. (A. M. Delathuy), *Missie en Staat in Oud-Kongo, 1880-1914. Witte Paters, Scheutisten en Jezuïeten*, Berchem, EPO, 1992.

——, *De Kongostaat van Leopold II, 1876-1900. Het verloren paradijs*, Antwerpen, Standaard Uitgeverij, 1989.

——, *E. D. Morel tegen Leopold II en de Kongostaat*, Berchem, EPO, 1985.

Maxwell, A., *Colonial Photography and Exhibitions: Representations of the Native and the Making of European Identities*, London, Leicester University Press, 1999.

McFadden, S., "Good Housekeeping," *The Bulletin*, 1 October 2010, pp. 50-51.

McLeod, H., *Religion and the People of Western Europe 1789-1989*, Oxford, Oxford University Press, 1997.

"Mechelen – Schuttersvest – Koloniaal standbeeld Mechelse pioniers der beschaving," delcampe.be, n.d., https://www.delcampe.be/nl/verzamelingen/postkaarten/belgie/mechelen/mechelen-schuttersvest-koloniaal-standbeeld-mechelse-pioniers-der-beschaving-530543531.html, (accessed 18 June 2018).

"A la mémoire du général Molitor," *La Revue coloniale belge*, no. 261, November 1956, p. 835.

Mémoires du Congo et du Ruanda-Urundi, n.d., http://www.memoiresducongo.be/revues/, (accessed 8 January 2019).

Mémoires du Congo et du Ruanda-Urundi, "Presentation," n.d., http://www.memoiresducongo.be/en/, (accessed 16 December 2018).

Meriwether, J., *Proudly We Can Be Africans: Black Americans and Africa, 1935-1961*, Chapel Hill, University of North Carolina Press, 2002.

Mertens, J., W. Goedertier, I. Goddeeris, and D. de Brabanter, "A New Floor for the Silenced? Congolese Hip-Hop in Belgium," *Social Transformations*, vol. 1, no. 1, 2013, pp. 87-113.

Metcalf, B., and T. Metcalf, *A Concise History of India*, 2nd ed., Cambridge, Cambridge University Press, 2006.

Meunier, M., "Africa Dreams, l'ombre du roi," *Jeune Afrique*, 22 March 2010, http://www.jeuneafrique.com/Articles/Dossier/ARTJAJA2566p020-028.xml1/rd-congo-belgique-colonisation-bande-dessineeafrica-dreams-l-ombre-du-roi.html, (accessed 25 June 2014).

——, "Colette Braeckman visiteuse du «Soir»," *Jeune Afrique*, 22 March 2010, http://www.jeuneafrique.com/Articles/Dossier/ARTJAJA2566p020-028.xml2/presse-rd-congo-joseph-kabila-kinshasacolette-braeckman-visiteuse-du-soir.html, (accessed 18 July 2014).

——, "Une histoire belge," *Jeune Afrique*, 22 March 2010, http://www.jeuneafrique.com/Articles/Dossier/ARTJAJA2566p020-028.xml0/ue-rwanda-rd-congo-burundiune-histoire-belge.html, (accessed 3 July 2014).

Meurant, G., *Dessin Shoowa: textiles africains du Royaume Kuba*, [Brussels], Crédit Communal, 1986.

Mnookin, R., "Ethnic Conflicts: Flemings & Walloons, Palestinians & Israelis," *Daedalus*, vol. 136, no. 1, 2007, pp. 103-119.

Mobe, A., "Le Congo, la Belgique et la Grande guerre," *L'Express*, 4 October 2013, http://www.lexpress.fr/actualite/monde/afrique/le-congo-la-belgique-et-la-grande-guerre-1914-1918_1288104.html, (accessed 8 August 2014).

Mobe Fansiama, A., "En marge d'une exposition au Musée royal de l'Armée de Bruxelles: Lisolo na Bisu. Les soldats congolais honorés," *L'Année Francophone Internationale*, 2011-2012, pp. 61-64.

Mobil'Art, "Claude Lyr," n.d., http://www.mobilart.be/claude_lyr, (accessed 11 June 2018).

Mobutu, roi du Zaïre, dir. T. Michel (135 minutes), 1999.

Mommen, A., *The Belgian Economy in the Twentieth Century*, London, Routledge, 1994.

Monaville, P., "The Untraceable Colonialist: Autobiographical Practices and Colonial Ideologies in Belgium," in D. Ramada Curto and A. Rappas, (eds.), *Colonialism and Imperialism: Between Ideologies and Practices*, European University Institute Working Paper HEC No. 2006/01, San Domenico di Fiesole, EUI, 2006, pp. 59-66.

Moniteur belge, 12 June 1914, pp. 3729-3733.

Monroe, J., "Surface Tensions: Empire, Parisian Modernism, and 'Authenticity' in African Sculpture, 1917-1939," *American Historical Review*, vol. 117, no. 2, 2012, pp. 445-475.

"Mons: les mains coupées s'agrippent à la statue de Léopold II," lavenir.net, 13 September 2017, https://www.lavenir.net/cnt/dmf20170913_01054469?pid=3388079, (accessed 15 June 2018).

Monseur, L., "La Colonisation belge: une certaine image officielle (les manuels: 1919-1939)," Master's thesis, Université de Liège, 1984-1985.

"Monument commémoratif en l'honneur des Troupes des Campagnes d'Afrique 1885-1960," n.d., http://balat.kikirpa.be/object/20027278, (accessed 11 July 2018).

"Un monument Léopold II," *La Revue coloniale belge*, no. 239, 15 September 1955, p. 649.

"Monument Leopold II (Kolonel Dusartplein)," 2019, http://hasel.be/monument-leopold-ii-kolonel-dusartplein, (accessed 9 January 2019).

Le Mouvement antiesclavagiste, Brussels, J. Goemaere, 25 March 1894, p. 119.

Murphy, A., "Landscapes for Whom? The Twentieth-Century Remaking of Brussels," *Yale French Studies*, no. 102, 2002, pp. 190-206.

"Musées – Museums, Namur," 2 April 1997, http://www.promin.be/belvil/nammus.htm, accessed at http://archive.today/mPHj4, (accessed 11 August, 2014).

Musonda Milundu, D., "La circulation des objets d'art: La commercialisation," in Léon Verbeek, (ed.), *Les arts plastiques de l'Afrique contemporaine: 60 ans d'histoire à Lubumbashi (RD Congo)*, Paris, L'Harmattan, 2008, pp. 269-293.

Mycock, A., "After Empire: The Politics of History Education in a Post-Colonial World," in M. Carretero, S. Berger, and M. Grever, (eds.), *Palgrave Handbook of Research in Historical Culture and Education*, London, Palgrave Macmillan, 2017, pp. 391-410.

Naipaul, V. S., *A Bend in the River*, Harmondsworth, Penguin, 1979.

Naissance de la peinture contemporaine en Afrique centrale, 1930-1970, Tervuren, MRAC, 1992.

Namikas, L., *Battleground Africa: Cold War in the Congo, 1960-1965*, Stanford, Stanford University Press, 2013.

Ndaywel È Nziem, I., "L'historiographie congolaise: un essai de bilan," *Civilisations*, vol. 54, 2006, pp. 237-254.

——, *Histoire générale du Congo: De l'héritage ancien à la République démocratique*, Paris, De Boeck & Larcier, 1998.

——, *Histoire du Zaïre: De l'héritage ancien à l'âge contemporain*, Louvain-la-Neuve, Duculot, 1997.

Nederlands letterenfonds, "Jef Geeraerts: Gangrene – Black Venus," n.d., http://www.letterenfonds.nl/en/book/530/gangrene-black-venus, (accessed 18 July 2018).

Nolan, F., "Frère Mathieu, (Jean-Baptiste Brichaux), 1871-1944," n.d., *Les Missionnaires d'Afrique*, http://peresblancs.org/frere_mathieu.htm#gb, from *Petit Echo* no. 1071, 2016, (accessed 8 January 2019).

Nora, P., *Les lieux de mémoire*, 3 vols., Paris, 1984-1992.

Nord, P., *Paris Shopkeepers and the Politics of Resentment*, Princeton, Princeton University Press, 1986.

Omasombo Tshonda, J., "Lumumba, drame san fin et deuil inachevé de la colonisation," *Cahiers d'Études africaines*, vol. 44 (1-2), nos. 173-174, 2004, pp. 221-261.

Omfloerste histories, verhalen nabij de Leie, "Het ontluisterd monument," 24 April 2018 https://omfloerst.wordpress.com/2018/04/24/het-omstreden-monument/, (accessed 30 June 2018).

Oostindie, G., *Postcolonial Netherlands: Sixty-five Years of Forgetting, Commemorating, Silencing*, trans. A. Howland, Amsterdam, Amsterdam University Press, 2011.

L'Opinion publique belge: Le parlement, l'Europe, les finances publiques, la politique culturelle, Brussels, Institut de Sociologie, Université Libre de Bruxelles, 1971.

"The Ostende Historical Museum De Plate," *deplate.be*, 2018, https://www.deplate.be/stadsmuseum/ostend-historical-museum-de-plate, (accessed 19 June 2018).

"Le Parc Duden," *Bruxelles Environnement*, n.d., https://environnement.brussels/fiche/parc-duden, (accessed 8 June 2018).

Park, R., "A King in Business: Leopold II of Belgium, Autocrat of the Congo and International Broker," *Everybody's Magazine*, vol. 15, no. 5, November 1906, pp. 624-633.

Pavlakis, D., *British Humanitarianism and the Congo Reform Movement, 1896-1913*, Surrey, Ashgate, 2015.

Peemans, J.-P., "Imperial Hangovers: Belgium-The Economics of Decolonization," *Journal of Contemporary History*, vol. 15, no. 1, 1980, pp. 257-286.

Peeters, B., "A Never Ending Trial: Hergé and the Second World War," trans. P. Newman and H. Frey, *Rethinking History*, vol. 6, no. 3, 2002, pp. 261-271.

Périer, G.-D., "Rendons les Fétiches aux Noirs!," *Les Beaux-Arts*, no. 18, 21 November 1930, p. 1.

Pétré, R., "Monuments aux morts congolais et Belges de la Force publique," *Bel-Memorial*, www.bel-memorial.org/books/mon_congolais_et_belges_de_la_force_publique_Rene_PETRE.pdf, (accessed 11 July 2018).

Petridis, C., "René and Odette Delenne," *Tribal People*, no. 61, 2011, pp. 118-123.

Pinkney, D., *Napoleon III and the Rebuilding of Paris*, Princeton, Princeton University Press, 1958.

"Place du Trône – Statue du roi Léopold II," *La Régie des Bâtiments*, 3 September 2007, http://www.buildingsagency.be/realisatieberichten_fr.cfm?key=84, (accessed 23 October 2013).

Planche, J.-C., "*Rwanda 1994*, par le Groupov: Une réparation symbolique," *Périphéries*, May 2000, http://www.peripheries.net/article245.html, (accessed 2 July 2014).

Planche, S., "Le 'Roi colonisateur' à l'école: portrait ambivalent d'un (anti)héros," in V. Dujardin, V. Rosoux, and T. de Wilde d'Estmael, (eds.), *Léopold II. Entre génie et gêne. Politique étrangère et colonisation*, Brussels, Racine, 2009, pp. 269-284.

Plancquaert, M., "Les Yaka: Essai d'histoire," *Annalen: Menselijke wetenschappen*, no. 71, Tervuren, MRAC, 1971.

Plasman, P.-L., interview, "Léopold II, roi maudit?," Matin Première, *RTBF.be*, 1 December 2009, http://www.rtbf.be/info/emissions/article_matin-premiere-leopold-ii-roi-maudit?id=5408883, (accessed 2 July 2014).

Plasman, P.-L., and S. Planche, "Le «cas» Léopold," *Louvain*, no. 184, 2010, p. 28.

Poddar, P., R. S. Patke, and L. Jensen (eds.), *A Historical Companion to Postcolonial Literatures—Continental Europe and its Empires*, Edinburgh, Edinburgh University Press, 2008.

Pollain, J., "L'immigration en chiffres," *La Revue nouvelle*, vol. 36, no. 9, 1980, pp. 139-146.

Poncelet, M., *L'invention des sciences coloniales belges*, Paris, Karthala, 2008.

"Ponthier, Pierre," *Connaître la Wallonie*, n.d., http://connaitrelawallonie.wallonie.be/fr/lieux-de-memoire/ponthier-pierre#.WyPaSIonZhE, (accessed 8 January 2019).

Porter, B. *The Absent-Minded Imperialists: Empire, Society, and Culture in Britain*, Oxford, Oxford University Press, 2005.

"Programme des manifestations de propagande coloniale 1952-1953," *Cercle colonial de Louvain. Koloniale kring van Leuven: Seizoen/Saison 1952-1953: Programme*, Kessel-Lo, Belgium, Van der Poorten, [1952].

Puttemans, P., *Modern Architecture in Belgium*, trans. M. Willert, Brussels, Marc Vokaer, 1976.

Quaghebeur, M., and E. Van Balberghe (eds.), with N. Fettweis and A. Vilain, *Papier blanc, encre noire: Cent ans de culture francophone en Afrique centrale (Zaïre, Rwanda et Burundi)*, 2 vols., Brussels, Labor, 1992.

Quanten, K., *Operatie Rode draak*, Antwerp, Manteau, 2014.

Rahier, J., "The Ghost of Leopold II: The Belgian Royal Museum of Central Africa and Its Dusty Colonialist Exhibition," *Research in African Literatures*, vol. 34, no. 1, 2003, pp. 58-84.

——, "*Métis/Mulâtre, Mulato,* Mulatto, *Negro, Moreno, Mundele Kaki,* Black, . . . The Wanderings and Meanderings of Identities," in P. Hintzen and J. Rahier, (eds.), *Problematizing Blackness: Self-Ethnographies by Black Immigrants to the United States*, New York, Routledge, 2003, pp. 85-112.

Ranieri, L., *Léopold II: Urbaniste*, Brussels, Hayez, 1973.

Raxhon, P., *Le débat Lumumba: histoire d'une expertise*, Brussels, Labor, 2002.

Renard, H., "Matonge, Congolese Wijk in Brussel," *Knack*, 7 May 2010, p. 47.

Renders, L., "In Black and White: A Bird's Eye Overview of Flemish Prose on the Congo," *Tydskrif vir Letterkunde*, vol. 46, no. 1, 2009, pp. 109-122.

——, "In Flanders' Fields: Postcolonialism, Multiculturalism and the Limits of Tolerance," in M. Lacy, C. Gehring, and J. Oosterhoff, (eds.), *From De Halve Maen to KLM: 400 Years of Dutch-American Exchange*, Münster, Nodus Publikationen, 2008, pp. 1-14.

Renders, L., and H. Roos, "The Congo in Literature," *Tydskrif vir Letterkunde*, vol. 46, no. 1, 2009, pp. 8-10.

Review of Reynebeau, M., *Een geschiedenis van België* (2003), *Knack*, 15 October 2003.

Revue belgo-congolais illustrée, 1948, 1967.

Reynebeau, M., *Het klauwen van de leeuw: de Vlaamse identiteit van de 12de tot de 21ste eeuw*, Leuven, Van Halewyck, 1995.

Rich, J., " 'Tata otangani, oga njali, mbiambiè!': Hunting and Colonialism in Southern Gabon, ca. 1890–1940," *Journal of Colonialism and Colonial History*, vol. 10, no. 3, 2009, https://muse.jhu.edu/article/368536, (accessed 23 August 2018).

Roberts, A., *A Dance of Assassins: Performing Early Colonial Hegemony in the Congo*, Bloomington, Indiana University Press, 2013.

Rosoux, V., "Le Mémoire de la colonisation: fer de lance ou talon d'Achille de la politique étrangère belge?," in S. Jaumain and E. Remacle, (eds.), *Mémoire de guerre, construction de la paix*, Brussels, Peter Lang, 2006, pp. 157-179.

Rosoux, V., and L. van Ypersele, "The Belgian national past: Between commemoration and silence," *Memory Studies*, vol. 5, no. 1, 2011, pp. 45-57.

Rusesabagina, P., with T. Zoellner, *An Ordinary Man: An Autobiography*, New York, Viking, 2006.

"Rwanda 94, Extraits de presse," [2014], http://groupov.be/index.php/spectacles/extraits/id/9?symfony=45b532bead34f0c0e520698017abfc00, (accessed 2 July 2014).

Ryckmans, F., "Congo: 50 ans de l'indépendance," *RTBF.be*, n.d.

———, *Mémoires noires: Les Congolais racontent le Congo belge*, Brussels, Racine, 2010.

Salmon, P., "Les retours en Belgique induits par la décolonisation," in J.-L. Miège and C. Dubois, (eds.), *L'Europe retrouvée: les migrations de la decolonisation*, Paris, 1994, pp. 191-212.

Sanchez, A., "Most statues of Leopold II have plaques in Flanders," *The Brussels Times*, 17 August 2018, http://www.brusselstimes.com/belgium/12258/most-statues-of-leopold-ii-have-plaques-in-flanders, (accessed 30 August 2018).

Sanderson, J.-P., "La démographie du Congo belge sous la colonisation belge," PhD Thesis, Université Catholique de Louvain, 2010.

Sarlet, C., "Vingt ans après: Le retour du refoulé. Les Belges au Congo," *Textyles*, no. 14, 1997, pp. 95-110.

Schildkrout, E., and C. Keim (eds.), *The Scramble for Art in Central Africa*, Cambridge, Cambridge University Press, 1998.

Schoonvaere, Q., "Étude de la Migration congolaise et de son Impact sur la Présence congolaise en Belgique: Analyse des principales données démographiques," Group d'étude de Démographique Appliquée (UCL) & Centre pour l'égalité des chances et la lutte contre le racisme, 2010.

Schorske, C., *Fin-de-Siècle Vienna: Politics and Culture*, New York, Alfred A. Knopf, 1980.

Service Public Fédéral Finances, "Donation Royale," *www.belgium.be*, n.d., https://finances.belgium.be/fr/sur_le_spf/institutions_qui_dependent_du_spf_finances/donation_royale#q1, (accessed 8 January 2019).

Shultz, T., "Europe Worries Young People Are Going Abroad to Seek Jihad," *National Public Radio Morning Edition*, 8 May 2013, http://www.npr.org/2013/05/08/182175929/europe-worries-young-people-are-going-aboard-to-seek-jihad, (accessed 18 July 2014).

Seressia, J., and E. Daniel, *Manuel d'histoire de Belgique*, 7th edn., Brussels, Centre d'études juridiques, législatives et pédagogiques, 1970.

Sikitiko: The King's Hand, dir. P. De Vos (8:54 minutes), YouTube.com, uploaded 26 July 2010, http://www.youtube.com/watch?v=AYqwg1aR3nA, (accessed 8 August 2014).

Silverman, D., "Diasporas of Art: History, the Tervuren Royal Museum for Central Africa, and the Politics of Memory in Belgium, 1885-2014," *Journal of Modern History*, vol. 87, 2015, pp. 615-667.

———, "Art Nouveau, Art of Darkness: African Lineages of Belgian Modernism, Part III," *West 86th: A Journal of Decorative Arts, Design History, and Material Culture*, vol. 20, no. 1, 2013, pp. 3-61.

——, "Art Nouveau, Art of Darkness: African Lineages of Belgian Modernism, Part II," *West 86th: A Journal of Decorative Arts, Design History, and Material Culture*, vol. 19, no. 2, 2012, pp. 175-95.

——, "Art Nouveau, Art of Darkness: African Lineages of Belgian Modernism, Part I," *West 86th: A Journal of Decorative Arts, Design History, and Material Culture*, vol. 18, no. 2, 2011, pp. 139-81.

Simenon, G., *African Trio: Talatala, Tropic Moon, Aboard the Aquitaine*, trans. S. Gilbert, P. Auster, and L. Davis, New York, Harcourt Brace Jovanovich, 1979.

——, *Le blanc à lunettes*, Paris, Gallimard, 1937.

Simons, P., "Spektakel van Hugo Claus," *Ons Erfdeel*, vol. 14, 1970-1971, p. 147.

Slade, R., *King Leopold's Congo: Aspects of the Development of Race Relations in the Congo Independent State*, London, Oxford University Press, 1962.

Solvel, F., "Ces inconnus du métro," *Brusselslife.be*, 28 July 2015, https://www.brusselslife.be/fr/article/ces-inconnus-du-metro, (accessed 20 June 2018).

"Souverain (square du). Vorstsquare," n.d., http://www.urba.be/Rues/rues_S.htm, accessed at *Archive.today*, http://archive.li/R7Hbw#selection-1527.0-1571.197, (accessed 7 June 2018).

Spaas, L., "The Congo in Brussels: Exploitation and Enterprise," in N. Aubert, P.-P. Fraiture, and P.-P. McGuinness, (eds.), *La Belgique entre deux siècles: laboratoire de la modernité, 1880-1914*, Oxford, Peter Lang, 2007, pp. 51-65.

Spectres, dir S. Augustijnen (104 minutes), 2011.

Stanard, M., "African Art and Post-Colony Belgium: Political Decolonization versus Cultural Integration," in B. Sèbe and M. Stanard, (eds.), *Decolonising Europe? Popular Responses to the End of Empire*, Routledge, forthcoming.

——, "Lumumba's Ghost: A Historiography of Belgian Colonial Culture," in M. Farr and S. Barczewski, (eds.), *The MacKenzie Moment: Essays Presented to Professor John M. MacKenzie*, Basingstoke, Palgrave Macmillan, 2019.

——, "Après nous, le déluge: Belgium, Decolonization, and the Congo," in M. Thomas and A. Thompson, (eds.), *The Oxford Handbook of the Ends of Empire*, Oxford, Oxford University Press, 2019, pp. 144-161.

——, "Revisiting Bula Matari and the Congo Crisis: Successes and Anxieties in Belgium's Late Colonial State," *Journal of Imperial and Commonwealth History*, vol. 46, no. 1, 2018, pp. 144-168.

——, "'Boom! Goes the Congo': The Rhetoric of Control and Belgium's Late Colonial State," in M. Thomas and R. Toye, (eds.), *Rhetorics of Empire: Imperial Discourse and the Language of Colonial Conflict after 1900*, Manchester, Manchester University Press, 2017, pp. 121-141.

——, "The colonial past is never dead. It's not even past: Histories of Empire, Decolonization, and European Cultures after 1945," *Jahrbuch für Europäische Geschichte*, vol. 17, 2016, pp. 151-174.

——, "Belgium, the Congo, and Imperial Immobility: A Singular Empire and the Historiography of the Single Analytic Field," *French Colonial History*, vol. 15, 2014, pp. 87-110.

——, "Digging-In: The Great War and the Roots of Belgian Empire," in A. Jarboe and R. Fogarty, (eds.), *Empires in World War I: Shifting Frontiers and Imperial Dynamics in a Global Conflict*, London, I.B. Tauris, 2014, pp. 23-48.

———, "Violence and Empire: The Curious Case of Belgium and the Congo," in R. Aldrich and K. McKenzie, (eds.), *The Routledge History of Western Empires*, London, Routledge, 2013, pp. 454-467.

———, "King Leopold's Bust: A Story of Monuments, Culture, and Memory in Colonial Europe," *Journal of Colonialism and Colonial History*, vol. 12, no. 2, 2011, https://muse.jhu.edu/article/448312, (accessed 11 January 2019).

———, *Selling the Congo: A History of European Pro-Empire Propaganda and the Making of Belgian Imperialism*, Lincoln, University of Nebraska Press, 2011.

———, "Interwar Pro-Empire Propaganda and European Colonial Culture: Toward a Comparative Research Agenda," *Journal of Contemporary History*, vol. 44, no. 1, 2009, pp. 27-48.

———, "Imperialists without an Empire: Cercles coloniaux and colonial culture in Belgium after 1960," in C. Koos and C. Granata, (eds.), *The Human Tradition in Modern Europe*, Lanham, Md., Rowman & Littlefield, 2008, pp. 155-170.

———, "'Bilan du monde pour un monde plus déshumanisé': The 1958 Brussels World's Fair and Belgian Perceptions of the Congo," *European History Quarterly*, vol. 35, no. 2, 2005, pp. 267-298.

"Standbeeld Leopold II overgoten met rode vloeistof," *Brussel Deze Week/BRUZZ*, 29 January 2018, https://www.bruzz.be/samenleving/standbeeld-leopold-ii-overgoten-met-rode-vloeistof-2018-01-29, (accessed 22 June 2018).

"Statistieken van de bezoeken aan het museum in 1979," *Africa-Tervuren*, vol. 26, no. 1, 1980, p. 3.

"Une statue de Léopold II déboulonnée à Forest," RTBF journal télévisé (19h30), *RTBF.be*, 11 January 2018, https://www.rtbf.be/auvio/detail_une-statue-de-leopold-ii-deboulonnee-a-forest?id=2297924, (accessed 8 June 2018).

"Une statue de Léopold II peinte en rouge à Bruxelles," *RTBF.be*, 9 September 2008, http://www.rtbf.be/info/societe/divers/une-statue-de-leopold-ii-peinte-en-rouge-a-bruxelles, (accessed 24 January 2011).

"Les statues parlent aussi," *RTBF.be*, 8 March 2013, http://www.rtbf.be/lapremiere/emissions/programmes/detail_les-statues-parlent-aussi?emissionId=999&programId=118850, (accessed 11 August 2014).

Stearns, J., *Dancing in the Glory of Monsters: The Collapse of the Congo and the Great War of Africa*, New York, PublicAffairs, 2011.

"Stèle à un combattant de 1914-1918 et stèle à un martyr du Congo, Elsaute (Clermont-sur-Berwinne)," *Bel-Memorial*, n.d., http://www.bel-memorial.org/names_on_memorials/display_names_on_mon.php?MON_ID=2536, (accessed 8 January 2019).

Stengers, J., "Belgian Historiography after 1945," trans. F. Perlin, in P. C. Emmer and H. L. Wesseling, (eds.), *Reappraisals in Overseas History*, Leiden, Leiden University Press, 1979, pp. 161-181.

———, "Sur l'aventure congolaise de Joseph Conrad," *ARSOM-KAOW, Bulletin des Séances/Mededelingen der Zittingen*, vol. 17, no. 4, 1971, pp. 744-761.

Stinglhamber, G., and P. Dresse, *Léopold II au travail*, Brussels, Éditions du Sablon, 1945.

"Studiedag voor Jonge Historici," 20 March 2008, 25 March 2011, *CEGESOMA*, http://www.cegesoma.be.

Symons, T., and J. Houssiau, "The Everyday Things of Life," in G. Pluvinage, (ed.), *Expo 58: Between Utopia and Reality*, Brussels, Racine/Brussels City Archives, 2008, pp. 41-50.

Taithe, B., "Missionary Militarism? The Armed Brothers of the Sahara and Léopold Joubert in the Congo," in O. White and J. Daughton, (eds.), *In God's Empire: French Missionaries and the Modern World*, Oxford, Oxford University Press, 2012, pp. 129-50.

Thompson, A. (ed.), *Writing Imperial Histories*, Manchester, Manchester University Press, 2013.

Thomas, M., B. Moore, and L. Butler, *Crises of Empire: Decolonization and Europe's Imperial States, 1918-1975*, London, Hodder, 2008.

Thomas, P., "Belgium's North-South Divide and the Walloon Regional Problem," *Geography*, vol. 75, no. 1, 1990, pp. 36-50.

"Thys, Albert," *Connaître la Wallonie*, n.d., http://connaitrelawallonie.wallonie.be/fr/lieux-de-memoire/thys-albert#.WyfCWoonZhE, (accessed 8 January 2019).

Thys van den Audenaerde, D., "In Memoriam, Lucien Cahen," *Africa-Tervuren*, vol. 28, no. 4, 1982, pp. 3-4.

Tipo-Tipo, M., *Migration Sud/Nord, Levier ou Obstacle? Les Zaïrois en Belgique*, Brussels, Afrika Instituut-ASDOC/Institut Africain-CEDAF, 1995.

"Tokopesa Saluti!," 20 November 2013, http://www.sinthendrikdeinze.be/227-geschiedenis-3e-graad, (accessed 8 August 2014).

Tollebeek, J. (ed.), *Mayombe. Rituele beelden uit Congo*, Tielt, Lannoo, 2010.

Tousignant, N., "L'évolution des représentations du passé mis en exergue par le gouvernement belge depuis 1999," conference presentation, 2005, www.vimeo.com/21365702, (accessed 18 September 2013).

———, "Les Manifestations publiques du Lien colonial entre la Belgique et le Congo belge (1897-1988)," PhD Thesis, Université Laval, 1995.

Toussaint, E., "Les crimes de la Belgique coloniale au Congo: Devoir de mémoire," *CADTM*, 29 October 2007, http://cadtm.org/spip.php?page=imprimer&id_article=2922, (accessed 2 July 2014).

Toussaint, J., "Le Musée africain," *Côté Jambes*, no. 47, 2004, pp. 8-9.

La Tribune congolaise, 18 October 1913, no. 35.

Truyts, J., "Nieuw infobord bij omstreden standbeeld van Leopold II in Oostende," *DeRedactie.be*, 11 September 2016, https://www.vrt.be/vrtnws/nl/2016/09/11/nieuw_infobord_bijomstredenstandbeeldvanleopoldiiinoostende-1-2764959/, (accessed 19 June 2018).

Tshitungu Kongolo, A., "Commémoration du soldat inconnu congolais," *CADTM*, [11 November 2008], 26 November 2008, http://www.cadtm.org/spip.php?page=imprimer&id_article=3896, (accessed 7 January 2019).

———, "Colonial Memories in Belgian and Congolese Literature," trans. C. Labio, *Yale French Studies*, vol. 102, 2002, pp. 79-93.

T'Sjoen, Y., "'Koloniseren is een smaak die je moet leren'—Hugo Claus en *Het leven en de werken van Leopold II* (1970)," *Tydskrif vir Letterkunde*, vol. 46, no. 1, 2009, pp. 151-166.

Turner, T., *Ethnogenèse et nationalisme en Afrique centrale: aux racines de Patrice Lumumba*, Paris, L'Harmattan, 2000.

Union royale belge pour les pays d'Outre-Mer – Koninklijke belgische unie voor de overzeese landen, n.d., http://www.urome.be/, (accessed 7 January 2019).

Vanacker, S., "'As Befits Men': The Creation of Masculinity in the Crime Fiction of Jef Geeraerts," in E. O'Beirne and A. Mullenci, (eds.), *Crime Scenes: Detective Narratives in European Culture since 1945*, Amsterdam/Atlanta, Rodophi, 2000, pp. 241-253.

Van Beurden, S., *Authentically African: Arts and the Transnational Politics of Congolese Culture*, Athens, Ohio University Press, 2015.

——, "The Value of Culture: Congolese Art and the Promotion of Belgian Colonialism (1945-1959)," *History and Anthropology*, vol. 24, no. 4, 2013, pp. 1-21.

van Bockhaven, V., "Leopard-men of the Congo in Literature and Popular Imagination," *Tydskrif vir Letterkunde*, vol. 46, no. 1, 2009, pp. 79-94.

Vancraenbroeck, M., *Les médailles de la presence belge en Afrique centrale 1876-1960*, Brussels, Bibliothèque Royale de Belgique, 1996.

Van Damme-Linseele, A., "From Mission 'Africa Rooms': Frans M. Olbrechts's Rediscovered African Collection," *African Arts*, vol. 41, no. 2, 2008, pp. 38-49.

van de Craen, P. "What, if Anything, Is a Belgian?," *Yale French Studies*, no. 102, 2002, pp. 24-33.

Van De Mieroop, D., and M. Pagnaer, "Co-Constructing Colonial Dichotomies in Female Former Colonizers' Narratives of the Belgian Congo," *Journal of Linguistic Anthropology*, vol. 23, no. 2, 2013, pp. E66-E83.

Van den Braembussche, A., "The Silence of Belgium: Taboo and Trauma in Belgian Memory," *Yale French Studies*, vol. 102, 2002, pp. 34-52.

van den Weghe, J., *Djiki-Djiki*, Brecht/Antwerpen: Uitgeverij De Roerdomp, 1972.

Vanderbeeken, R., "Documentary as Anti-Movement: On *Spectres* by Sven Augustijnen," *Afterall*, vol. 31, 2012, pp. 94-105.

VanderKnyff, R., "Parlor Illusions: Stereoscopic Views of Sub-Saharan Africa," *African Arts*, vol. 40, no. 3, 2007, pp. 50-63.

van der Krogt, R., and P. van der Krogt, "Josef en Lieven Vandevelde met Sakala," *Statues – Hither & Thither*, n.d., http://statues.vanderkrogt.net/object.php?webpage=ST&record=beov019, (accessed 19 July 2018).

van der Krogt, R., and P. van der Krogt, "Roi Léopold II," *Statues – Hither & Thither*, n.d., http://statues.vanderkrogt.net/object.php?record=bena033&webpage=ST, (accessed 14 July 2018).

Van Doorslaer, R., "De ondergang van de kolonialen," *Bijdragen tot de Eigentijdse Geschiedenis-Cahiers d'histoire du temps présent*, no. 11, 2003, pp. 161-175.

Van Ginderachter, M., "Belgium: Too many pasts, too many memories," in B. De Wever, (ed.), *Belgium's Diverging Memories. Is this so? If so, why? And is it a problem?*, [Brussels], Re-Bel, 2015, pp. 7-14.

——, *Le chant du coq: Nation et nationalisme en Wallonie depuis 1880*, trans. M. Paret, Ghent, Academia Press, 2005.

Van Goethem, H. *Belgium and the Monarchy: From National Independence to National Disintegration*, trans. I. Connerty, Brussels, UPA, 2010.

Vangroenweghe, D., "The 'Leopold II' concession system exported to French Congo with as example the Mpoko Company," *Revue belge d'Histoire contemporaine*, vol. 36, nos. 3-4, 2006, pp. 323-372.

——, *Voor rubber en ivoor: Leopold II en de ophanging van Stokes*, Leuven, Van Halewyck, 2005.

——, *Du sang sur les lianes: Léopold II et son Congo*, Brussels, Didier Hatier, 1986.

——, *Rood Rubber: Leopold II en zijn Kongo*, Brussels, Elsevier, 1985.

Vanhee, H., and G. Castryck, "Belgische historiogafe [sic] en verbeelding over het koloniale verleden," *Belgisch Tijdschrift voor Nieuwste Geschiedenis*, vol. 32, nos. 3-4, 2002, pp. 305-320.

Van Hoecke, S., and J.-P. Jacquemin, *Africa Museum Tervuren 1898-1998*, Tervuren, MRAC, 1998.

Van Nieuwenhuyse, K., "Towards a Postcolonial Mindset in a Post-Colonial World? Evolving Representations of Modern Imperialism in Belgian History Textbooks (1945-2017)," in K. Van Nieuwenhuyse and J. Pires Valentim, (eds.), *The Colonial Past in History Textbooks: Historical and Social Psychological Perspectives*, Charlotte, NC, Information Age Publishing, 2018, pp. 155-176.

Van Reybrouck, D., *Congo: Une histoire*, trans. I. Rosselin, Arles, Actes Sud, 2012.

——, *Mission suivi de l'Ame des termites*, trans. M. Nagielkopf, [Arles], Actes Sud, 2011.

——, *Congo: een geschiedenis*, Amsterdam, De Bezige Bij, 2010.

——, interview, Festival Theaterformen, *Presence of the Colonial Past: Afrika auf Europas Bühnen*, Hannover, 2010, pp. 12-14.

Van Schuylenbergh, P., "Trop-plein de mémoires, vide d'histoire? Historiographie et passé colonial belge en Afrique centrale," in P. Van Schuylenbergh, C. Lanneau, and P.-L. Plasman, (eds.), *L'Afrique belge aux XIXe et XXe siècles. Nouvelles recherches et perspectives en histoire coloniale*, Brussels, Peter Lang, 2014, pp. 31-71.

——, "Découverte et vie des arts plastiques du bassin du Congo dans la Belgique des années 1920-1930," in P. Van Schuylenbergh and F. Morimont, *Rencontres artistiques Belgique-Congo, 1920-1950*, Louvain-la-Neuve, Université catholique de Louvain, 1995, pp. 1-62.

Van Schuylenbergh, P., and M. Zana Aziza Etambala (eds.), *Patrimoine d'Afrique centrale. Archives Films: Congo, Rwanda, Burundi, 1912-1960*, Tervuren, MRAC, 2010.

Vansina, J., *Through the Day, Through the Night: A Flemish Boyhood and World War II*, Madison, University of Wisconsin Press, 2014.

——, *Living with Africa*, Madison, University of Wisconsin Press, 1994.

Vanthemsche, G., "Belgian royals on tour in the Congo (1909-1960)," in R. Aldrich and C. McCreary, (eds.), *Royals on Tour: Politics, Pageantry and Colonialism*, Manchester, Manchester University Press, 2018, pp. 169-190.

——, "The Belgian Colonial Empire (1885/1908-1960)," in M. Gehler and R. Rollinger, (eds.), *Imperien und Reiche in der Weltgeschichte: Epochenübergreifende und globalhistorische Vergleiche*, vol. 2, Wiesbaden, Harrassowitz, 2014, pp. 971-997.

——, *Belgium and the Congo, 1885-1980*, trans. A. Cameron and S. Windross, revised by K. Connelly, Cambridge, Cambridge University Press, 2012.

——, "Van de *Belgische Koloniale Biografie* naar het *Biografisch Woordenboek van Belgen Overzee*," ARSOM-KAOW, *Bulletin des Séances/Mededelingen der Zittingen*, vol. 57, nos. 2-4, 2011, pp. 215-235.

——, "The Historiography of Belgian Colonialism in the Congo," in C. Lévai, (ed.), *Europe and the World in European Historiography*, Pisa, Pisa University Press, 2006, pp. 89-119.

——, "De Belgische socialisten en Congo 1895-1960," *Brood & Rozen: Tijdschrift voor de geschiedenis van sociale bewegingen*, vol. 2, 1999, pp. 31-65.

——, *Genèse et portée du "plan décennal" du Congo belge (1949–1959)*, Mémoires in-8°, new series, vol. 51, no. 4, Brussels, ARSOM, 1994.

Vellut, J.-L., *Congo: Ambitions et désenchantements, 1880-1960. Carrefours du passé au centre de l'Afrique*, Paris, Karthala, 2017.

——, "Rénovation du Musée royal de l'Afrique centrale," *La Libre Afrique*, 8 December 2017, https://afrique.lalibre.be/12013/renovation-du-musee-royal-de-lafrique-centrale/, (accessed 7 June 2018).

——, "Itinéraires d'un rêveur," in F. Rosart and G. Zelis, (eds.), *Dans l'atelier de l'historien contemporanéiste: Parcours d'historiens de l'Université catholique de Louvain*, Louvain-la-Neuve, Harmattan-Academia, 2012, pp. 135-160.

——(ed.), *La mémoire du Congo. Le temps colonial*, Tervuren, MRAC, 2005.

——, "European Medicine in the Congo Free State (1885-1908)," in P. Janssens, M. Kivits, and J. Vuylsteke, (eds.), *Health in Central Africa since 1885: Past, Present, and Future*, Brussels, King Baudouin Foundation, 1997, pp. 67-87.

——, "Ressources scientifiques, culturelles et humaines de l'africanisme en Belgique: Perspectives sur un patrimoine d'outre-mer et sa mise en valeur," *Cahiers africains-Afrika Studies*, 9-10-11, 1994, pp. 115-144.

——, "La peinture du Congo-Zaïre et la recherche de l'Afrique innocente. Présentation du livre de J. A. Cornet, R. De Cnodder, I Dierickx & W. Toebosch: «60 ans de peinture au Zaïre»," *ARSOM-KAOW, Bulletin des Séances/Mededelingen der Zittingen*, vol. 36, no. 4, 1990, pp. 633-659.

——, review of H. Eynikel, *Congo belge: Portrait d'une société coloniale*, in *The Journal of African History*, vol. 26, no. 2, 1985, p. 277.

——, "Mining in the Belgian Congo," in D. Birmingham and P. Martin, (eds.), *History of Central Africa: Volume Two*, London, Longman, 1983, pp. 126-162.

Verbeeck, G., "De Lumumba-commissie: Geschiedschrijving en collectieve herinnering," *BMGN – Low Countries Historical Review*, vol. 122, no. 3, 2007, pp. 1-17.

Ver Boven, D., *De rode aarde die aan onze harten kleeft*, Brussels, Reinaert, 1962.

Verhaegen, B., "La Colonisation et la décolonisation dans les manuels d'histoire en Belgique," in M. Quaghebeur and É. Van Balberghe, (eds.), with N. Fettweis and A. Vilain, *Papier blanc, encre noire: Cent ans de culture francophone en Afrique centrale (Zaïre, Rwanda et Burundi)*, 2 vols., Brussels, Labor, 1992, vol. 2, pp. 333-379.

Verlinden, P., *Weg uit Congo: Het drama van de kolonialen*, Leuven, Davidsfonds, 2002.

Verlinden, P. and S. Hertsens, *Belgisch-Kongo: 50 jaar koloniale herinneringen*, Leuven, Davidsfonds, 2010.

Vermeulen, J., "Ontstaan van de post-koloniale roman in 1959-1970," *Vlaanderen*, vol. 38, no. 225, Roeselare, Christelijk Vlaams Kunstenaarsverbond, 1989, pp. 82-89.

Verswijver, G., and H. Burssens, "Hidden Treasures of the Tervuren Museum," *African Arts*, vol. 28, no. 3, 1995, pp. 22-31.

Les Vétérans coloniaux. Bulletin mensuel, no. 3, March 1939, p. 3.

Viaene, V., "King Leopold's Imperialism and the Origins of the Belgian Colonial Party, 1860-1905," *Journal of Modern History*, vol. 80, 2008, pp. 741-90.

Viaene, V., B. Ceuppens and D. Van Reybrouck (eds.), *Congo in België: koloniale cultuur in de metropool*, Leuven, Leuven University Press, 2009.

"Victor Roelens," *BALaT Belgian Art Links and Tools*, n.d., http://balat.kikirpa.be/object/70159, (accessed 5 July 2018).

"Vielsalm honore ses pionniers," *Mémoires du Congo et du Ruanda-Urundi*, no. 39, September 2016, p. 44.

Ville de Namur, "Agenda 2003 – June," www.ville.namur.be/agenda/manifestation/06.html, (accessed 6 May 2003).

Vints, L., *Kongo made in Belgium: beeld van een kolonie in film en propaganda*, Leuven, Kritak, 1984.

Visages de Paul Panda Farnana, dir. Mona MK/Afrikavision (10:05 minutes), 21 April 2011, https://www.youtube.com/watch?v=4e2OUUp10Ao, (accessed 10 January 2019).

"Volont, Jules, Joseph," *Bulletin de la Société royale de Géographie d'Anvers*, vol. 32, Antwerp, J. Van Hille-de Backer, 1908, pp. 466-467.

Volper, J., "Of Sculptures & Skulls: The Émile Storms Collection," *Tribal Art*, vol. 17, no. 66, 2012, pp. 86-95.

Vrelust, J., et al., *Antwerp, World Port: On Trading and Shipping*, trans. G. Shipton, [Antwerp], BAI/MAS Books, 2012.

Walschap, G., *Oproer in Congo*, Amsterdam, Elsevier, 1953.

Wastiau, B., *ExItCongoMuseum: An essay on the 'social life' of the masterpieces of the Tervuren museum*, Tervuren, MRAC, 2000.

Weightman, C., and A. Barnes, *Brussels: Grote Markt to Common Market*, Brussels, Paul Legrain, 1976.

Weverbergh, J., *Leopold II van Saksen Coburgs allergrootste zaak*, Paris, Manteau, 1971.

White, O., and J. Daughton, "Introduction: Placing French Missionaries in the Modern World," in O. White and J. Daughton, (eds.), *In God's Empire: French Missionaries and the Modern World*, Oxford, Oxford University Press, 2012, pp. 3-25.

Wiener, M., "The Idea of 'Colonial Legacy' and the Historiography of Empire," *Journal of the Historical Society*, vol. 13, no. 1, 2013, pp. 1-32.

Wigley, A., "Marketing Cold War Tourism in the Belgian Congo: A Study in Colonial Propaganda, 1945-1960," Master's thesis, Stellenbosch University, 2014.

William, "Neem deel aan de 8ste editie van Congo In Vlaanderen op 28-juni-2014," 31 May 2014, http://congoinvlaanderen.be/neem-deel-aan-de-8ste-editie-van-congo-in-vlaanderen-op-28-juni-2014/, (accessed 25 June 2014).

Wills, C., *Lovers & Strangers: An Immigrant History of Post-War Britain*, London, Allen Lane, 2017.

Wils, L., *Histoire des nations belges*, trans. C. Kesteloot, Ottignies, Quorum, 1996.

——, *Vlaanderen, België, Groot-Nederland: Mythe en geschiedenis*, Leuven, Davidsfonds, 1994.

——, "Introduction: A Brief History of the Flemish Movement," trans. J. Fenoulhet and T. Hermans, in T. Hermans, (ed.), *The Flemish Movement*, London, Athlone Press, 1992, pp. 1-39.

Wintle, C., "Decolonizing the Smithsonian: Museums as Microcosms of Political Encounter," *American Historical Review*, vol. 121, no. 5, 2016, pp. 1492-1520.

"De witte neger," http://www.standbeelden.be/standbeeld/973, 26 October 2010, (accessed 28 June 2018).

Wrong, M., "The famous things they never said," *NewStatesman*, 4 September 2008, https://www.newstatesman.com/africa/2008/09/famous-quotation-wrong-lumumba, (accessed 12 December 2018).

Wynants, M., *Des ducs de Brabant aux villages congolais: Tervuren et l'exposition coloniale 1897*, trans. C. Kesteloot, Tervuren, MRAC, 1997.

Young, J., *The Texture of Memory: Holocaust Memorials and Meaning*, New Haven, Yale University Press, 1993.

Zaïre 1885-1985: Cent ans de regards des belges, Brussels, Cooperation par l'Education et la Culture, 1985.

"Zon en schaduw over Vlaanderen," *De Autotoerist*, 1 July 1965.

Index